FROM AROUND THE GLOBE

Secular Authors and Biblical Perspectives

Edited by

Seodial Frank H. Deena
Karoline Szatek

University Press of America,® Inc.
Lanham · Boulder · New York · Toronto · Plymouth, UK

Copyright © 2007 by
University Press of America,® Inc.
4501 Forbes Boulevard
Suite 200
Lanham, Maryland 20706
UPA Acquisitions Department (301) 459-3366

Estover Road
Plymouth PL6 7PY
United Kingdom

Library of Congress Control Number: 2006937943
ISBN-13: 978-0-7618-3627-8 (paperback : alk. paper)
ISBN-10: 0-7618-3627-6 (paperback : alk. paper)

Dedication

To my friend and colleague Gay Wilentz
(September 1, 1950—February 6, 2006) scholar, pioneer, and teacher.
We shared many conversations.
Gay was small in stature, but she cast a large shadow, and her shadow gave
voice and power to the poor, exploited, marginalized, and oppressed across the
world.

Contents

Section 2: Europe

Section 3: Asia and the Middle East

Section 4: Africa

Section 5: African American

Preface

From Around the Globe: Secular Authors and Biblical Perspectives is a collection of 24 essays written by a cross-discipline of scholars from universities across the globe — North America (including Boston U, Baylor U, U of California Santa Barbara, U of Michigan, U of MA Amherst, UNC, UNLV, and Pace U), Singapore, Italy, Spain, England, South Africa, the Caribbean, and Botswana. These scholars' essays explore a broad range of contemporary and cutting-edge connections between the Bible and diverse, global literature. Their fields of study range from classical western literature to multicultural: medieval, modern, Native American, African, Asian, and Caribbean, for instance. The analyses explore various literary genres—tracts, novels, plays, poems, and letters.

"From Around the Globe: Secular Authors and Biblical Perspectives" is a revolutionary study that treats literature, criticism, and the Bible from a global perspective. Through the centuries writers from both East and West and from both industrialized nations and the developing world have employed the Bible as an analogue or have drawn allusions from it to compose their prose, poetry, drama, and other documents. Most often, these authors draw clear references to the biblical matter, as do John Milton, John Bunyon, William Shakespeare, T. S. Elliot, Richard Wright, Toni Morrison, Derek Walcott, Wole Soyinka, Zora Neale Hurston, and others. Other authors, however, lean toward the more guarded and camouflaged reference. Some non-western writers might even be unaware of the allusions they generate, and western writers, while delving into allegorical shadows might, in fact, unwittingly layer deep biblical references. These submissions seek to actively engage in a (re)assessment of authors' biblical references.

Acknowledgements

Putting together a global and multicultural collection of essays like *From Around the Globe: Secular Authors and Biblical Perspectives* is not an easy task. As with all things difficult, a number of people made this book possible. Many thanks go to my co-editor Karoline Szatek, who is always fun to work with and to her spouse Matt for his continuous support. We would like to thank the contributors to this book for their hard work, patience and understanding through what seemed, at times, an unending process. Several of my graduate assistants—Ashley Noble, Robley Shepherd, Randy Marfield, and Elizabeth N. McArthur—worked on this project. Special thanks to Robley and Elizabeth for their attention to detail and unending dedication that brought this project to completion. The editors owe you many thanks.

East Carolina University, Harriot College of Arts and Sciences and Dean Alan White, and the Department of English and Chair Bruce Southard have been very supportive. To my friends, Reggie Watson, Rick Taylor, Laureen Tedesco, Lester Zeager, Andy Sargent, John Bradley, Tope Bello, Ravi Paul, Lionel Etwaru, Naresh Samaroo, Lokenauth Ramkissoon, Frederick Jeffers, Andrew Husbands and my pastor John Zabawski for all their support and many happy memories.

Most importantly my children—Shivaun, Esther, Rachel, and David—were part of this sacrifice. Unfathomable gratitude to my wife, Debbie, for her encouragement and support. Finally, many thanks to the author of the Bible for inspiring a life-giving book for all times, peoples, and places.

1   The Bible as Babel: The Suspicions
of Dorothy L. Sayers
Crystal Downing

Many people enter Scripture as though it was sacred space. Assuming that the Bible's carefully carved verses build toward a unified whole, like the masonry of a Medieval cathedral, they believe the text encompasses and contains the very mind of God. For these people, even profane words like "ass" and "damn" are sanctified once they enter the holy space of Scripture. It is no coincidence that the word "profane" has architectural roots, distinguishing that which is outside the "fane," or temple, from the sacred enclosed within.

The Bible itself, however, contains a cautionary tale that might warn against the sanctification of its own language:

> Now the whole earth had one language and the same words. And as they migrated from the east, they came upon a plain in the land of Shinar and settled there. And they said to one another, "Come, let us make bricks, and burn them thoroughly.". . . Then they said, "Come, let us build ourselves a city, and a tower with its top in the heavens, and let us make a name for ourselves; otherwise we shall be scattered abroad upon the face of the whole earth." (Genesis 11:1-4; NRSV)

The end of the story is famous: God disapproves of the people's attempt to reach the heavens and confuses their language, creating multiple tongues so that their brick-like signifiers can no longer attain the transcendental signified. God, we might say, deconstructs their Babel.

Jacques Derrida, famous for the phrase, "transcendental signified," as well as the "deconstruction" it elicits, often invoked the metaphoric relationship between language and architecture. In his "Introduction to Hegel's Semiology," for example, he notes how the "body of the sign" becomes for Hegel "the monument in which the soul will be enclosed, preserved, maintained, kept in maintenance, present, signified" (83). And he implies that this monument functions as a stand-in for Christ: "the sign, as the unity of the signifying body and the signified ideality, becomes a kind of incarnation" (82). For Derrida, however, the body of the sign, the monument attempting to enclose the soul--even when found in the Bible--is merely Babel. As he notes in "Des Tours de Babel,"

> The "tower of Babel" does not merely figure the irreducible multiplicity of tongues; it exhibits an incompletion, the impossibility of finishing, of totalizing, of saturating, of completing something on the order of edification, architectural construction, system and architectonics. (3)

Heedless of both Babel and Derrida, societies continue to erect towers of signification, assuming that their verbal monuments have attained the heaven of truth. Reinhold Niebuhr recognized this problem in 1937, publishing an essay entitled, "The Tower of Babel," to discuss how communities sanctify their own interpretations of God's work. Failing to recognize that all vocabularies are human constructions--like the Tower of Babel--such societies naively assume that language, though historically contingent, contains truth that transcends the ground upon which it is situated. Niebuhr demurs:

> Religion, declares the modern man, is consciousness of our highest social values. Nothing could be further from the truth. True religion is a profound uneasiness about our highest social values. Its uneasiness springs from the knowledge that the God whom it worships transcends the limits of finite man, while this same man is constantly tempted to forget the finiteness of his cultures and civilisation and to pretend a finality for them which they do not have. Every civilisation and every culture is thus a Tower of Babel. (28)

Reading Niebuhr and recommending to others the book that contains "The Tower of Babel," famed detective fiction writer Dorothy L. Sayers (1893-1957) recognized in him a kindred spirit. Her suspicions about cultural constructions, and the language with which they are built, affected not only the suspects within her detective novels, but also the way she viewed, as well as used, the Bible.

Sayers' awareness that cultures are finite, that their vocabularies only "pretend a finality which they do not have," arises, I suspect, from her Oxford education. Attending Somerville College from 1912 to 1915, Sayers earned First Class Honors in French, specializing in the Medieval period. In fact, before she turned to detective fiction in 1921, she taught modern French and German in high school, beginning to translate the 11th century *Chanson de Roland* in 1916 and the 12th century *Tristan of Brittany* in 1917. Though the translations were not published until much later, Sayers was obviously immersed in the vagaries of language--the cultural situatedness of both translation and interpretation--long before she created Lord Peter Wimsey, her famous fictional sleuth.

Detective fiction, by its very nature, focuses upon interpretation, since the best interpreter tends to solve the case. This is what makes the genre so attractive: as readers enter the text and follow the narrative, they get to join a fictional detective in the analysis of clues, assessing the difference between red herrings and reliable data in order to arrive at the *proper* interpretation. The pursuit of the *proper*, however, is the genre's greatest weakness. As Sayers was to note in 1941, after having written twelve mystery novels, readers love detective fiction because it presents life in terms of an obvious problem— usually in the form of a murder—which has "a predictable, final, complete and sole possible solution" (*Mind* 188): "pretend[ing] a finality," to use Niebuhr's words, which life does "not have." In *The Mind of the Maker*, Sayers actually quotes Niebuhr as she establishes the dissimilarity between the crises of detective fiction and the those of real life: "The problem of good and evil cannot be completely resolved in history. -- Reinhold Niebuhr: *Beyond Tragedy*" (*Mind* 205).

Even in her very first detective novel, *Whose Body?* (1923), Sayers undermines clear-cut distinctions between good and evil, creating parallels between the novel's protagonist and its villain. Both Lord Peter Wimsey and Sir Julian Freke do research on dead bodies as an avocation, Freke preferring dissection to his medical practice (105), and Peter's preferring detection to aristocratic languor (119). In fact, when Freke tells Detective Inspector Parker that "Dissection is the basis of all good theory and all correct diagnosis" (105), we could substitute "detection" for "dissection" to get a sense of Peter's avocation. Significantly, Peter ascertains that Freke has murdered the victim when a medical student describes, part by part, the body he was dissecting in Freke's lab (147-50): dissection therefore becomes detection. Sayers even has the student comment on similarities between the way Peter talks about the assembly of fictional tales and how Freke dissects a body (145).

Both Freke and Peter are intelligent interpreters of data, but their conclusions differ according to their particular worldviews. As a scientific materialist, Freke believes that all religious emotion, including guilt and joy, is biological, the work of nerves and cells (106). Therefore his murdering and dissecting of Sir Reuben Levy cannot be condemned as an absolute "evil" anymore than religious piety can be praised as an absolute "good." Freke murders to dissect, causing us to wonder how our own interpretations, as in Wordsworth's famous poem, might do the same: "Our meddling intellect / Misshapes the beauteous forms of things:--/ We murder to dissect" ("The Tables Turned").

The plot of *Whose Body?* is thus predicated upon hermeneutic ambiguity, forgrounding the situatedness of interpretation. To signal that this is her intent, Sayers includes a discussion about Biblical hermeneutics between Lord Peter and his friend Detective Inspector Parker. When Peter discovers Parker reading a Bible commentary on the Epistle to the Galatians, the amateur sleuth expresses skepticism about the legitimacy of the author's interpretation. He tells Parker that scholars of the Bible interpret according to their own particular "bias" (118). Not long afterwards, Parker and Lord Peter discuss the same issue in their assessment of murder suspects; first Peter admits his own "bias," then he acknowledges that of Inspector Sugg, paralleling him with the Bible scholars that Parker has been reading (120, 122). Quite significantly, when Sugg's interpretation of the murder is first mentioned in the novel, Parker dismisses it saying, "Sugg will build up a lovely theory, like the Tower of Babel, and destined so to perish" (22). Sayers implies that understanding itself, whether of the Bible or of a murder, is Babel: a construction built on biased foundations. It may be no coincidence that the person who finds the murder victim is an architect.

Nevertheless, certain biases seem better than others. Inspector Sugg situates his interpretation upon one site on the body. Noticing that the victim in the bathtub is circumcised, he assumes it must be the body of the missing Jewish financier, Sir Reuben Levy. Peter, however, discovering flea-bites and severely decayed teeth, realizes that the corpse, though Jewish, could not be that of a wealthy man. While Sayers originally referred to the victim's circumcised flesh quite explicitly, her publisher had her censor the allusion (Reynolds 101), leaving only an oblique reference by Peter's mother to Jewish circumcision (42).[1] Parker's reading of Galations provides the greater clue, for the book repeatedly chides the Galatians for putting too much emphasis on circumcision-- as did Inspector Sugg, who erected a Tower of Babel. Facts, though empirically verifiable and irrefutably true, like that manifest on the victim's flesh, can be misinterpreted according to one's bias.

Sayers therefore implies that Freke's scientific interpretation of life, based upon empirically verifiable facts, might be inaccurate as well. While Freke understands existence by taking things apart (via dissection), Parker understands existence by putting things together (via Bible commentaries). Sayers makes one a foil to the other by way of their mutual reference to footprints. Parker uses a metaphor from his profession, detective investigation, to describe how commentaries he studied in college seemed to be so obsessed with finding a "burglar" in the house—something foreign to the construction—that they didn't pay attention to the "foot-prints" that were already there: those of the "household" (118). He thus echoes Freke, who had earlier told him that he studies a patient's emotional excesses to ascertain a body's biology the same way Parker studies "the footsteps of the criminal" in order to ascertain a body's murderer (106). By thus paralleling detection with physiology and Bible study, Sayers suggests that some footprints are better to follow than others: Freke's belief that all action can be physiologically explained eliminates moral responsibility--even for murder; Parker's belief that the Bible is worth studying reflects his sense of responsibility in a created universe where murder in cold blood is wrong--even though he cannot empirically verify a Creator. After all, the two most famous verses in the epistle Parker studies state, "For all the law is fulfilled in one word, even in this: Thou shalt love thy neighbour as thyself "; and "Whatsoever a man soweth, that shall he also reap" (Galatians 5:14, 6:7).[2] Freke, who does not love his neighbor as himself, ends up as dead as the body he murders, reaping what he has sown. Though all knowledge is marked by interpretive bias, Sayers implies that some interpretations have better consequences than others.

Sayers thus signals in her first secular novel that interpretive ambiguity does not mean one gives up searching for the truth, whether in the Bible or about a murder. She has Parker, a paragon of integrity, exhort, "If you've any duty to society in the way of finding out the truth about murders, you must do it in any attitude that comes handy." Peter responds, "I don't think you ought to read so much theology" (121), as though in recognition that detection is the task of all humans who are looking for clues--not just about solving a death, but more importantly about the meaning of life.

Sayers also interweaves the Bible, bias, and the meaning of life in her fifth detective novel, *The Documents in the Case* (1930), for which she consulted Dr. Eustace Barton, a physician who had helped other detective fiction writers with scientific technicalities. In *The Documents in the Case*, Sayers has Munting, her protagonist, ask a group of scientists, "What is Life?" Multiple interpretations are provided, varying according to whether the speaker is a biologist, a behaviorist, a chemist, or a clergyman. The Rev. Perry and his curate both ascribe to Biblical definitions, but Waters, the chemist, replies that life "is a kind of bias--a lop-sidedness" (214). By this Waters refers to the evolution of inorganic molecules to organic compounds, explaining that the former are visually symmetrical while the latter are asymmetrical--or "lop-sided." This difference in molecular structure, Waters explains, seems to have occured at the moment biological forms first appeared on earth, their symmetry having been twisted into asymmetrical form. Scientists have reproduced this "twist" only through the "exercise of deliberate selective intelligence," an intelligence which itself gives evidence of "life" (214). Waters' explanation provides a clue not only to life but also to death--for the novel's murder was achieved through the "exercise of deliberate selective intelligence" when Munting's friend Lathom intentionally laced the murder victim's food with a poison that was inorganic and hence symmetrical. The compound became asymmetrically organic (and hence undetectible) as it went through the victim's digestive track.

Waters, unaware of the murder at this point, thinks only of life, implying several times that the evolution from inorganic to organic compounds necessitated "an intelligence behind it all"--what Rev. Perry calls "God" (217). Sayers thus intentionally laces her text with a biblical interpretation of the origins of life. We recognize her intentionality during the lab scene in which a pre-digested sample of mushroom stew eaten by the victim, Harrison, is tested for inorganic synthetic poison. During the experiment, Munting keeps humming to himself--drums and all--Biblical passages from Hayden's *Creation*, culminating with the phrase from Genesis 1: "Let there be light (Pomty-pom) and there was--" (220).

"Light" is exactly what Munting desired in the experiment. For if light came through the polarizing microscope when viewing the stew Lathom fed Harrison, that would mean there was no symmetrical inorganic poison added to it, and Lathom, Munting's friend, would be innocent. As the experiment begins, Waters turns off the lights, leaving only a sodium flame. Munting reports, "In that green, sick glare a face floated close to mine--a corpse face--livid, waxen, stamped with decay" (225). In the weird light, Munting's imagination has overlaid the face of the dead Harrison onto the face of Waters, causing him to take pity on a man he had formerly disdained. When the experiment proves that Harrison was murdered by Lathom, we realize that Munting's imaginative projection of Harrison's face on that of Waters functions as though "the spirit of God moved upon the face of the waters" (Genesis 1:2), enabling Munting to feel love for a victim he formerly despised. Sayers even prepares us earlier in the chapter for this important biblical pun: she has Waters state that the author of Genesis was uncannily accurate when he established the origin of life "on the face of the waters" (212). Furthermore, it is Waters who defines "Life" as a kind of "bias," and then undermines Munting's bias toward the innocence of Lathom.

Sayers reinforces throughout *The Documents in the Case* that life is filled with biases and thus interpretive lop-sidedness. She structures the novel through an epistolary format, such that we get conflicting, obviously biased, perspectives on the same events. Then, during the party at Perry's house, she includes a biblical incident to confirm that interpretation is not innocent. When Matthews, a biologist, off-handedly refers to germs as a judgement from God, Perry's curate protests that the Bible warns against interpretations that claim assurance about God's judgements, and he gives the example the tower of Siloam (211). His allusion is to an incident recounted in the Gospel of Luke, when Jesus denounces those who interpret pain and suffering as punishments from God: "those eighteen, upon whom the tower in Siloam fell, and slew them, think ye that they were sinners above all men that dwelt in Jerusalem? I tell you, Nay" (Luke 13: 4-5a). This tale of a tower, like that of Babel, deflates any assurance that one can reach the mind of God. Nevertheless, with the repeated phrase from Genesis, "Let there be light," Sayers once again implies that searching for the light, even in the face of bias, is imperative. And some biases, like that seen through the polarizing microscope, get us closer to the truth than others.

Like the tower of Siloam, a tower becomes slayer in Sayers' tenth detective novel, *The Nine Tailors* (1934). Unlike the tower of Siloam, however, Sayers establishes this tower as the novel's constitutive symbol, key to solving the mystery of *The Nine Tailors*. Rising to an great height, the tower has the Bible inscribed on its walls. Etched under its windows is a statement that echoes verses from Psalm 19: "There is no speech nor language, where their voice is not heard. Their line is gone out through all the earth" (3-4a). These "voices" with neither speech nor language come from the tower bells, themselves inscribed with text, as though they were commentaries on the textual tower that contains them. The Scripture-bearing tower becomes sanctified through the church that supports it, Fenchurch St. Paul, which Sayers explicitly associates with the sacred space of Noah's Ark. Responding to the life-saving call of the tower bells, village people escape a devastating flood by congregating, along with their farm animals, within the church walls.

Sayers begins the flood account with an epigraph from Genesis: "Of clean beasts, and of beast that are not clean, and of fowls, and of everything that creepeth upon the earth there went in two and two unto Noah into the ark -- Genesis VII. 8, 9" (367). And she glosses the next chapter, recounting the rise of the waters, with a verse from the Psalms: "Deep calleth unto deep at the noise of thy waterspouts: all thy waves and thy billows are gone over me -- Psalm XLII. 7" (377). Five out of the novel's twenty chapters begin with Bible verses, significant in light of the fact that none of Sayers' other eleven novels employ Scriptural epigraphs. Inscribing both the church tower and the novel that contains it with Bible verses, Sayers seems to impute the sacred containment of the tower onto her novel, implying that, like Noah's Ark, the text contains life. As the "sign" is to Hegel, the tower qua novel is a "monument in which the soul will be enclosed, preserved, maintained, kept in maintenance, present, signified" (Derrida, "Hegel" 83).

However, by the end of the novel, we discover that the Scripture-inscribed tower, which signals the means to salvation, was also an instrument of death. Two characters had bound Geoffrey Deacon in the tower, seeking to enclose, preserve, and maintain his life until they could smuggle him out of the village. Before they can rescue him, however, a group of bell-ringers start a nine-hour course of bells that kills Deacon through the ear-splitting intensity of the noise. Sacred space, the fane of a church, thus becomes complicit with the pro-fane. As Derrida might describe it, "the completely other is announced as such--without any simplicity, any identity, any resemblance of continuity--within what is not it" (*Of Grammatology* 106).

Sayers implies that no tower or text, including the Bible, can be an absolute Ark-like refuge that makes present the transcendental signified; it either contains that which it speaks against, or it fails to legitimize its own absolute authority.

As she wrote one correspondent,

"[W]here is your Scriptural authority for the Scriptures themselves? On what texts do you rely for the make-up of the Canon as we have it?" (*Ltrs* 2. 367). Eschewing what David Jeffrey describes as "a tendency among post-Reformation and evangelical Protestants to elevate the Bible to the status of a shibboleth, seeing it in effect as *autopistos*--drawing its authority from itself" (xviii), Sayers recognized that Scripture is not self-interpreting. In her mind, if the biblical canon is contingent upon Church history, Christians should study the traditions and evaluate the proclamations of those who formulated the canon. As she tells another correspondent, all too many "crude and erroneous ideas about doctrine" have come from people who interpret the Bible without having an informed understanding of exegetical contexts and hermeneutical history (*Ltrs* 2. 288).

Interpretation, Sayers recognized, is always situated--like a tower. This statement explains why no one has the right to take another person's life, for killing implies one can build a tower that reaches the level of God's transcendent perspective on life and death. Significantly, in several of Sayers' novels, including *Whose Body?*, Lord Peter has a nervous breakdown when he realizes that his discovery of a murder has led to the perpetrator's death. Though the criminal deserves punishment, Peter is not so sure the murderer deserves the death penalty, and he is traumatized by his own complicity in taking the life of another human being. As Niebuhr notes and Sayers quotes in *The Mind of the Maker*, "The problem of good and evil cannot be completely resolved in history." And all humans—from murderers to the sleuths that capture them—are situated in history.

The theological implications of good and evil led Sayers to abandon detective fiction--not out of distaste for Peter Wimsey, but because she found it far more exciting to explore the interpretive ground upon which cultural constructions stand. Her transition into a new kind of writing was inspired, in fact, by a literal construction—the architecture of Canterbury Cathedral.

In the autumn of 1936, Sayers was asked to write a play for the annual Canterbury Festival, and thus to follow in the footsteps of Charles Williams, who wrote *Thomas Cranmer* for the 1936 festival, and T. S. Eliot, whose *Murder in the Cathedral* was produced in 1935. Sayers, understandably, felt intimidated by the task. Even though she had written her first staged drama the year before (*Busman's Honeymoon*), it was about a subject she knew well—dectective fiction—and was done in collaboration with a specialist in drama who taught at the Royal Academy of Dramatic Art. Nevertheless, Sayers finally agreed and wrote a play about William of Sens, the architect who designed and coordinated the reconstruction of Canterbury Cathedral after its choir burned down in 1174. Called *The Zeal of Thy House*, the play was a rousing success. When it went on tour in 1938, Sayers became the focus of increased media attention. In response to one interview, she wrote an essay for the *Sunday Times* proclaiming that Christ's death and resurrection, as recounted in the Bible, was

"The Greatest Drama Ever Staged."[3] This proclamation elicited additional offers to write plays about Christian subject matter and then to speak and write about related biblical and theological issues. Almost against her will and definitely to her chagrin, the secular detective novelist became known as a "Christian writer" —which eventually got her into trouble, for she still regarded the Bible as Babel.

Though earnest about her Anglo-Catholic convictions, Sayers had no patience for low-church biblicism. When one correspondent apparently asked for Bible passages with which to exhort an errant sibling, Sayers responded, "honestly, if anybody implored me 'in every letter' to read the bible and quoted texts at me, I should feel an unregenerate urge to throw the sacred volume straight out of the window!" Sayers suggested that the sibling might find more edification in secular literary art. After all, she notes, the Scriptures don't always seem to help those who know it best, and she gives the example of the New Testament Pharisees, who "might have done better to wrestle with the great human problems of Aeschylus or Euripedes or Virgil" (*Ltrs* 3. 524-25). Though this statement was written late in her life--1950--Sayers' reference to Pharisees echoes an incident she wrote into a play commissioned by BBC radio soon after *The Zeal of Thy House* garnered acclaim. *He That Should Come*, broadcast on Christmas Day 1938, places its characters in a crowded inn on the night of Jesus' birth. One tenant, a Pharisee, disparages a Jewish Gentleman who is dressed in the most fashionable Roman style, asserting that such clothes insult God and "bind a foreign yoke and a pagan custom upon our necks in flat defiance of the Law of Moses" (154). Though Sayers was surely as disturbed by the Roman oppression of the Jews in the first century as she was to be about the Nazi oppression in 1939,[4] she quite clearly shows that this Pharisee is not dismayed by the "foreign yoke" so much as by the loss of traditional readings of Scripture.

In contradistinction to the Pharisee, Sayers has a Roman Centurion praise Rome because it tolerates the gods of foreigners (161). His welcoming attitude is reinforced when he takes compassion on Mary and Joseph, who have been told there is no room in the inn. Approaching the landlord about possible accommodation in the inn's stable, the Centurion asks, "Is there any *room there*?" In contrast, the Pharisee makes no room for those outside his constructed worldview: "*What room* will there be for such as you in the great day of redemption when the Lord's Messiah comes?" (150, 158; emphasis mine). Of course, Sayers implies that the Pharisee is so obsessed with a traditional interpretation of the Messiah that he fails to see the new Word when it appears before his very eyes.

While some may regard Sayers' distinction between the Pharisee and the Centurian as religiously biased, Sayers clearly shows that the Pharisee's problem is not his faith position so much as his interpretive rigidity. She wards off accusations of anti-Semitism by making the fashionably dressed "Jewish Gentleman" turn out to be Joseph of Arimathea, who will, in an act of love and respect, eventually provide room in his tomb for the crucified Christ. However, just as he disparages Joseph's Roman clothes, the Pharisee responds to Arimathea's praise of Roman theatres with disgust, describing all play-acting not only as inethical and un-Jewish, but also as an "abomination" before God (157). Significantly, Sayers gives the same opinion to another Jewish character: one of the play's shepherds. He describes disturbing things he has heard about Roman theater—masking, cross-dressing, scripts laced with "smut and nastiness"—ending his description with "It ain't right, to our way of thinking" (167). Through his humble reference to "our way of thinking," the Jewish Shepherd acknowledges the situatedness of his ethic, providing a radical contrast to the Pharisee, who puts himself on a tower presuming to reach the mind of God.

The Pharisee's problem is not his Jewishness but his lack of epistemological humility. Indeed, a dozen years later Sayers was to give a similar personality to a Christian character, Arius, in *The Emperor Constantine* (1951), her lengthy play about the fourth century formulation of the Nicene Creed. She provides Arius biblical justification for his view that Jesus, though one with God, was God's creation, showing that it is his supercilious attitude, not his doctrine, that makes him distasteful. When he is asked to present his views at the Council of Nicaea, he makes a condescending pronouncement about the insufficiency of those members of the Council who understand neither the Greek language nor the Scriptures as well as he, archly stating, "Our Latin friends who have no definite article in their woolly language may be excused for woolly thinking; but for those who speak Greek there is no excuse" (143-44). Like her Pharisee in *He That Should Come*, Sayers' Arius assumes his reading of Scripture is superior to the interpretive fashions which come out of Rome, brought by "our Latin friends."[5] For both, their construction of the Bible is an impregnable tower.

Rather than the elevation of a tower-like text that mystifies one's own interpretive ground, Sayers establishes that belief should not be in a book but by way of identification with an interpretive community--like the "our way of thinking" formulated at the Council of Nicaea. Because makers of creeds construct meaning in the process of representing it, they must approach their task as a communal enterprise wherein the integrity of the work relies on majority assent. "Dogma," as Sayers often notes, means an "*opinion*" endorsed by the whole body of believers.[6] Sayers therefore felt no need to shore up her own faith, admitting that, like a tower, it is situated: "To me, Christian dogma seems to offer the only explanation of the universe that is intellectually satisfactory. . . . [E]verybody has to approach a subject from some point of view or other, and that one happens to be mine" (*Ltrs* 2. 401). By this Sayers did not mean to imply that faith is a matter of individual preference, of *personal* opinion. Instead, her "point of view," her "bias," was aligned with that of an ancient interpretive community. In fact, whenever she was asked her own opinion about theological issues, she deferred to church dogma, repeatedly repudiating the "personal" in discussions of theology as frivolous. When an acquaintance of hers indicated that he was more interested in her personal opinion about Christianity than in Church doctrine, she got positively enraged, exploding in a letter, "[D]amn it all! It's hardly flattering to be told that you are interested in my opinion, but not in the subject I am talking about" (*Ltrs* 3. 295). Explaining that Christianity is the construction of "a society of persons" in response to the Person of Christ, Sayers established church dogma, "the subject I am talking about," as the bottom line. For her, that meant the Bible should not be hallowed as an immutable container of absolute truth; it is the guide to faith and practice for an interpretive community, providing narratives that explain how and why that community came into being. Realizing there was nothing sacred about the language that communicated this history, Sayers' own diction, as we see, often got salty, damn it all, when discussing doctrinal issues. Eventually, however, her damns hit the fans.

In 1940 Dr. James Welch, Director of Religious Broadcasting for BBC radio, commissioned from Sayers a series of radio plays about the life of Jesus. She wrote twelve plays, starting with the nativity story, proceeding through famous incidents in Christ's life, until the last play dramatized Biblical accounts of post-resurrection appearances. She includes not only extra-biblical interpretive traditions--such as the names of the two thieves on the cross and the identification of Mary Magdalen with Mary of Bethany--but also numerous fictitious events and incidents that she created to contextualize or elaborate upon Gospel material.

By December of 1941 the broadcasts were ready to be announced, and Welch set up a press conference to advertise the series. As part of the publicity, Sayers read an extra-biblical passage from her fourth play, *The Heirs to the Kingdom*, in which the disciple Philip has just admitted to the rest of the disciples that he got short-changed at the market. A working class Matthew responds: "Fact is, Philip my boy, you've been had for a sucker. Let him ring the changes on you proper. You ought to keep your eyes skinned, you did really" (105). When members of the press reported that Sayers put slang into the mouths of Christ's disciples, they sensationalized her dismissal of the King James Version of the Bible. As a result, before the first play was even aired, a censorship campaign was mounted by the Protestant Truth Society and the Lord's Day Observance Society (LDOS), who sent petitions to the Archbishop of Canterbury, as well as Winston Churchill, demanding that the plays be banned. Sayers, famous for Peter Wimsey's sleuthing of suspicious behavior, was now the suspect; the brilliant creator of a secular detective was suspiciously secular.

The controversy over Sayers' play cycle parallels that surrounding Martin Scorsese's 1988 screen rendition of Nikos Kazantzakis' novel *The Last Temptation of Christ*. In both cases, the most vociferous protests came from Christians who had heard about, but not heard, the scripts.[7] Like protesters who regarded the film as "the most blasphemous, evil attack on the church and the cause of Christ in the history of entertainment," the LDOS asserted that Sayers' "proposed theatrical exhibition will cause much pain to devout people, who feel deeply that to impersonate the Divine Son of God in this way is an act of irreverence bordering on the blasphemous." Because radio "impersonations" depend entirely upon the spoken word, protesters attacked Sayers' "spoliation of the beautiful language of the Holy Scriptures which have been given by inspiration of the Holy Spirit."[8] The beautiful language for them was King James English, as though to say the Holy Spirit inspired authors of the Bible to write Shakespearean prose. The protestors obviously did not realize that the King James Bible was based, in part, on translations from the Latin for which William Tyndale had been persecuted almost a century earlier. The so called "Authorized Version" was merely one babel among many.

Sayers makes a very similar point in her introduction to the published version of the play cycle, *The Man Born to be King* (1943), employing an architectural metaphor to repudiate "the general air of stained-glass-window decorum" that surrounds accounts of the biblical Jesus (6). She despaired over people who mystify the Bible, entering it with hushed tones as though entering the sacred space of a cathedral, its language like precious stained-glass. In fact, she regarded the Christian insistence upon the Authorised Version a "singular piece of idolatry" (3). For her, the language of the Bible should be as vulgar as the people it describes. Sayers, in fact, relished vulgarity, addressing a club in 1936 with a speech she titled "The Importance of Being Vulgar," by which she meant "the importance of a writer's being able to speak to the comon emotions and desires of all human beings" (Kenney 41). For her, sacralizing of the Bible's contents-- whether the people it describes or the language it uses--eviscerates the text's ability to speak to the common emotions and desires of all human beings. She parodied such mystification in a letter to a clergyman who had praised her fourth play in the cycle, facetiously writing "Christ wasn't born into history—He was born into the Bible (Authorized Version)—a place where nobody makes love, or gets drunk, or cracks vulgar jokes, or talks slang, or cheats, or despises his neighbours, but only a few selected puppets make ritual gestures symbolical of the sins of humanity" (*Ltrs* 2. 354).

Several years earlier, Sayers had employed the puppet metaphor to describe her secular creation, admitting that the Lord Peter Wimsey of her early novels was merely a manipulated marionette:

> I plugged confidently on, putting my puppet through all his tricks and exhibiting him in a number of elegant attitudes. But I had not properly realized . . . that any character that remains static except for a repertory of tricks and attitudes is bound to become a monstrous weariness to his maker. ("Gaudy" 210)

Similarly aware that most people felt monstrously weary with what they perceived to be mere puppets in the Bible, Sayers had a difficult task before her.

Just as she had "perform[ed] a major operation" on Lord Peter, turning him into a "complete human being" in her later novels ("Gaudy" 211), she wanted to make biblical characters seem like real people. This meant writing dialogue consonant with how people talked in her own day, as well as hiring the best possible actors for the broadcasts, actors who would not make their characters sound like ventriloquized puppets.

For Sayers, a good actor who did not believe one word of the Bible was preferable to a poor actor who had memorized the Bible as an earnest believer. She makes this quite clear in an essay written while she was working on *Man Born to Be King*. In "Why Work" she tells of a "dear old pious lady" who had seen *The Zeal of Thy House* and asked whether the actors who played the angels were selected "for the excellence of their moral character." Sayers responds that "the right kind of actor with no morals would give a far more reverent and seemly performance than a saintly actor with the wrong technical qualifications" (*Creed* 79, 80). It was therefore to Sayers' delight that the BBC hired a secular crew with the right technical qualifications for an effective performance. The producer was the brilliant Val Gielgud, brother of the famous actor John Gielgud; Mary Magdalen was played by a young Hermione Gingold, perhaps best known for her superb role as the priggish mayor's wife in the classic film *The Music Man* (1962); and the music was composed by Benjamin Britten.

Sayers believed that the characters in her Bible plays should be puppets of their creator no more than a humans should be of their Creator. This reflected her theory of art as fleshed out in *The Mind of the Maker* (1941): when humans create they are most like Creator God, fulfilling the *Imago Dei*. Studying the creative act, then, "we gain a kind of illumination upon the variety and inconclusiveness of the world about us" (*Mind* 52). And for Sayers, the world of the Bible was as inconclusive as our own. As she noted to the clergyman who praised her fourth play in the cycle:

> There must have been all sorts of different grades of "belief" -- belief that this was the Messiah, implicit confidence in this remarkable person, acceptance of the teaching, a dim sense that here was a man with something unearthly about him -- according to the religious and social background of the believer. (*Ltrs* 2. 353)

Belief is situated and hence is multiple--like the babel that gives the Tower its name.

In *The Man Born to Be King* Sayers implies that, like belief *in* Jesus, the belief *of* Jesus is also situated--situated in his humanity. Sayers affirmed the traditional doctrine, established at the Council of Nicaea, that Jesus was both fully human and fully divine. However, she felt that too many Christians ignore this dogma of the church, feeling uncomfortable with Jesus as an embodied being who experienced all the pains, impulses, and desires that the flesh is heir to. In contrast, she whole-heartedly endorsed Hebrews 4:15: "For we have not an high priest which cannot be touched with the feeling of our infirmities; but was in all points tempted like as we are, yet without sin." The temptation of Jesus was imperative to her theology, which itself was situated in traditional church dogma. She made this clear in a letter to the Editor of *Punch*, several years before the *Man Born to Be King* scandal. In the letter she mentions the problem of Docetism in the early Church: a view (later proclaimed heretical) which held that Christ's flesh only *appeared* to be mortal and therefore his suffering and death were only illusions. In order to avoid this heresy, Sayers asserts, Christians must accept that Christ had a real body that experienced actual pain and real temptation. She then comments on the biblical accounts of the temptations, noting a parallel between Satan's temptation of Jesus on a tower of the temple (Matthew 4:6, Luke 4:9) and the thief's words to Christ on the cross (Luke 24:39). Satan stated "If Thou be the son of God, cast Thyself down," while the thief taunted "If Thou be the Son of God, come down." According to Scripture, of course, Jesus resisted both: remarkable only if he is considered truly and completely human (*Ltrs* 2.73).

Sayers therefore repeatedly illustrates in *The Man Born to Be King* that Jesus, although one with God, did not always know the mind of God, most famously demonstrated by his prayer in the Garden of Gethsemane: "If it be possible, let this cup pass from me" (Matthew 26:39). In her eleventh play of the cycle, *Man of Sorrows*, she has the apostle John despair over Jesus' agonized words on the cross: "My God, my God, why hast Thou forsaken me?" (Matthew 27:46). John asks the extra-biblical Proclus, a Roman soldier, "What horror could wring that cry out of him? He was always one with God" (303), as though to signal a dawning awareness that his own interpretation of Christ's nature has been too narrow. In her notes to the ninth play of *Man Born to Be King*, Sayers explains her own theory about the nature of Jesus:

> In the Upper Room, the God-consciousness and the Man-consciousness are very closely fused, with the God-consciousness often coming to the top. In the Garden, it seems as though the Man-consciousness became permanently uppermost, and I think it must be played with a very strong and real sense of the human horror at physical death. (230)

Her phrase "permanently uppermost" implies that the Man-consciousness remained with Jesus through his death, such that the agonized prayer on the cross might also reflect his human horror at physical death. And, as Sayers notes in her Introduction to the published version of *The Man Born to Be King*, "There is no reason to suppose that a thing is unauthentic because [a Gospel writer] does not mention it" (19). Interpretive speculation, as long as it does not undermine church dogma, deconstructs the text's sanctified status. Furthermore, if Jesus, called the Word of God in John 1: 1, was fully human, then might the Bible, called the word of God, also be fully human.

Ironically, those people who assert the sanctity of every word in the Bible actually, if unwittingly, end up glorifying themselves more than Scripture. Their attempts to protect the Bible are, more often than not, a protection of their own hermeneutic scaffolding—as though to say they, like the builders of Babel, can reach the mind of God. Sayers warns against such interpretive arrogance through the character of Judas in *Man Born To Be King*. She makes him intensely devoted to the mission of Jesus, at times the most admirable disciple. But, as the play cycle progresses, we discover that Judas is more committed to his own hermeneutic than to trusting Christ. Like Inspector Sugg, Judas "will build up a lovely theory, like the Tower of Babel, and destined so to perish" (*Whose Body?* 22).

His demise comes soon after the so-called "Triumphal Entry," reported in all four Gospels, which Sayers has Judas interpret in a peculiar way. Seeing Jesus ride into Jerusalem on an ass as the crowds yell "Hosanna," Judas comes to the conclusion that Jesus has "sold himself" to a political, rather than spiritual, revolution. Out of pure idealism, then, Judas willingly betrays Jesus, believing that his spiritual savior has fallen to political temptation. He tells Caiaphas, in all earnestness, that Jesus is "corrupt to the bone. . . . I suppose I was a fool to trust him" (220). Judas does not realize that the act he regards as Jesus's failure actually signals his strength.

In an incident Sayers made up to foreground the ambiguity of interpretation, Jesus actually resists temptation by renouncing an offer to lead a revolt against the Romans. An extra-biblical character, "Baruch, the Zealot," sends Jesus a message stating that he and his cohorts are ready to follow Jesus into battle. All they need is a sign: Jesus is to ride into Jerusalem on a war-horse that the Zealots have saddled and hidden for him; as soon as they see the sign they will join him with weapons drawn. However, Baruch disdainfully adds, if Jesus is not courageous enough to be their Messiah, he should enter Jerusalem instead on the back of an ass that is as weak as he (203).

Sayers creates this extra-biblical story to show that Jesus' ability to resist temptation is interpreted differently depending upon where one is situated. Judas sees only the ass, not realizing the renunciation it represents--just as, two decades earlier, Inspector Sugg saw only circumcised flesh, misinterpreting which body it represented. Similarly, detractors of *The Man Born to Be King* heard only Sayers' smart-ass slang, misinterpreting the author's intentions. Sayers' commitment to making the Bible sound as secular as possible did not mean she was "corrupt to the bone"; instead it signalled her desire to make the Gospel story dramatically interesting--especially to those people bothered by the pietistic protectivism of the Protestant Truth Society and the Lord's Day Observance Society. As she had written several years before,

> Let us, in Heaven's name, drag out the Divine Drama from under the dreadful accumulation of slipshod thinking and trashy sentiment heaped upon it, and set it on an open stage to startle the world into

> some sort of vigorous reaction. If the pious are the first to be
> shocked, so much the worse for the pious . . . . (*Creed* 24)

The excessively pious were, indeed, shocked by *The Man Born to Be King.* Sayers received "abusive anonymous letters," including one which began "You nasty old sour-puss" (*Ltrs* 2. 375). Most of the listening world, however, was startled into vigorous endorsement of the plays. Sayers was inundated with accolades from Christians and secular listeners alike, praising her ability to make the Bible come alive.

Instead of constructing a tower that pietistically protected conventional biblical language, thus deferring to those who thought King James English got closer to God, Sayers presented a babel of tongues in *Man Born to Be King,* bringing God down to earth--which is what the Gospel story is all about in the first place. Sayers, the one-time secular writer, had made God secular.

In its earliest English usage (13th century), the word "secular," meaning "of or pertaining to the world," referred to "members of the clergy," distinguishing those that lived "in 'the world'" from those who choose "monastic seclusion" (*OED*). Secular Christians lived outside the fane of protective architecture, mingling among the profane. However, daunted by what they encountered outside of sacred space, many built towers of religious behavior into which they herded all who might be saved, guarding them from the babel of multiple interpretations. For those in the 13th century, the tower was constructed out of the sacraments—an architecture sometimes literalized by the tower-like shape of the Eucharistic pyx that contained the Host. For Protestants in Sayers' day, the tower was the Bible. In contrast, Sayers, a genuinely secular Christian, demonstrates throughout her writing career that no human construction can capture the mind of God. While for some, as Derrida wrote, "the sign, as the unity of the signifying body and the signified ideality, becomes a kind of incarnation"; for Sayers, the only incarnation worth believing was that of the secular God.

NOTES

1. I thank Barbara Reynolds for the detail about the publisher's censorship. However, she inaccurately states that Peter notices the corpse to be "uncircumcized" (101). Though Sayers is, indeed, unclear in this portion of her novel, probably due to her publisher's proscription, the context implies that what Peter notices are the fleabites and decayed teeth. Some people have commented upon the anti-Semitism in Sayers' works, but this is mitigated somewhat by the fact that the (unrequited) love of Sayers' life was a Russian Jew. Sayers was writing *Whose Body?* as she fell in love with him, and her inclusion in the novel of Sir Reuben Levy's marriage to a Christian woman may have been a projection of her own desires.

2. Since the Revised Standard Version of the Bible was not yet available when Sayers was writing, I quote the King James through the remainder of this essay.

3. This is the title she gave the essay, first published 3 April 1938, and republished in *Creed or Chaos?*

4. Throughout her writings during the war, Sayers uses the Nazis to exemplify "sheer barbarism" ("Religions Behind the Nation" 69).

5. My comparison of Arius with the Pharisee echoes a discussion from my book *Writing Performances: The Stages of Dorothy L. Sayers*, 119-21.

6. See, for example, *Ltrs* 2. 170.

7. James W. Welch, in his "Foreword" to the British edition of *The Man Born to be King*, repeatedly cites the fact that protesters had not heard or read the plays. I discovered that Catherine Kenney also alludes to the parallel between Scorsese's film and Sayers' plays, but she does not explain the similarity (228).

8. Commenting on Scorcese's script is James Dobson in a "Focus on the Family" radio broadcast. The two protests against Sayers' scripts are quoted by Coomes (18).

Works Cited

Coomes, David. *Dorothy L. Sayers: A Careless Rage for Life*. Batavia, IL: Lion, 1992.

Derrida, Jacques. *"The Pit and the Pyramid: Introduction to Hegel's Semiology."* In *Margins of Philosophy*. Trans. Alan Bass. Chicago: U Chicago P, 1982. 69-108.

——. *Of Grammatology*. Translated by Gayatri Chakravorty Spivak. Corrected edition. Baltimore: Johns Hopkins UP, 1998.

Dobson, James. *Focus on the Family*. Radio Broadcast: 11 July 1988.

Downing, Crystal. *Writing Performances: The Stages of Dorothy L. Sayers*. New York: Palgrave, 2004.

Jeffrey, David Lyle. *People of the Book: Christian Identity and Literary Culture*. Grand Rapids: Eerdmans, 1996.

Kenney, Catherine. *The Remarakable Case of Dorothy L. Sayers*. Kent: Kent State UP, 1990.

Niebuhr, Reinhold. *Beyond Tragedy: Essays on the Christian Interpretation of History*. New York: Scribner's, 1937.

Reynolds, Barbara. *Dorothy L. Sayers: Her Life and Soul*. New York: St. Martin's, 1993.

Sayers, Dorothy. *Creed or Chaos?* Manchester, NH: Sophia Institute, 1974.

——. *The Documents in the Case*. With Robert Eustace. 1930. New York: Harper and Row, 1987.

——. "Gaudy Night." 1937. In *The Art of the Mystery Story: A Collection of Critical Essays*, Ed. by Howard Haycraft, 208-221. New York: Simon and Schuster, 1946.

——. *He That Should Come*. 1939. In *Two Plays about God and Man*, 123-186. Noroton: Vineyard, 1977.

——. *The Letters of Dorothy L. Sayers*. Vol. 2, *1937 to 1943: From Novelist to Playwright*. Ed. by Barbara Reynolds. New York: St. Martins, 1997.

——. *The Letters of Dorothy L. Sayers*. Vol. 3, *1944 to 1950: A Noble Daring*. Ed. by Barbara Reynolds. Cambridge: Dorothy L. Sayers Society, 1998.

——. *The Letters of Dorothy L. Sayers*. Vol. 4, *1951 to 1957: In the Midst of Life*. Ed. by Barbara Reynolds. Cambridge: Dorothy L. Sayers Society, 2000.

——. *The Man Born to be King: A Play-Cycle on the Life of our Lord and Saviour Jesus Christ.* 1943. Grand Rapids: Eerdmans, 1979.

——. *The Mind of the Maker.* 1941. San Francisco: Harper, 1979.

——. *The Nine Tailors.* 1934. New York: Harcourt Brace, 1962.

——. "The Religions Behind the Nation." In *The Church Looks Ahead: Broadcast Talks*, 67-78. London: Faber, 1941.

——. *Whose Body?* 1923. New York: Avon, 1961.

——. *The Zeal of Thy House.* 1937. In *Four Sacred Plays*, 7-103. London: Gollancz, 1948.

Welch, James W. Foreword to *The Man Born to be King: A Play-Cycle on the Life of our Lord and Saviour Jesus Christ*, by Dorothy L. Sayers, 9-16. London: Gollancz, 1946.

2

Yvette Nolan's *Job's Wife*:
The Center's Reaction
Jana Karika

In *God is Red*, Vine Deloria, Jr., cites a 1973 *Washington Post* article, which describes a modern astronomers' quest to study the "Crab nebula supernova" explosion of July 4, 1054. He notes that the supernova was "one of the spectacular events of celestial history" and was "clearly observable at various parts of the planet" (152). The *Post* article further notes that cave paintings and rock carvings in California, Arizona, and New Mexico dated around this event and depicting a bright light beside the moon may be evidence that North Americans saw it. Deloria points out that there are "very few references to this event in Europe, where the social science of history was fairly advanced" (152). He calls this a "startling victory of faith over experience" and gives the following explanation:

> For many centuries peoples of Western Europe believed that the heavens, being made by God at creation, were constant. The appearance of meteors and comets was thus a great embarrassment, since these phenomena seemed to indicate that the heavens were not all that stable. . . . The reason that there are very few records in Europe [concerning the supernova] is that everyone believed that the heavens were constant. Thus people did not really see what they

were seeing. (153)

Whether one is inclined to accept Deloria's explanation and assumptions concerning the beliefs and methods of European astronomers, it is difficult to ignore the conclusion he draws from the illustration: "If men become so blinded to their observations that their beliefs override their actual experiences, would it not seem possible that the whole method of interpreting events needs drastic revision?" (153). This conclusion raises an interesting question about the nature of the relationship between one's religious beliefs and one's perceptions of the world, a particularly important issue for postcolonial writers engaging in Biblical re-appropriation as a means of counter-discourse. It can be a difficult undertaking to create a work that forces an audience to reexamine the previously unquestioned interpretations of stories that are at the center of their religious beliefs and social hierarchy. Because the Bible has been used for so many centuries by European colonial powers to justify the oppression and religious conversion of native peoples, traditional interpretations which emphasize God's favor and blessings on the Israelites are of central importance, not only to the Christian religion, but to the whole social structure of colonial life. If the assumptions about God's chosen people, God's role in daily life, or even God's blessing in holy war are questioned, then the assumptions concerning colonial authority are interrogated as well.

Canadian playwright Yvette Nolan artfully implicates Biblical characters in this postcolonial cause through simple, yet provocative references to them in her short one-act play *Job's Wife*. The references are provocative primarily because there is virtually no explanation accompanyies them. The title, *Job's Wife*, for example, has no concrete tie to the play itself. The female character, Grace, is not married and is dating a man named Paul who is, according to the dialogue, "native."[1] The subtitle, "The delivery of Grace," is also veiled since we learn that pregnant Grace never delivers her baby; she miscarries. And finally, when God appears in answer to Grace's prayers, he is a "native Indian" who tells Grace to call him "Josh." Kimberly Blaeser, author of "Pagans Rewriting the Bible," observes that this type of spiritual and intellectual challenge is characteristic of many Native American writers. She writes, "Recent works [in contemporary native fiction] position us on the shifting grounds of religious and spiritual understandings, requiring us to reconsider, reevaluate, re-imagine what these terms mean or have meant to Indian people as well as what they might come to mean to all people" (13). Blaeser's statement is particularly relevant to the examination of *Job's Wife* because it reflects the reality that in a postcolonial society, as the marginalized find their way back to the center, they will influence society as often as they will be influenced. *Job's Wife* portrays the confrontation of a white Catholic woman with a Native God; hence, it represents the collision of orthodox Christianity with native spirituality–an inevitable occurrence in a multi-cultural society. Just as Walcott incorporates the traditions from his varied ancestral roots in *Ti-Jean and His Brothers*, Nolan explores the hybridization of Christianity and Native American traditions, not as an adversarial encounter, but as a quest for renewal. Blaeser writes, "It is the stasis and monologic quality of orthodox dogma that much contemporary Native American literature opposes, whether manifested in Christian or in tribal religions. What it upholds is heterodoxy, which implies instead responsiveness, a dialogic engagement, an involvement in spiritual relationships" (23).

The power of *Job's Wife* lies in the Biblical allusions that are left hanging in the air for the audience to contemplate privately. Each one represents a possibility for spiritual evolution, and if the audience member is to make sense of the reference, he must set aside the single-minded nature of the interpretations set forth in traditional church education. The stories must be revisited in a way that considers the various contradictions within the Biblical narrative and expands the realm of possible readings to include those congruent to Native American theology.

Before examining the allusions further, it is important to acknowledge the context into which they are introduced. The play opens with Grace, a white woman pregnant with her native boyfriend's baby, on her knees with her rosary. She cries out to God, "Oh please where are you? Why can't I find you now?" (19). God first appears on stage in a white mask and doesn't acknowledge Grace. When Grace falls asleep, God appears "laid out flat" on a scaffold upstage and accompanied, according to the stage directions, by the sound of "bones against bones and a rattle that sounds like a snake." He is described as "a big man, obviously native Indian" who "wears a cape made of rags and bones" which rattles as he rises up to the sitting position (20). This God awakes Grace from her sleep in order to answer her prayerful calls to him, but when she sees him, he is so different from her perception of what God should be that she believes he is a robber and pleads for her safety. Grace lets her beliefs override her actual experience, the first indication of Grace's spiritual stasis. She gives several arguments opposing the possibility that this could actually be her God. First she says, "I'm a Catholic, born and bred, and you're, you'll excuse my saying it, you're not exactly my idea of God" (22). Then she tries to redirect God to her boyfriend: "Perhaps you have the wrong room. Paul is asleep in the other room. You'd probably measure up to his idea of god" (22). Finally, God says, "No Grace, I am for you. Paul doesn't ask for things, he just gives thanks frequently" (22).

The first two hundred or so lines go on in this manner with several exchanges between Grace and God that establish the postcolonial conflict of acknowledging the possibility that God is multi-racial. Nolan simultaneously manipulates casting and costumes to give the audience visual and aural cues and designs a dialogue that clearly lays out the basic themes targeted in her counter-discourse. There is nothing covert in Nolan's delivery of the basic premise of her work: the assumption made by white Christians that God must also be white is the result of European cultural tradition, and that tradition unjustly privileges white people, their concerns, and their methods of worship above all other cultures and religions. However, the potency of Nolan's work extends beyond these simple, almost glib, exchanges between the native God and the white woman unwilling to accept him as the answer to her prayers. Several times throughout the play, the dialogue becomes almost predictable in its shots at Catholicism with remarks like, "All that free will and they choose Catholicism . . . between a rock and a hard place" (27). Although it is important to recognize these cues and exchanges that illustrate the obvious differences in European and Native religions and traditions, it is the less obvious connections that might spur on the spiritual debate.

The first Biblical reference is in the title, *Job's Wife*. The Old Testament book of Job is the story of a man who is stricken with great physical pain and emotional loss and yet is ultimately restored and blessed by God. Since the title is the only place referring to Job, the burden is on the audience to make the connection between the Old Testament Job and this postcolonial play. The generally accepted "moral" of the story of Job's life, as evidenced in expressions like "He has the patience of Job," is that if one trusts God and keeps humility and faith even in the midst of seemingly undeserved hardship, God will ultimately prove His goodness. While there may be elements of this message at the surface of the play, to stop interpreting would ignore the complex spiritual questions raised by Job's affliction. Those in the audience willing to set aside the pre-packaged morals passed down through orthodox Christianity will detect Nolan's use of the Book of Job to prompt a debate over the nature of God's involvement in daily life and her rejection of the fear of punishment that often motivates Judeo-Christian behavior. Just as Grace is emotionally conflicted over her pregnancy and confused about God's role in her life, the Book of Job is fraught with internal contradictions. The tension, for example, between Job's bitter tone and his refusal to curse God contributes to the endless debate within the Church concerning God's ways in the world. Several questions raised about the cause for Job's suffering. In the very first lines of the story he appears as "blameless and upright; he feared God and shunned evil" (Job 1:1). Yet Satan immediately suggests that Job bases his righteousness on the comfortable life he has been given. Satan says, "But stretch out your hand and strike everything he has, and he will surely curse you to your face" (Job 1:10). And so the initial assertion is that Job's affliction tests his faithfulness. Job's friends, however, contend that God only punishes those who deserve it; therefore, Job must have done something evil. An added element of irony exists in the pious words Job's friends offer him during his time of suffering. Even as they spew forth verses of praise for God's justice and condemnation of Job's unwillingness to admit his wrongdoing, they cannot name Job's transgressions nor to relay firsthand experience with the type of suffering Job endures. In *Exploring the Hebrew Bible*, John Carmody, Denise Lardner Carmody, and Robert L. Cohn assert that the apparent hypocrisy of the speeches can make them sound like "cheap wisdom, the sort of impure advice offered to the poor by the rich over cocktails" (294).

In a similar fashion, the counsel Grace receives from her priest is completely unhelpful. When she goes to confession, she tells the priest that she has engaged in sexual relations outside of marriage. He responds, "The church does not condone relations before marriage. (lewdly) How often?" (29). When she tells him she's pregnant, he responds, "You made your bed, you lie in it. . . . Well, you will have to marry as quickly as possible. Go now and sin no more." Although she calls after him—"Marry? I don't want to marry. He won't want to marry. Father, please. Father?"—the priest does not respond (30). The priest is not the only representative of orthodox religion that fails Grace, however. Grace's father represents her mother, whose voice is never heard throughout the play. When Grace reveals her pregnancy to her father, the thrust of his response suggests that the statement will kill her mother. He says his wife will never accept Paul, the baby's father, as a member of the family because "he's the kind of person [she] is used to helping, with her church group or whatever" (25). He seems more concerned that the pregnancy will embarrass the family in front of the church than that his own daughter is at an important emotional crossroads. A parallel can be drawn between the advice given to Job by his friends and the advice given to Grace by representatives of orthodox religion – they are both spiritually hollow.

The Native God, on the other hand, delves into the essence of Grace's dilemma, manifested in the father of her child who sleeps on the couch rather than in the couple's bed, and says, "What odd customs you have. Instead of apologizing to the one you have wronged and making restitution to that one, you go into a little box and whisper your mistakes to someone who doesn't know you and doesn't care about what you've done, and he tells you it's all right" (30). That exchange brings to the foreground a difference in a European Christian theology that emphasizes individual spirituality and a Native American theology that emphasizes the community – what Blaeser calls "a cyclical understanding of the spiritual relationship between each being and all other elements of creation" (18). Further into their conversation, the Native God extracts an even more revealing confession from Grace. She unwittingly acknowledges that she is more comfortable within the constructs of her hollow rituals than with the opportunity she has been given for genuine interaction with God:

> HIM: Do you feel cleansed when you come out of that little
>   box?
> GRACE: (doubtful) Well, yes.
> HIM: Really? Then what do you need me for?
> GRACE: I don't need you! I never asked you here! I'm not
> even convinced that you are here. (30)

For safety's sake, Grace clings to the Church's rituals rather than to venture into the multi-cultural world where things are, another clue to Nolan's allusion to Job. Job 11 records an accusatory speech from a friend who feels certain Job has transgressed. No matter how many times Job reiterates his innocence, his friends are still eager for him to confess something. Carmody, Carmody, and Cohn write, "[His friends] would rather hear 'correct' answers in which he does not believe than his honest emotions – a constant danger for 'orthodox' piety of any tradition" (295).

Recognizing the ambiguity and depth of spiritual conflict within the Book of Job allows the postcolonial audience also to recognize the potential of the text to aid in usurping the authority of Western interpretations and reach a deeper understanding of God's relationship with the world. Carmody, Carmody, and Cohn argue the following about the Book of Job:

> In this book the tentative, self-critical, argumentative character
> of the Bible and Israelite religion is very obvious, so reading it can
> help us appreciate that other books of the Bible share these
> characteristics, and that biblical religion as a whole is much more
> provisional than dogmatic, much more tolerant of conflict and
> diversity than concerned to lay down a single party line. This
> appreciation will be all the more valuable if our experience of the

people who profess to follow biblical religion, be they Jews, Christians, or Muslims, has suggested that biblical religionists are not always tentative and tolerant but, on the contrary, often seem sure of themselves to the point of simplemindedness. (308)

Certainly the Christianity of the colonizer is one of the religions that seem so sure of its authority that completely disallows intolerance of alternative views. Nolan uses the parallels between Job's wrest with God and Grace's struggle with her pregnancy to highlight the danger of stasis in the Christian psyche. Her alignment of the Christian priest in the confessional with the hypocritical friends of Job signals the spiritual deficit of the colonizer's Christianity.

The second Biblical reference is to Joshua, the Old Testament hero whose army brought down the walls of Jericho. As Grace first begins to understand that this "native Indian" claims to be God, she says, "You're saying you're God" and he replies, "Oh I so hate labels. Call me Josh. . . . I always kinda liked Josh" (21). A knee-jerk reaction would be to assume the native speaks sarcastically since the churce associates Joshua with the kind of holy war in which, like the Manifest Destiny theories of Europeans in North America, the Israelites were "chosen" by God to take possession of a "promised land" regardless of the cost to the people currently inhabiting it. But this would again be reciting the Church's interpretation without any consideration of an alternative view. Upon closer examination, one can see that many aspects of the Book of Joshua parallel Native American spiritual elements. For example, the focus of the Book of Joshua occurs on the land and great care (and considerable text) is devoted to the explanations of land allotments among the tribes of Israel.[2] Not only does the text remind us of the often neglected reality that the Israelites were divided into tribes, each with their own folklore and traditions, as opposed to one cohesive "chosen" people as often represented in the Church's memory, but it also indicates that different tribes had different folklore and emotional ties to their land, as in the story of Acsah in chapter 15 verses 17-19.[3] This would indicate a commonality with Native American spirituality, which is strongly tied to the land. In fact, Vine Deloria, Jr., who devoted the majority of his book *God is Red* to a discussion on the relative merits of a spatially oriented culture (like Native Americans) over a chronologically oriented culture (like Christianity), acknowledges that at the time of Joshua, the Hebrew priority was more inline with the Native American priority. He contends, "It is with the emergence of the Hebrews as a migrating nation into Canaan that the community and the land merge into a psychic and religious unity" (162). Not until Christians transfer their image of the "promised land" from a geographical position to a spiritual position in the after-life that they diverge from that tradition. In addition to these similarities between the Book of Joshua and Native American religion, some scholars speculate that the Judeo-Christian tradition does not represent the sociology and politics of the time. The sociological theories of Norman K. Gottwald, in his book *The Tribes of Yahweh,* suggest that the Israelite success in Canaan was due in large part to a multi-cultural effort to overthrow the oppressive governments in the area, which were ruled by kings. The traditional Judeo-Christian interpretation claims the victory clearly belonged to the Israelites; however, Gottwald contends that a fairly large number of native Canaanites inspired by the political theology of "Yahwism" which paid allegiance only to God and not to kings perhaps joined the Israelites (See in particular Gottwald's chapters 4 & 5). In any case, the success of the invasion of Canaan led to a shift in government "by tribal elders rather than centralized kings" (Carmody 122). In light of these considerations, the Book of Joshua has a considerably multi-cultural flavor.

Placing the spiritual conflicts of Job and the tribal land issues of Joshua within the context of the conversation between Grace and "Him" gives evidence that when released from the constraints of European social conventions and simplistic, self-serving interpretations, Biblical text can reflect some of the same concerns of Native American literature.

Job's Wife, more so than the other two works discussed here, seems to focus on the ways in which native spirituality can positively influence the colonizer's stale religious customs. Placing a white woman in a sympathetic position and making her the sole source of wise counsel that of a Native American creates a story which not only (re) centers the wisdom of the native culture, but also shows how that wisdom can influence and transform the stale spirituality of orthodox Christianity. Where Catholicism and white society failed Grace during her crisis, the wisdom of the Native God reassured her that she was not being punished. When the white God turned away from her, the Native God came to her and stayed in spite of her initial disbelief. And even in the end, when the Native God leaves with the Baby Spirit that Grace miscarried, the lack of admonishment or emotional anguish seems to be an implied promise that someday the world will be ready for a baby born of a Native father and white mother. The unspoken promise is acknowledged when Grace leaves a pile of tobacco, a traditional Native American gift of respect, on the floor behind her as she leaves for the hospital with Paul.

Kimberly Blaeser says that the work of Leslie Silko and Louis Owen, "like much of Native American literature, finally implicate the reader, refuse to remain a consumable product, and become instead a spiritual force" (13). In *Job's Wife*, Yvette Nolan has joined that effort to (re) center Native American spirituality so that it may, too, become a spiritual force and influence the spiritually stagnant Center.

NOTES

1. This is Nolan's term. It should be noted that the terms First Nation and Aboriginal are more commonly used terms in Canada.

2. Eight of the 24 chapters of Joshua are devoted to a detailed account of the land appropriation. (Joshua 12-19)

3. For a more detailed commentary of the tribal and land divisions in Joshua, see John Carmody, Denise Lardner Carmody, and Robert L. Cohn, Exploring the Hebrew Bible (Englewood Cliffs, NJ: Prentice Hall, 1988).

Works Cited

Barker, Kenneth, ed. *The NIV Bible*. Michigan: Zondervan Bible Publishers, 1985.

Blaeser, Kimberly. "Pagans Rewriting the Bible: Heterodoxy and the Representation of Spirituality in Native American Literature." *Ariel* 25.1 (1994): 13-31.

Carmody, John, Denise Lardner Carmody, and Robert L. Cohn. *Exploring the HebrewBible*. Englewood Cliffs: Prentice Hall, 1988.

Deloria, Vine, Jr. *God Is Red*. New York: Dell, 1973.

Gottwald, Norman K. *The Tribes of Yahweh: A Sociology of the Religion of Liberated Israel, 1250-1050 B.C.* New York: Orbis, 1979.

Nolan, Yvette. *Job's Wife. Blade, Job's Wife, and Video.* Toronto: Artbiz Communications, 1995. 17-34.

Ridington, Robin. "Cultures in Conflict: The Problem of Discourse." *Canadian Literature, Special Edition: Native Writers and Canadian Writing.* Ed. W.H. New. Vancouver: UBC P (1990): 273-289.

Walcott, Derek. *Ti-Jean and His Brothers. Dream on Monkey Mountain and Other Plays.* New York: The Noonday P, 1970. 81-166.

3   Djuna Barnes's *Nightwood* : The Biblical Perspective

Trish Clark

The biblical allusions in Djuna Barnes's *Nightwood*, too great to be dismissed, leave the reader questioning Barnes' view of the Church and formal religion. The ambiguous nature of *Nightwood* allows the reader certain flexibility in analysis. A key point in *Nightwood* is the reference to bowing down and what this action can reveal to the reader. The characters' observances of this action may seem to some to be a form of punishment for pursuing the Adamic nature (referring to the fall of Adam and suppressing human desires) or a celebration of embracing human nature.

Barnes begins *Nightwood* by introducing Guido Volkbien, a Jew of Italian descent. Although a Jew, he and his son Felix desperately hide their ancestry and adopt a lineage from Austria "to uphold his story . . . [with] a coat of arms that he had no right to and a list of progenitors (including their Christian names) who had never existed" (Barnes 3). Felix, like his father, becomes obsessed with burying his past and finally must answer for this false identity in the rearing of his son, who Barnes describes as being "born to holy decay" (107). The idea of Guido's birth being of holy decay can be interpreted in two ways. One, Guido could be reaping the final results of Felix and Grandsire Guido's attempts at burying the true nature of their family's religious origin. Another explanation for young Guido's decay is the absence of sacrilege in his mother Robin. She embraces the animalistic nature that humanity fervently warns to avoid in the Bible. In fact, Dr. O'Connor later describes her as "outside the 'human type' – a wild thing caught in a woman's skin" (146).

Barnes' introduction of Guido renouncing his religion is in complete contrast to the introduction to the New Testament, the book of Matthew. The four gospels, "Matthew," "Mark," "Luke," and "John," give the account of Christ's life, ministry, death, and resurrection (Henry 2, vol. 5). However, Jews were hesitant to accept this self-proclaiming Messiah. Therefore, Matthew devotes the first chapter to tracing Christ's lineage to King David and Abraham, "that nation and family out of which the Messiah was to arise" (3, vol. 5). Henry also explains that the Jews "were very exact in preserving their pedigrees" (3, vol. 5) which again shows the profound contrast in identity-claiming seen in the gospel of Matthew and Barnes' characterization of the Volkbien patriarchy. *Nightwood*'s opening chapter devotes itself to hiding true family heritage (which, in itself is a Jewish pride) in order for the Volkbien family to be accepted, while Matthew's beginning chapter defends Christ's lineage in Judaism in order for Jews to accept him as the Messiah.

Another interesting step in Barnes' portrayal of Christianity is the suggested biblical references in the chapter headings of *Nightwood*. For one, "Bow Down," the first chapter in the novel, introduces a kaleidoscope of characters who could be interpreted as modern Sodomites who defame God and may likely be humbled and forced into obeisance. Guido and Felix are both fixated on erasing all traces of their Jewish history, thus Christianity could interpret them as denying the omnipotence of God. Barnes describes Frau Mann as "unsexed as a doll" and as having a "bulge in the groin" (13); later, Frau Mann refers to Doctor O'Connor as *Herr Gott*, or Mister God (25). Frau Mann's character can be described as androgynous due to the reader's inability to distinguish her as man or woman. Her acknowledgement of O'Connor as God dismisses the sacredness of the title and gives honor to a man who really wishes to be a woman. Doctor O'Connor overtly refers to God throughout the novel but never indicates true worship of Him. His tone is somewhat sarcastic, especially in light of his blaming God for being born a man instead of a woman. He thinks of God as a prankster with a bag of tricks, seeing whose lives can be destroyed through his magic. Bowing down refers not only to an act of reverence but also (and more importantly in *Nightwood*) to a movement forced by God. The Sodomites were characterized as a self-indulgent people, living for the moment, only caring for the desires of self; they had no reverence for God. The characters thus far parallel the people of Sodom. This chapter merely offers the reader a glimpse into the state of society depicted in the novel; Barnes' characters will either bow down in penance for their defamation or bow down in reverence to themselves for portraying the self in all of its confusion.

Another chapter that continues the allusion to bowing down is "Where the Tree Falls." In this chapter, Felix expounds upon Guido's condition as well as his own emotional state concerning Robin and Guido. We not only hear Felix's personal convictions of these topics but also the somewhat unbiased judgments of O'Connor. Felix asks the doctor if Guido will be able to survive knowing that others have said he is not "sound of mind" (120). The doctor tells Felix that "'Guido is not damned...Guido...is blessed – he is peace of mind – he is what you have always been looking for – Aristocracy'" (121). However, Barnes previously describes Guido as "mentally deficient and emotionally excessive, an addict to death" (Barnes 107). O'Connor's statement could mean that Felix has accomplished making Guido the fine, Christian-born son he has always wanted his family to be and that Felix should do something else other than worrying to death about his son and who he wishes him to be. However, O'Connor could also have been saying, "You got exactly what you wanted: a son just as screwed up as any aristocrat could be. His mother doesn't love him and his father is worried what others will say about his past." Felix worships his faux heritage and Robin enough to allow it to consume not only his life, but also the life of his son. The title of this chapter could be a reference to a verse in Isaiah, "Shall I fall down to the stock of a tree?" (*King James Bible*, Isa. 44.19). Henry explains that trees were used to carve out gods for idol worship and the one who creates it "gives divine honours to it, prostrates himself before it in the most humble reverent posture, as a servant, as a suppliant; he prays to it, as having a dependence upon it, and great expectations from it ("he saith, Deliver, me, for thou art my god" [v. 15])" (246). The one posing the question is asking if God would want him to fall down before a tree stump – a senseless, lifeless, helpless thing – like those who created these images (246). Here, "Where the Tree Falls" comes to signify Felix's bowing down to his graven images: lineage and Robin. He cannot help but worship them both. His entire life is devoted to burying religious tradition; he also tells the doctor that Robin is with him through Guido (117) and further describes her intently, almost stalkingly, through images in his remembrance of her, such as the way she walks, the way she wore her clothes, and her silence (117). The conclusion of the chapter shows Felix embarrassed for being himself as he looks at whom he believes to be the Grand Duke Alexander of Russia, the epitome of prestige and great family tradition. Barnes describes him leaving as "an animal . . . turn[ing] its head away from a human, as if in mortal shame" (123). Felix does not understand that the denial of his lineage is the denial of his true self; the masking of his identity only humanizes, or stifles, the potential of his true, or animalistic, nature. He has fallen down to the idol of humanity, casting away his true self.

Nightwood may also explain the worst of all sins: imitation. Someone may replicate another's experiences in hopes of either deceiving herself or others. In either case, this impersonation ultimately leads to the destruction of personal desires and convictions. Jenny Petherbridge cannot survive on her own. She lives vicariously through the lives of others or others' possessions. In fact, she seems to have no idea of self at all. Her description bears resemblance to an attempt to make one doll out of many. "She had a beaked head and the body, small, feeble, and ferocious...they did not go together. Only severed could any part of her have been called 'right'" (64). Barnes also explains her conversations as "words that...seemed to have been lent to her" (66). The concept of borrowed possessions does not only apply to verbal and physical aspects, but also to emotions. Barnes states that, "No one could intrude upon her because there was no place for intrusion. This inadequacy made her insubordinate – she could not participate in a great love, she could only report it" (68). Jenny's lack of self-recognition or self-fulfillment leaves her with no other choice than to steal recognition and fulfillment from others. Her surroundings are the lives of many, having a

> continual rapacity for other people's facts . . . defil[ing] the very meaning of personality in her passion to be a person; somewhere about her was the tension of the accident that made the beast the human endeavour. (67)

In other words, Jenny is the beginning of the end for self-indulgence.

Jenny, along with the fourth chapter, is known as "The Squatter." This title also refers to bowing down, or at least the imitation of it. Barnes states that, "she was a 'squatter' by instinct" (68) and only capable of mimicry. Jenny forgot long ago how to seek her own indulgences. Thus, in her continual shadowing of others' experiences, she has forgotten her own desires. Even O'Connor describes her as the "poor and lightly damned" (138). She desperately wants Nora's prized possession, Robin. When she claims Robin as her own, she desires to experience Robin's life; however, she can only view it through Robin's actions. She will never be able to experience it for herself. Squatting can only imitate bowing down. Jenny squats because she cannot bow down to her natural instincts; according to Barnes, she has none. The descriptions of her physical framework, her relationship with others, and her self-less nature seem to result in Jenny being a failed human being. Barnes even describes her as one who, "seemed to be steaming in the vapours of someone else about to die; still she gave off an odour to the mind (for there are purely mental smells that have no reality)" (65). Although she could literally be defined as dead, something, at least enough to know how to mimic, exists within her mind. Therefore, Jenny pretends to bow down to fool others and herself.

One might even wonder if Jenny knows the difference in squatting and bowing down; both bowing and squatting appear to be the same physical position, but Jenny is always one moment behind because she must watch her assailants' every move to be in sync with her surroundings. Barnes may include Jenny's character as a mimic to give parallel to Christianity's hypocrite. The hypocrite may seem as spiritual as any other devout person; however, the individual knows this action or experience to be a lie. In the Bible, even Job questions, "What is the hope of the hypocrite, though he hath gained, when God taketh away his soul?" (27.8). Although Job's inquiry seems to parallel Jenny's outcome, Jenny surpasses the hypocrite to a somewhat more pathetic level; although she knowingly seeks the possessions of others, she never realizes that denying her own desires will literally be the "death of her" (a phrase she so carelessly uses to describe others' afflictions as her own) (66). God does not have to take away her soul; she loses it through her own actions of self-denial.

Dr. Matthew O'Connor earnestly seeks his true identity, but can only experience it superficially; although born a man, Matthew understands himself to be a woman. Throughout *Nightwood*, O'Connor embraces femininity. For example, his medical "specialty" is gynecology, although he holds no formal license. He also refers to himself (among other female references) as "the Old Woman who lives in the closet," suggesting his transgendered secret (138). In the chapter entitled, "Watchman, What of the Night?" Nora comes to O'Connor in search of an answer that might somehow explain Robin's nightly tendencies. In the book of Isaiah, an Edomite asks, "Watchman, what of the night?" and then repeats the question: the watchman answers, "The morning cometh, and also the night; if ye will inquire, inquire ye" (21.11-12). Henry explains the job of the watchman as "somebody that was more concerned for the public safety and welfare than the rest, who were generally careless and secure" (Henry 114, vol. 4). The watchman's duty required him to "make discoveries and then give warning...in this they must deny themselves" (114, vol. 4). O'Connor's unofficial duty in *Nightwood* is to care for all of the others. He plays counselor to all of Robin's scorned lovers. He conducts himself as any good watchman should. He explains his discoveries of Robin to Nora and Felix through trite stories that eventually come to explain his own character. However, everyone ignores his vain endeavor to seek direction, thus his failure to deny himself. Nora and Felix are so soundly secure in their humanistic behaviors that even O'Connor's tirades of animalistic nature cannot save them from their own destruction. For example, O'Connor explains, "Our bones ache only while the flesh is on them . . . it serves to ache the bone . . . We will find no comfort until the night melts away; until the fury of the night rots out its fire" (85). To this explanation, Nora says that she will never understand Robin, that she will always "be miserable – just like this" (85). The point of O'Connor's statement serves to exhort Nora to find her own comfort, to burn out her obsession with owning Robin and seek her own identity instead of analyzing Robin's.

O'Connor's quest for simplicity comes to fruition in "Go Down, Matthew" where he explains how a priest inadvertently cajoles O'Connor to masturbate in a church. The priest tells O'Connor to "Be simple . . . be simple as the beasts in the field; just being miserable is not enough – you have got to know how" (131). The doctor interprets this as a call to his natural behavior, forsaking all human inhibitions, yet neither he nor Tiny O'Toole is able to perform. He then questions God, "Have I been simple like an animal, God, or have I been thinking?" (133). Thinking inevitably separates humanity from the animal kingdom. O'Connor's thoughts, whether they be from guilt or embarrassment, ultimately keep him from being able to perform the natural function of erection or orgasm. Readers slowly witness O'Connor's decline into self-pity. As he rambles about his life discoveries in a bar to an ex-priest, the doctor forgoes his role as watchman to curse those who could not see the truth. "May they all be damned! The people in my life who have made my life miserable, coming to me to learn of degradation and the night" (161). He then also realizes that his life has been for naught. Although he knows he has the soul of a woman, he is a man; in his quest for his identity, he finally sees it as his curse, "It's all over, everything's over, and nobody knows it but me . . . now nothing, but wrath and weeping" (166). Therefore, O'Connor bows down, more importantly breaks down, after realizing his fight with himself and God is over.

Although I am concentrating more heavily on those characters who actively bow down, it is just as important to relate one's denial of the self as well. Nora merely acts as observer of all acts in *Nightwood*. She watches Robin indulge in a lifestyle somewhat foreign to her own. Rarely does she venture out with Robin. She waits for Robin to return from her gallivanting and play. She wishes to taste of Robin's lifestyle, but is unwilling to completely divulge in Robin's animalistic behavior. Nora parallels Lot in the observance of Sodom and Gomorrah's behaviors. He also does not seek the "iniquity of the city," but cannot draw himself from observing the self-indulgent behaviors of man (Gen. 19.15). Nora witnesses first-hand Robin's complete return to primitivism. She forever links herself to Robin by sharing in this experience, thus fulfilling O'Connor's prophecy: "Nora will leave that girl someday; but though those two are buried at opposite ends of the earth, one dog will find them both" (106). The only response given to Robin's transformation is Nora's attempt to touch Robin; and at that moment, Robin transcends at lightning speed (169). Robin's slight brush with humanity seems to hasten Robin's return to the natural; Nora inadvertently aids in Robin's animalistic transformation (an ideal time for Nora to accept her own innateness. Nora neither bows down to the self in submission nor in reverence; on the contrary, does she, unwilling to wake Robin from her nightmare, continue to walk in the denial of the day.

Of course, Robin acts in complete rejection of the rules of humanity. *Nightwood* concludes with Robin's complete metamorphosis into a dog. This transformation takes place in the most sacred of religious surroundings, a church. The interpretation of this change relates to how one views nature. The Christian world may view Robin's "possession" as a final curse for her denial of all sacredness in God and her life (lesbian relationships, neglecting her child, etc.). Robin's final "digression" might appear analogous to the fate of the Philistine's god, Dagon. When the Philistines captured the arc of the covenant, they brought it to the temple of Dagon. The next morning when they went to the temple, Dagon's image was fallen on its face. The Philistines simply set Dagon in his place again. However, the second morning, they found

> Dagon was fallen upon his face to the ground before the ark of the Lord; and the head of Dagon and both the palms of his hands were cut off upon the threshold; only the stump of Dagon was left to him. (I Sam. 5.4)

Robin's desire to embrace her Adamic nature could be interpreted as proof of her defying God, or at least her attempt to project the self above religion; therefore, her attempt to worship the self brings about the degradation of prostrating in penance against her will. However, Robin invites the physical transformation into a dog; she willingly accepts it. Robin controls where this conversion takes place; she chooses her life to begin in the church. Therefore, this is her spiritual awakening. Robin embraces her natural self. Christianity may view this bowing down as a dog to be her punishment from God. On the contrary, Robin wills this change to happen; she refuses to deny her true self.

In light of the embedded religious allusions in *Nightwood*, Barnes must have had a rooted message to the reader concerning religion. If not, why would Barnes purposely utilize Christianity, like her characters, unconventionally? She contorts the dogmatic nature of religion and creates her own sense of worshipping the self in its natural sense. What might appear as the deterioration of Christianity may serve as a revelation of a purer form of religion: one without thought or consciousness. On the other hand, Barnes may have viewed Christianity as one realm untouched, but adhered to, by women. The church's structure and formality has been tried and tested in various ways. For instance, the Protestant Reformation, Martin Luther specifically, dared to question the authority of the church and who has the right to interpret scripture for the common man. However, the church's foundation of male-domination is still accepted dogma; possibly, Barnes' contortion of religion in *Nightwood* may be an attempt to deliver the reader, especially women, an alternative to organized religion.

Mary Daly, a former Catholic theologian turned postchristian feminist philosopher, explains that "the struggle for the equality of the sexes have often seen the Catholic Church as an enemy . . . for Catholic teaching has prolonged a traditional view of woman which at the same time idealizes and humiliates her" (Daly 53). The Bible gives specific instructions for women and their roles in everyday life; these instructions all derive from a state of obedience and submission. Women are made from man; women are the cause for the curse of man and the final dismissal from Eden; women must submit themselves to their husbands, and women must keep silent in churches. However, Catholicism idolizes the Virgin Mary for the Immaculate Conception. Daly expounds upon this irony, a view among progressive Catholic theologians known as the "myth of the 'eternal feminine'" (147).

Although Catholic theologians explain this idea as a compliment to women, Daly explains the eternal feminine as a means to "keep a woman on a pedestal at all costs, paralyzing her will to freedom and personhood" (148). In order for Mary to keep her picture-perfect image as the mother of Christ, then women need to subject themselves to a low, unnoticeable profile. Daly continues to explain that, "on all fronts the Eternal Woman is the enemy of the individual woman looking for self-realization and creative expansion" (150). Robin, for a short time, attempts, yet ultimately fails, the conventional lifestyle of the eternal feminine. She marries and delivers a son, but holds no regards to playing the role of submissive wife or doting mother. In fact, when deciding to leave Felix, Robin exclaims furiously, "I didn't want him!" and slaps Felix across the face (49). Robin's actions defy all characteristics of the Eternal Woman.

Upon discovering that she is pregnant, Robin begins aimlessly visiting churches, praying incessantly. However, while kneeling, "Robin, trying to bring her mind to this abrupt necessity [of prayer], found herself worrying about her height" (46). Prayer, a reverential act in religion, holds no regard for Robin; her preoccupation with trivial matters such as height denotes her lack of focus conversing with God. Even the nuns realize that Robin looks as if she "would never be able to ask for, or receive, mercy" (46). Again, the nuns represent the Eternal Woman, and their idea of mercy, if granted to or solicited by Robin, would eventually desecrate the religious mythology Barnes creates: one that does not recognize rigid gender identities, humbling acts of obedience, or fixed iconography. Although Robin searches for answers through the structure and history of organized religion, she inevitably leaves empty-handed and draws closer to the realization that only she controls or, as Barnes may argue, creates her own divine experience.

However, Barnes attempts to not only liberate women from the confinement of the Eternal Woman, but also men from the responsibility of manhood. Notice, for example, O'Connor's effeminate nature. Robin's scorned lovers do not seek manly passion from O'Connor; on the contrary, they welcome his loving compassion (or so they perceive it as compassion) and ability to be a good listener. O'Connor fits the historically effeminate behavior, willingly listening to one's problems then carelessly spreading that same information as gossip to other characters. The doctor's gender-psyche surpasses triviality; he has "in [his] heart...the wish for children and knitting," even telling God, "I never asked better than to boil some good man's potatoes and toss up a child for him every nine months" (91). His desire for a husband and children parallel the stereotypical desires of women. Even his complaint of not being a woman is a historically feminine quality: women are never satisfied with what they have.

Barnes' attempts at gender-meshing in *Nightwood* may only begin to reveal her true thoughts of the Church. Why would Robin choose her final conversion to take place in a church? Barnes possibly wanted the reader to understand that religion is more than a building. Barnes' work gives adequate support to her possible attack on organized religion, but that message still is multi-faceted. However, one message remains clear: religion is an experience, not one to be imitated or controlled, but one to be created through instinctive, sensual transcendence. Barnes' religion is created by the participants and adheres to the laws of nature, which inadvertently, has no laws to follow. In the book of Romans, Paul writes that those "who changed the truth of God into a lie, and worshipped and served the creature more than the Creator" are given "over to a reprobate mind" (1.25, 28). In contrast, Barnes relishes the idea of reprobation, for it denounces all constraints of purity and goodness, the epitomes of

Christianity. An institution or revered text would merely restrict the essence of spirituality that Barnes' religion offers.

Works Cited

Barnes, Djuna. *Nightwood*. New York: New Directions, 1961.

Daly, Mary. *The Church and the Second Sex*. New York: Harper Colophon, 1968.

Henry, Matthew. *Matthew Henry's Commentary*. 6 vols. Old Tappan: Revell, 1964.

King James Bible. Grand Rapids: Zondervan, n.d.

Djuna Barnes's Revision of Biblical Genealogies in her Novel *Ryder*
Martina Stange

Nothing Sacred.
- Angela Carter -

It seems to be a truism by now that Djuna Barnes (1892-1982) produced some of the most imaginative, outrageous, and significant avant-garde art of the twentieth century; notably, her novels *Ryder* (1928) and *Nightwood* (1936) are an individual and an individualistic contribution to the modernist period, a period well known for the overwhelmingly male aesthetic that characterizes much of its so-called canonical literature.

In *Ryder*, Barnes traces the history of the Ryder family, comprising Sophia, the Grandmother, Wendell (her son) and his two wives, Amelia and Kate-Careless, and of course, Wendell's numerous known and unknown offspring. At first glance, the reader is offered in the novel the neat filial order of a family chronicle. This fact seems to be underlined by *Ryder*'s solidly patronymic title, but one soon discovers by the fourth chapter that "not paternal authority, but rather interruption and conscious rejection of patrilinearity" (Miller 130) are at the centre of the text. Wendell's mother Sophia "gave him no father's name but stayed by her own"[1] and embodies "[i]n her rejection of patriarchal authority and her affiliative conception of motherhood, the decadence of filial genealogy and the rise of a new, independent womanhood" (Miller 130).

Barnes self-consciously includes and parodies other texts and traditions, especially patriarchal conventions, in her novel. She was extremely well read, and created an intertextual world in many of her works, but in this multi-faceted novel, she arranges as if in a stylistic display case various parodies of cosmogonies, Eastern myths, and the Holy Scriptures. In *Ryder* the reader meets parodies of Chaucer's Tales (chap. 10), the epistolary novel of the eighteenth-century (chap. 12, 25 and 35), a short drama (chap. 41), a lullaby (chap. 22), cosmogonies (chap. 44), a fairy tale (chap. 27), a pulp-fiction version of a sentimental girl's novel (chap. 24)[2] and of course, the Bible (chap. 1, 46). The style is "copy" in the double sense this term had in Early Modern English: *Copiousness* as a lusty expressiveness of language, and, of course, the text is a parody of other works, a true copy.

In its explicitly intertextual organization, *Ryder* also comments on its own technique by showing "intertextuality is not just used [here] as one device amongst others, but is foregrounded, displayed, thematized and theorized as a central constructional principle" (Pfister 214). The walls in Sophia Ryder's room are covered with numerous drawings, etchings and lithographies.

> There smiled forth the women she admired: George Eliot, Brontë, Elizabeth Stanton, Ouida, the great Catherine, Beatrice Cenci, Lotta Crabtree, and the great whore of the spirit, the procuress of the dead, the madame of the Bawdy-house-of-the-Shades, the miracle worker - 'Caddy-Catch-Can.' There were the men she admired for this and for that, - Proudy, the railroad magnate, . . . Burgoyne[3], Pepys, Savonarola, a massive head of a Samoan chief, . . . a pencil sketch of the Divine Dante, to say nothing of those later celebrities who may have found themselves on her walls because of the beauty of their prose, Stedman, Browning, Wilde and Thompson.[4] (23)

An interesting collection of historical but also fictitious persons is assembled on the walls. At first this seems to be an arbitrary selection, a confusing get-together, but the various pictures touch upon central themes developed in the novel.

The actress Lotta Crabtree (1847-1924) and the authors Robert Browning (1812-89) and Oscar Wilde (1854-1900) were members of a radical reform movement in London, and well known to Barnes' paternal grandmother, Zadel Barnes, a spiritualist and early feminist, who was also the autobiographical source for the Sophia-character in *Ryder*. Savonarola is notorious for being a fanatic religious reformer. These people exemplify the subversive potential of *Ryder* – a novel whose aim is to break down encrusted ideas of gender roles in parodistic form.

In 1895, a book published in New York caused a sensation: *The Woman's Bible* by Elizabeth Cady Stanton. It included commentaries written by women on selected chapters of the Bible. Zadel, a good friend of Stanton, introduced Barnes to the work of Elizabeth Cady Stanton, who, as the editor of *The Woman's Bible,* was definitely not sanguine about the possibility that the biblical records contained any nonpatriarchal faith. Therefore, when Barnes took up the Holy Scriptures as a textual model for *Ryder*, she was aware of feminist[5] critical assessments of biblical texts as sexist that began at the end of the nineteenth century. The influence exercised on *Ryder* by an exegesis of dogmatic texts from a feminist perspective constitutes a subversive potential not to be underestimated because it clearly serves to undermine the monolithic block of gender roles. The Bible[6] often symbolizes the founding text of patriarchal culture, and Barnes realized the cultural significance of the text which serves as an important influence and model for her style, events, characters and genres. Furthermore, she recognized the "problems and possibilities of women's authority in a culture shaped by the masculine hegemony that the Bible has come to represent," and made them the root of her intertextual interaction or carryover with the Bible (Brown 163). She started to question, to renew, and to update traditional images of the Divine and/or theological aspects in various ways:

1. The figure of the grandmother called Sophia/Wisdom is consciously woven according to the female image for God in Scripture, Divine Wisdom.

2. One of the central characters called Molly Dance constructs a reversionary cosmogony from a female point of view by eliding Eve and tracing original sin to men.

3. Another female character also retells the Fall myth, imagining a female and lesbian paradise, lost through Wendell's introduction of heterosexuality and rivalry among women.

4. *Ryder* is a novel with illustrations by its author, some of mock religious character.

5. And, in one of the central chapters of the novel, Barnes deliberately takes up the overall structure of the biblical genealogies from the Bible and changes it to suit her reversionary intent from a feminist standpoint. As this aspect has never been discussed in critical assessments of Barnes' novel before, it will be the focus of my essay.

Barnes enfolds what Mikhail Bakhtin has described as the difference between "authoritative discourse" and "internally persuasive discourse." Authoritative discourse is "the word of the fathers"; it is a "prior discourse," a discourse "given" with its own "special language" not to be "profaned" (Bakhtin 342). Evidently, the Bible as the ultimate form of patriarchal textual authority bears many traits of such an authoritative discourse. By contrast, an internally persuasive discourse is a "word that is denied all privilege . . . and is frequently not acknowledged in society (not by public opinion, nor by scholarly norms, nor by criticism)" (Bakhtin 342). As Bakhtin underlines, authoritative discourse is inflexible and rigid, forbidding a "play with borders," quite in contrast to the supple and fluid quality of internally persuasive discourse (Bakhtin 343-346).

But, as Bakhtin also notices, "both the authority and discourse and its internal persuasiveness may be united in a single word – one that is simultaneously authoritative and internally persuasive – despite the profound difference between these two categories" (Bakhtin 342). I think that Djuna Barnes rewriting of Biblical stories offers such a double-voiced discourse; here, the authoritative and internally persuasive discourses merge and open up a "hybrid construction" (Bakhtin 342-344). However, before I start to describe Barnes' revisionary method in more detail, let me first provide some information about her model: the biblical genealogies.

According to the overwhelming majority of written records of the Bible, Israel saw its sociological structure based on kinship. Kinship must have been of decisive importance not only for determining descent, but also for conceptions of social prestige, job order and ethnical and political relations.

It is also quite obvious that Israel had a patrilinear form of society; women neither played a role in the regarding the identity of a person nor in matters of inheritance, though some women were in higher social positions. In such an ordering of society, man (the male) is given all authority in the family: he is the lord and the owner of his wife (or wives) and his children. Women only appear as objects of exchange in the social interactions as, for instance in Genesis 34,8-10: "Hamor appealed to them in these terms: 'My son Shechem is in love with this girl; I beg you to let him have her as a wife. Let us ally ourselves in marriage; you shall give us your daughters, and you shall take ours in exchange.'"

If we take these two propositions for granted, it makes available a discussion of genealogies in the Bible:

1. Most of the genealogies are found in the Tetrateuch and the Chronistic Books, "but they are also incorporated in the Deuteronomistic redaction" (Plum 74). If we talk about genealogies in the Bible, we have to be aware of the fact that a lot of these texts are constructions; they are not providing historical facts but they are time-bound and narrative-laden. One can deduce from them information on social, political, economical and ethnic ideals. Normally we have to ascertain the extent to which the genealogical form was utilised by the author of a particular book to communicate characteristic theological convictions.

Let me very briefly give an example: the Priestly historians first realized a complete genealogical system describing the degrees of relationship among the individuals in the historical tradition of Israel. These sections in the Pentateuch reveal the most complex and comprehensive genealogical speculation, that "knits together all of the important figures of the Israelitic traditions of the primeval and patriarchal periods by means of a continuous genealogical tree, the culmination of which was probably the inauguration of the cultus with its Aaronic priesthood and also an enumeration of the main clans that constituted the people of Israel" (Johnson 37).

Therefore, we can sum up the function of the genre "genealogy" mainly as etiological and/or legitimatory.

On a more general level genealogies have to do with developments, outcomes, begettings and the belief in God's sovereign and detailed control of history. They always exhibit a sense of movement within history toward a divine goal. In their externally demonstrated fertility they are signs of Yahweh's blessing that will continue (Gen 5).

A genealogy can be constructed either in an ascendant form, X1, the son of X2, the son of Xn or in a descendant. X1 begot X2; or, these are the names of the sons of X1: X1.1. Descendant genealogies can be further subdivided into straight linear ones as in Gen 4,1, in diachronical ones as in Gen 5,1-32 or as a kind of spreading as in the Table of Nations in Gen 10 (Fechter).

2. As women play no important role in a patrilinear society for questions of personal identity, these genealogies mainly present rows of male descent (Gen 4:1f; Gen 5:1-32 and Gen 10).[7] As profound androcentric texts they are theological interpretations, argumentations, projections and selections rooted in a patriarchal society. Normally, they need to be read critically for their theoretical-theological androcentric tendencies, and they must be evaluated historically in terms of their own time and culture. But this was not the way the American authoress Djuna Barnes dealt with the biblical genealogies.

Wendell Ryder is introduced in Chapter. 1 of the novel as "Jesus Mundane," a kind of mock-saviour. His label "Jesus Mundane" points to special pretexts: the gospels of the New Testament. The gospels according to Matthew (1:1-17) and Luke (3:23-38) introduce Jesus via genealogies, "which have been created in full realization of the Old Testament genealogical system and the possibilities of the genre" (Plum 87). Wendell is promised, "Thy life and the lives that thou begettest, and the lives that shall spring from them, world without final. . . . [t]hose multitudes that shall be of thy race begotten, unto the number of fishes in thin water, and unto the number of fishes in great waters" (3). But this "ordinary" Jesus is an ambivalent figure, though he is praised and lifted above the other people like Abraham to whom God gave the covenant: "I will bless you abundantly and greatly multiply your descendants until they are as numerous as the stars in the sky and the grains of sand on the seashore" (Gen 22,17), he is also rebuked:

> Go now, and lift up thy cries from about me, for I have done with thee awhile and thy ways, and thy ways' ways, and the things that thou hangest about the places of the soul. . . . Knowest thou if thou hast troubled me, or how thou hast inconvenienced me for thy sake? Or if thou hast pleased me in any way, or hast not? . . . These things are as the back of thy head to thee. Thou hast not seen them. (5)

The speaker in the passage is difficult to pin down: in its diction, it resembles God from Genesis, floating above the waters, impenetrable and without a (textual) body. Only a reading of the whole novel offers a clue to the identity of "me." The pronoun signals the summarized protest of all women against Wendell. He is the one who has never paid attention to their anguishes and their pain, especially their labour pains: "[T]hink not that it [= the labour pains] is a tithe of the loosening and the tightening that was among the bowels" (4). Wendell's elevation to the title and position of a new Jesus, blessed with fertility like Abraham, constantly "scattering [his] seeds" (198), is the curse lying on the women in the novel. But they are nonetheless able, as we will see, to take their revenge on him.

The intertwining of the themes of numerous progeny, fertility and continuity, released by God's "Be fruitful and increase" in Gen 1,28, is further elaborated in *Ryder*, most of all in chapter 46, "Ryder - His Race", where the genealogies of the Bible are consciously and stylistically evoked. Here, Wendell Ryder's possible descendants are endlessly enumerated in the structure of a genealogy. The 'fathering' of offspring is presented as the central event in Wendell's life, assuming a historical importance. His longing for paternity, his wish to reproduce himself indefinitely, perpetually remaking the world over in his image is a means of overcoming uncertainty and mortality. Additionally, his wishful thinking invokes a hitherto unknown greatness and fertility by documenting a direct line of descent.

> I, my love, am to be Father of All Things. For this was I created, and to this will I cleave. Now this is the Race that shall be Ryder – those who can sing like the lark, coo like the dove, moo like the cow, buzz like the bee, cheep like the cricket, bark like the dog, mew like the cat, neigh like the stallion, roar like the bull, crow like the cock, bray like the ass, sob like the owl, bleat like the lamb, growl like the lion, whine like the seal [...]. Never before have all these sounds been common to the human, but I shall accomplish it; [...] Some shall be prophets, some sophists, some scoundrels, some virgins, some bawds, some priests, some doxies, some vassals, some freemen, some slaves [...]. (210/211)

In the first place, Wendell's dream reflects the sociology of patriarchal societies; that is, those societies like the biblical Israel dominated by male, property-holding heads of families: "I make you father of a host of nations. I will make you exceedingly fruitful; I will make nations out of you" (Gen 17,6). Second, his whole status is legitimised by way of this genealogy that resembles in its totalising claim Ishmael's genealogy in Gen 25,12-17. Nevertheless, Wendell takes up a model written in the authoritative style of the Bible; he challenges it internally through the persuasive discourse. In his fantasy, the uncrossable zone between animal and human is broken down. By attributing the ability to produce animal sounds to his future children, Wendell renegotiates and extends the possibilities of the process of creation and disrupts the order and hierarchy willed by God. As a result, the stability of a neat 'chain of being' as exemplified by the authoritative discourse of the biblical genealogy gets shifty and undetermined. What's more, Wendell's position as patriarch and ruler of a future genealogy is pulled into this maelstrom of a now uncertain hierarchical ordering.

Moreover, Wendell disregards the dichotomy of good and evil in the diverse 'professions' his children are going to take up. In a combination of conventionality – there is nothing to argue against a prophet and a virgin – and humorous violation – a scoundrel and a bawd are less desirable subjects for a society – Wendell again overturns his own master plan. Thus, we encounter in this passage an example of Bakhtinian double-voiced discourse, where two different intentions, one in the style of the authoritative discourse and the other in the internally persuasive discourse, are expressed simultaneously. In such a hybrid construction the authoritative discourse looses his status as an inviolable and unchallengeable norm.

Wendell who has cast himself in the role of biblical patriarch and an American Noah has unwittingly undermined his secure position, and is now a vulnerable victim for some women in the text. Accordingly, two women further thwart his plan, because he seems to have forgotten one of the basic premises of nature: that the continuity of history is depending on both sexes. And "where choice triumphs over determination the female sex is represented" (Plum 85) as already the biblical examples of Rebecca, Naomi and Bathseba have amply illustrated.

The first incident is recounted in the aforementioned central chapter 46. Wendell comes one day to Lady Terrance Bridesleep, proposing to sleep with her. Lady Bridesleep, "well into her sixties" (206), yet "vastly pleased with nature at its most natural", accepts because "[w]ho was she at sixty that upon the turnspit of her attraction a man should baste and be a man for all that" (208). After she has taken pleasure from Wendell, he wants to talk about a probable name for their future child. Not surprisingly, he as the creator of the new member of his famous race wants to give the child its name (211).

In analogy to religious/cosmological beliefs fathers are thought to be the sole creators and begetters of their children; Carol Delaney calls this a "monogenetic" theory of procreation (3): "[P]aternity has not meant merely the recognition of a physiological link between a man and a child . . ., paternity has meant begetting; paternity has meant the primary, creative, engendering role the *logos spermatikos*, the seminal word of God" (11). Women are reduced in this theory to 'vessels', merely giving birth and nurturing the children.

But Lady Bridesleep refuses the role in which Wendell would cast her – a new Sarah, a late-blooming childbearer. "[B]eing a woman of wit" (206), she casts down the "crowing," post-coital Wendell, telling him that their son, of course it should have been a son, shall be called "Nothing and Never" (211). The chapter ends with Wendell's stunned response, a singular occurrence of silence in this otherwise extremely loquacious text: "Wendell opened his mouth, but no sound came" (211).

The other incident, where his aspirations as the father of a real genealogy are refuted is told in chapter 44 entitled "Fine Bitches All, and Molly Dance." Molly Dance, a dog breeder, is a female version of Wendell Ryder, with many children and a veritable sexual appetite. Molly takes her (sexual) pleasure as it comes and makes no effort to ascertain the paternity of her children. This transgressive female constantly casts doubt upon the legitimacy of children and introduces uncertainty into a patriarchal system, making "of Society a Dupe" (26). Wendell, who is deeply troubled by her behaviour, wants to procure some certainty: He will 'beget' her next child, and then she will know its father. But again, his 'master-plan' comes to naught. "For Molly reveals the power of female promiscuity to unravel the symbolic order of patrimony" (Miller 135): "'Well,' said Molly . . . , 'how shall she, or I, or you, or another know but that Dan, the corner policeman, be he? For not two nights ago he had the same idea, and that only goes to show you,' she added, ' that one man's thoughts are not worth much more than another's" (199).

These are only two examples, but in the course of the whole novel, Wendell is clearly reduced to an interchangeable part in a strictly maternal cosmos. Taking up the biblical structure of genealogy implies patrilinearity as wishful thinking on his side, but this is completely rejected by some of his desired mates. Lady Bridesleep and Molly Dance overturn patriarchal society, already crumbling through Wendell's hybridisation of the sacred text, by literally 'unfathering' his children.

His defeat is made explicit because both women take away from him the chance and the right of naming the desired (male) child. The act of naming signifies recognition of identity, an endowment of new essence and being, and it also implies that the namer has authority over the named. Yahweh changes Abram's name to Abraham (17:5) in his direct dialogue with him, yet the names of his wife and his son, which are also determined by Yahweh, are to be given by Abraham, who represents God's authority as husband and father (Fuchs 120). Wendell will never be able to proceed to establish paternal authority over a newborn son by naming him, and by adding him to his desired genealogy: "Without the woman's oral designation of the father, paternity remains indeterminate" (Boheemen 31).

The book of Genesis marks the revelation that there is only one principle manifested at the divine level: Without a partner, God created the world. God gave Adam the power to continue creation, by means of his "seed"; and Genesis in his various genealogies is the record of the genealogical procession of seed e. g. who begot whom. The male role in procreation as documented in the genealogies reflects on the finite level God's power in creating the world. Divinity in Genesis is creativity and potency – a principle animating the universe – and implicitly or explicitly masculine. It is also presented in the form of authoritative discourse that has the status of taboo zone, seeking to avoid dialogue. In *Ryder*, creativity and potency is newly constituted in Wendell's way to bring the authoritative discourse into contact with the internally persuasive discourse. At last, a league of memorable female characters completely redefines creativity and potency. These textual manoeuvres allow for a re-reading of the biblical texts, not necessarily profaning them but, in Adrienne Rich's phrasing, "what's sacred tries itself/ one more time" (25-31).

NOTES

1. Djuna Barnes, *Ryder*, Elmwood, IL: Dalkey Archive Press 1990, p. 17. Hereafter, quotations from the novel are cited parenthetically in the text by page number.

2. The chapter is reminiscent of the "Nausicaa"-episode from James Joyce's *Ulysses*.

3. John Burgoyne (1722-92) was a 'second-rate' Georgian playwright.

4. This is probably an allusion to the poet Francis Thompson (1859-1907), who has written severals poems and essays with a religious content. His style is characterized by an expressive imagery.

5. The term "feminist" signifies a certain set of views, which could also be held by men about the equality of the sexes and the need for example for non-hierarchical relationships.

6. In quoting the Bible, I have taken the New English Bible as my text. For the sake of convenience throughout this essay I speak of "the Bible" though I am quite aware of the fact that there are at least four: the Jewish, Catholic, Eastern Orthodox and Protestant Bible. Likewise, I refer to the "Old Testament" and "New Testament" as established and familiar terms though, of course, the Jewish Bible has no "New Testament" and Jews do not regard their sacred text as an "Old Testament." For a lively discussion in written form on this contested ground in the field of Biblical Theology, see Christoph Dohmen and Thomas Söding (eds.), *Eine Bibel – Zwei Testamente*, Paderborn: Schöningh 1995.

7. In Matthew 1, 2-7 four women "enter the stage" via the linear genealogical list: Tamar, Rahab, Ruth and Bathseba. For a lucid commentary, see Hubert Frankemölle, *Matthäus-Kommentar*, Düsseldorf: Patmos-Verlag.

Works Cited

Barnes, Djuna. *Ryder*. Elmwood Park, Il.: Dalkey Archive Press, 1990.

Bakhtin, Michael. *The Dialogic Imagination: Four Essays*. Ed. Michael Holquist. Austin: U of Texas P, 1981.

The New English Bible with the Apocrypha. Oxford/Cambridge: Oxford and Cambridge UP, 1970.

Boheemen, Christine van. *The Novel as Family Romance: Language, Gender, and Authority from Fielding to Joyce*. Ithaca/London: Cornell UP, 1987.

Brown, Amy Benson. *Rewriting the Word: American Women Writers and the Bible*. Westport/Connecticut/London: Greenwood Press, 1999.

Carter, Angela. *Nothing Sacred: Based on Fathers and Sons by Iwan Turgenev* [a play]. Toronto: Couch House Press, 1988.

Delaney, Carol. *The Seed and the Soil: Gender and Cosmology in Turkish Village Society*. Berkeley et al.: U of California P, 1991.

Fechter, Friedrich. *Genealogie im Alten Testament*. 31. Aug. 2000. ⟨http://www.phil.uni-freiburg.de/SFB541/B1/fechterdoc.html⟩.

Fuchs, Esther. "The Literary Characterization of Mothers and Sexual Politics in the Hebrew Bible." *Feminist Perspectives on Biblical Scholarship*. Ed. Adela Yarbro Collins. Chico, California: Scholars Press, 1985. 117-136.

Herring, Phillip F. *Djuna: The Life and Works of Djuna Barnes*. New York/London: Viking, 1995.

Johnson, Marshall D. *The Purpose of the Biblical Genealogies: With Special Reference to the Setting of the Genealogies of Jesus*. Cambridge: Cambridge UP, 1969.

Miller, Tyrus. *Late Modernism: Politics, Fiction, and the Arts between the World Wars*. Berkeley/Los Angeles/London: U of California P, 1999.

Pfister, Manfred. "How Postmodern is Intertextuality." *Intertextuality*. Ed. Heinrich F. Plett. Berlin/New York: de Gruyter, 1991. 207-24.

Plum, Karin Friis. "Genealogy as Theology." *Scandinavian Journal of the Old Testament* (Aarhus) 1 (1989): 66-92.

Rich, Adrienne. "The Desert as Garden of Paradise." *Time's Power, Poems 1885-1888*. New York: Norton, 1989. 25-31.

Stange, Martina. *'Modernism and the Individual Talent': Djuna Barnes' Romane* Ryder *und* Nightwood. Essen: Die Blaue Eule, 1999.

Wilson, Robert R. "The Old Testament Genealogies in Recent Research." *Journal of Biblical Literature* 94 (1975): 169-189.

5   The Measure of (Un)marked Vows
in Two Early Modern English Dramas
Karoline Szatek

Whether avowed Protestants or recusant Catholics, Elizabethan and Jacobean citizens shared one common characteristic – swearing. Much of what we know about the early modern English indicates that their swearing often occurred when they name-called, as in "horeson!" or to swear *at* someone. Cursing also included, "By Jove!" to swear *by*; and they testified in a court of law to swear *against* a defendant. For especial effect, they loved spouting blasphemy. They frequently called upon some part of God's body and/or crucifixion. "Zounds," they exclaimed, for Christ's wounds; "S'blood," for His blood, and "S'heart!" for, of course, Christ's heart. As with oath-makers today, the early modern English citizens employed oaths to vocalize surprise, disappointment, anger, jubilance, as well as other emotions.

The English propensity for oath-making hearkened back at least to the medieval period, "the time of Joan of Arc," when "the French labeled the English, 'les Goddems,'" Geoffrey Hughes points out in *Swearing: A Social History of Foul Language, Oaths and Profanity in English* (1).[1] Although through the years the clergy imposed religious injunctions against the early moderns, the English nonetheless continued to use off-color speech.

The popularity of swearing in early modern England may be blamed on Elizabeth I. She had a strong appetite for and prolific use of both secular bawdry and religious swearing.[2] Nathan Drake claims that Elizabeth I never "spared an oath in public speech or in private conversation when she thought it would add energy" (qtd. in Shirley 10). Elizabeth, in fact, advocated swearing and suppressed any injunctions opposing oath-making in public, in court, or even on the stage.[3] Consequently, swears, curses, and vows of both the secular and religious kind appear in preponderance in the period's written artifacts, specifically, the dramas.   Playwrights like Thomas Heywood and even Shakespeare, to name but two, gave Elizabeth and their other audience members what they wanted to hear—swearing—and in a variety of forms and situations.

In addition to Queen Elizabeth, the Bible also seems to have influenced what the English said. Although during the sixteenth and seventeenth centuries most English people were illiterate, they, ironically enough, did learn about swearing from the Bible during obligatory Sunday services. Ironically, the same queen who advocated cursing required her subjects attend church; otherwise, they would either be financially penalized or tossed into jail for a time. While at church, Anglican preachers delivered sermons on God's covenant with Moses and Abraham, God's vow to toss Adam and Eve out of Eden, Jesus' promises of heaven, Noah's oaths to his family, and Abraham's contracts with Sarah and Hagar.

Church, though, was not the only place the English learned about the biblical oaths. Fathers and mothers schooled their children from the Bible; some fathers even told or read their children Bible stories from either the Geneva or King James versions.   Merchants, ship captains, farmers, and unschooled peasants often cultivated biblical principles in their children. And while some–the most irreverent–did not carefully follow biblical doctrine, they did know of the Good Book's stories well enough to refer to them at will in their oath-making. And humans, being what they are, imperfect, often make promises and almost as often break them whether they vow to remain married, economically stable, law-abiding, or even child-bearing.

Most early moderns knew both about covenant-making and of the many biblical vows and oaths stated in the Bible, therefore. And the dramatists being commentators on social practices, alluded to biblical covenant, or swearing-an-oath, in their plays.[4] Early modern dramas' characters who represent all socio-economic stations, articulate many of the profane oaths stated in the Bible. Both men and women in the dramas utter various agreements and write contracts that relate in one way or another to the Old and New Testaments.

Non-foul-mouthed covenants, which may be spattered throughout with profanity, occurs in Thomas Heywood's *The Wise-Woman of Hogsdon*, a tale concerning patient women, witchcraft, profligate fiancees, and, ironically, biblical allusion by way of characters' swearing, breaking oaths, and experiencing consequences for having done so.

Wise-Woman's initial scene opens with Boyster, Young Chartley, and several gallants throwing dice and expressing profanities. These young men ask for blessings and damn the dice to which young Chartley while asserting a feigned morality admonishes, "Nay, Swear not, lets play patiently" (I.i. 106). A good looking young man of privilege Chartley squanders his father's money and his own inheritance. Heywood labels Chartley a "wild-headed gentleman" in the "Dramatis Personae." Because he thoroughly enjoys his lifestyle, Chartley swears never to marry.   Whether we consider Chartley merely irresponsible and therefore too young to marry, or whether we simply view him as a coward, Chartley foreswears wedding. To Chartley being married must have meant imprisonment, considering the etymology of the word. The word "wedlock," derives from the Anglo-Saxon "wedd," meaning "a pledge" and "locc," or, to lock in (OED). A married person, if not careful, can lose independence of thought and action. To others—biblical characters, early modern people, playwrights, and characters—marriage was a serious promise that certainly united not only a man and a women but also established covenants that carried with them legal, political, social, and commercial power—and implications. Marriage, then, was a matter not to be taken as lightly as Chartley does.

Some early moderns, Elizabeth I as an example, secretly vowed not to marry. However, when Chartely makes his personal oath, he is already betrothed to a young country gentlewoman, Second Luce. Prior to the Act I, scene I Chartley abandoned Second Luce and headed for the city where he wooed and became engaged two other young ladies, Gratiana and a goldsmith's daughter, First Luce, who appears in I. ii and whom I'll call "Sempter Luce" to avoid the unnecessary confusion.

In the biblical era, the early modern period, and even today, keeping promises measured a person's honor, upbringing, dignity, and, all too often, the depth of someone's purse. Second Luce trusted Chartley's vow and wanted to preserve her honor follows Chartley to the city dressed as a page. In the course of her journey to mend the breach in her wedding engagement, Second Luce befriends the Wise-Woman of Hogsdon. Wise-Woman eventually concocts a scheme to trick Chartley into marrying Second Luce; or, to state this in another way, Wise-Woman causes Chartley to honor his covenant with Second Luce.

In Hebrew, "covenant" means "berith" and may be defined as "a treaty, alliance of friendship, a pledge, an obligation between a monarch and his subjects, a constitution. . . [,] a contract" (*Complete Word*). Biblical scholars claim that both Old and New Testament covenants followed specific rules. First, a covenant occurred between people, governments, the deity and an individual, or the deity and a single nation. Second, the promises made were considered spiritually and legally binding. Shylock alludes to biblical precedents when he defends his "bond" when he literally translates both the Old Testament and Venetian law. Last, to make a covenant, an individual or government promised, vowed, and swore an oath either verbally or in writing: The Ten Commandments in Old Testament, the Epistles in the New Testament, and in court in early modern England where two parties would swear for their legal right to enact one end of a contract, or to be foresworn, disavowed, and sometimes legally manipulated, as in Shylock's case.

Obedience to God's covenants meant blessings. Ruth, a Moabite, one of Lot's descendants and a Gentile, sacrificed her personal freedom by committing herself to Naomi, her Israeli mother-in-law's well-being and to her second husband, Boaz, Naomi's relative. Ruth also quietly promised to honor God. For her steadfast promises and loyalty God rewards Ruth with children, a sign of His silent covenant with her. Moreover, this once barren woman became the great-grandmother of King David and an ancestor of Jesus of Nazareth (Matt 1:5). Also, Abraham became the Father of a Nation, Noah and his family lived through the Flood, and God restored Job's home, family, and finances far beyond Job's expectations.

To the Hebrews and Israelites pledges, promises, oaths, vows, and swearing had a direct connection with God, even if God was not literally included in the oath. Had King Saul's son Jonathan not placed his own life in jeopardy to honor his pledge with King David, King David of course might not have lived, but Jonathan might have risked being punished by David or possibly by God, since God chose David to be one of Jesus' ancestors.

Whether by individuals or by God, covenants ordinarily consisted of three additional components: signs, sacrifices, and oaths "which sealed the relationship" between two parties (*Complete Word*), or, to state this in another way, "to cut a covenant," or "karat b'rit." In Hebrew, "b'rit" means "to cut." A sign of a covenant could have been a burning pot, a fiery bush, a parting of a sea; biblical sacrifices involved the slaying of a young lamb, goat, a ram. In the case of Abraham, God required Abraham he lay his son Isaac an alter as an offering to Him. After the parties participated in the first two components, they then made a solemn convenant, an oath or a swearing of a promise. If one of the parties broke a covenant, the promise-breaker could suffer consequences.

Some biblical characters may have kept their oaths, but being human and therefore prone to imperfection they often broke their vows, whether they promised to remain married, economically stable, law-abiding, or even child-bearing. Judas betrayed Christ for political, religious, and financial reasons. David violated his marriage vows when he committed adultery with Bathsheba. The Hebrews only saw the promised land but never walked into it because they glorified graven images and disbelieved God's promises to deliver them fully. As with the Hebrews, David, Judas, and others suffered consequences; David grieved terribly for separating himself from God; and Judas committed suicide.

To seal his betrothal to Second Luce, Young Chartley probably gave her a sign of his intent – a ring or other gift, perhaps a public reading of their marriage bands. Young Chartley, though, understood that marrying Second Luce would have meant his sacrificing his free-wheeling ways, something he clearly sought to avoid. What he does not acknowledge is that he has to pay a penalty also for his lover affairs with Sempter Luce and Gratiana, his lying to the young ladies and his friend Boyster, and his dishonorable manner of spending his father's money. Chartley will not be rewarded as he failed to remain obedient to his marriage vows.

Although not of biblical proportions, Chartley in *Wise-Woman* must suffer consequences. Heywood, wittingly or no, follows scripted, biblical, covenantal law. Chartley therefore becomes a marked man not only from a biblical perspective but also from an early modern and gender-related one.

According to Deborah Tannen and rightly or wrongly, men lean towards being confrontational because they are challenge-oriented. They tend to respond truculently whether a statement or question is meant contentiously (Tannen, *Understanding* 31). And when men hear what they interpret to be an order, they are inclined to resist it. This assertive behavior allows men to feel hierarchically superior, claims Tannen (*Understanding* 30). To accept a "low-status position" in "a relationship" can cause some males to react "intense[ly] uncomfortab[ly]" (30). In Heywood's play Boyster nearly loses the sempter's daughter, Luce, because he confided in Chartley and trusted he had a mutually-agreed covenant with Chartley.

Chartley, though, thoroughly enjoys competing, as evidenced by his gaming. Chartley personally vows himself that he will win Sempter Luce, and he does. Also, Chartley loves the high stakes of simultaneously juggling more than one young lady's affections. When Chartley's friends and lovers confront him at the end of the play and require he make restitution, Chartley strenuously resists them simply by concocting more lies. When Gratiana asks Chartley, "What drew you to this folly" regarding his courting of her and Second Luce, Chartley answers,

> Who but the old dotard thy Father, who when I was honestly married to a civill maide, hee perswaded mee to leaue her, I was loath at first, but after intreating vrging, and offering mee large proffers, I must confesse I was seduc't to come a wooing to the. (V.iv.2175-80)

To counter Chartley, Heywood employs the Wise-Woman as his foil. Wise-Woman, a witch and self-proclaimed charlatan, arranges for Chartley to face Boyster, Sempter Luce and Second Luce, Gratiana, and even his own father who has been searching for his prodigal son. Wise-Woman craftily arranges for all the other characters to confront Chartley at once about each of his contractual breaches. These men and women pressure Chartley into telling the truth. They circle him and hurl large verbal stones at him that he finally cannot avoid any longer. They also provide proof: Gratiana's father, Chartley's father, and Second Luce, to name three.

Subsequently, Chartley comes clean:

> I had best bit out my tongue, and speake no more; what shall I doe, or what shall I say, there is not out-facing them all: Gentlemen, Fathers, wiues, or what else, I haue wronged you all. I confesse it tht I haue, what would you more? Will any of you rayle mee? Ile beare it. Will any of you beate mee? So strike not too hard, Ile suffer it. Will any of you challenge mee? Ile answer it. What would you haue mee say, or doo? One of these I haue married, the other I haue betrothed, yet both maides for mee. Will you haue mee take one, or leaue t'other? I will. Will you haue mee keep them both? I will. (V. iv. 2214-24)

Chartley publically dashes what little pride he had left, his honor, and his manliness. He sees his "conscience blush[es] inwardly then [his] face outwardly" (2294-95) after having admitted to his father:

> . . . if I should say I would become a new man, you would not take
> my word. If I should sweare I would amend my life, you would not
> take mine oath. If I should bind my selfe to become an honest man,
> you would scarce take my bond. (2285-89)

Although his father initially refuses to value Chartley's new covenants, Second Luce does, for she swears to marry him after all.

Whereas at the end of the play Chartley's oaths restore him him to his bride, his father, and his friends because they see an honest change in him as a result of Wise-Woman's intercession, Chartley's earlier oaths seemed to empower him, or so he thought. No woman will give him orders; no man will control him either through trust or money, Chartley's attitude and behavior suggests. One person in the play has power over him, however– Wise-Woman, a social outcast.

Wise-Woman lives like a hermit, supposedly casts spells, has little money, and to some degree typifies the early modern patriarchal perception of women. Second Luce actually wears breaches, but she still subordinates herself even to Wise-Woman who operates "as a key trope for imaging social disorder" (Chedgozoy 9). To misogynists, Wise-Woman symbolizes the uppity, disorderly woman suggestive of Eve, Jezabel, and even Queen Elizabeth, but Wise-Woman as opposed to these women and Chartley kept all the covenants she swore.

At the end of Act V Chartley learns his lessons, and the other characters admire Wise-Woman for being remarkable and raise her status regarding her economic, her social, and her gender. Chartley even tells her "theres some loue for you" (V.iv.2324).

And Wise-Woman did not even cross-dress.

Wise-woman represents female ingenuity, strength, endurance and power. She depicts, too, women placed at the margins of early modern society–the farmers' wives, fishwives, and Billingsgate's prisoners. The patriarchy's titles for these women marked their lower-class status; even so, these women challenged early modern politics, economics, and culture (Chedgzoy 16).

Wise-Woman is also an older version of Heywood's Diana, whose own markedness bewilders each of the characters in the last act of Shakespeare's *All's Well that Ends Well*.

The plot of *All's Well that Ends Well* focuses primarily on Diana, along with Helena and Bertram who sharse Chartley's sentiments about marriage. Chartley, though, marries at the end of *The Wise-Woman of Hogsdon*, while Bertram weds in the beginning of *All's Well*. Bertram also attempts to escape his commitment to his betrothed, Helena, a young orphaned woman reared in the court and who healed the dying King of France's fistula. In return the King bestowed a valuable ring to Helena and granted Helena's wish to marry a very reluctant Bertram, Count of Rossillion. Bertram regarded Helena, an orphan whom Bertram's mother's ward, more as a servant than an economic and socio-political equal.

After publically carrying out the marriage covenant with Helena, Bertram flees the court then subsequently woos Diana, who, unaware of Bertram's vows until she meets Helena. Helena left the court after Bertram violated his oath and coincidentally took up temporary lodgings with Diana and her financially-strapped, widowed mother. Diana and her mother were once part of the upper class. Helena learns of Bertram's seductive plan for Diana and carefully informs and the two other women of her court wedding to Bertram then carefully lays out a plan for Bertram to reestablish his vows to Helena in public and significantly reward Helena with title, rank, power, and influence.

After a turn of events, Diana wears the ring the King of France had given Helena. When Diana encounters the King at the end of the play, Diana refuses to relay the events of the situation in a direct manner; rather, she speaks in riddles. Diana asserts that Bertram is both guilty and not guilty of the crimes of which she accuses him. Furthermore, Diana claims, Bertram abused her—but did not defile her; and, she points out, she is neither a virgin nor ruined. Diana also bluntly admits she owned the King's ring, but did not possess it, buy it, find it, steal it, or borrow it (V. v. 267-304).

To the French King and court Diana's riddling linguistically signifies her as "some common customer" (l. 286), "an easy glove" (l. 277), and therefore deceitful, crafty, even evil, and the King calls for an exorcist. Until Helena, rumored dead, miraculously appears (l. 304-05). Before France sees Helena Diana's infuriating discourse causes him to threaten Diana with imprisonment and her execution:

> King: Unless thou tell'st me where thou hadst this ring,
> Thou diest within this hour.
> Diana: I'll never tell you. (V.v. 282)

Diana must riddle, however. If she speaks deliberately or if she perjures Helena's case, she would risk breaking her own vows both to Helena and her mother. Plus, she would tarnish her family's name.

Especially when measured against Diana's verbal convolutions, Bertram hears a challenge and responds bluntly, directly, and brusquely. Bertram, as with Chartley, imagines he is" following "his own free will" (Tannen, *Understanding* 29-31). To evidence his own power the King of France also speaks sharply.

But Diana's words, phrases, sentences—her rhetorical and logical complexities—significantly empower her, so in the play's last moments the King of France admires her, tells her to select a courtier for a husband, and though not stated, restores Diana and her mother economically. He also rewards the two with name and respect.

Diana's linguistic machinations also seal the vows and covenants she committed to her mother and Helena. Moreover, Diana's riddles successfully demarcate Bertram as a fraud, an adulterer, a liar, a coward, and a youngster unable to keep sworn oaths, forcing Bertram to call out, "Oh, pardon" (V.v.309). Biblically, at great risk Diana sacrifices herself to the court for Helena by showing France Helena's ring marks her position in the matter among Bertram, Helena, and her. Politically and socially she also honors her oath to Helena.

The terms "marking," "marked," and "unmarked" refer to the Trubetzkoy and Prague school of linguistics, which Roman Jakobson developed and Deborah Tannen applies. According to linguists, "voicing," or verbal expressions, tones, and sounds, are usually either marked or unmarked utterances. Each articulation characterizes individuality, gender difference, cultural and public identity, and social rank.

Christine Knoeller, in *Voicing Ourselves*, defines "voicing" and therefore "marking":

> If voicing is in fact language attributed explicitly or by implication to someone other than the speaker, how is it that what is not otherwise attributed is understood to be "unvoiced," without any explicit "attribution" to the speaker? . . . What is "unvoiced," that is one's own words, is linguistically unmarked, whereas voicing another's words is necessarily marked as such by attribution [an] explicit attribution. (48-49)

In western and some eastern cultures, the unmarked and unvoiced operate synonymously with each other and with the silenced and absent; so, too, the marked and the voiced with the privileged and present. The marked/unmarked establishes "hierarchical relationships"; the marked utterance usually establishes predominance over the unmarked (Jakobson 261; Tannen *Working* 108). Therefore, linguists often view root words—"wit," "inform," "cat"—unmarked. They also consider prefixes and suffixes *un*-marked because they have significance or "no meaning on their own" (Tannen, *Working* 108). Other language experts view the addition of affixes and suffixes to root words as marking the base of a word because these empower newly formed words— "wittingly," "uninformed," "cattiness."

The understanding of linguistic markedness can be slippery at best because the meaning of a root word or its related word can based on the connotation of each interpreter.

When regarding marking and gender Tannen writes that "the unmarked forms of most English words" (*Talking* 109), like "prince," "chef," and "murder," denote male rather than female. In other words Tannen refers to a male word as "the unmarked case"; endings, such as "ess and ette, . . . mark words as female (109). Unfortunately, marking words for female also, by association, tends to mark them for frivolousness" (109). And "any marked form can pick up extra meaning beyond what the marking is intended to denote. The extra meanings carried by gender markers reflect the traditional associations with the female gender: not quite serious, often sexual" (109). Marking is a flexible tool, then, for discussing discuss early modern dramas' characters' vows, oaths, and gendered utterances.

In *All's Well* Diana is a marked figure from both a patriarchal and linguistic standpoint. Indeed, Diana's seeming equivocations in front of the King and the court distinguish her as incredible and therefore insignificant, so much so that the King would easily throw her in prison. Rare, was it, that the early modern court took women seriously. Moreover, the court viewed women's oaths as untenable; They considered women fickle, coy, and therefore, often without merit. Parliament frequently required Elizabeth I defend her words, especially when she first stepped onto the throne. But Parliament's demands on Elizabeth were not unprecedented. Ancient patriarchal attitudes written into the Old and New Testaments influenced early modern ideologies toward male/female markedness. The early moderns new that Joseph nearly caused the stoning of Mary, the mother of Christ, because she was pregnant. Mary claimed she had laid with no man. Instead of believing Mary upheld her vows with him, Joseph treated Mary like Mary Magdalene, a common prostitute. As did the Virgin Mary *All's Well's* Diana punctuates her claims with proof. After waiting for the right moment to present her evidence Diana no longer speaks in riddles but directly and pointedly says, "Good mother, fetch my bail" (V.v.295). Diana 's mother leads Helena into the court and astounds everyone present, especially Bertram. Diana switched her verbal position from conventionally-viewed female speech to male to expose Bertram's crimes and to spite the King's specific orders to send her to prison.

Infrequently do women adjust their speech patterns and practicies, but they do so if in the company of men, and especially if the men play any games. "The very games" women "play are more likely to be men's games than women's" (Tannen, *Understanding* 29, 31, 235). Diana knew the games Bertram played, so she chose a similar one to marks both him and Helena.

Helena also takes on the male speech and behavioral patterns when she confronts Bertram with his written oath that he thought he gave to Diana but handed to Helena instead. Helena reads the letter to the court, specifically directing it to Bertram: "'When from my finger you can get this ring / And are by me with child" (V.v.314-15). Marginally convinced, Bertram finally accepts Helena as his wife, but will divorce her should she be lying about her pregnancy. She is not, but Bertram attempts to take the upper hand; but he cannot because Helena, with Diana's help, vows with certainty she carries Bertram's child. Together, then, Diana's and Helena's evidence substantiates the case against Bertram. They also buttress Diana's riddles while also clearly establishing the hierarchy between unmarked/marked and male/female. What a woman vows, promises, and swears has intentionality and thereby takes on power.

A male with a reputation to uphold, Bertram does not want to lose face; meaning, he wishes to continue his involvement in a patriarchal world where men mark women in a definite subordinate position, and where some men subordinate other men based on their social rank. If violating his oaths and opposing Diana's riddling assaults means his achieving his second objective, so be it. If he can mark himself as superior, he will be in control of the circumstances in which he finds himself, and he will control the kind of relationship he will have with Helena. Bertram therefore swears that

> If she, my liege, can make me know this clearly,
> I'll love her dearly, ever, ever dearly.
> (V. iii. 315-16)

Bertram's first line signifies his right as a male to choose whether he actually is Helena's husband. Here, he certainly (and ironically) appears "one-up" on Helena (Tannen *Understanding* 24). The second line, and the more powerful, portrays a wretched, young man who will assume a subordinate role to Helena if she is indeed his wife and expecting his child. He tries to convince his audience that he will adhere to whatever oath he swears. He sounds like a sycophant, though, and clearly marks himself again as female. Bertram becomes "one-down" (*Understanding* 24).

Unintentionally, Bertram unmarks his position, and he leaves Helena with the last, marked words that raise her position in her marriage, just as Bassanio allows Portia to control their marriage. But in Diana Helena had more superior help than Shakespeare's Portia of *The Merchant of Venice*. Portia relied on Nerissa, a waiting woman who stayed in the background mainly. Nonetheless the women in both plays worked cooperatively and through negotiation.[5]

By working/assisting each other, women move from being unmarked to marked, thereby upsetting the established hierarchies, particularly of male and female. Many men continue to view women as unmarked because they perceive "'women's language' as 'powerless language'" primarily because of its indirectness (Tannen, *Understanding* 225). As demonstrated especially by Diana's fulfilling her promise to Helena in *All's Well* and Wise-Woman in Heywood's play, women's language authorizes many women to assert their markedness—and to covet the dominant position—without being direct or oppositional. From many male's perspectives, "a woman who appears forceful, logical, direct, masterful, or powerful, . . . risks undercutting her value as a woman" (Tannen, Understanding 241). But women who can operate from the male-attributed, unmarked positions—Helena, Diana, and even Cressida, Kate, Rosalind, and Beatrice, from the plays–Ruth, Deborah, Mary, Mary Magdalene, from the Bible, find not only companionship, rapport, solidarity, and cooperation, but also a prominent markedness. As Tannen asserts, "there is no unmarked woman" and "indirectness does not reflect powerlessness" (Talking 110; Understanding 226). And what a woman vows, promises, and swears has intentionality and thereby takes on power, especially when in the vows that women purposefully speak directly and markedly.

NOTES
1. I am indebted to Geoffrey Hughes for his detailed look at the history of swearing and oath-making in England.

Regarding blasphemy, one of Sir John Harington's epigrams published in 1615 refers to the English fondness for blasphemy since the middle ages. Harington also comments on the "shift from the religious to secular swearing" (Hughes 102):

> In elder times an ancient custom was,
> To swear in weighty matters by the Masse.
> But when the Masse went down (as old men note)
> They sware then by the crosse of this same grote
> And when the Crosse was likewise held in scorne,
> Then by their faith, the common oath was sworn.
> Last, having sworne away all faith and troth,
> Only God damn them is their common oath.
> Thus custome kept decorum by gradation,
> That losing Mass, Crosse, Faith, they find damnation.
> (qtd. in Montagu 162)

2. Archbishop Parker called Elizabeth to task once after her having "greatly feasted" with his wife and him:

> And you, Madam, I may not call you, and Mistris I am ashamed to call you, so I know not what to call you, but yet I do thank you" (qtd. in J. E. Neale 101)

3. Because of pressure from Queen Elizabeth's suppression of a 1601 bill to the Commons to censor swearing, English government did not interfere with public speech until 1606 when the "Act to Restraine Abuses of Players" and in later in 1623 when Puritans directives demanded cessation of both religious and common cursing. Once these two decrees were in place, the English, rather than invoking God, Christ, or the Virgin Mary, began referring to a Greek or Roman deity instead.

4. I employ the words "swearing," "covenant," "vow," "oath," and so forth interchangeably in the remainder of the paper. The distinction between profanity and biblical allusion to covenants are clearly noted.

5. Tannen writes repeatedly in several of her books about women and their willingness to cooperate. See this paper's bibliography for the titles of two of those books.

Works Cited

Bevington, David, ed. *The Complete Works of Shakespeare.* 5th ed. Chicago: U of Chicago P, 2004.
The Complete Word Study Dictionary: Old Testament. Chattanooga: AMG, 1992.
Chedgzoy, Kate. "Impudent Women: Carnival and Gender in early

Modern Culture." The Glasgow Review 1(1993): 9-22.

Heywood, Thomas. *The Wise-Woman of Hogsdon. The Critical Edition of Thomas Heywood's The Wise Woman of Hogsdon.* Ed. Michael H. Leonard. New York: Garland, 1980.

Holy Bible. The New International Version. Nashville: Broadman & Holman, 1986.

Hughes, Geoffrey. *Swearing: A Social history of Foul Language, Oaths, and Profanity in English.* 1991. London: Viking, Penguin, 1998.

Jakobson, Roman. *On Language.* Ed. Linda R. Waugh and Monique Monville-Burston. Cambridge: Harvard UP, 1990.

Knoeller, Christian. *Voicing Ourselves: Whose Words We Use When We Talk About Books.* Albany: SUNY, 1998.

Shakespeare, William. *All's Well That Ends Well.* Bevington 370-413.

——. *Twelfth Night, or What You Will.* Evans 437-76.

Shirley, Frances. *Swearing and Perjury in Shakespeare's Plays.* London: Allen and Unwin, 1979.

Tannen, Deborah. *Talking from 9 to 5: How Women's and Men's Conversational Styles Affect Who Gets Heard, Who Gets Credit, and What Gets Done at Work.* New York: William and Morrow, 1994.

——. *You Just Don't Understand.* New York: Ballentine, 1990.

6 The Country House Poem and the Christian Ethos
Eric Sterling

Genre is not merely a mode of classifying literature, but also a manifestation of authorial intention and manner of thinking. Thus, Rosalie Colie says that "as an expression of Renaissance culture relevant to more than its belletristic production, the notion of genre is historically significant" (2). Heather Dubrow adds that the "country house poem exemplifies this intimate relationship between literary history and literary forms" ("Country-House" 153). According to most accounts, this intriguing and influential but often neglected genre began in England with Ben Jonson's "To Penshurst" and "To Sir Robert Wroth" in *The Works of Benjamin Jonson* (1616), although recent scholars, such as Susanne Woods and Patrick Cook, have argued that Jonson was inspired by Aemilia Lanyer's "Description of Cooke-ham" (1611). Such poems by Jonson, Lanyer, Robert Herrick, Thomas Carew, and Andrew Marvell all manifest the values that the writers deemed praiseworthy: the utility of the estate, hospitality and charity, respectful and affectionate relationships between the owners and their neighbors, and the house's reflection of its owners' virtues. The country house owners embody these four interrelated concepts, which allow them to act as Christians toward their neighbors, the poor, and the poets who visit them at their estates. Previous scholarship on this genre discusses these themes from social and historical perspectives yet largely overlooks the religious ethos of the poetry. Richard Harp, for instance, observes that although Don E. Wayne, like other scholars who have studied Renaissance country house poems (especially Jonson's "To Penshurst"), derives his information from social, ethical, and intellectual "contexts of the sixteenth and seventeenth centuries, the one area that he almost completely ignores is . . . the religious" (74). Although these poems have often been considered as mainly secular, they generally include epideictic praise of patrons for their Christian virtues. The descriptions of the houses frequently echo the Book of Genesis and intimate life before the Fall, yet also allude to passages and beliefs from the New Testament. The values the poets present contain religious and Biblical connotations, and thus the verse of this genre may valuably be read as highly religious poetry; furthermore, because of the Christian values of the estates' owners, the house represents not only a dwelling, but also a metaphorical church.

A primary concern of the country house poets is the estate's purpose. The ideal country house should be constructed modestly; it should be comfortable and enjoyable for all its inhabitants. Dubrow notes that "a distrust of artifice is one of the most common themes of pastoral, and 'To Penshurst' channels that distrust into a condemnation of elaborate and costly architecture" ("Country-House" 167). In "To Penshurst" Jonson initially praises Robert Sidney's estate by describing what Penshurst is not: "Thou art not, *Penshurst*, built to envious show / . . . but stand'st an ancient pile" (ll. 1, 4).[3] By juxtaposing the Sidney estate with extravagant and impractical architectural wonders, Jonson not only praises the home, but also permits Penshurst to appear more laudatory by contrast. In addition, Jonson's praise by negation allows for moderate praise instead of flattery. If Jonson were to extol the Sidney family directly, his praise would appear as sycophancy. Jonson avoids the mistake of immodestly praising modesty by extolling the virtues of the Sidney family indirectly by lauding the unpretentiousness of their estate at Penshurst and employing what Dubrow calls the "negative formula, [which] deserves much of the credit for the singular lack of sycophancy in the poem" ("Country-House" 161).

Tomas Carew borrows Jonson's use of the Horatian "negative formula" in "To My Friend G.N., from Wrest"; Carew claims that although the Wrest Park manor is smaller than other country houses, it is superior, for it

> more numerous traines
> Of noble guests daily receives, and those
> Can with farre more conveniencie dispose
> Than prouder piles, where the vaine builder spent
> More cost in outward gay embellishment
> Than reall use, which was the sole designe
>   Of our contriver, who made things not fine,
> But fit for service. (108)[1]

These lines not only confirm the importance of utility, but also justify the values of "use" by stating that such a concern is Divine in nature: God desires us to use what He provides and to live in a practical, not an ostentatious, fashion. Kari Boyd McBride observes that the country house ideally was constructed in order to maintain "a moral economy wherein all classes and all peoples lived in right relationship with each other and with the rest of creation" ("Introduction"

5). To construct a serviceable and practical country house for the benefit of one's family, friends, and community is virtuous; contrariwise, to build an architectural marvel to win prestige subverts God's "sole designe" (Carew 108).

Several critics have discussed the ostentation and vanity that other houses exhibit. G.R. Hibbard, for instance, states, "Houses like Holdenby and Wollaton Hall were not designed to meet the needs of the households living in them, but for the reception of Elizabeth and her court and as an expression of their owners' sense of their own importance. Splendour and impressiveness rather than utility were what they aimed at and frequently achieved" (160). Each of these monumental structures has an "an inflated bauble, an architectural symbol rather than a house" (Summerson 41). Renaissance country house poets therefore consider pretentious, impractical architectural structures to be affectatious and wasteful. Thus the speaker in Marvell's "Upon Appleton House" asks:

> Why should of all things Man unrul'd
> Such unproportion'd dwellings build?
> . . . .
> What need of all this Marble Crust
> T'impark the wanton Mote of Dust,
> That thinks by Breadth the World t'unite
> Though the first Builders fail'd in Height?
> (ll. 9-10, 21-24)

The speaker alludes to the proud constructors of the Tower of Babel (Genesis 11) who vainly attempted to create an edifice far beyond their means. By living in similarly impractical structures, the owners of ostentatious country houses strive to be as gods—a hubristic desire, for it denies implicitly the omnipotence of God by their wish to supplant or replace Him. Their ostentatious display of wealth indicates that they disregard the principle that "[i]t is easier for a camel to go through the eye of a needle, than for a rich man to enter into the kingdom of God" (Matthew 19:24).

Renaissance country house poems praise hospitality partly because the poets of the time considered it a dying virtue. Daryl W. Palmer claims that the "seventeenth-century spawned the country-house poem, a genre devoted, in part, to eulogizing ancient hospitable practices" (34). The use of the word "eulogizing" indicates Palmer's belief that the poets wrote about hospitality at a time in which it was a waning virtue—expiring because of disuse. Alastair Fowler concurs regarding the demise of Christian hospitality in Renaissance England, stating that "[l]iterature sometimes addresses values most directly when they are under threat" (8 Introduction). Joseph Hall's satire entitled "Housekeeping's Dead" (1599), for instance, is one of many Renaissance works that portray the unfortunate demise of hospitality: people who have the ability to aid others

> Have penned themselves up in the private cage
> Of some blind lane; and there they lurk unknown
> Till th'hungry tempest once be overblown;
> Then like the coward, after his neighbour's fray,
> They creep forth boldly, and ask where are they? (40)

A gradual decline in Christianity was discernible to many, and perhaps this movement away from hospitality derived partly from the enclosure laws. Poets, such as Jonson, Carew, and Herrick, discerned this unfortunate trend, which they may have likened symbolically to a decline in patronage, and wrote their epideictic works in part to call attention to the waning Christian hospitality they witnessed and to attempt to show their readers and the owners the importance of this virtue. The poets lauded the estate owners for their magnanimity and wanted to manifest that hospitality is important and that others who have the means should act in the same generous manner. The country house enabled some owners to provide the Christian hospitality the poets celebrated.

Country houses, these poets believed, should provide hospitality and charity and thus benefit the owners' community. Throughout the Old and New Testaments, God tells human beings to act benevolently toward others. The Scriptures state, "If ye fulfil the royal law according to the scripture, Thou shalt love thy neighbour as thyself, ye do well" (James 2:8). Likewise, Jonson extols the virtue of generosity when he praises the Sidney hospitality in "To Penshurst," once again by negation, claiming that he is

> not Faine to sit (as some, this day,
>   At great mens tables) and yet dine away.
> Here no man tells my cups; nor, standing by,
>   A waiter, doth my gluttony envy:
> But gives me what I call, and lets me eate.
> (ll. 65-69)

Significantly, the reference to the poet sitting at a great man's table yet being forced to dine again elsewhere alludes to the literal mistreatment Jonson suffered at the Earl of Salisbury's house (*Discoveries* 14). Jonson thus juxtaposes his humiliation at the Earl's table with the royal treatment he receives from the Sidneys. The Sidneys "[u]se hospitality one to another without grudging" (1 Peter 4:9). We admire the hospitality of the Sidneys even more when we realize how injuriously the poet has been treated elsewhere.

The country house poet's consciousness of the religiosity of hospitality also appears in Carew's "To Saxham." At Little Saxham, Carew considers the fires that keep the house warm in the winter:

> Those chearfull beames send forth their light
> To all that wander in the night,
>   And seeme to becken from aloofe

The weary pilgrim to thy roof;
Where, if refresht, he will away,
Hee's fairly welcome, or, if stay,
Farre more. (35)

The first two lines echo Matthew 5:16, which reads, "Let your light so shine before men, that they may see your good works, and glorify your Father which is in heaven." Dubrow observes that "Carew's 'To Saxham' and [Jonson's] 'To Penshurst' celebrate the friendly interaction between the house and potential guests that the poems celebrate while avoiding the sycophancy common in epistles directed to aristocrats" ("Politics" 76). Carew views the hospitality and charity expressed toward weary travelers as godly and a glorification of God. Christ will say to the righteous, "Come, ye blessed of my Father, inherit the kingdom prepared for you from the foundation of the world: For I was an hungred, and ye gave me meat: I was thirsty, and ye gave me drink: I was a stranger, and ye took me in" (Matthew 25:34-35).

A correlation exists between the landowners' hospitality and their homes, for charitable and benevolent people live in an estate designed for hospitality, not for ostentation. Mark Girouard says that seventeenth- and early eighteenth-century landscape painters portrayed country houses as hospitable edifices: "[t]he panoramic views certainly seem to have had more behind them than pride of possession; like the country house poems written a little earlier by Ben Jonson and others, they suggest a deliberate attempt to project country houses as the hospitable centres of a fruitful countryside" (*Town and Country* 224). In Carew's "To My Friend G.N., from Wrest," the speaker states that Wrest Park possesses

an usefull comelinesse,
Devoide of art, for here the architect
Did not with curious skill a pile erect
Of carved marble, touch, or porpherie,
But built a house for hospitality. (107)

The estate owners who build houses that enhance their hospitality, a godly virtue, exhibit piety as well as generosity.

Some critics of country house poems, such as Raymond Williams and Don E. Wayne, believe that the splendor and the wealth of the estate owners exemplify their parasitic relationships with the poor, implying that the Sidneys and other such home owners exploit lower-class workers—shamefully improving their estates through the labor of the poor. Raymond Williams, for instance, observes that despite details suggesting an abundance of food at Penshurst, Jonson fails to mention in his poem that any laborers are working (30). The critic suggests that in Jonson's efforts to praise the Sidneys, the poet chooses purposefully to avoid mentioning the laborers who work hard to ensure that the Sidneys possess a large surplus of food.   Wayne adds that "To Penshurst" is Jonson's "attempt to rationalize the accumulation of wealth and the maintenance of certain relations of exchange" (121).   Such comments indicate that some critics overlook the religious nature of the poems.   The plenitude of food—seemingly obtained without human labor—may serve as Jonson's tribute to the Creator for providing the food the people eat.   Richard Harp says that Jonson had "biblical and theological support for showing a nature that may be fruitful even when man rests from his labor" (81).   One such example derives from "That All Good Things Come from God" (from *The Book of Homilies*, originally published in 1574), which states "It is not the increase of fruits that feedeth men, but it is the word, O Lord, which preserveth them that trust in thee" (258).   The reader, therefore, should consider the possibility that Jonson does not consider the laborers essential to his poem because it is the mercy and generosity of God that causes the food on their land to be plentiful. Williams and Wayne also fail to realize that the laborers do not work all the time; in fact, they are not working because they are dining at Penshurst on the food that they have cultivated and harvested because the estate owners kindly invite them to share the meal in the communal hall and provide the workers with time to relax.   Dubrow notes that laborers and neighbors "are welcomed within [the house], guests at its table and in its vision; and the poor, rather than sneaking through the door to steal, receive charity at it" ("Politics" 75).   Readers of "To Penshurst" and other country house poems may be reminded of 1 Peter 4.9, which says, "Use hospitality one to another without grudging" and Luke 14: 13-14: "When thou makest a feast, call the poor, the maimed, the lame, the blind: And thou shalt be blessed."

The estate owners freely share their food with the workers and the poor who live in the vicinity; they are generous and benevolent.   The wealthy patrons in these poems do not acquire more pelf by employing their power for covetous ends.   The speaker in Herrick's "A Panegerick to Sir Lewis Pemberton," for instance, tells Pemberton:

> Safe stand thy walls, and Thee, and so both will
> Since neithers height was rais'd by th' ill
> Of others; since no Stud, no Stone, no Piece,
> Was rear'd up by the Poore-mans fleece:
>
> (ll. 115-19)[2]

These lines echo "To Penshurst": "And though thy walls be of the countrey stone, / They'are rear'd with no mans ruine, no mans grone" (ll. 45-46).   The Cavalier poets stress that the landowners, as Christians, do not prosper at their neighbors' expense; their homes manifest, in contrast, the benevolence of the estate owners and justify the respect they receive.

In Jonson's poem, the Sidneys' neighbors flock to visit them. The poor members of the community like the Sidneys so much that they bring food to the rich estate owners, without desiring any recompense:

> all come in, the farmer, and the clowne:
> And no one empty-handed, to salute
>   Thy lord, and lady, though they have no sute.
> Some bring a capon, some a rurall cake,
>   Some nuts, some apples;
>   (ll. 48-52)

The gifts that the Sidneys receive obviously have little monetary value, but the presents illuminate the neighbors' harmonious relationship with the Sidneys and connote the laudable behavior of the noble family. We admire the Sidneys not only because the poet does, but also because the rustic neighbors do.

A touching example of poetic praise of a country estate resident appears in Aemilia Lanyer's "Description of Cooke-ham." Therein the speaker admires her patron (the Countess Lady Clifford) and is jealous that a tree, and not she, has received a kiss from the patron; "Scorning a sencelesse creature should possesse / So rare a favour, so great happinesse" (ll. 167-168), the speaker kisses the tree, absorbing from it the kiss it has previously received, thereby demonstrating her adoration for the Countess.[4] "Description of Cooke-ham" differs from other country house poems in that the owner and the speaker are women. The poem is designed to provide a female perspective on country houses as well as the spirituality and sisterhood that the house and the owner inspire. Hugh Jenkins says that in the poem, Lanyer describes Cooke-ham as "the female Eden" (161) and that the poem suggests "a specifically female spirituality. . ." (163). Elaine V. Beilin claims that unlike Jonson, who praised virtuous women to make a point about human nature and to call attention to himself as a poet, "Lanyer wrote specifically to praise women, and more precisely, to redeem for them their pivotal importance as Christians" (179). Susanne Woods points out that the virtue of the Countess, along with the contemplation and meditation enkindled by Cooke-ham, allows Lanyer to discover "her vocation as a religious poet" and inspires her "to produce her story of Christ's passion" (118). Lanyer confesses in the poem that the country house, with its presence of the Countess, is "where I first obtain'd / Grace from that Grace where perfit Grace remain'd" (ll. 1-2). Patrick Cook suggests that "Lanyer offers us a portrait of Lady Clifford's piety through a meditative engagement with her own salvational history, using the idea of conversion through freely bestowed grace pervasive in Protestant religious lyric (105). This country house poem suggests that a bond exists between the Countess's spirituality and the natural surroundings at Cooke-ham. The trees and flowers flourish in the Countess's presence because Lady Clifford possesses spiritual beauty and divine grace; God, who created this natural beauty, allows it to thrive only while she resides at Cooke-ham. The natural beauty in this Edenic country house begins to decay when the Countess leaves. The subsequent decay at Cooke-ham, like that in the Garden of Eden, is inevitable. Indeed, Beilin says that "realizing a Christian vision means relinquishing earth's beauty, facing death, and believing in immortal life" (204).

The country house poem blurs distinctions between social classes; this concept is unusual in an era that possessed sumptuary laws and distinct social castes. Although the social classes are by no means equal in these poems, the distance between them diminishes. In Jonson's "To Sir Robert Wroth," Wroth's country estate at Durrants is a place where

> The rout of rurall folke come thronging in,
> (Their rudenesse then is thought no sinne)
> Thy noblest spouse affords them welcome grace;
> And the great *Heroes*, of her race,
> Sit mixt with losse of state, or reverence.
> Freedome doth with degree dispense.
> (ll. 53-58)

Similarly, Wayne says that at Penshurst the walls do not "function as *walls* or barriers; instead they are described as so open that 'all come in' (l. 48) who so desire" (67). Communal eating, in which people of various social classes sat down and shared a meal together, plays a significant role in "To Penshurst." Alastair Fowler believes that the communal feasting involving the estate owners and their neighbors and servants represents "Christian practice, related to the Eucharist and obedient to Deuteronomy's injunction, 'the stranger . . . shall eat and be satisfied'" (Introduction 8). The blurring of social classes is also manifest in the construction of country house architecture. Hibbard notes that Renaissance country houses contain a large hall that "was the common ground for members of the family and their servants and, very often, their tenants as well" (160). The paths of the landowners, tenants, guests, and servants intersect frequently, and people of different social classes are not segregated. William A. McClung notes that "the dependents of an ideal English manor are part of the family" (35). Mark Girouard concurs with McClung, saying that during the Renaissance, "when someone talked about his family he meant everyone living under his roof, including his servants; by the nineteenth century he meant his wife and children" (*Life* 10). Thus, people living in country house estates during the Renaissance shared, to some extent, a sense of equality with their fellow Christians, despite their differing socioeconomic backgrounds. This sense of family, prevalent in country house poems, should remind readers of Galatians 6:10, which reads, "Let us do good unto all men, especially unto them that are of the household of faith" and Psalms 133:1, which reads, "Behold, how good and pleasant it is for brethren to dwell together in unity." Girouard adds that "[t]he country house [functions] as the centre of its neighbourhood, rather than as a secret world apart" (*Town and Country* 223). Girouard emphasizes a distinction between Renaissance and eighteenth-century country houses: the latter but not the former include parks immediately adjacent to the home whose "main function was to set off the house" (*Town and Country* 224). Thus, eighteenth-century country house owners desired parks to separate themselves from nearby dwellers of lower classes, but Renaissance country house owners did not have parks to set themselves apart from their neighbors. The classes also blur because the owners treat members of lower social classes as fellow Christians rather than as inferiors. They adhere to the golden rule: "Therefore all things whatsoever ye would that men should do to you, do ye even so to them: for this is the law and the prophets" (Matthew 7:12).

Because of this emphasis on mutual charity, Herrick and Jonson consider country dwellings more peaceful and more suitable for spiritual reflection than urban life. In "A Country life: To his Brother, M. Tho: Herrick," the speaker praises the peaceful life his brother has chosen:

> Thrice, and above, blest (my soules halfe) art thou,
> In thy both Last, and Better Vow:
> Could'st leave the City, for exchange, to see
> The Countries sweet simplicity:
> And it to know, and practice; with intent
> To grow the sooner innocent:
> By studying to know vertue;
> (ll. 1-7)

The speaker implies that country life is more peaceful than urban life and that rural dwellers, unlike city inhabitants, are innocent. When Thomas Herrick leaves the city for the country, the speaker describes his consequent moral improvement as if he has recently experienced a religious conversion, as if he has become a better Christian while having lived in the country. In contrast, Herrick, Jonson, and Carew—among other country house poets—portray urban life as corrupt and rural dwelling as pure. Jonson considered "the country as the place where civilized leisure forms the basis of the virtuous life" (Elsky 1). Girouard notes that many people during the Renaissance began to consider the activities of the owner on a country estate "virtuous and prestigious" (*Life* 215). Girouard asserts that although some country estate owners started to spend more time in London (since the court was the power base), the most virtuous owners remained in their rural estates and maintained their faith in the simple Christian values that they found in the country. He says that poets such as Jonson and Marvell "constantly urged landowners to live on their estates, and praised and glamorized the lives of those who did . . ." (*Life* 5). The rural inhabitants in these poems are benevolent and virtuous people who inherently possess Christian virtues. Robert C. Evans says that in "To Sir Robert Wroth," God's presence "reminds Wroth of his own place in the larger scheme of things. This order, with God at its head, provides an alternative to the corruption the poem depicts" in the city (119). Since the country dwellers reside in an environment untainted by the artificial, evil city and resembling, to some extent, the Garden of Eden before the Fall, they naturally act in a moral and godly fashion.

A correlation exists between these estate owners and their homes. Sara Van den Berg says, "Durrants, the country estate Wroth chose as his chief residence, mirrors his moral values. It becomes, in Jonson's poem, a metaphor for the ideal interior state of its lord" (120). Focusing on the previously mentioned lines of Marvell's "Upon Appleton House" ("What need of all this Marble Crust / T'impark the wanton Muse of Dust" [ll. 21-22]), Robert Cummings similarly claims that "While the estate might originally 'impark' the house, in the proposed analogy the house 'imparks' the body: the 'Marble Crust' of the house is now construed as the surrounding estate, and the body is construed as the house" (26). Cummings notes that 2 Corinthians 5:1 is one of many "instances of the house conceived as the soul's castle" (26). In Marvell's poem, the virtuous Fairfax family replaces the religiously hypocritical nuns on the property; the speaker declares that "Though many a *Nun* there made her Vow, / 'Twas no *Religious House* till now" (ll. 279-80). A property, therefore, is not religious because of what it represents or the occupation or religion of the inhabitants, but because of the owner's Christian behavior.

Because the estate owners embody Christian values, their houses serve as symbolic churches. St. Peter, for instance, suggests that the church is spiritual and figurative, saying that the Lord is "a living stone" and that Christians, as "living stones, are built up a spiritual house, to be a holy priesthood, to offer up spiritual sacrifices, acceptable to God through Jesus Christ" (1 Peter 2.4-5). Richard Harp adds that the church "is not essentially a building at all but rather a group of individual Christians, called by St. Paul 'the temple of the living God,' to whom 'God hath said, I will dwell in them, and walk in them' (11. Cor. 2:16)" (76). Thus, houses such as Penshurst contain dwellers who live their lives as Christians, offering hospitality and charity to the less fortunate. This behavior makes their impressive but unpretentious estates metaphorical churches; God dwells within because the owners and their guests comport themselves as true Christians.

A link also exists between the virtue of the country house owners and the prosperity of their lands. God rewards generous and hospitable landowners by blessing their estates with a plenitude of game, food, and beautiful natural surroundings. The Christian charity of the patrons helps create their good fortune. In "To Sir Robert Wroth," the speaker claims that God rewards the landowner for wisely utilizing his property at Durrants:

> God wisheth, none should wracke on a strange shelfe:
> To him, man's dearer, then t'himselfe.
> And, howsoever we may thinke things sweet,
> He alwayes gives what he knowes meet;

> Which who can use is happy.
>
> (ll. 95-99)

Alastair Fowler states that "the estate enjoys a providential plenitude, whereby bountiful nature seems almost to offer itself . . . of its own free will . . . This bounty is distributed through the landlord's generous hospitality" ("Country" 2). Jonson praises the Sidneys' hospitality indirectly by listing the numerous wild and domestic animals that make Penshurst their home and by cataloguing the plenitude of orchard fruits that grow there:

> Fat, aged carps, that runne into thy net.
>> And pikes, now weary their owne kinde to eat,
> As loth, the second draught, or cast to stay,
>> Officiously, at first, themselves betray.
> Bright eeles, that emulate them, and leape on land,
>> Before the fisher, or into his hand.
> . . . .
> The earely cherry, with the later plum,
>> Fig, grape, and quince, each in his time doth come:
> The blushing apricot, and woolly peach
>> Hang on thy walls, that every child may reach.
>
> (ll. 33-38, 41-44)

This passage echoes Genesis 9:2-3, where Adam is told about the fowls and "all the fishes of the sea; into your hand are they delivered. Every moving thing that liveth shall be meat for you." Life at the country estates is more than a peaceful pastoral existence—it is Edenic. Country house poets portray life at the estates as resembling life before the Fall, manifesting the Christian virtues human beings should exhibit in their everyday lives. The celebration of Christian values in these works was quite necessary in this turbulent era, which included religious and political upheaval such as the execution of Charles I, the Interregnum, and the decline of the power of the Puritans. Because Christianity played a significant role in Renaissance estate poems from Jonson through Marvell, it therefore should not be surprising "that the genre dies out when religious stability is basically restored to English life with the return to the throne of Charles II in 1660" (Harp 86).

NOTES
1. All quotations from Carew's poetry are from this edition and are cited by page number because no line numbers are provided.
2. All quotations are from this edition and are cited by line number.
3. All quotations from Jonson's poetry are from this edition and are cited by line number.
4. Quotations from Lanyer's poetry derive from this edition and are cited by line number.

Works Cited

Beilin, Elaine V. *Redeeming Eve: Women Writers of the English Renais-sance*. Princeton: Princeton UP, 1987.

Carew, Thomas. *The Works of Thomas Carew, Sewer in Ordinary to Charles the First*. Edinburgh: W. and C. Tait, 1824.

Colie, Rosalie. *The Resources of Kind: Genre-Theory in the Renaissance*. Ed. Barbara K. Lewalski. Berkeley: U of California P, 1973.

Cook, Patrick. "Aemilia Lanyer's 'Description of Cooke-ham" as Devotional Lyric." In *Discovering and (Re)Covering the Seventeenth Century Religious Lyric*. Eds. Eugene R. Cunnar and Jeffrey Johnson. Pittsburgh: Duquesne UP, 2001. 104-18.

Cummings, Robert. "The 'Mose of Dust' in Marvell's Upon Appleton House." *English Language Notes* 24 (1986): 25-27.

Dubrow, Heather. "The Country-House Poem: A Study in Generic Development." *Genre* 12 (1979): 153-79.

——. "The Politics of Aesthetics: Recuperating Formalism and the Country House Poem." In *Renaissance Literature and Its Formal Engagements*. Ed. Mark David Rasmussen. New York: Palgrave, 2002. 67-88.

Elsky, Martin. "The Mixed Genre of Ben Jonson's 'To Penshurst' and the Perilous Springs of Netherlandish Landscape." *The Ben Jonson Journal* 9 (2002): 1-35.

Evans, Robert C. *Ben Jonson and the Poetics of Patronage*. Lewisburg: Bucknell UP; London: Associated UPs, 1989.

Fowler, Alastair. Introduction. *The Country House Poem: A Cabinet of Seventeenth-Century Estate Poems and Related Items*. Edinburgh: Edinburgh UP, 1994. 1-29.

——. "Country House Poems: The Politics of a Genre." *The Seventeenth Century* 1 (1986): 1-14.

Girouard, Mark. *Life in the English Country House: A Social and ——. Town and Country*. New Haven: Yale UP, 1992.

Hall, Joseph. "Housekeeping's Dead." In *The Country House Poem: A Cabinet of Seventeenth- Century Estate Poems and Related Items*. Ed. Alastair Fowler. Edinburgh: Edinburgh UP, 1994. 39-44.

Harp, Richard. "Jonson's 'To Penshurst': The Country House as Church." *John Donne Journal* 7 (1988): 73-89.

Herrick, Robert. *The Poetical Works of Robert Herrick*. Ed. F.W. Moorman. London: Oxford UP, 1921.

Hibbard, G.R. "The Country House Poem of the Seventeenth Century." *Journal of the Warburg and Courtland Institutes* 19 (1956): 159-74.

Jenkins, Hugh. *Feigned Commonwealths: The Country-House Poem and the Fashioning of the Ideal Community*. Pittsburgh: Duquesne UP, 1998.

Jonson, Ben. *The Complete Poetry of Ben Jonson*. Ed. William B. Hunter,

Jr. New York: W.W. Norton, 1963.

———. *Discoveries, 1641; Conversations with William Drummond of Hawthornden, 1619.* Ed. G.B. Harrison. New York: E.P. Dutton, 1923.

Kelsall, Malcolm. *The Great Good Place: The Country House and English Literature.* New York: Columbia UP, 1993.

King James Version. All Biblical quotations are from this version and are cited in the text.

Lanyer, Aemilia. *The Poems of Aemilia Lanyer: Salve Deus Rex Judæorum.* Ed. Susanne Woods. New York: Oxford UP, 1993.

Marvell, Andrew. *The Poems of Andrew Marvell Printed from the Unique Copy in the British Museum with Some Other Poems by Him.* Ed. Hugh Macdonald. London: Routledge and Kegan Paul, 1952. Quotations from Marvell's poetry are from this edition and are cited by line number.

McBride, Kari Boyd. *Country House Discourse in Early Modern England: A Cultural Study of Landscape and Legitimacy.* Aldershot, England: Ashgate, 2001.

———. Introduction: The Politics of Domestic Arrangements. In *Domestic Arrangements in Early Modern England.* Ed. Kari Boyd McBride. Pittsburgh: Duquesne UP, 2002. 1-14.

McClung, William A. *The Country House in English Renaissance Poetry.* Berkeley: U of California P, 1977.

Palmer, Daryl W. *Hospitable Performances: Dramatic Genre and Cultural Practices in Early Modern England.* West Lafayette: Purdue UP, 1992.

Summerson, John. *Architecture in Britain 1530-1830.* 4th ed. Baltimore: Penguin, 1963.

"That All Good Things Come from God." In *The Book of Homilies.* Oxford: Oxford UP, 1859.

Van den Berg, Sara J. *The Action of Ben Jonson's Poetry.* Newark: U of Delaware P, 1987.

Wayne, Don E. *Penshurst: The Semiotics of Place and the Poetics of History.* Madison: U of Wisconsin P, 1984.

Williams, Raymond. *The Country and the City.* New York: Oxford UP, 1973.

Woods, Susanne. *Lanyer: A Renaissance Woman Poet.* New York: Oxford UP, 1999.

7   Biblical Allusion through an Ironic Filter
in Swift's *Gulliver's Travels*
Edward J. Rielly

A phenomenon concerning Swift scholarship is the usual separation of Swift the author of *Gulliver's Travels* from Swift the clergyman. The most vivid gauge of this separation appears in the Bible. As an Anglican clergyman who took his duties seriously, Swift would have had almost daily contact with the Bible in prayer, meditation, liturgical services, or sermon preparation. It is logical to assume, therefore, that he would have made at least some use of it as he wrote his masterwork, *Gulliver's Travels*. On the whole, however, scholars either have ignored the Bible as a source for the *Travels* or have looked without success for a relationship between Swift's book and Scriptures. The *Index to the Prose Writings,* for example, notes only one Biblical allusion in the *Travels*, the reference in Part II to the existence of "Giants in former Ages," which reflects the account of giants in Genesis, VI, 4.[1] More emphatically, Charles Beaumont, in his monograph *Swift's Use of the Bible*, flatly states that "Swift has no Biblical quotations or allusions *in Gulliver's Travels*" (53).

One study that stands out prominently against this common separation is Roland Mushat Frye's "Swift's Yahoo and the Christian Symbols for Sin." Frye shows that Swift follows scriptural and homiletic traditions in his scatological depiction of the Yahoos in Part IV of the *Travels*, traditions that viewed man's physical deformity and filth as symbols of fallen man's moral corruption. Frye also associates the Yahoos with Leviticus, pointing out that most of the food that they eat Leviticus proscribes as unclean.

Unfortunately, Frye's discoveries have not been carried much further, perhaps because, as C. F. Daw points out in his article "Swift's Favorite Books of the Bible," Swift was reluctant to spice his conversation and writing with scriptural tags and cliches of the profession.[2] According to Daw, Swift's "explicit references to the Bible usually occur when he has temporarily cloaked himself in an adopted identity that screens him from charges of priestly self-interest in citing Scripture as an authority for his position" (201). Daw has in mind principally *A Tale of a Tub* with its satiric attack on Catholicism and nonconformity through the allegory of the three brothers, Peter, Martin, and Jack. Daw's observation calls to mind "A Letter of Advice to a Young Poet," which Swift probably wrote.[3] In the letter, the author urges the young poet to make himself conversant with the Scriptures, not as something to believe, but "as a Piece of necessary Furniture for a *Wit* and a *Poet*." Without the Bible, he adds, he does not know what "our *Play-wrights* would do for images, Allusions, Similitudes, Examples, or even Language it self" (329-30). Swift's message should be taken ironically, intending chastisement of the practice that he cites rather than a literal following of his advice. Possibly Swift may have avoided Biblical quotations and overt references to the Bible in the *Travels* in order to avoid falling into company with those that he considers self-serving wits and playwrights.

Nonetheless, Biblical allusions not only occur in *Gulliver's Travels*, but figure importantly in the thematic development of Gulliver's second voyage and in the depiction of Gulliver as a sinful man who in his moral pride proves as obstinate as the Biblical pharaoh himself. "A Voyage to Brobdingnag" thus includes, with considerable appropriateness, most of the plagues of Exodus, the plagues with which God afflicted the Egyptians because of the pharaoh's refusal to acknowledge God's divine authority and follow His commands as relayed through Moses and Aaron. In the Authorised Version of 1611, the standard version of the Bible for Swift, these plagues appear as bloody waters, frogs, lice, flies, murrain, boils and blains, hail, locusts, darkness, and the death of the first born.

The first plague in Exodus, the turning of water into blood, occurs as Aaron stretches out his rod "upon the waters of Egypt, upon their streames, upon their rivers, and upon their ponds, and upon all their pooles of water, that they may become blood, and that there may be blood throughout all the land of Egypt, both in vessels of wood, and vessels of stone" (VIII, 19). Swift uses this plague as he does the others, transforming Biblical details in accord with the demands of the fictional narration in which Gulliver is both sightseer and a victim of the plagues. Instead of changing water to blood, the narrative instead places Gulliver as an onlooker at an execution. Swift puns on the word *vessel*, substituting for the vessels of wood and stone the two human vessels for blood--veins and arteries:

> The Malefactor was fixed in a Chair upon a Scaffold erected for the
> purpose, and his Head cut off at a blow with a Sword of about forty
> Foot long. The Veins and Arteries spouted up such a prodigious
> quantity of Blood, and so high in the Air, that the great *Jett d'eau* at
> *Versailles* was not equal for the time it lasted; and the Head when it

fell on the Scaffold Floor, gave such a bounce, as made me start, although I were at least an *English* mile distant. (II, 88)

Then, as now, *vessel* was a common synonym for *vein* or *artery*.[4] In Swift's version, the altered vessels cause the plague to have a personal impact on the tiny Gulliver as they empty themselves of blood rather than being filled, as were the vessels in Exodus. The effect is that Gulliver's own small world is fully as ensanguined as was the Egyptians' larger world.

The plague of frogs follows the bloody waters in both Exodus and the "Voyage to Brobdingnag." In Exodus, God tells Moses to warn the pharaoh that "the river shall bring foorth frogges abundantly, which shall goe up and come into thine house, and into thy bedchamber, and upon thy bed, and into the house of thy servants, and upon thy people, and into thine ovens, and into thy kneading troughes." Further, "the frogges shall come up both on thee and upon thy people, and upon all thy servants" (VIII, 3-4).

In the *Travels*, while Gulliver was sailing his toy boat in a trough that the Queen had ordered built for him, a frog slipped into the trough from a pail of water that a servant was carrying and climbed aboard the boat, nearly overturning it. The frog then hopped back and forth, daubing Gulliver's face and clothes with slime. Despite its size, which "made it appear the most deformed Animal that can be conceived," Gulliver states, "I banged it a good while with one of my Sculls, and at last forced it to leap out of the Boat" (II, 92). The frog thus literally follows its Egyptian ancestors into a man's trough, albeit not into a kneading trough. As with the plague of blood, Swift shows that humor and word play can be useful satiric tools, even in a Biblical context.

In a single passage in Chapter IV, Swift draws upon two more plagues, those of lice and of boils and blains. According to the Bible, God commanded Moses to sprinkle handfuls of ashes toward heaven, which "became a boile breaking forth with blains, upon man and upon beast" (IX: 8-11); earlier, God had called down the plague of lice, ordering Aaron to strike the earth with his rod, whereupon the dust "became lice, in man and in beast" (VIII, 16-17).

Gulliver recalls in the *Travels* how he often went riding with his companion Glumdalclitch and her governess. On one trip, a group of beggars crowded around the coach when it stopped at some shops. For Gulliver, these beggars provided "the most horrible Spectacles that ever an *English* Eye beheld":

> There was a Woman with a Cancer in her Breast, swelled to a monstrous size, full of Holes, in two or three of which I could have easily crept, and covered my whole Body. There was a Fellow with a Wen in his Neck, larger than five Woolpacks, and another with a couple of wooden Legs, each about twenty Foot high. But, the most hateful Sight of all was the Lice crawling on their Cloaths. I could see distinctly the Limbs of these Vermin with my naked Eye, much better than those of an *European* Louse through a Microscope, and their Snouts with which they rooted like Swine. (II, 71-72)[5]

The reader should not be surprised to find these two afflictions united in a portrait of beggars. What may be more startling to a reader, however, is that, from Gulliver's point of view, the person most harmed by these afflictions, as by the plague of blood, is Gulliver himself. And he suffers, not because he feels sympathy for the criminal or the beggar, but because the sight startles or disgustes him.

The plague of flies, the fourth affliction in Exodus, is the first of the Biblical plagues to appear in *Gulliver's Travels*. God's promise, conveyed through Moses, is that if the pharaoh will not free the Israelites, "beholde, I will send swarmes of flies upon thee, and upon thy servants, and upon thy people, and into thy houses: and the houses of the Egyptians shall bee full of swarmes of flies, and also the ground whereon they are" (VIII, 21). Pharaoh, of course, rejects the warning:

> And the LORD did so: and there came a grievous swarme of flies into the house of Pharaoh, and into his servants houses, and into all the lande of Egypt: the land was corrupted by reason of the swarme of flies. (VIII, 24)
>
> Gulliver likewise suffers the affliction of flies: The Kingdom is much pestered with Flies in Summer, and these odious Insects, each of them as big as a Dunstable Lark, hardly gave me any rest while I sat at Dinner, with their continual humming and buzzing about mine Ears. (II, 63)

Gulliver further notes how the flies would leave their excrement on his food and sting him about the face. He adds that "it was the common Practice of the Dwarf to catch a number of these Insects in his Hand as School-boys do among us, and let them out suddenly under my Nose on Purpose to frighten me, and divert the Queen" (II, 64).

In Chapter V, Gulliver confronts the plague of hail, the seventh plague of Exodus, which falls with unusual severity. In Exodus:

> And the haile smote throughout all the land of Egypt, all that *was* in the field, both man and beast: and the haile smote every herbe of the fielde, and brake every tree of the field. (X: 25)

In Brobdingnag:

> ANOTHER day *Glumdalclitch* left me on a smooth Grass-plot to divert my self while she walked at some istance with her Governess. In the mean time there suddenly fell such a violent shower of Hail, that I was immediately by the force of it struck to the Ground: And when I was down, the Hail-stones gave me such cruel Bangs all over the Body, as if I had been pelted with Tennis-balls; however I made a shift to creep on all four, and shelter my self by lying flat on my Face

> on the Lee-side of a Border of Lemmon Thyme, but so bruised from
> Head to Foot that I could not go abroad in ten Days. (II, 79-80)

The eighth plague in Exodus, the infestation of locusts, becomes in the *Travels* the swarm of wasps that robs Gulliver of his food. The main curse of the Biblical plague of locusts is their insatiable appetite that devoured "every herbe of the land, and all the fruit of the trees, which the haile had left, and there remained not any greene thing in the trees, or in the herbes of the field, through all the land of Egypt" (X: 15). The wasps in Brobdingnag are no less voracious. Gulliver states that as he sat down to breakfast one morning,

> above twenty Wasps, allured by the smell, came flying into the
> Room, humming louder than the Drones of as many Bagpipes. Some
> of them seized my Cake, and carried it piece-meal away; others flew
> about my Head and Face, confounding me with the Noise, and
> putting me in the utmost terror of their Stings. (II, 65)

In substituting wasps for locusts, Swift may have seen in the wasp an adversary more dangerous to the individual Gulliver than is the locust, whose immediate victim is chiefly the land itself. Throughout the second voyage, it should be remembered, the sinful Gulliver suffers most of the effects of the plagues, not the Brobdingnagians, who would have been the primary sufferers from a plague of locusts. Swift may also have had in mind the position of the locust in Leviticus as a clean animal (XI: 22). Swift, who followed the Levitical list of clean and unclean animals while composing Part IV of the *Travels* (as Frye has demonstrated), may well have had the same Biblical passages in mind when he drew this plague and wanted as much as possible to associate the figure of Gulliver with moral corruption.

The plague of murrain seems to be the one plague that Swift does not use in this voyage. Swift quite possibly considered this plague, given its usual animal victims, inappropriate, and followed Psalm CV in dropping it from the list.[6]

The ninth and tenth plagues of Exodus, the thick darkness that fell over the land of Egypt and the death of the first born of each Egyptian family, are the most symbolic and effectual of the Exodus plagues and maintain their considerable importance in *Gulliver's Travels*. Their value within the whole frame of the Exodus story and also within the narrative of the "Voyage to Brobdingnag" is apparent by their parallel position at the end of the two series of plagues, where they have, of course, a great effect on the pharaoh and Gulliver. In the last chapter of Part II, Gulliver journeys to the seashore, accompanied by a page. But while Gulliver is asleep in his box, an eagle lifts him high in the air, as Gulliver surmises, to drop the box "like a Tortoise in a Shell, and then pick out my Body and devour it" (II, 143). Assaulted by other eagles, however, the giant bird drops the box into the ocean.

A central image of Gulliver's period afloat in the water is that of darkness, the ninth Biblical plague. The darkness in Exodus is unique in that it is both visual and physical, a "darkenesse over the land of Egypt, even darkenes which may be felt" (X: 21). Gulliver's darkness has the same qualities: "My Fall was stopped by a terrible Squash, that sounded louder to mine Ears than the Cataract of *Niagara*; after which I was quite in the dark for another Minute, and then my Box began to rise so high that I could see Light from the tops of my Windows" (II, 143-44). Gulliver fears the waves, and feels the lack of air, which almost stifles him until he can open the slip-board on the roof. Gulliver recalls, however, that after four hours,

> I heard, or at least thought I heard some kind of grating Noise on that Side of my Box where the Staples were fixed; and soon after I began to fancy that the Box was pulled, or towed along in the Sea; for I now and then felt a sort of tugging, which made the Waves rise near the Tops of my Windows, leaving me almost in the Dark (II, 147).

Darkness was a prominent moral and religious metaphor in Swift's time, as he certainly would have known. Benjamin Keach, for example, in his *Tropes and Figures* discusses six metaphorical meanings of darkness based on the Scriptures: "(1.) The State of Nature, or Unregeneracy, or deep Alienation from the Life of God (2.) Several Sins wherein wicked Men live. (3.) Desertion. (4.) The Grave. (5.) Hell. (6.) Afflictions" (383-84). Evidently Gulliver's descent into the water in his box may convey all of these meanings.

At the moment of Gulliver's greatest fear, however, rescue is imminent. When he senses the pull on his box, he feels, despite the darkness, "some faint hope of Relief" (II, 147). The tenth plague important to remember because it occasioned the death of multitudes also concerns Passover, the sparing of the children of the Israelites, and ultimately, the deliverance of Israel from bondage. At this point in the second voyage, an incident has already occurred in which comic echoes of the tenth plague resound. Immediately after the hail incident in Chapter V, Gulliver recounts "a more dangerous Accident," how "a small white Spaniel belonging to one of the chief Gardiners, having got by accident into the Garden, happened to range near the Place where I lay." He adds that the dog "came directly up, and taking me in his Mouth ran strait to his Master, wagging his Tail, and set me gently on the Ground." Fortunately, the dog was so well trained that it did not harm even his clothes (II, 81). In Exodus, God foretells the death of the first born of all Egyptian men and animals: "But against any of the children of Israel, shal not a dog move his tongue, against man or beast: that ye may know how that the LORD doth put a difference betweene the Egyptians and Israel" (XI: 7). The incident with the dog reads almost like a comic parable of the divine promise.

So Gulliver survives; death passes him over, and he is delivered in words and images, like the plagues drawn from Exodus. The eagles, seen first as a threat, are in reality the immediate agents of Gulliver's rescue from the captivity of Brobdingnag. Gulliver mentions "the clapping of Wings" and the "the noise and flutter of Wings" (II, 142-43); in Exodus, God tells Moses, "Ye have seene what I did unto the Egyptians, and how I bare you on Eagles wings, and brought you unto my selfe" (XIX: 4).

It should be pointed out that Gulliver suffers many other indignities and dangers throughout Part II in addition to the incidents drawn from Exodus. Swift does not rely solely on afflictions borrowed from the Bible in punishing Gulliver. Gulliver's smallness in relation to the Brobdingnagians makes him susceptible to any number of mishaps, from being temporarily kidnapped by a monkey to falling into a mole hill to landing up to his knees in cow dung. These more or less natural disasters are not so far removed from the plague images as one might think, given that the plagues in Exodus are based on types of events that did occur in the natural world. God presumably could have afflicted the pharaoh with additional plagues had He so desired.

Although Gulliver's rescue parallels the deliverance of the Israelites, as the primary sufferer and object of the plagues, he more closely resembles the pharaoh of Exodus. Gulliver's failure, and the reason why he suffers the plagues, is the sin that brought disaster to the pharaoh—moral pride, the pride that blinds a person to one's own moral and intellectual imperfections, permitting complacency even when one directly opposes to the rule of God. This disobedience and opposition (so characteristic of the pharaoh's behavior) eighteenth-century moral critics viewed as a form of implied self-sufficiency, even, by extension, self-deification. The model for such sin was identified as Satan, especially as described by Milton in Book V of *Paradise Lost*, who, seeing the Son of God "proclaim'd/*Messiah* King anointed, could not bear/Through pride that sight, and thought himself impair'd [that is, rendered inferior]" (ll. 663-65). Very early in *Paradise Lost*, Milton writes of Satan's "obdurate pride," (I,58), a phrase that applies as well to Gulliver.[7] Swift's character also follows Satan and the Egyptian pharaoh into a refusal to accept his own imperfections and acquiesce in God's plan for him.

Part of Gulliver's refusal, of his "obdurate pride," occurs when he refuses to recognize and correct his behavior and values, including acknowledging the weaknesses of his own people. Even after his many audiences with the king of Brobdingnag, and the king's denunciation of Europeans as "the most pernicious Race of little odious Vermin that Nature ever suffered to crawl upon the Surface of the Earth" (II, 121), Gulliver assures the reader that "I artfully eluded many of his Questions, and gave to every Point a more favourable turn by many Degrees than the strictness of Truth would allow." Gulliver adds, "I would hide the Frailties and the Deformities of my Political Mother, and place her Virtues and Beauties in the most advantageous Light" (II, 123). Similarly, when the Brobdingnagian ruler rejects as heinous Gulliver's proffered gift of gunpowder, Gulliver responds incredulously to what he considers a "STRANGE Effect of *narrow Principles* and *short Views*," and accuses the king of "a *nice unnecessary Scruple*, whereof in *Europe* we can have no Conception. . ." (II, 127).

As Gulliver refuses to acknowledge his own failures and those of his nation, so does he fail to see what Swift certainly recognized, God's hand in what occurs. Being rescued repeatedly after a string of unsuccessful sea journeys is something that Gulliver should have recognized as the result of divine Providence, not merely fortunate human occurrences.

The failure of Gulliver continues to mount throughout the *Travels*. Like the protagonist of Daniel Defoe's *Robinson Crusoe*, Gulliver presents his spiritual autobiography, but in this case without realizing precisely what he is undergoing. Unlike Crusoe, no final recognition of sin, repentance, and acceptance of God's direction exists. Although Gulliver repeatedly delivers from his troubles after each of the four parts of the book, he slides increasingly downward into pride, hardening his heart against God's Providence, which is the most dangerous stage in the type of spiritual autobiography widely popular with English readers during the seventeenth century. [8] Finally, he rejects even his own human nature at the end of Part IV in his insane desire to become a houyhnhnm, or rational horse, and he barely tolerates having humans around him. In a final irony, what Gulliver castigates humans for above all else is their pride (IV, 198-99). He does not, of course, see God's hand in his deliverance, not only from the land of Brobdingnag, but from his subsequent catastrophes. He recognizes no dependence on God, thus implicitly declaring himself not only superior to the Brobdingnagians and to fellow humans, but to God as well. His behavior implies the same self-deification recognized in the Satan of *Paradise Lost* and the pharaoh of Exodus.

Ultimately, Gulliver, a type of Egyptian pharaoh, and a sometime representative of the Israelites in his deliverance from Brobdingnag, becomes an Everyman. Swift's concern is not merely to present a character who fails to understand himself but also to offer a lesson for readers. Swift as satirist both exhibits the follies and vices of humankind and affects reform, even if only indirectly. As a clergyman as well as satirist, Swift knew the importance of accepting divine Providence and cultivating the virtues, including humility.

The shifting roles that Gulliver plays are consistent with Swift's use of irony, where the coin keeps rotating but the result is always either heads up or tails down. In Chapter VI of Part I of the *Travels*, for example, Swift has Gulliver describe a long series of laws and customs in Lilliput. Those morally sound practices differ from English practice, while the evil practices parallel English life (I, 92-107).

Swift thus draws a moral picture of humankind, a portrait in which the plagues symbolize people's propensity for sin, and most importantly, the moral pride that hardens the sinner's heart even in the face of moral instruction and God's repeated attempts to lead the sinner into obedience of the divine will. The "Voyage to Brobdingnag" becomes in part a sermon on moral pride, a sermon with its own Scriptural base, the plagues with which God punished that earlier example of moral pride, the Egyptian pharaoh.

NOTES

1. See *Index to the Prose Writings of Jonathan Swift* (89). The Biblical reference occurs in *Gulliver's Travels* on page 133 of the 1726 first edition, the edition referred to throughout this paper. All Biblical quotations are drawn from the Authorised Version of 1611, the standard Bible for Anglicans in Swift's time, and certainly the version that he knew best. I have used the edition by William Aldis in five volumes.

2. Nonetheless, certain observations are pertinent to this study. Ernest Tuveson, for example, perceives that the separation of Jonathan Swift the satirist from Dr. Swift the Dean is the primary reason for some of the greatest misunderstandings of Swift's writings. Kathleen Williams, although not recognizing the imagistic pattern of the plagues discussed in this paper, does identify the pride that Swift satirizes as "the pride of the 'wicked' of the Old Testament; it is vanity and delusion" (156).

3. For "A Letter of Advice to a Young Poet," see *The Prose Writings*, volume 9, 327-45. Davis discusses the letter, including its authorship, in the Introduction to the volume, pp. xxiv-xxvii.

4. Samuel Johnson, in his *Dictionary of the English Language*, 4th ed., defines vessel as "the containing parts of an animal body." N. Bailey, in *An Universal Etymological English Dictionary*, 17th ed., offers the following meaning: "a little Conduit or Pipe for conveying the blood or other Humours of the Body."

5. This passage also demonstrates another important source for the *Travels*— the inventions and experiments of science, including the popular use of the microscope. For a development of this subject, see Marjorie Nicolson's collection of essays *Science and Imagination*.

6. Psalm CV also excludes the plague of boils and blains, but includes the other eight, although in a somewhat different arrangement.

7. For the ways in which seventeenth- and eighteenth-century readers responded to Milton, see B. Rajan's Paradise Lost *and the Seventeenth-Century Reader* and John Shawcross's edited collection, *Milton, 1732-1801: The Critical Heritage*.

Useful studies of Swift's pride include Paul Fussell's "The Frailty of Lemuel Gulliver" and Samuel Holt Monk's "The Pride of Lemuel Gulliver." Fussell examines Gulliver's sufferings, including some of the disasters mentioned in this paper. Although he does not perceive the Biblical allusions, he does show that the sufferings are concrete and physical emblems of Gulliver's intellectual or moral corruption. A significant overview of pride in Swift's time is Arthur O. Lovejoy's "'Pride' in Eighteenth-Century Thought."

8. An outstanding study of the patterns found in spiritual autobiography is George A. Starr's *Defoe and Spiritual Autobiography*.

Works Cited

Aldis, William, ed. *The Authorised Version of the English Bible, 1611.* 5 vols. Cambridge: Cambridge UP, 1909.

Bailey, N. *An Universal Etymological English Dictionary.* 17th ed. London, 1759.

Beaumont, Charles. *Swift's Use of the Bible: A Documentation and a Study in Allusion.* Athens: U of Georgia P, 1965.

Daw, C. F. "Swift's Favorite Books of the Bible. *Huntington Library Quarterly* 43 (1980): 201-12.

Defoe, Daniel. *The Life and Strange Surprizing Adventures of Robinson Crusoe.* London, 1729.

Ehrenpreis, Irvin, ed. *Index to the Prose Writings of Jonathan Swift.* Oxford: Basil Blackwell, 1968.

Frye, Roland Mushat. "Swift's Yahoo and the Christian Symbols for Sin." *Journal of the History of Ideas* 15 (1954): 201-17.

Fussell, Paul. "The Frailty of Lemuel Gulliver." *Essays in Literary History.* Ed. Rudolf Kirk and C. F. Main. New Brunswick: Rutgers UP, 1960. 113-25.

Johnson, Samuel. *Dictionary of the English Language.* 4th ed. London, 1773.

Keach, Benjamin. *Tropes and Figures.* London, 1682.

Lovejoy, Arthur O. "'Pride' in Eighteenth-Century Thought." *Essays in the History of Ideas.* Baltimore: Johns Hopkins P, 1948. 62-68.

Milton, John. *Paradise Lost. Complete Poems and Major Prose.* Ed. Merritt Y. Hughes. New York: The Odyssey Press, 1957. 173-469.

Monk, Samuel Holt. "The Pride of Lemuel Gulliver." *Eighteenth-Century English Literature: Modern Essays in Criticism.* Ed. James L. Clifford. New York: Oxford UP, 1959. 112-29.

Nicolson, Marjorie. *Science and Imagination.* Ithaca, NY: Great Seal Books, 1956.

Rajan, B. *Paradise Lost and the Seventeenth-Century Reader.* London: Chatto and Windus, 1947.

Shawcross, John T., ed. *Milton, 1732-1801: The Critical Heritage.* Boston: Routledge and Kegan Paul, 1972.

Starr, George A. *Defoe and Spiritual Autobiography.* Princeton: Princeton UP, 1965.

Swift, Jonathan. *The Prose Writings of Jonathan Swift.* Ed. Herbert Davis. 13 vols. 1959. Oxford: Basil Blackwell, 1965.

Tuveson, Ernest. "Swift: The Dean as Satirist." *University of Toronto Quarterly* 22 (1953): 368-75.

Williams, Kathleen. *Jonathan Swift and the Age of Compromise.* Lawrence: U of Kansas P, 1958.

8

Members of God's Body:
Charles Williams's Theory of Co-inherence
Melissa Matyjask

Introduction

Charles Williams is not a name often spoken in literary discussions about the most influential writers of the twentieth century. If his name is known at all, it is in relation to his Arthurian poetry or in connection with the group of Oxford Christians and theologians called the Inklings. Relatively few people have read his fantasy novels, even though he published five of them. Remarkably, WIlliams is such an obscure name today when, between 1908 and his death in 1945, his job as an editor at the Oxford University Press allowed him to mingle with and befriend many well-known authors. C. S. Lewis, T. S. Eliot and W. H. Auden were among the authors that chanced to meet and work with Williams. In his introduction to Williams's final, posthumously published novel, *All Hallows' Eve*, T. S. Eliot reminisces: "To have known the man would have been enough; to know his books is enough; but no one who has known both the man and his works would have willingly foregone either experience" (xi). Despite the praise he received from his friends and colleagues, Charles Williams's fiction is not known, although, like his fellow Inklings C. S. Lewis and J. R. R. Tolkien, his novels are available in bookstores today. Although Williams's books are still in print and his reputation among well-read authors was so great, readers do not approach his fiction is a curiosity worthy of investigation.

When the 1960s brought a revival of interest in fantasy fiction, Williams, Lewis and Tolkien once again entered the fiction arena. The responses of literary scholars to Williams's work were polar extremes: either they loved the novels or they hated them. There is a good possibility that part of the reason Williams's fiction is not very popular concerns the response he received from these critics. Even critics that enjoyed Williams's work contend it is difficult to read because he employs nearly every narrative technique available to him. If it pleased critics, they could write entire studies that focus on the repetition or a setting description or on the use of such paradoxical terms as "terribly good." In fact, several long and laborious studies such as these have been written and are useful in their efforts to explain Williams's rhetorical style. However, even the many layers of Williams's writing cannot fully account for its lack of readers. Anyone who has read the fiction knows that a reader need not understand, or even consider, these sorts of mechanics to enjoy the work. The fiction is perfectly readable; one novel could easily be read in a single afternoon if a reader so determined.

Far more unsatisfactory to critics is the way in which Williams incorporates fantastic elements in his fiction. Perhaps they want his work to resemble that of his companion Inklings'. Tolkien's creation of Middle Earth, with great wizards, dwarfs and other fantastic creatures and Lewis's space trilogy are nothing at all like Williams's earthly fiction. Williams is most often criticized because he uses fantasy and the occult in otherwise realistic writing. He sets his novels on Earth in the twentieth century; and the characters he develops are people the reader might run into at the grocery store. A typical Williams narrative begins like any other realistic novel. Suddenly, with only a few hints, if any at all, something completely out of the ordinary will happen. Many readers and critics find the shift unsavory and cannot understand why Williams chooses such an unconventional technique. Traditionally or conventionally, readers expect that all of their senses will be excited by concrete descriptions, which create the scene for them. With Williams, however, the reader is given mostly abstract descriptions, reminiscent of the infamous "unspeakable" H.P. Lovecraft often used in his fiction. For Spacks, unconventional use of perspective and description shows that Williams lacks "the language of the novelist" (156). She claims the supernatural events disrupt the realistic narrative, ruin the plot of the novels by making them predictable, and are themselves not developed enough to ignite the imagination. A reader of Williams's novels must remember that Williams considers the supernatural as usual. Strange occurrences happen in real life; there are always phenomenon and weirdness that cannot be explained rationally. Instead of demonstrating a lack of ability, the descriptions prove that Williams holds a high opinion of his readers and requires his readers to participate vicariously in his work. Williams consciously chooses to leave the descriptions of supernatural events vague because, in doing so, he allows his reader to create his or her own image. The visions of the imagination are more fantastic, terrible or beautiful than any he could describe for his readers. T. S. Eliot gives, perhaps, the best rationale for Williams's rich rhetoric and use of fantastic elements. He claims that Williams had no choice but to bend the rules of technique because "What he had to say was beyond his resources, and probably beyond the resources of language, to say once for all through any one medium of expression" (AHE xi).

The theme Charles Williams labored to express has, perhaps, done the most to hold back his work from being more popular because it has caused his fiction to be inescapably labeled. All seven of his novels, all forty of his publications for that matter, have the same theme of Heaven versus Hell. While Patricia Meyer Spacks admits she enjoys reading the novels, she finds the theology in Williams's work disruptive to the actual writing. Later in "Charles Williams: The Fusions of Fiction," she claims: "The little sermons which keep intruding into his fiction suggest his greater concern with ends than with means" (159). Williams was born in 1886 and raised as a member of the Anglican Church. He never hid his devotion to the church and many of his essays are discussions of Christian doctrine. Critics like Spacks most likely know about the writer's background in Christianity and, to some extent, are familiar with the fact that Williams's had written theological essays. These critics will close their minds to the fiction because the themes openly build upon Christian doctrine and many of them will decide the writing is poor for that very reason.

However, Charles Williams's fiction is very much about human nature, behavior and interaction. In the introduction to *The Novels of Charles Williams*, Thomas Howard contends: "a man does not have to believe in heaven and hell in order to admit that these words conjure the most powerful pictures available to human imagination of states of being that manifestly belong to our human society" (22). Howard surmises that the images of heaven and hell are simply recognizable ways of describing the kind of life a person could have, depending upon the choices she makes. One could choose to try and live a life of goodness and respect other people without being a Christian. True, for Williams, the way of goodness meant the Christian way, and many of the images and characters he uses, and the references he makes are Christian in origin. Still, his teachings appear similar to some teachings found in other religions and could be used as a general guide for creating good relationships. Thomas Howard remarks that like any poet "Williams has nothing strictly new to say . . . by refurbishing the old images and setting them out freshly, wake[s] the rest of us up once more to the tang and bite of human experience" (16).

During the last three years of the 1930s, Williams labored to give definition to the theological beliefs he began to develop in his fiction. He created the word *co-inherence* to name the relationship between all matter and non-matter, which existed to create a larger existence in God. Co-inherence means that everything exists in a great, connected web. His fiction was written to develop the idea and give examples that would demonstrate the kind of life and values that the acceptance of the idea of co-inherence commands. Readers discouraged by Christian themes could approach Williams's novels with a more humanistic view, however, far from being a disruption or a cause of failure in the novels, the ideology upon which the novels were written is quite remarkable and makes his fiction all the more worth reading. Ultimately, Williams does not concern himself with the methods by which one gets into Heaven, as some critics commonly assume embodies all Christian writing. Williams instead attempts to teach how people might create a better life for themselves through what he believes comprises the real meaning of love.

Co-inherence is the underlying principle behind all of Charles Williams's theological beliefs. In this discussion, the definition given for co-inherence is far too simplistic for what Williams meant by co-inherence. In the essay "The Way of Exchange," Williams explains the intricate connection in creation: "we ought to be 'members of one another'–*membra,* limbs, not members of the same society. . . . Men and women are not members of a club; they are 'members' of mankind, which is not a club" (*Charles Williams* 210). He takes the concept from the Christian belief in the Holy Trinity. Christians believe that God exists as Father, Son, and Holy Ghost; that is, they are separate yet, all part of the same being. However, each has a role in the salvation of humans. The Son is to be the sacrifice for humans' sin; the Holy Ghost, the spirit that moves among humans and fills their hearts with love for God; and God, the creator offering forgiveness (Hefling 18). Humans should strive to live in the image of the Trinity and become part of the connection. However, people are not to sacrifice their individuality for the sake of becoming connected. The arm, though a member of the body, cannot be any other part of the body but an arm. Williams makes the claim in "The Way of Exchange" that co-inherence should not serve "as a lessening of individuality or moral duty but as the very fundamental principle of all individuality and all moral duty" (*Charles Williams* 209).

Williams must have known the concept of co-inherence would be difficult, or overwhelming, for people to understand. At the very least, he knew his theology would be met with resistance from those who believed the individual was to be valued over all else. The early twentieth century marked a time in literature when the individual was celebrated. Stream-of-consciousness writing was used to discuss sexuality, psychology and civil rights for all people. Williams would have had to defend his belief against many questions. His answer was that Christians had always believed in the connection of existence. The idea was, in fact, the very foundation of the doctrine; only the church had strayed from the idea. He wrote "The Order of the Co-inherence," an essay claiming that teaching and understanding co-inherence "in nature and in grace, without and within Christendom, should be, now, one of our chief concerns" (*Charles Williams* 148). The essay then proposes that an order be created in the church to ensure the teaching and outlines the seven statements that such an order would believe and live by. The statements serve as the best means for explaining the principles of co-inherence.

Williams borrowed Augustine's City of God, called "Union," to use as an image for the web he envisioned between humans. The image is appropriate because a city is made up of thousands of people and depends upon each person to do his or her part to ensure its vitality. The first two statements for the order of co-inherence describe the act of exchange, one of the two means by which what he calls The City should operate. Williams writes:

1.   The Order has no constitution except in its members. As it was said: *Others he saved, himself he cannot save.*
2.   It recommends nevertheless its members shall make a formal act of union with it and of recognition of their own nature. As it was said: *Am I my brother's keeper?* (*Charles Williams* 149)

Exchange depends very much upon recognition of others. In "The Way of Exchange," Williams explains that merely admitting that all humans come from the same source is not enough. He contends: "But the very first condition of admitting that [other people's] existence is as real as our own is to allow that they have, as individuals, as much right to act in the way that they decide as we have" (*Charles Williams* 205). Williams defines the simple acceptance of individuality: every person has a will and is entitled to make his or her own choices. "Am I my brother's keeper?" People, by admitting that others exist in the world and, as Williams puts it, "ceasing to resent their existence," then become champions of their neighbor's will (205). An individual makes the exchange when a person not only realizes she is her brother's keeper, but her brother is also her keeper. "Others he saved, himself he cannot save." The City depends upon people working for each other. "The Way of Exchange" is "an active 'sympathy,' and it spoke of . . . an active and non-selfish love. It went even farther. It declared a union of existences. It proclaimed that our own lives depended on the lives of our neighbors" (206). The exchange is not only our being charitable and accepting of others as individuals, but also realizing that others also act, and work, in ways charitable and accepting of us.

Co-inherence does not merely stop with human interaction, but encapsulates all existence. Williams wrote many essays explaining the value of physical existence. He believed that all matter was created; therefore, even physical matter was part of what he called "Natural Goodness." Charles Hefling definses the implication in his collection, *Charles Williams*, as "The sheer fact of existing, physically or spiritually, is meaningful" (8). Williams writes the third and fourth statements for the Order of Co-inherence to explain the idea of "Natural Goodness" as well as give reasoning for the first two statements. He writes:

3.   Its concern is the practice of the apprehension of the Co-inherence both as a natural and a supernatural principle. As it was said: *Let us make man in Our image.*
4.   It is therefore, *per necessitatem*, Christian. As it was said: *And whoever says there was when this was not, let him be anathema.* (*Charles Williams* 149)

Williams uses the Athanasian Creed as foundation for the belief that the Incarnation was the result of God's co-inherence with man. He became physical matter, not only for the salvation of humankind, but because he created all matter for the very reason of becoming part of it. The Athanasian Creed says, as quoted in Stephen Medcalf's essay, "Athanasian Principle in Williams's Use of Images": "God and Man were united 'not by conversion of the Godhead into flesh: but by taking of the Manhood into God'" (28). From the Incarnation, people are to learn that God did not create humans in order to test them, but rather to exist with them. "Let us make man in Our image." Man represents God's perfection. As Medcalf further explains, by the Incarnation:

> God is not made less perfect, but humanity has open to it the possibility of perfection. God is not divided into the moments of time, but humanity is made conscious of the fullness of eternity. God is not subjected to mechanical causation, but humanity fulfills God's purpose. Christ's humanity has all the limitations of humanity . . . but it is taken into God, and with it, if we accept the possibility, so are we. (28)

God did not become anything less than God through the incarnation. Instead, because he created man as his companion, the incarnation exemplified the perfection that he created in man.

Williams calls believing and seeing that God creates every spirit and every bit of matter and part of Him "The Way of Affirmation of Images." Many Christian churches have valued the existence of the spirit or soul above that of the body. The result, Williams asserts in "Sensuality and Substance," is "The great world and energy of the body have been either deprecated or devotionalized . . . turned into a pale imitation of 'substance,' of spirit. . . . But soul ought not to be allowed to reduce the body to its own shadow–at any rate, in the Christian church" (*Charles Williams* 114-115). Williams felt he must remind the church of The Way of Affirmation because the practice of what the termed "The Way of Rejection of Images" had become overvalued in Christianity. The Way of Rejection is to scoff at all physicality–to deny all the images of creation in matter–and focus completely on what is spiritual. Neither way can exist alone, according to Williams. Also between the Way of Affirmation and the Way of Rejection, there is exchange. Hence the maxim: "This also is Thou, neither is this Thou," which appears over and over in Williams's fiction. Charles Hefling best presents an explanation of the maxim in his collection of Williams's theological writings called *Charles Williams*. He writes: "To affirm an image as a revelation of God is to say, 'this also is Thou.' But because an image conceals even as it discloses, any such affirmation must always be corrected by adding its opposite: 'neither is this Thou'" (15). Depending solely upon images is idolatry, to deny an image altogether is to deny creation. "And whoever says there was when this was not, let him be anathema" (*Charles Williams* 149). Most often critics take the statement as Williams's assertion that Christianity is the only way. Of course, for him, no other way existed. But, because Williams makes his statement to the church and not in effort of conversion, he reminds the church that the foundation for Christian belief had been these very ideals of acceptance. The church had long ago forgotten to live by the Athanasian Creed of the apostles, and the result, Williams tells us in "Sensuality and Substance," is "The great world and energy of the body have been either deprecated or devotionalized . . . turned into a pale imitation of 'substance,' of spirit; thus losing their own powers and privileges" (*Charles Williams* 114). Because the church had forgotten the foundation of the Creed, the exchange between Affirmation and Acceptance of Images had been disrupted.

Although practicing exchange steps towards the Way of Affirmation of Images, substitution is even more necessary as it moves the individual closer toward the acceptance of one's place in The City. Substitution is just what it implies, a willingness to take someone's place. God loved humans enough to take on humanity's limits and offer his life as an example. To die for another human being constitutes the supreme testimony of love for them. Williams explains in statements five and six for the Order:

> 5.   It recommends therefore the study, on the contemplative side, of the Co-inherence of the Holy and Blessed Trinity, of the Two Natures of the Single Person, of the Mother and Son, of the communmicated [sic] Eucharist, and of the whole Catholic Church. As it was said: *figlia del tuo figlio.* And, on the active side, the methods of exchange, in the State, in all forms of love, and in all natural things such as childbirth. As it was said: *Bear ye one another's burdens.*
>
> 6.   It includes in the Divine Substitution of Messias [sic] all forms of exchange and substitution, And it invokes this Act as the root of all. As it was said: *We must become, as it were, a double man.* (*Charles Williams* 149)

Practicing substitution need not be as dramatic as dying in place of another person, but it requires as much commitment. Not as easily explained as exchange, substitution actually begins with exchange. In his essay "The Practice of Substituted Love," Williams lists the three requirements for substitution. They are: "(1) to know the burden; (2) to give up the burden; (3) to take up the burden" (*Charles Williams* 224). The person offers to accept the burden and actually know and feel it which requires commitment in that the person must assume the other's role completely. The giver's part is equally as important and difficult. As Williams notes, "It is habitual to us therefore to prefer to be miserable rather than to give, and to believe that we can give, our miseries up" (225). People do not believe in their neighbors. One more commonly practices to distrust others or even fear neighbors; we believe, therefore, only in ourselves. However, the act of substitution is required to make life on Earth livable and the participation in the co-inherence of The City complete.

Of course, the reward for living in accordance with the statements outlined in "The Order of Co-inherence" is the promise of eternal life in Heaven. However, the seventh and final statement corrects any notion that exchange and substitution should be done just to ensure one's place in Heaven. Williams states:

> 7.   The Order will associate itself primarily with four feasts: the Feast of Annunciation, the Feast of the Blessed Trinity, the Feast of Transfiguration, and the Commemoration of All Souls. As it was said: *Another will be in me and I in him.* (*Charles Williams* 149-150)

While people should certainly try to please God and be aware of the eternal consequences of their behavior, the purpose of living as Williams has set forth in preceding statements means working toward the acceptance of creation as perfection. Stephen Medcalf explains perfection in "The Athanasian Principle in Williams's Use of Images." He claims Williams's writing demonstrates:

> In various forms, the sense that everything and every person, is haunted by its own perfection; that that perfection not only is possible but exists actually; and that in certain states of consciousness, conspicuously–but by no means only–in falling in love, we are immediately aware of the perfect forms of things, of other people, and of ourselves. (27)

The logic follows thus: God is perfect. God created Man in his image. Man, therefore, represents God's perfection. If people willingly believe in co-inherence, practice exchange and substitution, their reward will be on Earth. In "The Practice of Substituted Love," Williams explains: "it may be possible to be astonished at the self as at everything else, when that which is God is known as the circle whose center is everywhere and the circumference nowhere" (*Charles Williams* 230). One can have a rewarding and happy live by striving to accept others and building good relationships.

None of Charles Williams's ideology is original. He admits that the major premises he expounds are borrowed. In the essay "The Way of Exchange," Williams claims that not only Christianity, but also all of the "great religions" believed in co-inherence as it applied to one's relationship with other human beings. "Much though they differed in their definitions of God, they did, generally, agree on their definitions of our duty towards our neighbor, even if they did not always agree on the exact definition of our neighbor" (*Charles Williams* 206). This quotation somewhat ambiguously defines "great religions," but Williams had, in his earlier essay "The Index of the Body," explicitly named religions that held co-inherence as foundation. The essay argues for the recognition of the body as a tool used to better understand the spirit. It reads:

> Man was "the workshop of all things," "a little world," . . . It is a very ancient idea; it was held before Christianity and has been held during Christianity; it was common to Christians, Jews, and Mohammedans; and, for all I know, the scientific hypothesis of evolution bears a relation to the union of the two . . .. [I]ts general principle remained constant; that man was the rational epitome of the universe. (*Charles Williams* 127)

The whole of Williams's theology can be broken down to this: because we are all part of the same existence, or because we are all forced to live together on Earth, we should realize and accept that all humans, as different as they may be from ourselves, are still human. Because each person has the free will to make choices in life, each person is individual, but must always remember that other people are individuals as well. Mutual human respect and with it respect for all things, in other words, Williams's process of exchange, merely enables us to live together without misery. Substitution, as complicated as it at first seems, simply builds more stable intimate relationships. Basically, everything comes down to love.

The following discussion focuses on what Williams believed are the only two alternatives for humans as Williams viewed them: Heaven or Hell, as represented in the novels, *War in Heaven* and *Descent into Hell*. I will begin by examining Williams's first published novel *War in Heaven* as a study in human behavior and statement on individuality, focusing on the novel's characters. In the novel, the characters form two groups fighting for possession of the Holy Grail. A comparison of these opposing groups will explain the way Williams believed people should interact with every person they meet. Also, the Holy Grail and the occult as they are used in the novel are integral parts to understanding character motivation. They will be touched upon also. In examining *Descent into Hell*, the discussion will turn to Williams's concept of co-inherence and substitution as they affect intimate relationships. Because the novel focuses on romantic relationships as well as familial and friendly ones, we ought to understand how each character loves, the more difficult task Williams undertakes in *Descent into Hell*. By the time he wrote the novel he had a better definition of his theological beliefs worked out and had begun to have his writings about the church and its doctrine published. The novel broadens the definition of reality and explains real love through his characters. Placing Williams's characters and their interactions in the foreground allows for a reading of his novels that recognizes the value of his doctrine as it examines how one spends their life, not their afterlife.

Descent into Hell

As Williams began spending more time with writers at Oxford, his fiction began to change. Seven years after the publication of *War in Heaven*, he began to explore the process of damnation. The result, *Descent into Hell*, a novel considered by many critics to be his best work. Thomas Howard remarks, "In *Descent into Hell* Williams came closer than in any of his other tales to giving us a real novel. The action is all of a piece. There is very little of the clutter we find in his earlier fiction" (247). Judith J. Kollmann agrees. In her study of Williams's language, "Complex Rhetoric for a Simple Universe," she claims the ideas of co-inherence reach their "most complete expression" in this, his second to last novel. Ironically, Williams's publisher refused to produce this novel, and its publication was put off until T.S. Eliot convinced his publisher to pick it up. Certainly, if not the best of Williams's novels, *Descent into Hell* critics favor the novel because it accomplishes so much. A scholar can indeed fill many pages by focusing on the phrase "terrible good," used to repeat theme in the novel or by devoting herself to determining Williams's theories on the position of a poet in society. Even though the writing is complexly interwoven, the reader need not be well versed in literary studies to appreciate what *Descent into Hell* accomplishes. With this novel, Williams takes to task an examination of the value of individuality in the City and its place in love.

A good place to begin to understand the workings of the City as they involve daily interactions between acquaintances at work or strangers on the street is *War in Heaven*. However, because Williams focuses very much upon self-abnegation, he gives little attention to the individual beyond the fact that she has a free will to make choices and is, therefore, equal to everyone else. Co-inherence could almost be read as some distorted form of communism. Every person is equal, deserving of respect, deserving to have just as much or as little as every other person. Very little room for self-expression, self-love or self-respect appears. If every person works for every other person, he or she cannot possibly be working toward any form of identity. Williams bases his ideal City, however, on the assumption that one creates an identity through intimate relationships and actions performed out of love.

Science fiction theorist Kathleen Spencer argues that Williams's essay "Images of the City," although focusing on authority and obedience in society, goes a long way in elaborating exactly how an individual may live for others while loving herself. In Williams's City, a hierarchy more akin to the free-love ideals of the sixties exists. Although seemingly a contradiction, the hierarchy ensures not only equality, but also a clear definition of exactly who she is. Spencer admits: "individual pride or desire must be subordinated to the demands of the task at hand, for the task is significant in a way that no individual can be" (22). This is the principle theme of *War in Heaven*. The responsibility of the individual rests solely on the individual to choose whether to take on the task. Again, the most supreme of all tasks for Williams was love. Yet, even in a City devoted to love, not everyone can have exactly the same amount of everything.

For example, there are kings, teachers, priests, street sweepers and garbage collectors. They will never be afforded the same means. There will always be an authority, and some will have more material goods. Life works as such. Spencer points out that even in these workings equality exists: "It is love that guards against the terrible dangers of authority and obedience, the great potential in each for abuse – love which, in authority, places limits upon itself and which, in obedience, still retains judgment and choice" (23). The key to the whole idea- - we will keep ourselves from ruling others, or allowing ourselves to be ruled by others who have any other purpose than love and the good of the City. Also, even though we may be in obedience in one relationship in our lives, we may also be the authority in another. As Williams explains it in "Image of the City": "He who is a good master of his craft in music may do ill enough in the theatre; and the Prime Minister must be docile to an expert scullion" (Spencer 23). The relationship is not total release of self to others but, an acceptance of one's individual place with others. Love is the means by which a person defines and accepts herself, thereby creating her position in the City. The process of self-discovery through love is central to *Descent into Hell*.

Love exists in Williams's theology on many different fronts. At the mention of the word *love,* one immediately calls to mind the sort of romantic, sexual union between lovers. Of course, there are romantic relationships in the novel, and Williams worked many years developing what he called "Romantic Theology" which focuses on marriage as an identification of human love for Christ. Williams believed a good, balanced and healthy relationship between lovers was akin to the relationship for which one should strive to accomplish with Jesus. Yet, intimacy cannot stop with lovers; it includes all personal relationships.. *Descent into Hell offers* a good representation of many different types of intimate relationships.

The plot of the novel centers around the production of a play in a middle class suburb of London called Battle Hill. Williams takes particular care to point out that "the poor, who had created it, had been as far as possible excluded, nor (except as hired servants) were they permitted to experience the bitterness of others' stairs" (9). Williams chose to exclude poor characters from the novel because he represents the community of Battle Hill as a selfish one and their exclusion of poor people merely part of their characterization. The people of Battle Hill are, in fact, so self-absorbed, they are oblivious to any other thing but themselves.

The citizens living in the community do not even realize that Battle Hill is not like most suburbs. They share the space they live in with many, many other people that walk among them unnoticed except by a few. The area receives its name from a hill that throughout history has been the stage for many battles. Williams describes Its history in the second chapter:

> The Hill's chronicle of anguish had been due, in temporalities,
> to its strategic situation in regard to London, but a dreamer might

> have had nightmares of a magnetic attraction habitually there
> deflecting the life of man into death. . . .Prehistoric legends, repeated
> in early chronicles, told of massacres by revolting Britons and
> roaming Saxons . . . a medieval fortalice had been built, and a score
> of civil feuds and pretended loyalties had worn themselves out
> around it. The Roses had twined there, their roots living on the blood
> shed by their thorns. . . .[A] peasant farmer, moved by some
> wandering gospeller, had, under Mary Tudor, grown obstinately
> metaphysical, and fire had been lit between houses and manor that he
> might depart through it in a roaring anguish of joy. Forty years later,
> under Elizabeth, the whispering informers had watched an outlaw, a
> Jesuit priest, take refuge in the manor, but when he was seized the
> Death of the Hill had sent him to its Type in London for more
> prolonged ceremonies of castration. . . . (25)

The history of Battle Hill has more effect on the place than merely namesake. Chapter two aptly named "Via Mortis," or the Way of the Dead, reveals that ghosts as well as the living occupy Battle Hill. In a manner we know as typical of Williams's writing, this seems out of place in the more realistic portrayal of the community as well as working against his Christian beliefs. However, one must remember Williams's own experience in the occult. If there is indeed one creator of all creation, and if all of creation is part of the same whole, how could death mean the end of interaction? "But," Williams writes, "if the past still lives in its own present beside our present, then the momentary later inhabitants were surrounded by a greater universe. From other periods of its time other creatures could crawl out of death, and invisibly contemplate the houses and people of the rise . . . awaiting the hour when they should either retire to their own mists or more fully invade the place of the living" (DIH 25-26). Williams believed spirit and body were a whole; once the body could no longer maintain, the spirit continued to live in a place for the dead that was still attached to the physical world because it was all part of the larger whole of creation. Similar to Purgatory, the dead would wait until they were ready for their fate of Heaven or Hell. The dead of Battle Hill are essential to the novel because they offer the reader a measure for the living characters, and they prove that the Hill is "favourable to apparitions beyond men; a haunt of alien life" (21).

As in *War in Heaven*, many characters, both living and dead, interact throughout the novel. Of course, as with any writing by Williams, each character adds something significant, but the novel focuses on two characters. Pauline Anstruther appears most often in the action of the novel. Williams instroduces her in the first chapter, "Magus Zoroaster," and the reader knows immediately she is struggling in her life. After Peter Stanhope reads his play for the group, an argument between Mrs. Parry, the producer and director, and Adela Hunt, the leading actress ensues about what Stanhope meant by including a chorus and whether or not they were significant or symbolic. Myrtle Fox unthinkingly calls nature "terribly good." Stanhope calls her on it by asking if she truly meant "terribly" as it means full of terror. She meant no such thing, but Stanhope insists it is the correct description. Pauline contemplates this "terrible good" while the others continue to argue: "She had never considered good as a thing of terror, and certainly she had not supposed a certain thing of terror in her own secret life as any possible good" (DIH 19). The "certain thing of terror" that haunts Pauline is a *doppelgänger*. Since very young, Pauline has run into an apparition that looks exactly like her. She had found a poem by Shelley about a Magus Zoroaster who also "met" himself, "But she had always hated Shelley since for making it so lovely, when it wasn't loveliness but black panic" (19). Now, after considering the "terrible good" Stanhope claims exists, she begins to wonder if Magus Zoroaster might not have enjoyed meeting his dopplegänger.

Pauline's double turns out to be part of herself that she has not been able to face because she has not learned about love. She tried to tell her mother when she was young, but it caused an argument and she has never spoken of it since. Because of her mother's refusal to help, a denial to love, Pauline has felt this was a burden she must carry alone. She even yearns to shut herself inside the house forever to be free of her double-she so lacks the courage to face it. She finally allows herself to confide in Peter Stanhope about her double, and he, in turn, offers her substituted love. Stanhope offers to carry Pauline's fear of the dopplgänger, which of course sounds ludicrous to Pauline. Stanhope explains the process of substitution: "Listen – when you go home from here, when you're alone, when you think you'll be afraid, let me put myself in your place, and be afraid instead of you . . . . It needs only the act. For what can be simpler than for you to think to yourself that since I am there to be troubled instead of you, therefore you needn't be troubled" (DIH 98). What it boils down to is a simple matter of trust. If Pauline wants to finally have peace, she must trust Peter Stanhope enough to allow him to give her love. Not romantic love here, but a friend's love. He reminds her that love is why existence was created. He tells her: "If you want to disobey and refuse the laws that are common to us all, if you want to live in pride and division and anger, you can. But if you will be part of the best of us, and live and laugh and be ashamed with us, then you must be content to be helped" (99). Pauline does what he asks that very afternoon and is surprised when she walks home free from fear and actually enjoying what she sees on her way. It works, the substitution takes place, and all Pauline does is trust and promise she will offer to do the same for someone else one day.

Once she trusts Stanhope, Pauline opens up to others. She arrived at Battle Hill just two years earlier, after her parents' deaths, to live with her grandmother. Pauline had never grown close to Margaret Anstruther, although her grandmother was full of love and "Her good will diffused itself in all directions" (54). After Pauline accepts Stanhope's offer of substituted love, she is given the opportunity to assist Margaret in offering help to another person, actually, the ghost of a man who hanged himself during the building of the manor house on the hill. All of his life he had felt no love and, even in death he cannot find peace. Margaret and Pauline show the worker how to love. It is all part of Pauline's education and movement toward the eventual meeting with the *doppelgänger*.

Pauline does not only need to learn how to allow herself to be loved, she must also learn exactly how far she can go in doing for herself before she is fully prepared to encounter her double. She must learn to resist the temptation to deny love in favor of the self. Lily Sammile, in the form of another of Battle Hill's living residents,. presents the temptation. Just before Stanhope carries Pauline's fear for her, Mrs. Sammile appears at her house and offers to help her as well. She offers an escape from the world. She says she believes there should be a choice in what happens in a person's life, and she could give Pauline security in a wonderful life. Lily assures Pauline that she could have every want and desire fulfilled, if only Pauline would come and see her. She says she can make a new "tale" for the younger woman, change her life. The proposition sounds enticing: "Everything lovely in you for a companion, so that you'd never be frightened or disappointed or ashamed anymore. There are tales that can give you yourself completely and the world could never treat you so badly then that you wouldn't neglect it" (61). Total rejection of the world to have everything you have desired in life- Mrs. Sammile's character exemplifies temptation incarnate. In *The Novels of Charles Williams*, Thomas Howard connects her with Lilith, a figure from Jewish tales. Lilith is said to have been Adam's wife before Eve. She grew impatient and unhappy with life in Eden and was, therefore, sent out. When God replaced her by Eve, Lilith returned to seduce both Adam and Eve. She is supposedly the serpent from Genesis and, so some say, continues to hate all that motherhood stands for; she curses infants and children. As Howard puts it, "She is the archetype of all wicked fairy godmothers and enchantresses" (271). She targets Pauline target because she lacks the knowledge of an adult. She, in her ignorance of love, is an infant.

Luckily, Stanhope stops in at just this moment with Myrtle Fox, diverting Lily's attention. However, another option is presented to Pauline. Myrtle says bad dreams never plague her because she simply tells herself, "Sleep is good, and sleep is here . . . .. I say the same thing every morning, ... Life is good and Life is here. Life is good" (64). Both ladies offer a solution we commonly hear. Life is what one makes of it, or people create their own fate--all of those sayings inspire because the individual has some say in what happens to her is what both Myrtle and Lily believe. Of course, Williams believes people do indeed choose their own fate, however, and to do what either woman proposes is self-deceit. Returning for a moment to Stanhope's "terrible good," sometimes we will become frightened, hurt, or angry. Simply, we must learn to live with what life hands us. Kathleen Spencer, in her guide to reading the novel, explains the idea as follows: "But to reject facts – even unwelcome facts like death and disappointment – is to reject the world and therefore all possible good . . . the secret of happiness is to accept those joys the universe offers, rather than trying to compel the universe to offer you joys of your own definition" (68). This is not to say a person cannot work to better herself and her lot, but while she works toward it, she should not let it consume her life. Work earnestly toward something, make good choices, but do not forget to enjoy what you do have. Pauline could choose Lily Sammile's offer, but she would miss the opportunity to learn love from Stanhope. She could choose Myrtle's method, but then she would be no better off because she would be denying facts, refusing to admit the existence of her double.

After Peter Stanhope's offer of substituted love, Lily Sammile returns only once more to tempt Pauline. When Pauline rejects the offer and returns to Margaret's bedside, she has her lesson in carrying another's burden with the dead man, all preparation for the moment she meets her *doppelgänger*. She has another encounter with the dead. This time it is her ancestor, the peasant burned for his beliefs on the Hill. She has always been amazed and confused by John Struther's tale. She has heard that he exclaimed, "I have seen the salvation of my God," as he was put through the flames. When she meets him, Pauline knows her time to carry his burden of fear has arrived. She cannot-she fears the fire as well. Then the *doppelgänger* appears and takes it for both of them. For the first time in her life, Pauline feels joy: "This then, after so long, was their meeting and their reconciliation: their perfect reconciliation, for this other had done what she had desired, and yet not the other, but she, for it was she who had all her life carried a fear" (DIH 170). The *doppelgänger* comprises a part of Pauline that she could not accept because she did not know love. To state this in another way, the courage it takes to participate actively in the reciprocal relationship of love had long since been foreign to Pauline. It had turned into the double and followed her. Her fear only made it pursue her more ardently because it was her courage and self-satisfaction. The cycle then is a very tangled one. A person may do much good, Pauline had never treated another person poorly, but peace in life, or Heaven on Earth, depends upon love. Love must be willingly given and willingly taken. However, love cannot be given until one has accepted both herself and life. She must also have learned she is worthy to be loved.

This complicated cycle can easily lose somone because it demands much effort from an individual. Lily Sammile and Myrtle Fox both offer much simpler ways. Yet, choosing those ways is a mistake as evidenced by the second main character's, Lawrence Wentworth's experience. His plot intertwines with Pauline's as he also encounters a double that is not his own image, but takes the form of the outspoken, selfish Adela Hunt. Wentworth choses a path that opposes Pauline's; he wends his way into Hell on Earth.

Wentworth, a famous name in Battle Hill, is a well-respected military historian, second only to a Mr. Aston Moffatt. He and Moffatt argue over a small detail of a battle, which matters very little to Wentworth who only only wants to prove himself correct; "In defense of his conclusion he was willing to cheat in the evidence" (DIH 39). He attributes a recurring nightmare he has to this conflict with Moffatt and his interest in Adela Hunt. His practice had always been to make up stories of his success and fame to lull him to sleep. Lately his dreams turned to a more distressing situation, his climbing down an infinitely long rope. He descends very slowly, but consistently. This dream does not terrify him; rather, it dissatisfies him more than those he creates for himself. He responds to the dream "not [with] *fear*; no monstrosity awaited him. On the other hand, he did, waking, remember to have felt the very slightest distaste, as if for a dentist. He remembered that he wanted to remain on the rope, . . . that was impossible" (37). His wanting to remain on the rope in his dream could be caused by his dread of approaching old age and death. Staying alive would be far better. But, more so, it represents his indecision of action. He has become infatuated with Adela Hunt, but has yet decided what he should do about it. Adela often visits with other young people of the community at Wentworth's house to talk with him about history and philosophy. He is smitten, but never tells her, and when she shows an interest in a young Hugh Prescott, it enrages Wentworth. Truthfully, he appears far less distraught that she is interested in Hugh than that Hugh can command things of her. Wentworth observes, "It was what he had never had – consent, yes, but not this obedience" (41). Similar to the situation with Moffatt, Wentworth's interior motives are hidden from even himself. He wants more than anything to be an authority, to have power over all that he possibly can.

Thus begins Wentworth's path to self-destruction. Williams likens Wentworth's decisions to an actual seeking of Hell. In the chapter "Quest for Hell," Wentworth seeks his own misery using Adela and Hugh. He has grown suspicious that the two of them have stood him up on the same night and, although Pauline tries to confide in him about the *doppelgänger*, he rages within himself about the situation. Ironically, he tells Pauline rather off-handedly that her friend who has seen a *doppelgänger* "was a very self-centered individual" (267). He succeeds in dismissing her and sets out to spy. Even as he spies, Wentworth lies to himself about his motives for doing so. He tries to convince himself, "He was not in ambush; he was out for a walk," but he really faces an ambush (51). He waits all night for the last train to see Adela and Hugh return from London, arm in arm. He wants to attribute his loss to something other than Hugh being Adela's preference. "He will seek the furtive and murky world of this solitary spying," Thomas Howard explains, "finding a ghastly nourishment by feeding on the tidbits of satisfaction that angry souls pick, vulture-like, from successes such as catching their rivals red-handed in deception" (267). What Howard means is that it becomes more satisfying for Wentworth to believe that Hugh has tainted Adela rather than believe that he has lost. He has begun to tell himself a new tale, like Lily Sammile and Myrtle Fox are convinced Pauline should do.

The lies he tells himself about Adela are not completely untrue. She and Hugh did conspire to trick him. Adela's character appears very much like Wentworth's. She, too, cares only for herself; perhaps the main reason he feels smitten with her. She possesses the self-confidence Pauline lacks, plus she looks ambitious and pretty. But, Adela, also willing to lie, refuses to compromise any goal to enter into love. Wentworth really does not want this real Adela. Instead, when the Adela-double shows up in "Return to Eden," she is everything he truly wants. "Wentworth understood that Adela was not enough, that Adela must be something different even from Adela if she were to be satisfactory to him, something closer to his own mind and farther from hers" (DIH 82). This succubus lures him into further rejection of society. She tells him: "You don't think about yourself enough" (DIH 82). It seems perfectly logical to him. In fact, he can reason her existence. An incredible passage in the novel concerns his reasoning because it could almost convince even the reader if it weren't so preposterous:

> The it that could be found if he thought of himself more; that was what he had said or she had said, whichever had said that the thing was to be found, as if Adela had said it, Adela in her real self, by no means the self that went with Hugh; no, but the true, the true Adela who was apart and his; for that was the difficulty all the while, that she was truly his, and wouldn't be, but if he thought more of her truly being untruly away, on whatever way, for the way that went away was not the way she truly went, but if they did away with the way she went away, the Hugh could be untrue and she true, the he would know themselves, two, true and two, on the way he was going, and the peace in himself, and the scent of her in him, and the her, meant for him, in him; that was the she he knew, and he must think the more of himself. (DIH 83)

Obviously, these are the ramblings of an insane man trying to reason his own insanity. Wentworth, a scholar supposedly dedicated to finding facts in history, but actually lying about them, has now begun to rationalize his lying to himself. The succubus is not Adela but Lilith, or, rather, what Lilith in the shape of Lily Sammile had offered Pauline: "Everything that is lovely in you for a companion": "the she that was he, and all he in the she" that he has simply created as a new tale and has refused to admit that it was his desire and his fantasy being played out and not the factual Adela (89).

As the novel progresses, Pauline learns about love and about herself, and as Mrs. Parry's production of Stanhope's pastoral is nearly ready for performance, Wentworth spends more and more time with his creation. At the dress rehearsal, Wentworth is asked his opinion of the costumes of the guard in the play. They are all wrong, easily fixed, but wrong. It would take little effort for Wentworth to be honest, but it would mean he would have to admit some part of reality into his world. He would have to accept the true Adela, be in her presence and

Hugh's. It would mean he would have to be around others, in the world of truth, but he prefers his created one. When he meets Adela, her voice intrudes because the real Adela speaks. He does not hate; that would be to consider that it exists, and for him it does not. He reasons: "He need not resent the grossness of the world; . . .. He had his own living medicament for all trouble, and distaste and oblivion for everything else" (DIH 141). He returns to his house and his succubus, closing everyone else out for good.

The play is performed successfully. Catherine Parry expertly and skillfully produces the play. Stanhope, following the rules of authority and obedience, recognizes her authority and bows to it. Margaret Anstruther dies, almost joyfully; Pauline knows she was received into love. Harmony almost exists on Battle Hill, except for some. Williams uses the mysterious city of Gomorrah from the Bible to describe the Hill in the last few chapters of the novel. The Bible never really explains what happens in Gomorrah; it only relates the workings of its sister city, Sodom, and relates that God destroyed the two for their sinfulness. Here, Gomorrah stands for the very selfishness that excludes all others. The description reveals mirrors that reflect and abstract the world out of shape. something Wentworth and Myrtle Fox do.. We do not know about Adela Hunt's guilt until nearly the end of the novel also. She asks Pauline to help her persuade Stanhope to allow her to produce his play in London. Of course, this will allow her to interpret the play, as she has wanted to all along in her many arguments with Mrs. Parry. She will also be advancing her career and increasing her fame by using her connection with Stanhope. Pauline recognizes this and asks Adela to admit it. Adela responds, "We shall be as good for him as he will be for us," persistent in trying to convince herself she has the good of everybody in mind (183). As for her relationship with Hugh, she thinks it a good enough idea, but she thinks that she will have to "manage" him. In fact, she has in mind that she should "manage the world" (185).

When the play finishes, Lily Sammile faints. Later, when Hugh and Adela happen across her in the graveyard, they are offered truth. All around Mrs. Sammile graves open and coffins begin coming out of the ground and their occupants emerge. Adela runs. She runs from the coffins, she runs from Lily Sammile, and she runs from Hugh. She runs from reality straight to Wentworth's house. When he sees her, Wentworth denies knowing her, and she happens to catch a glimpse of his Adela-succubus. The reality is too much for Adela, and she becomes ill. Pauline comes to visit, and Adela asks her to find Lily Sammile. While Pauline knows she does not want to deal with the woman, she willingly does this for Adela out of love. She finds Lily Sammile and sees dead people surround her. Lily acts as mother, not to the living, but to the dead. Once again she offers to give Pauline everything she wants. Pauline refuses:

> "How can I tell you? I only want everything to be as it is – for myself I mean."
> "Change," said the shape. "I don't change."

> Pauline cried out: "And if it changes, it shall change as it must, and I shall want it as it is then." She laughed again at the useless attempt to explain. (209).

Lily, or Lilith, is defeated and sent into the void of Hell. Her own dissatisfaction with creation could not withstand total acceptance of existence that Pauline demonstrated.

The novel does not end with this triumph of acceptance over rejection. The last image resembles Wentworth. He has one last opportunity to accept a reality that he did not create. The final chapter, "Beyond Gomorrah," finds him rejecting even the succubus because he prefers to be alone. He does attend the knighting of Aston Moffatt, and instead of being happy, or trying to be happy that a historian has received such an honor, all he can think is, "I've been cheated" (219). He finally and totally rejects reality. At this, he moves beyond ennui and into nothing. Even his name has no meaning to him. He has withdrawn into himself totally and found without having accepted any part of reality even a bad one, he has absolutely no value. The novel closes on his revelation: "there came upon him a suspense; he waited for something to happen. The silence lasted; nothing happened. In that pause expectancy faded. Presently, . . . he was drawn, . . . through the bottomless circles of the void" (222). Wentworth does not die, but he also does not live. He just is not. Turning so far inward has provided him nothing but blackness and blankness.

Wentworth's descent as opposed to Pauline's ascent is the ultimate statement against self-centeredness. Even if one considers this occurrence without a pre-conceived notion that it relates to Christianity, it remains fact. Logically, if a person cannot accept the love others give her, can she ever accept herself? Isn't the denial to allow yourself to be loved a rejection of your existence as equal to theirs? If she chooses to accept the reality of existence, the possibility of rejection or disappointment always exists, but those things should not keep one away from herself or others. In fact, in choosing to create a world for herself, she rejects what she is already, either ashamed or dissatisfied with whom she is. Heaven, for Williams, does not necessarily mean golden streets or mansions, but a state on Earth where a person finds complete acceptance of everything. Not that one cannot work to change, but if the change comes, accept it just as she has accepted her current conditions. Hell, then, is the point in which an individual can never be satisfied. It is the constant searching she will have to do, and she will always look more and more inwardly while ignoring all of the good around her. She will be miserable and will continue to search until, finally, search will appear useless. Then there is nothing. No want, no search, no acceptance, no love, and, most of all, no reason to be; no existence.

Conclusion

Since Williams's death in 1945, only a small amount of criticism has been written about his novels. In 1991, Dennis Weeks wrote, "The major problem in researching Charles Williams is the lack of secondary sources," (79). Weeks provides a fairly extensive critical look at the secondary sources available at the time he was writing. From his analysis of the work done on Williams's novels, Weeks concludes, "Williams criticism, in book-length form, is composed of about ten volumes written by different authors. Each of the books tends to repeat the other critics, making the individual studies somewhat confusing as it becomes very difficult to remember who said what; it is rather like reading a Tolstoy novel" (85). Although it is a generalized assertion that Weeks makes, some truth in recognizing that a good deal of the criticism is similar exists. Many of the critics seem to be trying to do one of three things with Williams's work. They attempt to explain his writing technique, trace the myths included in his work, or validate (or discredit) the placement of Williams's writing in the canon. Very few critics have attempted to explain Williams's novels as they pertain to his theology, Weeks being one of these few. The result, usually an extensive look that tries to encompass every aspect of the novel, turning it into a summary or a biographical critique of the novels. The idea driving these critics concerns a reader's possible understanding of the theology, or the inspiration behind the writing. Consequently, she will appreciate and understand the work better.

This study attempts a final evaluation of Williams's work. Weeks uses the theories of C.G. Jung to explain the novels and how each of them corresponds to a separate step of Williams's process towards co-inherence. While an understanding of Williams's theology does indeed improve the reader's experience with the novels, it is less important to understand why Williams felt the need to write down his religion or how the novels directly reflect his personal Christian beliefs. Instead, by examining Williams's *Principles of Co-inherence*, *War in Heaven,* and *Descent into Hell*, this study shows that Williams's theology as well as his fiction concerns the human experience of living and not necessarily the process by which one can achieve rewards in the afterlife.

The term, "co-inherence" may be explained in strictly Christian terms. However, let us for a moment reconsider the concept. Peter Stanhope tells Pauline, "There's no need to introduce Christ, unless you wish. It's a fact of experience" (DIH 98). Co-inherence is the very idea that we are all the same--all humans occupying the same space of the earth. We know, in fact, we must learn to tolerate one another, accept differences and work together to achieve anything at all. Yet, this simple truth eludes us daily as evidenced by the racial tensions and conflicts still occurring about religious differences. Williams's utopian City would exist if every human could accept every other human, or in Williams's term, if each human would practice exchange more often. When we recognize of co-inherence, we allow for equal human rights.

From this global view, we move to a more personal look at the concept of co-inherence. Because we allow that everybody has the right to choose his or her own course of action and belief, it follows that we are individuals capable of making those choices. Logically, of course, humans will look out for their own interests; however, the principle of co-inherence suggests that people may behave in any way they wish so long as it does not infringe upon others' rights. One should value herself, but not above others because through others we can live fulfilling lives. What Williams calls substitution, is actually love. Without the love of others, we are alone. No greater hell exists than to be alone among the billions of humans on Earth.

This principle perhaps exemplifies the simplest summary of Charles Williams's theology, but when considered in even more simple terms, the theology seems almost a logical induction about human rights and life. Applying this simplified explanation to the novels also simplifies them. In *War in Heaven*, the Archdeacon and his group are not successful because they all believe in Christianity; rather, they succeed because they practice exchange and work together for the common goal of protecting the Grail despite their differences. Gregory Persimmons lives because he believed something; he had a goal to use the Grail to do something. Only Mannesseh was doomed, not because of his Christianness, but because he refused to work toward anything at all. He did not want to build the City, nor did he want to rule the City as Persimmons wished - he merely wanted to destroy. The inevitable disagreement between people does not cause the error, but the rejection of society altogether that, ultimately, will lead only to the eventual rejection of the self.

Descent into Hell focuses on the rejection of society, then. It is all well and good to have an identity; each person is entitled to her own beliefs and values. However, what happens when a person makes a choice to only accept what she wants? Wentworth's total rejection of reality causes his descent. And, Adela Hunt refuses the reality of her own identity. These two not only refuse to work accept others, but privilege what they want above all else to the point that they no longer see or experience reality. Instead, they create a reality based upon their own desires. The result, they doom themselves to face the rest of life alone. Neither character will ever find love; the reality that each of them has rejected abandoned them.

Williams has often been identified with his character, Peter Stanhope. we learn: "There was a story, invented by himself, that *The Times* had once sent a representative to ask for explanations about a new play, and that Stanhope, in his efforts to explain it, had found after four hours that he had only succeeded in reading it completely aloud: 'Which,' he maintained, '*was* the only way of explaining it'" (DIH 15). This examination , then, points out that all Christian beliefs are not necessarily Puritanical and judgmental. Here, Williams's own theology has been explored as it relates to the human experience. However, it does not intended to say that a reader must have any background about Williams or his personal theology to understand *War in Heaven* or *Descent into Hell*. Instead, the theology offers a possible reading free from any preconceived notions about Christianity or Christian writing and allows the novels to speak for themselves about life and love in the human world.

Works Cited

Eliot, T.S. Introduction. *All Hallow's Eve*. New York: Pellegrini & Cudahy, 1948.

Hadfield, Alice Mary. *Outlines of Romantic Theology*. Grand Rapids, Michigan: Eerdmans, 1990.

Hefling, Charles. Intro. Williams, *Charles Williams: Essential Writings in Spirituality and Theology*. 1-34.

Howard, Thomas. *The Novels of Charles Williams*. London: Oxford UP, 1983. San Francisco: Ignatius, 1991. 15-40, 79-108, 247-87.

King, Jr., Roma A. "The Occult as Rhetoric in the Poetry of Charles Williams." *The Rhetoric of Vision: Essays on Charles Williams* Eds. Charles A. Huttar and Peter J. Schakel. Crambury, NJ: Associated UP, 1996.

Kollman, Judith J. "Complex Rhetoric for a Simple Universe: *Descent into Hell*." *TheRhetoric of Vision: Essays on Charles Williams* Eds. Charles A. Huttar and Peter J. Schakel. Crambury, NJ: Associated UP, 1996.

Loomis, Roger Sherman. *The Grail from Celtic Myth to Christian Symbol*. 1963. Princeton: Princeton UP, 1991.

Medcalf, Stephen. "The Athanasian Principle in Williams's Use of Images." *TheRhetoric of Vision: Essays on Charles Williams* Eds. Charles A. Huttar and Peter

J. Schakel. Crambury, NJ: Associated UP, 1996.

Ridler, Anne. *Charles Williams: Selected Writings*. London: Oxford UP, 1961.

Spacks, Patricia Meyer. "Charles Williams: The Fusions of Fiction." *Shadows of Imagination*. Carbondale: Southern Illinois UP, 1969. 150-59.

Spencer, Kathleen. *Charles Williams: Starmont Reader's Guide 25*. Mercer Island, Washington: Starmont House, 1986.

Weeks, Dennis L. *Steps toward Salvation: An Examination of Coinherence and Substitution in the Seven Novels of Charles Williams*. New York: Peter Lang, 1991.

Williams, Charles. *Charles Williams: Essential Writings in Spirituality and Theology*.

Ed. Charles Hefling. Boston: Cowley, 1993.

——. *Descent into Hell*. 1937. Grand Rapids, MI: William B. Eerdmans, 1996.

—— . "The Index of the Body." In Williams, Charles Williams: Essential Writings in Spirituality and Theology. 124-35.

——. "The Order of the Co-inherence" In Williams, *Charles Williams: Essential Writings in Spirituality and Theology*. 146-50.

——. "The Practice of Substituted Love." In Williams, *Charles Williams: Essential Writings in Spirituality and Theology.* 216-30.

——. "Sensuality and Substance." In Williams, *Charles Williams: Essential Writings in Spirituality and Theology.* 113-23.

——. *War in Heaven.* 1930. Grand Rapids, MI: William B. Eerdmans, 1999.

——. "The Way of Exchange." In Williams, *Charles Williams: Essential Writings in Spirituality and Theology.* 204-15.

9

Intimations of Religious Mysticism in Virginia Woolf's *To the Lighthouse*
O. Quimby Melton

In Virginia Woolf's *To the Lighthouse*, Mr. Ramsay experiences one of the most famous and controversial internal struggles of Modernism via one of the movement's most famous metaphors: the intellectual strivings and achievements of "splendid mind[s]" in terms of the alphabet.[1] In this passage, Ramsay feels that he's reached Q: a level rarely reached by intellectuals; but he wants to go farther, all the way to Z which he believes to be a level "only reached once by a man in a generation" (47). Beyond Q, he sees a "number of letters the last of which [Z] is scarcely visible to mortal eyes" (47). In this passage, Wolf's use of the letter Q is provocative. If she had merely wanted to refer to the middle of the alphabet – half-way to the exalted, Z-thought *telos* – then why not use the letter M? Since the 26 letter modern Roman alphabet is easily broken in half at 13 (M's position), Q – a letter two positions beyond the midpoint – seems to serve some other purpose, one perhaps linked with a prevalent and ancient theory about the Synoptic Gospels of the New Testament.

Biblical scholars have long referred to the gospels of Matthew, Mark, and Luke as the "Synoptic Gospels"[2] because "they are so similar that their texts [in the original Koine Greek] can be read in parallel columns."[3] Other nontraditional gospels, such as the Gnostic gospel of Thomas,[4] also read very like Matthew, Mark, and Luke; and this phenomenon has lead scholars to believe there was a common source for these gospels: the theoretical "Q" source (after German *Quelle*: "source").[5] Though there are several major theories about Q, there is no extant record of it which, for those more well-versed in the Old

Testament than the New, can be likened to the largely theoretical Elohist ("E"), Priestly ("P"), Deuteronomic ("D"), and Yahwist ("J") authors/sources of the Pentateuch.[6] This idea of the Gospel Q source is certainly a concept with which Woolf's own father Sir Leslie Stephen and his literary equivalent Mr. Ramsay would have been familiar: both were/are Oxford dons in an older sense of the position. Essentially, Oxford dons of this time and for centuries before it were Anglican priests who just happened to teach a subject other than theology. The Q source debate is at least as old the fourth century C.E. so Victorian priests such as Stephen and Ramsay would have been well versed in the theory and the problems associated with it.[7] It seems reasonable, then, to read the Q in Woolf's alphabet metaphor within the shadow of the Gospel Q source theory.

Such a reading might hold that Ramsay, in fixating on Q, sees that he cannot actually get past the Q source: the fundamental basis of his own work. Were he to pass it, he would either be beyond the realm of originality and would enter nothingness and the absence of knowledge or he would transcend the source material itself and enter an intimate sphere of immediacy with whatever created Q. Ramsay's struggle seems to point to the latter as he clearly believes grand things exist beyond Q. Theologically, to pass Q would be to pass or transcend the very limits of the gospels, of textual representation and therefore to experience the source of Q itself, that is, the source of the source: Jesus' life unbound by mimesis. In Ramsay's view, to pass Q would be a similar experience. In moving to R, to S, and finally to Z, one could experience truly innovative thought unbound by cultural precedent and the trappings of intellectual precedent, that is, Q. In each case, passing Q is tantamount to transcending the ultimate limit, the ultimate basis of knowledge. Thus, passing it is to enter a realm of new experience and thought. Reaching the Q source is quite a feat in itself; in Biblical circles it exists as nothing more than a theoretical possibility and proving its existence would be a significant discovery. However, Mr. Ramsay is not satisfied with merely reaching Q; he wants to transcend the very realms of original knowledge and enter the source of that knowledge itself.

Another mystical aspect of the novel includes Augustus Carmichael's affinity for acrostics. He seems to use these as an avoidance technique and defense: "Mr. Carmichael shrank away from [Mrs. Ramsay] ... making off to some other corner where he did acrostics endlessly" (58). This passage is noteworthy for the purposes of this paper because of the acrostic's place in Qabalah, Christian, and Islamic mystical sects.[8] One example is the Christian ABRACADABRA acrostic. Christian mystics made it from the transliterated Hebrew words *Ab* (Father), *Ben* (Son), *Ruach Acadasch* (Holy Spirit) so it clearly grew out of older acrostics associated with Jewish and even Islamic mysticism and appeared on an amulet worn around the neck thusly:

ABRACADABRA
ABRACADABR
ABRACADAB
ABRACADA
ABRACAD
ABRACA
ABRAC
ABRA
ABR
AB
A

Woolf's assertion that Carmichael does acrostics (probably something like a word jumble) "endlessly" seems to suggest the mystical acrostic's endless repetition and self-contained pattern of letters and words. In the quoted passage, these acrostics protect him from a certain amount of intimacy and ward off others – especially women, with whom he has had problems – who might shatter his delicate sensibility or challenge his desire to become a poet.

A third mystical aspect of *To the Lighthouse* concerns Mrs. Ramsay's vision of the places she's not seen. She feels "herself pushing aside the thick leather curtain of a church in Rome" (86); and though this reference is clearly to a Christian church, there is a heavy Jewish connotation as well. In the days of the great Temple, before Rome destroyed it, there hung a heavy curtain that separated the *sanctus sanctorum* where the ark and thus the presence of God rested from the rest of the temple.[9] The Catholic tradition of keeping the Communion Host in a sacred room behind an ornate curtain where only Priests can enter and bring it out to the congregation grew out of this tradition. Furthermore, the Synoptic Gospels report that at the moment when Jesus died on the cross, the afore mentioned "holy of holies" temple curtain split in two.[10] Theologians make much of this event, essentially seeing it as a symbol of the death of the old covenant in exchange for the new, and it can also be read as the brisk departure of God's spirit from his holy room as not to be contained in one space room but in the spirits of all men. In either case, though, the curtain's split represents a sea-change in theology and in man's relationship to God. Likewise, Mrs. Ramsay seems to want to abruptly affront old theologies and values to either enter and discover truth for herself or expose falsehood. Relevant to this passage, there is also the "Holy Door" at St. Peter's Basilica in Rome which is only open during the Catholic Church's "jubilee" years which have been launched at irregular intervals since 1300. Officially, only the pope can open and close this door, but Mrs. Ramsay in wanting to rip through such barriers wants to break through religious tradition and break through barriers to mystical and spiritual revelation, to the deepest chambers of holy sites, and into the rooms where God's very presence lives. These barriers essentially represent the portals to mystical knowledge and realities, and Mrs. Ramsay wants to transcend her drab reality for something mystical, spiritual, and fulfilling. As she does with Carmichael and his acrostics and Mr. Ramsay and his obsession with transcending Q, then, Woolf uses heavily nuanced and connotated images, language, and situations that suggest certain intimations of religious mysticism relevant to Mrs. Ramsay's experience in the novel, namely the three characters' desire to escape drab reality through religious mysticism.

NOTES

This brief article grew out of a paper I wrote for Dr. Beth Rosenberg's Spring 2002 graduate seminar on the Bloomsbury Group which was held at UNLV. The paper was later presented, in an altered form, at the Fall 2002 MSA 4 conference in Madison, Wisconsin as part of a seminar entitled "Modernism and the Psychology of Religious Experience" led by Pericles Lewis. The paper has once again been altered and edited for this collection.

1. Virginia Woolf, *To the Lighthouse* (Oxford: Oxford UP, 1992), 47.

2. The term *Synoptic* may be defined as "having an approximately parallel point of view," and the term is derived from the Greek term συνopαν (transliteration: syn + horan = synoran; "see" + "together"). See *The Oxford Companion to* The Bible (Ed. Bruce Metzger and Michael Coogan. Oxford: Oxford UP, 1993), 724-27. The gospel of John is not a Synoptic gospel as it is associated with a different problem (the Johannine problem) and its language, structure, and theology are distinctly different from Matthew, Mark, and Luke. For more on theories surrounding the gospel of John, see *The Oxford Companion to* The Bible, 373-77.

3. Thomas Cahill, *Desire of the Everlasting Hills* (New York: Doubleday, 1999), 260.

4. See Marvin W. Meyer, *The Secret Teachings of Jesus: Four Gnostic Gospels* (New York: Vintage, 1984) and Elaine Pagels, *The Gnostic Gospels* (New York: Vintage, 1989) and *Beyond Belief: The Secret Gospel of Thomas* (New York: Random House, 2003).

5. See *The Oxford Companion to* The Bible, 726 and Meyer, xvii.

6. In certain ways like Q, these four authors/sources are distinguishable by their respective literary styles, their narrative structures, and by their uses of different terms for God. See Bernhard Anderson, *The Living Word of the Old Testament*, 4th ed. (New York: Longman, 1988), 18-23 and Lawrence Boadt, *Reading the Old Testament* (New York: Paulist Press, 1984), 89-108.

7. See *The Oxford Companion to* The Bible, 725-26.

8. See, for example, Colette Sirat and Nicholas de Lange, *Hebrew Manuscripts of the Middle Ages* (New York: Cambridge UP, 2002), 204-33.

9. See *Exodus* 26:31-34.

10. See Matthew 27:51, Mark 15:38, and Luke 23:45.

Kneading the Texts Through
the Practice of Misquotation
Alessandro Monti

Biblical reference constitutes a continuous backdrop in Kipling early script dealing with typical Anglo-Indian themes and issues. Several dialogic constructs are at work here, these including Sunday school or college recollections, or even family heritage, if we consider the Methodist background in John Lockwood Kipling, the "pater"[1], intratextual quotations, some of them taken from Chaucer, and finally catachrestic puns with reference to specific Anglo-Indian civil and military hierarchies and roles. A first instance of Biblical *mise en abîme* concerns the Anglo-Indian common definition of a rather disagreeable incident in everyday life, that is a recurrent enough, as it seems, case of more or less compulsory cuckoldry, whose archetypal pattern is to be found in a sourish remark in *The Chronicles of Budgepore, or Sketches of Life in Upper India* (1870), a loose collection of fictional sketches by an Anglo-Indian lawyer, Iltudus Prichard. He writes apropos of the visiting tour made by a Deputy Governor-General, "the day following that of Molyneux introduction, Cocker had orders to go out into the district and complete the work that his superior had left uncompleted. He went reluctantly enough, poor fellow"[2].

Of course the occurrence should remind the reader of King David sending Uriah to his death, because of Bathsheba (2 Samuel 11). It seems quite likely to me that in Anglo-Indian jargon "Uriah" designated collectively the victimized husbands belonging to the Indian Civil Service. My own guess is substantially based on a quatrain in *Leviora: Being the Rhymes of a Successful Competitor* (1888), by Francis Bignold, a Civilian in the Presidency of Bengal,

        "On a Simla Scandal".
        When David fell victim to Bathsheba's charms
        Uriah the Hittite was ordered to arms;

But now the offender bears justly the brunt
And only the villain is sent to the front"[3].

In this version the happy twist of the tale restores justice, given that the pun
in the text inverts the Biblical ending of the story line. Punishment is meted out
to the villain, exactly as it happens in *David Copperfield* (1849-50), when the
trickster and would-be seducer Uriah Heep is finally unmasked and given his
well-deserved retribution. Incidentally, it is worth observing that the inversion of
roles, in the double Biblical paronomasia David-Uriah, anticipates the disruptive
upside down conclusion in the Anglo-Indian epigram. However, Dickens
exchanges *de facto* roles between victim and persecutor, so as to switch the
focus of his story line from the sheer arrogance of power to the indictment of
high hypocrisy.

"The Story of Uriah" is also a poem collected by Kipling in *Departmental
Ditties* (1886). Here punishment is not endorsed by a higher mundane authority,
as Bignold seems to suggest, but rather evokes a more private and revengeful
final twist, if we consider the poisonous *cauda* contained in the last lines,
featuring as they do a very peculiar version of an Anglo-Indian Doomsday, since
at Resurrection the offended husband will take *personal* revenge against his
offender. The poem is aptly framed by a Biblical quotation, taken from 2
Samuel 12, "Now there were two men in one city: the one rich, and the other
poor," that is from the sequence narrating the aftermath of the transgressive act
of seduction committed by David. Besides emphasizing the hierarchical hiatus
that acts at the very core of the violence against Uriah, the quotation introduces
an implied intratext within the main Biblical reference, since it reproduces, by
way of "showing," the actual beginning of the admonitory story, concerning the
cruelly predatory slaughtering of a "little ewe-lamb," told to David by Nathan.
Whereas Bignold highlights self-pleased and congratulatory satisfaction for the
sanitizing rescue on the part of some unspecified higher authority, Kipling
rehearses a voice of admonition and announces retributive death for the
culpable.

By misreading the Biblical episode into a tale of personal revenge Kipling
anticipates his blemished representation of a very "private" Resurrection of the
Dead. In the First World War short story "A Madonna of the Trenches"[4] Kipling
makes use of disturbing misquotations from Saint Paul and the Anglican Burial
Service to motivate a further, and more subterranean as well, instance of illicit
and subversive love[5]. To me, the trend of the main story line, in which a woman
walks back from the dead to take away her secret lover, as previously agreed
between them, stands strongly in correlation with the act of sending someone to
his death, because of a domineering act of love. As a matter of fact in "A
Madonna of the Trenches" the Uriah archetype degenerates ultimately into a
sophisticated pathology of amorous vampirism and decadent recollections of
erotic fetishism. Thus, the too clever authorial management of the framing or
intratextual quotations includes a coterminous presence of such mixed texts as

the disreputable "Les Noyades" by the somewhat notorious Swinburne, together with the Epistles of Saint Paul and the correlated distorted fragments taken from the Anglican Burial Service[6]. I would like to focus, in particular, on Saint Paul, his First Letter to the Corinthians, not only 15:32 ("If after the manner of men I have fought with beasts at Ephesus, what advantageth it me, if the dead rise, if the men rise not? Let us eat and drink; for to morrow we die"[7]), but also 15:21 ("For since by man came death, by man came also the resurrection of the dead"), a statement that Kipling seems to interpret quite literally. In fact the two complementary acts of death and resurrection that take place in the short story are endorsed by a profane rush of passion, one which makes a dead woman come back from the tomb, in order to impose his lover the respect of a ghastly pact.

We may detect the inchoative stages of this catachrestic device, of misreading a Scriptural text by means of a framing quotation, in the early "The Mark of the Beast" (*Life's Handicap*, 1891), in which the apparently unproblematic epigraph taken from Revelation (16:2) "and there fell a noisome and grievous sore upon the men which had the mark of the beast", actually conceals an astute Anglo-Indian pun. In *The Chronicles of Budgepore* two characters are branded as follows, "Mr and Mrs Thomas, bearing U.S., the mark of the beast, although there was no external indication of it either in their dress, their demeanour, or their conversation"[8]. Of course, "U.S." stands for "Unconvenanted Service", the inferior and subaltern rung in the Indian Civil Service. So the idiom designates derogatively a second rate individual and as such it bears paradigmatic links of semantic dichotomy with the Anglo-Indian adjective "elysian" (from "Elysium", that is Simla, the well-known pre-Himalayan hill-station to which the colonial government moved in the hot season), with an implied reference to the upper hierarchies and spheres of power.

Of course, the surface story line deals with lycanthropy, given that the intoxicated Englishman behaves like a ravenous wolf. As a matter of fact, he is "tokened" by a "silver" leper, namely by a man whose skin attains a symbolical state of purity, since his body constitutes a uniform white surface, with no blotches or other marks indicating the plague (Kipling refers here to 2 Kings 5:27, the story of Naaman and Gehazi. His text repeats the Biblical "a leper as white as snow"). Here leprosy introduces difference (man *versus* beast) in the paradigm *"ôhar/"âmê*: the touch of the leper makes a beast of the man who has infringed a taboo by insulting, and desecrating as well, a Hindu God. If we consider the categories concerning abomination, such as expressed in the Leviticus, we can understand how fullness of pollution implies measures of metonymic transition from impurity to functional purity, given that it is quite impossible for us to misunderstand the real nature, or identity, of the polluted object or creature.

As a matter of fact, the "beastified" Englishman in the tale has moved fully across the pale of shared belonging within human society. His ravenous taste for raw meat breaks the dietary taboo regarding blood, thus expelling de facto the Englishman from the society of men. Such move also transfers his body, not his onthogenetic exterior shape but his (or rather its?) phylogenetic belonging, to the pack of wolves, whose organization may be considered similar to the human *oikumene*, although ruled by such antinomic values as sheer and competitive greediness or crude and unmediated violence. In "The Mark of the Beast" the implied reference to the Leviticus suggests an inverted or regressive rite of passage, a sort of missing contiguity (as far as sequences of cultural development are concerned) between man and brute. Such notorious yielding to regression and devolutionary backwardness is further loaded in "Beyond the Pale" (*Plain Tales from the Hills*, 1886). Here a concealed and cryptic pun taken from the Bible ("and little Bisesa would have been able to knead her own bread," surely an echo of 2 Samuel 13, in which Amnon entices his sister Tamar to his house, in order to rape her, and she "took floor and kneaded it, and made cakes in his sight," as said in 2.13:8) introduces racial miscegenation (Trejago mounting Bisesa) under cover of the astute "kneading" of the Biblical text, so as to mix the incestuous rape against Tamar with the Chaucerian bawdy tale concerning the too artful student, the excessively simple miller and his young wife Alison[9]. The "knedding tubbes" mentioned by Chaucer in "The Miller's Tale," as a parodic counterpart to Noah's Flood, motivate furthermore the transgressive meaning that is associated with the Biblical resonance suggested by the idiom "to knead," inasmuch as that it shifts the sense of guilt from the male rapist to a promiscuous figure of woman, one who moves beyond the *limina* established by decency, or by the cultural lag that in "Beyond the Pale" disrupts the meeting between the two clandestine lovers. Consequently, "to knead" stands high as a metaphor indicating an illicit sexual encounter. As such it introduces difference by evoking a forbidden change in the relationships that give balance and continuity to a domestic universe.

It seems a long way from the early and idiolectic satire against what has been termed corrupt "officialism" in the government of colonial India, or from the shaping of an Anglo-Indian Gothic tale through an inside joke grounded on the text of Revelation. "Beyond the Pale" extends the agency of Biblical punning to a wider range of meaning and purpose, since it equates the act of love to a "privetee joke," that is to a sin of forbidden knowledge. Consequently, to penetrate the darkened eastern world should be considered equivalent to the "privetee" intercourse with a seductress: Bisesa as the alter-ego of Alison in "The Miller's Tale". The woman in Revelation 17:4 ("full of abominations and filthiness of fornication") stands behind this radical anti-feminine indictment, whose misogynous *damnatio* will be finally ransomed by the self-sacrificing seductress Grace Ashcroft of "The Wish House", in which the "cancer" of love becomes a bountiful source of life, notwithstanding compelled solitude and the decay of stricken flesh.

NOTES

1. See Arthur R. Ankers, *The Pater. John Lockwood Kipling. His Life and Times, 1837-1911* (Otford, Kent: Hamthorns, 1988).

2. Iltudus Prichard (1826-74), *The Chronicle of Budgepore, or Sketches of Life in Upper India*, two volumes, (London: King, 1870 and 1900).

3. Thomas Francis Bignold (?-1888), *Leviora: Being the Rhymes of a Successful Competitor* (Calcutta: Thacker, 1888).

4. Collected in *Debits and Credits*, 1926. An ex soldier has broken down, having seen the ghost of his aunt who has died of cancer. She was carrying an affair with the soldier's sergeant and comes back from the dead in order to bring him away with her (the sergeant kills himself so as to be reunited with his lover).

5. The hysterical ex soldier misquotes in his delirious babbling a passage by Saint Paul (1 Corinthians 15:32), dealing with "the manner of resurrection". The incipit of 15:32 reads like this, "If after the manner of men I have fought with beasts at Ephesus, what advantageth it me, if the dead rise not?", whereas the ex soldier in Kipling says, "What advantage it [is for me] to fight beasts of officers if the dead didn't rise". The original passage has also been included in the Burial Service.

6. The poem "Les Noyades" elaborates on a procedure of mass execution quite common during the French Revolution: naked men and women were tied together and drowned in the river Loire. Swinburne imagines the perverted bliss of an old peasant who anticipates his eternal conjunction with the beautiful body of a lady he has been hopelessly in love with.

7. See note 5.

8. See note 2.

9. For a more detailed treatment of the similarities between "Beyond the Pale" and "The Miller's Tale" by Chaucer see Nora Crook, *Kipling's Myths of Love and Death* (London: Macmillan, 1989). Also Alessandro Monti, *The Time After Cowdust* (Alessandria: Dell'Orso, 2000).

11   Biblical Walls and Textual Enclosures as Borders in Kipling's Short Narrative

Esterino Adami

Implicit in Kipling's writing, Biblical references are exploited in a productive process so as to depict colonial India and assign intertextual codes. Not only does the Biblical metaphor anchor the text to a solid literal tradition and moral reassurance, but it also permits to detect the otherness of the colonial world, in its monstrous, grotesque or lascivious aspects. The narrative procedure activated by Kipling relies on the malleability of the word and the ultimate result is to be found in those characters that bring forth a semantic or onomastic shift, and evolve from their Biblical origin into witnesses of disturbing India. The creative act is complex and vigorous because, to cite Harold Bloom, "to shape by molding, to make a fiction is to fashion Adam out of the *adamah*, out of red clay"[1]. The archaic meaning of 'kneading the bread' with its corollary of transgressive echoes is juxtaposed to the practice of writing and highlights the clash of two cultures, the hysterical fear of corruption and the fantasy of orientalism.

The principle that governs such fiction focuses on the horror of miscegenation, the taboo topic that discriminates civilized men from primordial savages. This appalling image which may be exemplified through the yielding to practices of incestuous intercourse is conveyed by a metaphor of hybridization, a polluting contiguity that corrodes the social sphere of norms regulating English colonial life. Contravening the imposition of *decorum* and circumstantial rules leads to disastrous aftermath, cast into the unspeakable category of otherness. Those who move beyond the pale, to misquote Kipling, violate a static sense of division, and overturn impenetrable conventions: they are condemned to a condition of horror, being exiled to the margins of society or metamorphosed into horrendous creatures. The discriminating Biblical principle used to give order to society refers in particular to gender relationships or sex taboos: it is an attempt to delete the outrage against the authority of God and the sacredness of moral integrity of man and this is justified by the prohibition to intermix races, and consequently cultures as well. Reluctantly to a certain degree, the Bible refers to human love and sexual relationships by providing parables and meaningful episodes. In its effort to deal with godly matters within a mundane context, the original Hebrew text operates semantic slippages and stylistic rearrangements. With reference to Exodus and Deuteronomy, for instance, the key terms are *patah* and *chasak*: both indicate the undertaking of seduction and wooing, but unlike the former that sketches a "maid that is not betrothed", the latter ascribes a negative permutation of values and coincides with raping or sexual violence[2].

In Kipling's production, however, the issue of demarcation and its prescriptive strictness can be textualized through the imagery of hybridization and abrupt regression by focusing on a cartographic construction of spaces: villages, towns, but even fields and backyards or rooms may become the ideal sites for negotiating cultural identities and affecting reciprocally monolithic assumptions. In his oeuvre, the complex geographical description of India acquires the system of orientalist classification and bespeaks of an organic taxonomy necessary to define or at least approach a composite setting. Mapping the text mirrors the hierarchized space, enclosed in the scope of imperial homologation of territories and cultures. Likewise the representation of Cyprus in *Othello*, a specific island that is manipulated so as to represent a borderline zone, a crest between Occidental rationality and Oriental oddness, is partial and does not record reality. Two short stories like "On the City Wall" and "Naboth," can be read in this light. The former appeared in *In Black and White*, in 1888, while the latter was first published in the *Civil and Military Gazette*, on 26 August 1886 and then collected in 1891 in *Life's Handicap*[3].

"On the City Wall" betrays from the very title its closeness to Biblical heritage and substantiates it with an opening quotation concerning the Wall of Jericho, illustrated in the Book of Joshua (especially 5:10-15 and 6:1-27). Yet Kipling's elaboration of such momentous icon implies a different interpretation of the wall, which is no longer a symbolic and actual hindrance, a threatening structure of segregation, but rather a mechanism that regulates cultural exchanges between two poles. The wall as a spatial representation with no doors or windows constitutes the barrier that isolates or protects the subject, but scarcely does it allow a dialogic contact between the inner and the outer, the self and the other, the notion of being and belonging. We should remember that whilst, according to Roland Barthes, a 'blind' wall functions as the core of antithesis[4], in the tale its power annihilates the communication amongst different fractions of the multifaceted Anglo-Indian world.

Set in the re-invented location of Lahore, the story pivots on the unseizeable figure of Lalun, a mysterious and enchanting courtesan who may be regarded as an echo of Rahab, the prostitute mentioned by Joshua ("So she let them down by a rope through the window, for the house she lived in was part of the city wall",

2:15), who was spared from the destruction of the city of Jericho. The power and prestige of Lalun, revolving as it does around her salon, may even obfuscate or represent in part an alternative form of attraction and guidance, in competition with the British Raj. The woman, in her ambiguous characterization as a lover, mother and seductress, lives in a matchbox house perched on the eastern wall of the city, a symbolic place that mediates temporal phases and geographical or cultural collocations. It is a perspective on the present pictured in the pupils playing cricket at the Government College, and on the past as well, with the mute presence of the "red tombs of dead emperors beyond the river" (p. 221). The contrast that opposes the British viewpoint and rule and the native frayed imagination creates a dichromatic filter of white, the color of the colonizer by antonomasia, and black, the hue or metonymy that relates to the concealing darkness of the colony. On the one hand, Kipling depicts an ironic portrait of the colonial society, dominated by a looming "supreme Government", whereas on the other, he concentrates on the character of Lalun. Far from the decadent cliché of an alluring Salome, she takes up the role of Scheherazade and through the recitation of poems and the music of sitars she reigns in her private court, a 'nowhere' place in which she acquires a supernatural identity.

In a sarcastic manner, Kipling creates a lascivious personage that might stand as a counterpart to the figure of the Beloved taken from the Song of Songs 8:10 ("I am a wall, and my breasts are like towers. Thus I have become in his eyes like one bringing contentment"). From the incipit, we also learn about her intertextual kinship with Lilith, the first wife of Adam[5] according to Talmudic tradition, a connection which underscores her liminality and oscillating significance. She is the holder of majestic beauty and feminine mystery and her idyosincratic domain includes the ethnic and social fragments of India: "Shiahs of the grimmest and most uncompromising persuasions; Sufis who had lost all belief in the Prophet and retained but little in God; wandering Hindu priests passing southward on their way to Central India fairs and other affairs; Pundits in black gowns, with spectacles on their noses and undigested wisdom in their insides; bearded headmen of the wards; Sikhs with all the details of the latest ecclesiastic scandal in the Golden Temple; red-eyed priests from beyond the Border, looking like trapped wolves and talking like ravens: M.A.'s of the University, very superior and very voluble – all these people and more also you might find in the white room" (p. 225).

However, we should not focus exclusively on this heterogeneous cluster, but on the image of the wall encapsulating the house itself: it is not a fence, a line of divide but conversely a structure that functions in a position of 'in-betweenness', to use a term coined by Homi Bhabha in the field of postcolonial criticism. Such salient metaphor, the wall as a sort of camouflage that interplays with cultural agencies, implies a connotation of disorder, a chaotic display of hybridity. Indeed the thematic device enfeebles boundaries and reshapes the local set by interpolating the black town and the civil lines. The two terms indicate in the colonial jargon respectively the areas inhabited by natives and the districts controlled by white settlers, and also express an anxiety of forces at odd, on the backcloth of the imperialist project of establishing a hegemonic rule.

Elsewhere in Kipling's fiction, the menacing disarray of the contact with forms of alterity is rendered by a kind of epidemic regress, an abnormal return to type that contaminates the body: this is the case of "The Mark of the Beast", a story characterized by an obnoxious transmogrification which under the fake exoticism of Indian myths actually conceals a western and Biblical archetypal structure. The metamorphic process represents the breaking of a code or a taboo, the discarding of rules. It is an operation that implies the switching of linguistic registers, from the fabulous idiom of Indian folklore to the pregnant notions of Biblical matrix, and cultural tradition, the monstrous element of the Holy Writs, restored and grafted onto the ethnic narration. This type of discourse views the infectious quality of abomination of which Julia Kristeva speaks[6], with reference to Leviticus. Inserted in a post-Darwinian context, the story orchestrates the corruption of the body and of the soul through an almost Gothic figure of repulsion. The Biblical metaphor is here necessary to stabilize anew a civil order and contrast the overflowing textual interstices that hide a pernicious decadence.

The twist of turning the Biblical Wall of Jericho into the wall-house of Lalun brings to light the precarious balance of the English cultural supremacy in India. The code of social behavior of the English community abroad, supported by the myth of superiority and education, is profoundly affected by the cultural clash taking place in the city, and in Lalun's salon in particular. None escapes the mesmerizing aura that surrounds the insidious 'harlot': neither the narrator nor his friend Wali Dad can resist to her influence or uphold their own creed. The narrator will even contribute to the flight of a political prisoner, Khem Singh, during the violent riots ravaging across the city: in the end, like in a tale of the *Arabian Nights*, he will be awarded the title of Lalun's Vizier, a mental projection that carries an orientalist mirage. In spite of the ironic distance that Kipling deploys to illustrate the life of the British, 'marginalized in the colony', the fictional texture requires a semantic elaboration so as to furnish a dichotomy of values – Lalun's inebriant prerogative and the British sense of morality and self-control. The courtesan, who perhaps is modeled on the figure of some enchanting belle of the Punjab that Kipling might have beheld, evokes a concept of feminine pluralities, in the author's mind, not solely an opposite sign within a discourse of belonging and identity. However, we should take into account Lalun's collocation in an ideal repertoire, a catalogue of oriental curiosities that incorporates the anthropological description and follows the ethnic representation. This constitutes the practice of the Anglo-Indian society, whose frame of mind relies on a taxonomic principle: to stage the native character, and define their childish marginality and weakness, the writer conceals the British intention to constrain the wilderness of the colony in order to administer it properly and in thus doing he raises the stylized façade of enchanting colonial adventures and legendary exotic lands. The necessary endorsement of this narrative act derives from the Biblical citation that relocates the text and ascribes the *exemplum* within the British frame of mind.

In the end, Kipling considers the wall of Lalun as a fictional palimpsest that monitors a fragile equilibrium, a device that bisects the colonial scenario into illuminated pictures or fragments of memory, bound to be filed in a synthetic representation of the Orient. The geographical axe and spatial collocation, ranging from Lalun's elevated house to the stinky and dirty gullies of the native areas, from the imposing "blackened wall of Fort Amara which dominates the City" (p. 227) to the mephitic Muslim and Hindu areas, show a catachrestic function, one in which the single topographic component works as a border, a limit: to step across the symbolic line points out the perilous pathway of the trespasser. It is a violation of codified norms, an outrage against the British ability to interpret the local setting within a prescriptive framework. As a matter of fact, "the physical assault of the element is more than matched by the power of the native environment to disarm any rational scheme or assumption [and] the very physiography of native districts in Kipling's stories erodes our concrete sense of time and place"[7]. The serpentine or spidery map of Lahore with the murkiness of its ditches becomes a paradigmatic example.

We can probably extend our analysis of the wall as an impermeable enclosure to the notion of the compound, a typical Anglo-Indian lexeme that refers to the enclosed ground ,whether garden or waste, which surrounds an Anglo-Indian house. This may restore afresh a Biblical link and mark an emblematic edge. This is what occurs in "Naboth", a story named after the character from 1 Kings 21:28. He is the owner of a vineyard which is coveted by King Ahab and his wife Jezebel who bring false evidence of blasphemy against him. Consequently Naboth is stoned to death. However, Kipling inverts astutely the rationale of the events narrated in the Bible, since the colonial 'intruder' becomes the disposed, so as to justify the otherwise violent act of greediness operated by the royal couple by exchanging roles between culpable and victim. This inversion obfuscates the moral lesson contained in the original tale. The importunate, native sweetmeat seller, re-christened Naboth, who quietly and silently penetrates the narrator's domesticity, sets in motion a double textual procedure: he denounces the experience of colonialism, since he, the legitimate inheritor of the Indian land, is turned into an exile in his own country, and simultaneously he has his identity compulsively re-negotiated, since his sly act of encroaching makes an agent of subversive contamination of him. Such move also indicates a drastic shift in the border that discriminates the indescribable wilderness from the immaculate civilization, enclosed within the protective space of the master's bungalow. The text is purged from the powerful sense of revenge pictured in the death of Jezebel, devoured by dogs nearby the wall of Jezreel, though the imperative admonishment lingers in the revisited interpretation that Kipling gives of the Biblical apologue.

In Kipling's idyolectic re-writing of ancient stories we observe how the Anglo-Indian register, through the mechanism of irony, selects the didactic vignette in order to obtain a peculiar, oblique inversion, expressed in the epilogue by the laconic comment of the narrator: "I know exactly how Ahab felt. He has been shamefully misinterpreted in the Scriptures" (398). Naboth the colonial squatter substitutes idiosyncratically the villain Ahab in his parodic inversion of roles that broadens the scope of the original tale. The stain of covetousness dilates the narrative pace and subscribes the colonial view of the question of the land. Furthermore it is possible to deconstruct linguistic puns from the very name Naboth, and discern an analogy with the Anglo-Indian term Nabob, from the Hindustani Nawab (Arabic Naib), via the Portuguese Nababo. The term originally meant "deputy" and was used in the Mogul empire to indicate a feudal lord, acting as a semi-independent governor of a province. In the eighteenth century the epithet became familiar in England through a famous speech of Burke against Clive and the play *Nabob* by Foote (1768), and acquired general currency to designate an Anglo-Indian who returned with huge (and not always over-licit) fortunes made too quickly after exploiting the 'gorgeous' Est.

This could be the key of Kipling's metaphor, given that the suggested lexical transformation from 'Naboth' to 'nabob' should be read as a wordplay that replaces the derelict pauper with the wealthy schemer, in which the act of dispossession, a metaphor of swallowing, witnesses a blending of cultural signs and at the same time insists on the denial of difference. The narrative construction of the native may be compared to bacterial phenomena that propagate and elude enclosures or confines. Here we gather once more the idea of the wall or border as a stratagem to reinforce the inscriptions against hybridization. Born out of the Biblical tradition, the eponymous character is catapulted into a contrived correlation of disguised meanings induced by phonetic similarities: Naboth, crystallized by the colonizer, partakes of the symptom of pollution, in an anarchic re-drawing of edges and identities.

It is worth noticing that the same leitmotif, the dangerous stance of 'cannibalism' that eradicates the domestic dimension of the white character, is reiterated in postcolonial literature as a narrative backlash: to follow Salman Rushdie's catchphrase, the Empire writes back and thematizes the revengeful attitude of writers who dispossess English (another metaphoric example of expropriation) and dismantle the authoritative center in favor of the dynamic periphery. Articulated by the modes of narrating the experience of diaspora, the fluid reaction or displacement deletes the peaceful Victorian houses that make up the endless suburbs of metropolitan centers. The native, now made a nomad lost in an alienating environment, swaps social roles and overthrows a worn dichotomy. Let us look for instance at the play *Birds of Passage* (1983) by Hanif Kureishi: far from playing the part of a newly-arrived, shocked immigrant from the subcontinent, Asif is shown as a lodger who turns out to be a brilliant businessman determined to subvert the local hierarchies in suburban London. Indeed he takes over the house by plotting a pungent and highly ironic annexation, one in which the concept of ownership is formulated as a product or rather a reactive consequence of historical events. Here the bulimic search for possessions nears postmodern fiction and updates astute Naboth into scheming Asif.

An involuntary witness to Thatcherism, the personage traumatizes the western tranquility of urban life by virtue of his disturbing plans and postcolonial heritage. In his self-awarded capacity of entrepreneur, he coldly reflects on the transformation of the estate as he says "it's perfect for conversion into two flats. That'll mean work and money. Because structurally the place will have to be altered. In the meantime I've got eight Indian students moving in"[8]. Endowed by his rhetoric skills, Asif-Naboth empowers himself by exploiting the crisis of values in the western world and develops a chameleon-like tactic to deal with the English. On the intertextual level, Kureishi's stylistic device concerning the subversion of roles and the rise of subalterns, in which the lodger becomes the master and the landlord is neutralized into a parasitic spectator, adds further irony, being a controversial echo or partial adaptation of *Entertaining Mr. Sloan* (1968) by the English playwright Joe Orton.

To come back again to Kipling, I would like to conclude by noting how both short stories, "On the City Wall" and "Naboth", establish the uncertain interface of western and eastern cultural systems whereas his characters challenge their given roles and explore a hybrid zone of mutation: Lalun's house and Naboth's terrain become quasi-magical sites for undertaking cultural or even mythical, if we cling to the religious lore of the native population, performances. The writer's aim is grounded on the overlapping of the Biblical citation upon the orientalized construction of India and its panoply of prodigious troves. The meticulous archive that he delineates is more than a compilatory methodology since it also mitigates the obscurity and alienation of the colony[9]; indirectly it introduces the circuitous dialectic of imperial reinforcement. Furthermore, Kipling's justification of the metaphorical and geographical route leading to marvelous India is screened via the adventurous grand tour of the European traveler who set for eastern territories and crossed the lands of Judeo-Christian tradition, dramatized by the Book of books. Such secularized adjustment of frontiers is conveyed by the making of specific and distinct categories or subcategories: men, women, military, civilians, English, natives, Hindus, Muslims, castes, tribes, and so on. A whole miscellaneous imagined universe unfolds and requires a different, outlandish terminology so that the writer delivers a double procedure of code-mixing and code-breaking. Consequently, this kind of discursive form of displacement and incorporation artificially alternates intricate narratives and disordered chronicles and in thus doing celebrates the imperialist spirit that reverberates across Kipling's prose.

NOTES

1. Harold Bloom, *Ruin The Sacred Truths* (Cambridge, Massachusetts and London, England: Harvard University Press, 1991): 10.

2. *Ibid.*: 15.

3. "On the City Wall" is now collected in *The Man Who Would Be King and Other Stories* (Oxford and New York: Oxford University Press, 1987) and "Naboth" is contained in *Life's Handicap* (London: Macmillan, 1964). All quotations from the two stories refer to these editions with page reference indicated parenthetically. For a brief outline of their plots, see Norman Page, *A Kipling Companion* (Houndmills and London: Macmillan Press, 1985), in particular: 112-114.

4. See Roland Barthes, *S/Z* (Paris: Edition du Seuil, 1970).

5. A prototype of banshees and mermaids, Lilith is usually associated with female monsters and witches. Mothered by Adam, "she was supposed to have borne him a flock of devils as children, and later was regarded as an evil spirit presiding over desolate places and especially dangerous to women in childbirth". Abraham H. Lass, David Kiremidjian and Ruth M. Goldstein, *Dictionary of Classical and Literary Allusion* (Ware: Wordsworth Editions, 1994): 133. Such detail accentuates the ambiguous double nature of Lalun. Her name is extrapolated from a historical romance published in Bombay in 1884 titled *Lalun the Beragum: Or The Battle of Paniput*.

6. See Julia Kristeva, *Pouvoirs de l'horreur. Essays sur l'abjection* (Paris: Editions du Seuil, 1980).

7. Lewis D. Wurgaft, *The Imperial Imagination. Magic and Myth in Kipling's India* (Middletown, Connecticut: Wesleyan University Press, 1983): 133.

8. Hanif Kureishi, *Birds of Passage* (1983), now collected in *Plays One* (London: Faber and Faber, 1992): 210.

9. See Edward Said, *Orientalism* (1978), (London: Penguin Books, 1995). When Said coined the ground-breaking term Orientalism, he also postulated the projection of inner fears and mental attraction that the West has always constructed in order to encase the slippery symbols of the East, reduced into miniatures of otherness. Indeed, "in the system of knowledge about the Orient, the Orient is less a place than a *topos*, a set of references, a congeries of characteristics, that seem to have its origin in a quotation, or a fragment of a text, or a citation from someone's work on the Orient or some bit of previous imagining, or an amalgam of all these": 177.

12   Songs of Ascents and Descents:
Israeli Modernist Poets and the Hebrew Bible
Leonore Gerstein

The twentieth century has witnessed the revival of Hebrew as a spoken language after a period of roughly 2400 years during which it was the language of prayer and literature for the few alone.[1] Throughout the centuries during which oral Hebrew languished, the Bible was read and studied in the original and Jewish literature continued to be written in a language and style that hewed close to their biblical origins. Writers and readers knew the Hebrew Bible well enough to make biblical allusion, whether subtle or obvious, a *sine qua non* of literature written in Hebrew, and an entire aesthetic of allusive practice evolved over the centuries, with its own distinctions and conventions.[2] In *Canon and Creativity*, Hebrew literary scholar Robert Alter remarks on "the powerful propensity of Hebrew poetry for allusion to specific biblical texts" (Canon 136). In another study, he suggests that the Bible was for the Jews as much linguistic resource as the cornerstone of their religion and that the essential allusiveness of the Hebrew language and its poetry is the source of its particular character: "More than anything else, what makes Hebrew poetry different, is the vital presence of the Bible – through remembered words, verses, phrases, whole passages, themes and symbols – in the mind of every genuinely literate user of Hebrew [. . .] With the Bible always in the background, a skillful Hebrew poet can shift perspective or tone, introduce irony [. . .] with a carefully weighted allusion to a biblical text" (Tradition 248).

The tradition Alter describes continues to be exploited in the work of many modernist Israeli poets. Even the avowed secularists among them practice the ancient and self-conscious tradition of intertextuality that Alter describes. One can get a sense of the proliferation of biblical allusions in Israeli literature from the fact that there is an entire volume with over one hundred compositions inspired exclusively by story of the binding of Isaac.[3] The examples of biblical reference are so numerous that I have felt the need to limit my discussion in this essay to literal citation of biblical text, leaving aside subtler kinds of allusion, and concentrating on five twentieth century poets who exemplify a range of tone and technique.

The pervasive allusiveness of Hebrew literature flows from the core of Jewish culture. Judaism is a revelation religion, one in which almost nothing is written or thought that does not allude to its holy text, the Hebrew Scriptures. Lawrence Kushner, a contemporary practitioner of the interpretive tradition, calls Jewish civilization "a community consecrated to a book." He explains the relationship between the scriptural Ur-text and later Jewish thought: "Its words are more than holy, they are the memento and touchstone of the people. [. . .] These scriptural pieces are the traditionally proper point from which any teacher might venture a new idea" (xii). New ideas in Judaism were at times given the external form of scriptural commentary in order to decrease collective resistance to them. This is the case with the Zohar, for example, a thirteenth century mystical text that presents itself as a midrash, a free-form interpretation, of the Torah (the Pentateuch). Such subterfuge is no longer required, but as biblical allusions in modern Israeli poetry are almost always a response to something other than the Bible itself, they are in a sense a continuation of the subversive commentary tradition. In anticipation of what is to come in this essay, I offer the following example of subversion, a section from "Three Exegeses" by Yehuda Amichai, in which the poet uses the exegetical tradition against itself:

> 'Your name shall no longer be called Abram'
> I am Abram who once was Abraham
> But returned the H to his God,
> Like a man who proudly returns
> A medal to the sovereign state. (1-5; translation mine)

As was true during the years in the Diaspora, thorough familiarity with the Hebrew Scriptures is a given for Israeli poets and their readers. That the majority of Israeli intellectuals are largely nonbelievers, or secularists, as they say, has no relevance in this matter. The public school curriculum in Israel includes early and continuous exposure to scripture, and even second graders are able to read passages from the Bible in the original. Though modern Hebrew has produced some new grammatical forms, altering the biblical tense system, for example, and has greatly expanded the lexicon, it incorporates and builds upon the grammar and vocabulary of biblical Hebrew. Thus, Israeli poets have the means to play Modern Hebrew and the language of the Bible against each other. Israeli modernists in particular are in a position to exploit linguistic layering and the potential for dissonance to express emotional and intellectual ambivalences toward their tradition, as well as other conflicts.

Literary tradition aside, the infusion of biblical allusions into Israeli life and literature has had an ideological function, especially during the collectivist phase of Israeli history, when political discourse was especially active and fine oratory appreciated. Zionist ideologues, both religious and secular in orientation, raided the Bible in their search for Jewish nationalist slogans, and current Israeli political rhetoric continues this pattern. In the early years of statehood, Israeli culture, in constructing its self-image, preferred to link itself with the biblical period in Jewish history and leap over the intervening Diaspora experience altogether. To this day, Israeli archeology is marshaled to reflect and support this interpretation of the past.

* * *

The Israeli poets I will discuss were all well read in world literature and receptive to external influences. They share the Anglo-American and European modernists' complexity of tone and connotative subtlety, and it is the complexity, one's sense of the poet's desire to both acknowledge the tradition and control it in a love/hate relationship, that makes much of Israeli poetry so compelling. The Israeli modernists tend to be more easily understood by the common reader than their Anglo-American and European counterparts. More often than not, they are consciously inclusive, and scriptural allusions in their works would be considered anything but esoteric from the Israeli reader's point of view. Prior to the modernist period, Israeli culture expected poets to be willing and effective communicators, with a sense of mission and responsibility toward the community that entailed getting one's point across clearly (Sandbank, 16-17).[4] Even modernist Israeli poets for whom communicability is not a stylistic norm seem to want their readers to be able to appreciate their clever handling of biblical verses and confront their emotional ambivalence toward the evoked text. This ambivalence arises out of the very complex historical circumstances, shared by writers and readers, which accompanied the creation of the state of Israel in biblical territory.

Israeli poets approach the sacred text with outspoken skepticism. They seem to see their biblical borrowings as a raw material onto which they need to imprint their syntactic and thematic stamp through radical alteration. The semantic-syntactic changes can occur either following, or in the body of, the original quotation. The Israelis are no more creative than other modernists, such as Ezra Pound or T. S. Eliot, in their intertextual play, but they are often less reverential. In an Israeli poem, the use of scripture is often emblematic of a general struggle over personal and national identity, a struggle in which poets assert themselves by twisting the words of the elders symbolized by the biblical text. The Israelis do not use biblical citation or allusion to reveal an overlooked link between them and the past, but rather to confront a bond that is all too powerful and assert their freedom from it. Their programmatic aim is to establish distance from the Bible even as they engage with it dialogically. Most often, an allusion serves to express ambivalence toward the sacred, no matter whether the context is organized religion or it's twentieth century equivalent in Jewish life - nationalist ideologies.

A poet such as Yehuda Amichai, who is extraordinarily clever in his manipulations of sacred text, uses the quotations to develop a serious theme, often to do with the disparity between illusions and reality, or the struggle between superego and id. As is true for many Israeli modernists, biblical allusion for Amichai is in itself a metaphor for inner contradiction or, absent a specific inner struggle, a sense that all is not well with the world. Amichai once characterized his use of scriptural language as "making the low high and the high low." (Cohen 35). These tropes often entail an anachronistic representation of the once sacred, an approach that harmonizes with the extensive use of colloquial Hebrew in his poetry (35). The use of a deliberate strategy suggests the extent to which the poet found the extant cultural presuppositions about allusiveness to be both problematic and enriching. In many poems, Amichai reproaches the Bible for the illusions with which it has filled the Jewish imagination over the centuries. Surprising juxtapositions represent incompatible experiences, such as the poet going into battle and yet unable to forget the biblical message of peace. Of course, the reproach is anachronistic and not meant to be taken literally, but rather as a trope used to advance the poet's argument. One of Amichai's poems uses the image in Micah 4:4 of peace and security, "They shall sit every man under his vine and under his fig tree and none shall make them afraid," to introduce the theme of allusion: Here is the first stanza in Amichai's "I Want to Muddle the Bible":[5]

> The airplane flies above the fig tree
> which rises above the man lying under his fig tree.
> The pilot is I and the man under his fig tree is I.
> I want to muddle the Bible.
> I want so to muddle the Bible. (1-5; translation mine)

It is obvious that bedeviling the Bible is a symbolic act of protest secondary in its emotional intensity to the poet's response to war. The purported inner confusion is, in fact, a protest against conditions that force a peaceable individual to become a fighter. In an earlier, somewhat arch poem, "A Sort of Apocalypse," Amichai has the two men from Micah 4:4, one under the fig-tree, the other under the vine, communicating by phone about an impending battle, perhaps a more extreme jumbling of the Bible than in the above poem, but standing for a similar inner conflict:

> The man under his fig tree telephoned the
> man under his vine,

> "Tonight they definitely might come. Assign
> Positions. Armour-plate the leaves. Secure the tree [..]
> (1-3; trans. Bloch and Mitchell)

In "In the Full Severity of Mercy," Amichai begins by using the biblical promise of Genesis 22:17, "I will bestow my blessing upon you and make your descendants as numerous as the stars of heaven and the sand on the shore," to make a point about modern life:

> You can count them. They
> aren't like the sand on the seashore. They
> aren't like the numerous stars. They're like lonely people.
> On the corner and in the street. (1-5; trans. Kronfeld)

As the poem continues, the theme deepens and expands to encompass the speaker's disillusionment with an entire tradition. In her study of Israeli modernism, Chana Kronfeld has written a fine analysis of this poem and one by Zach referring to the same biblical passage. She suggests that Amichai's poem actually illustrates his anti-modernist side, in that he makes it very easy for the reader to identify with both the alluding and evoked text (Kronfeld 133). I think the same communicative ease can be found in most of Amichai's biblically allusive poems, but I am not sure that this makes them anti-modernist. She makes the extremely valuable point that allusion for Amichai and other Israeli poets places "specific significance on the mutual reinterpretation of the two texts activated in the allusive process," and notes that allusion itself can become a theme for Israeli poets (133). I differ with her only in my sense that what becomes the theme is not so much the allusive practice itself as allusion providing a metaphor for the layered and contradictory self. Perhaps I see more traces of romanticism in the Israeli modernists than Kronfeld does.

Amichai's ironic tone is abetted at times by a youthful coarseness that suggests a wish to *epater les bourgeois*. He chooses the least obscure verses, perhaps in order to communicate easily with a wide audience, but more likely, because these are phrases that have become a part of him, ones often heard in public, though perhaps not recited privately. The phrases "Every man under his vine and fig tree," and "If I forget Thee, O Jerusalem," for example, would be familiar to every Israeli teenager. Amichai takes verses from Psalm 121, alters the tense to conform to Modern Hebrew, and then immediately conjoins them with a deflating phrase. The biblical words are, "I turn my eyes to the mountains; from where will my help come?"/ Help comes only from the Lord [.. .]" (alternate translation: "If I lift my eyes to the hills,/ where shall I find help?"). Amichai's words are:

> I lift my eyes to the mountains. Now I understand
> What it means to lift eyes, what a heavy load

> It is. But those violent longings.
> The pain-never-again-to-be-inside.
> (1-4; trans. Amichai and Hughes)

Without quoting all of it, Amichai evokes the entire biblical passage, one so familiar to most readers that they would have trouble suppressing it. Replacing the pious question and response is the poet's subjectivity, a presence boldly announced with the words "Now I." While implicitly paying homage to the beautiful image of the original, Amichai partially empties the words by yoking them to a self-deprecating presentation of himself. As he cannot utter the religious vow and affirmation of the original text, he instead uses his syntactic collage to criticize both his heritage and his own character. He portrays himself, initially, with a certain degree of self-mockery, as weak and self-absorbed. Only then does he echo the tone of the evoked text, by introducing the theme of longing, perhaps for the lost biblical certainty, and perhaps for an erotic enmeshment.

In "If I Forget You, Jerusalem," Amichai again allows his quotation to evoke the contiguous verses in the original text. In Psalm 137:5, the words are "If I forget you, O Jerusalem,/ let my right wither;/ let my tongue stick to my palate." Amichai's poem begins with,

> Let my right hand forget.
> Let my right hand forget, and my left hand remember
> Let my left remember, your right hand close
> And your mouth open near the gate. (1-5; translation mine)

For readers familiar with the entire psalm, "Your mouth" arouses an association with "let my tongue stick to my palate" of the adjacent verse. Again, there is puncturing of rhetorical grandeur and a secular, all-too-human, recontextualization. No longer a vow of communal loyalty, now the words refer to a purely personal, erotic experience, albeit in Jerusalem (the *your* above is in feminine form in Hebrew). Somewhat sacrilegiously, the poet implies that Jerusalem is unforgettable for him because of its erotic associations and that the pleasure principle has taken place of religious piety in his life. But aside from the sacrilege, there is the sense that, living in Jerusalem, the poet must inevitably construct his experience in the language of another time, reflecting a past culture. Perhaps more than in the earlier example, the merging of past and present here is subtle and painful. Amichai illustrates a notion we might associate with T. S. Eliot: two distant moments in a tradition modify each other. (Of course, Eliot was not referring *only* to the use of quotation and explicit evocation). I now find it difficult to read the lines of the psalm without recalling Amichai's recontextualization.

With perhaps a less impassioned tone than in Amichai, a similar reciprocal relationship is expressed in several of Natan Zach's poems. In "Man's Days are

Like the Grass" there is a most subtle expression of the poet's love/hate
relationship with the Bible and what it represents. Zach shatters syntax, taking
apart and recombining verses from Job and Psalms, but does so adding no words
that are not found in the original text. Only the phrase "have no fear" is
appended to the lines from Job and Psalms, but this is such a common biblical
phrase that I feel is intended to be perceived as a quotation. By means of
repetition and rearrangement alone, the poet manages to question the meanings
of the words as intended in the original context. From Psalms, 103:15-16, Zach
borrows, "Man, his days are like those of grass," a verse followed by "he
blossoms like a flower of the fields: /A wind passes by and it is no more / its
own place no longer knows it." From Job 5:7 he takes, "Man is born to [do]
mischief,/ just as sparks fly upward" (*Amal*, which JPS translates as *do mischief*,
is more often translated as *trouble*. Here is what Zach does with the biblical
verses:

> Man's days are like the grass
> His days like the grass.
> The days of man are like grass
> His days
> Have no fear.
>
> Man is born to trouble.
> Born to trouble.
> Born to trouble is man
> Born.
> Have no fear.
>
> As sparks fly upward
> Fly upward sparks
> As sparks fly upward
> Fly upward
> Have no fear.
> (translation mine)

In her study of Israeli modernism, Chana Kronfeld says that imagism has
influenced the Israeli poets' use of scripture, and this poem's sparseness may be
a case in point. But the sparseness in Zach's poem differs from the pictorial self-
sufficiency we expect from imagism. Its ironic effect depends entirely upon
one's knowing the original biblical context. Zach's syntactic devices are bold
and original. His irony, which borders on cynicism, is most evident in his use of
the phrase "have no fear," here divested of its reassuring biblical sense. Yet,
accompanying this embittered attitude, there is an expression of love for the
language of the source in the very restraint Zach exercises in altering it. Zach
seems to be liberating the quotations by manipulating their syntax and creating
musicality through repetition, as if to reveal the Bible's hidden beauty even as

he subverts its message.

As I noted earlier, Zach has written a poem that also alludes to the biblical promise from Genesis 22:17 already encountered in Amichai's "With the Full Extent of Mercy." What is of special importance in this poem is the way in which Zach uses God's active Logos as an occasion to explore poetic language *per se*. God and humanity's enchantment with language is the subject of Zach's melancholy reflections in "As Sand," which open thus:

> When God in the Bible wants to promise,
> he points to stars. Abraham strolls
> from his tent at night
> and sees lovers. As the sand on the sea shore,
> God says. And man believes,
> even though he understands that to say
> *as sand* is merely a manner
> of speaking.
> And from that time on,
> sand and stars have been intertwined in
> man's net of images. But perhaps
> we shouldn't speak here of man.
> He wasn't mentioned there and then.
> (1-13; trans. Bargad and Cheyet)

Kronfeld asserts that when he "thematizes" allusion, Zach "empt[ies] the evoked text of any promise of meaning," expressing his "favorite radically modernist message about the meaninglessness of language" (137-139). I do not see Zach as emptying the evoked text of meaning as much as reluctantly acknowledging the hold that metaphor has on our imaginations. The metaphorical net of images in which the two symbols of infinite multiplicity are intertwined can suggest potency as well as entrapment. Zach seems to be implying that resorting to figurative language and alluding to a collectively recalled heritage of tropes are inescapable aspects of our humanity, perhaps both a blessing and a curse. At the end of the poem, as if illustrating his point about the power of figurative language, he uses the metaphor of water and the synecdochic "seed." Here is the second half of the poem:

> and yet it is said explicitly *as sand*
> from which we might infer
> the capacity for enduring. On the other hand,
> it's possible to believe
> that everything is then set free
> and there are no more - explicitly
> no - boundaries.
> As sand on the sea shore. But then,
> water is never mentioned.
> God does, however,

speak of seed. Which only goes to show
the ways of heaven,
And possibly those of nature. (14-26; trans. Bargad and Cheyet)

In Zach's brief lyric "Talitha Cumi" we have a rare example of an Israeli poet citing the Christian scriptures, first a phrase from Mark 5 that contains the Hebrew word "Cumi," the first for a contemporary Jerusalemite. Talitha Cumi is a lovely old building, dating from the late nineteenth century, built by European missionaries in the Jewish section of the city.[6] Here is the first section of the poem in T. Carmi's prose translation:

> *Talitha cumi*, I beg of you. You're an intelligent person, get up. Perhaps I was mistaken. I am certain that I didn't see. It's been a long time since then. Get up, this isn't what I intended, yes, perhaps, I admit it, but get up, *Talitha cumi. Eli, lamah shevaktani*, which means, why have you left me. My God, what made you do such a thing to me, which means why. Why didn't you stop me, which means water which means wind.

Zach transforms the story of Jesus' healing of the girl Talitha into a dramatic monologue about a quarrel between lovers. One infers that the couple has just made love and that the experience has caused the woman to break down in tears. Of course, the lover wants the crying to cease and so he reprimands her with the words, "you are an intelligent person," a colloquial expression in modern Hebrew meaning "shape up." His gradual admission of guilt is a comic moment that leads into a more serious, albeit it self-pitying, entreaty to God. This evolves into free associations about the elusive nature of words and the absurdity of all attempts to pin down meanings. The iconoclasm of the poem depends on our awareness of the Christian context, not a likely awareness for the common reader in Israel. This suggests that Zach is content to leave some connotative facets of the poem's meaning hidden from all but himself and a minority of his readers. Without intending to demean, Zach's "Talitha Cumi" secularizes the divine-yet-human voice of Jesus by putting his words into the mouth of the pathetically flawed, all-too-human speaker. And yet, at the poem's conclusion, Zach's speaker utters an abject, pleading call to his "Maker." This is T. Carmi's prose translation of the final lines of the poem:

> I didn't realize how greatly I troubled you with trivialities, my Maker. Make me null and void, my Lord. I didn't realize how little you made of me, my Lord, in my hunger. Talitha, cumi. (trans. Carmi 1983).

This ending forces one to ask: after all that came before, does Zach intend the speaker to be perceived as a true believer? I think not; and yet, the response the poem evokes is more complex than a simple yes or no. The speaker's identification with Jesus is not based upon his divinity, but on his suffering and sense of abandonment, and his turning to God is a confession of his moral shortcomings rather than a discovery of his relationship to the Divine. And yet, it is also possible that, *in extremis*, the secularist has discovered the limitations of his worldview and has come to feel things that cannot be expressed without the inclusion of God in the discourse.

I see represented in Zach and Amichai different temperaments and styles, one vociferous, the other reticent, both responding to the same cultural themes and one allusive textual source. Amichai replaces the lost meanings of the biblical text with richly elaborated fragments of his own experience, whereas Zach tends to leave the depleted, or questioned, biblical text to stand-alone and echo within the reader. In a sense, Zach's challenge to the tradition is more radical in its reticence, even though Amichai often sounds more openly iconoclastic.

Another notable nineteen-fifties iconoclast is David Avidan, a poet who likes to spin fantastical elaborations on a biblical person or theme but also quotes specific texts here and there. Perhaps he is the one poet from the State Generation who took the most extreme steps to liberate readers from biblical associations, achieving this with a sort of linguistic shock therapy, in parodies such as the sequence of poems called *Hit Songs About Samson*, which contains no biblical quotations or stylistic traits. In "A Green Tree is on Fire and is Not Consumed," the burning bush of Exodus 3 is clearly being evoked, as Avidan uses the biblical verb for "consumed" instead of the modern Hebrew equivalent. The alluding context is an urban scene, with sidewalks, telephones, and firefighters, and the diction surrounding the biblical verse is very colloquial. In a surrealistic juxtaposition, unspecified battlefield horrors intrude upon a spring day in the city. I quote a passage from the middle of the poem:

> They thus phone the firefighters,
> And in the meanwhile they look at the tree.
> A citizen goes down a very bright street.
> What's going on here.
> Nothing.
> Only a green tree burns-and-is-not-consumed.
> Is on fire and is not consumed.
> Very strange. Really strange. Really.
> Maybe God simply
> all of a sudden decided
> after so many years of snobbish distant isolation
> to repeat the Mount Horeb number.
> It was spring [. . .]
> (30-43; translation mine)

Later in the poem, Avidan describes the fiery tree as follows: "The branches/ screeched/ like a wild chorus/ in a weary, grown-up wind." In reconstructing the allusion, the reader must contrast this with God's voice emerging from the burning bush to announce His presence to Moses. Like Zach and Amichai, Avidan is quarrelsome and rebellious, but he tends to denigrate, or deflate, the biblical texts to which he alludes to a greater degree than they. In "Young Ecclesiastes," Avidan puns on the well-known words "Vanity, vanity, all is vanity" (also translatable more literally as *emptiness* or *exhaled air*) and uses it as the refrain that punctuates a young pseudo-intellectual's ruminations. The biblical *hevel havalim* (vanity of vanities) becomes *aval avalim* (but of buts), and thus *all is vanity* is transformed into *everything is contingent*. The poem continually plays with verses from Proverbs and Ecclesiastes, intermingling them with long ruminations on sexuality, art, and death, all handled with the semi-seriousness Avidan favors. Even more than Amichai and Zach, Avidan intends to make readers disconcertingly uncertain of the response expected of them.

* * *

Zach, Avidan and Amichai bring the Bible forward in time, indulging in varying degrees of anachronism in their identification with and interpretation of the Bible. On the other hand, Yonatan Ratosh and T. Carmi thrust themselves back imaginatively into the biblical period and illuminate a dark corner, the myths and rites that the Israelites absorbed from the surrounding Semitic cultures. Both, Ratosh typically and Carmi only occasionally, set aside the distancing ironic measures of the poets we have already discussed and exercise their negative capability instead. Generally speaking, they refrain from the "bringing down" of the holy book that Avidan, Amichai, and Zach practiced. They engage with the Bible as the product of a mythology-infused culture, hovering on the border between magical and religious beliefs. But it is also the case that both poets write from a fundamentally secular point of view. Neither of them is nostalgic for ancient superstitions and religious practices and yet, to judge by the vitality of their language, they are invigorated by their own evocations of the mythic way of thinking found here and there in the Hebrew Bible.

Ratosh assertively scrapes away the Priestly and Rabbinic glosses on the Bible, which present monotheism as an anti-mythic theology. He wants his Israeli readers to see their cultural beginnings with fresh eyes, as a Fertile Crescent civilization hardly distinguishable from the Canaanite culture that surrounded it. His biblical citations and evocations are inseparable from the main principles of his political philosophy. Ratosh was the chief poetic spokesman of the Young Hebrews, often referred to as the Canaanites, a movement that advocated a total rejection of Diaspora Judaism. Israeli critic, Dan Laor, prefaces his discussion of Ratosh's approach to the Hebrew Bible with the following comment: "The principle underlying Ratosh's theory is the need to clearly and absolutely distinguish between the scattered Jewish people and the 'Hebrews,' natives of a common territory . . ., sharing a single language and a culture that has nothing in common with Jewish culture" (Laor 101-102). Ratosh has no sympathy for the Zionist ideology, which sought to establish a renewed, healthier Jewish culture in a Jewish nation state. Of course, there is a fundamental contradiction between valorizing the new native culture and the rejection of the nationalist movement that brought Jews to the Middle East in the first place. Indeed, several historians have pointed out that the Canaanite movement was the logical extension of the criticism of Jewish culture voiced by the secularist Jewish reformers of the nineteenth century and the Zionist movement to which they gave rise.

Ratosh called Israeli (Jewish) writers who did not espouse his beliefs "Jews who write in Hebrew," not to be confused with authentically Hebrew writers, like himself. He saw himself as one of the pioneer Hebrew writers. And pan-Canaanite though he was, he nonetheless said absolutely nothing about the culture the Young Hebrews shared with the other Semitic inhabitants of the land, the Arabs. In general, the ideology to which Ratosh dedicated his life and many of his writings is not what makes him worthy of discussion in our context. Rather, it is his poetic achievement, including his unique use of the Bible that earns him a special place within secular Israeli modernism.

Ratosh forges two links with the earlier regional Canaanite culture, Canaanite polytheism and the Akkadian spoken in the city of Ugarit, a language closely resembling early Hebrew. In many of his poetic works, Ratosh presents YHWH, God of the Israelites, as merely one member of the Canaanite pantheon. In doing this, Ratosh was influenced by late nineteenth century European (non-Jewish) biblical scholarship, such as the writings of Julius Wellhausen, which emphasized the suppression of archaic Israelite religion by later forms of worship and finally by the redactors of the Hebrew Bible (Laor 103). Speaking of the actions of Gideon in Judges VI: 25-32, for example, Wellhausen explains, "The altar of a single stone, the flames bursting out of it, the evergreen tree, the very name of which, Ela, seems to indicate a natural connection with E l—all this was in the eyes of a later generation far from correct, indeed it was Baal-work. A desire that the piety of Gideon should be above suspicion gave rise to a second story, in which he erects an altar to Jehovah in place of the former altar of Baal" (Wellhausen 238).[7] Ratosh is also aware that the influence of the Canaanite culture is evident in biblical poetry, pervasively so in the imagery of the psalms, for example (Alter 1987, 244).[8]

Within the scriptures per se, while quoting and alluding to virtually every book in the Hebrew Bible, Ratosh valued the period of the Judges and the monarchy of David and Solomon above others. For him, the Bible is the primary documentary evidence of the Hebrew civilization, albeit one that the redactors used to promote the later YHWH-centered religion. The redactors' theological aims led them to distort the original content of the Hebrew religion, according to Ratosh, the result being the we must now give the Bible a contrarian reading if we are to uncover the original layer of meaning (Yizhaki 205). Ratosh's use of religious rhetoric and the revival of the Canaanite pantheon should not lead us to view him as approaching the Bible as a believer. His orientation is purely secular.[9] Not only did he reject every aspect of normative Judaism; while reviving the mythic content of Canaanite polytheism, nowhere does he advocate the revival of Canaanite worship, its rituals, prayers, and other practices.

The long poem, cast in the mold of Hebrew prophecies "Haholchei ba-hoshech, They Who Walk in Darkness," offers countless examples of Ratosh's use of archaic forms of Hebrew and of his portrayal of Hebrew religion as a syncretistic blending of belief in the ancient Israelite deity YHWH with the worship of the gods of Canaan, Baal, Astarte and Anat, primarily. In his essay on this 755 line-long polemical poem, Yedidyah Yizhaki offers a close analysis of this pseudo-religion along with Young Hebrew ideological themes, both of which are wedded to the Bible. "The general tendency of the poem's structure and language points to a deep connection to the Bible, with the intention of turning it toward its sources, its archaic stratum, both linguistic and thematic. The poem creates a syncretistic whole, composed of biblical and Ugaritic poetry, merging God with Canaanite deities. Thus the Bible is presented as a *later distortion* and the poem returns the traditional text to its original meaning, its pre-Jewish meaning, within its original Canaanite context, known to us mostly from Ugaritic writings" (Yizhaki 205). In the title itself, Ratosh draws on Isaiah 9:1, "The people that walked in darkness," but modifying the verb morphology to represent a form even more archaic than the biblical Hebrew that has come down to us (Yizhaki 199). Here is my prose translation of the first fourteen lines of the poem:

> I have seen the glory of Yahaweh in the moonlight of Tammuz, at dawn after a night of love in beautiful Milhamiyah, which is in the Jordan valley, facing Hermon and Gilead. And a thick cloud was beneath his feet and darkness on the face of the deep. A great cloud, very heavy, hangs as one huge lump above the peaks of Gilead, between heaven and my land. And like the vision of a flaming fire, he glows in the mist at the eastern edge. (translation mine)

In the very first line of this poem, Ratosh declares his subversive stand. He violates a basic tenet of Judaism proscribing the uttering of the name of God. Ratosh adds the diacritical marks that represent vowels to the consonants YHWH, God of the Israelites and of subsequent Judaism, making it pronounceable as Yah-ha-weh.[10] In the second line, he mentions the Canaanite god Tammuz, a word not found in Hebrew scripture but in later Hebrew the name of a spring month in the Jewish calendar. The phrase "a thick cloud was beneath his feet," is a citation from Psalms 18:10 and David's poem of thanksgiving in 2 Samuel 22:10. The description of the god appearing in the midst of clouds is a veiled reference to the god Baal, who is often described in

Ugaritic texts as riding a cloud. Immediately following is the quotation from Genesis 1:2: "and darkness on the face of the deep." There is also an allusion to Exodus 16:10: "and there in a cloud appeared the presence of the Lord," and Ezekiel 1:4: ". . . a huge cloud and a flashing fire." This verse from Ezekiel is also alluded to in "and as a vision of a flaming fire." The final phrase, "at the eastern edge," is a reference to the East as mentioned in Ezekiel 47:18 and other similar locutions in the Bible. This interweaving of paganism and sublime holy texts concludes the first scene in a poem of a deliberately prophetic cast, a scene charged with both mystical awe and defiance in the face of tradition. Ratosh quotes or alludes to biblical text with this frequency for several hundred lines. Then the discourse becomes more overtly political, still in biblical Hebrew but with fewer quotations, to become highly allusive again in the final two hundred lines.

Lines 27-28 of "They Who Walk," come from Exodus 34 verses 4 and 7, as well as a parallel passage in Numbers. These verses, spoken by God to Moses, describe two antithetical facets of His nature, as both "slow to anger, abounding in steadfast love" and as one who "does not remit all punishment." Many Jewish readers would recognize the entire four-verse passage, as it was transferred from the Bible to the prayer book. In Ratosh's poetic context, the characterization is meant to apply to the Canaanite god Baal as he appears in the speaker's prophetic vision:

> He stood at a great distance. His bow was not extended outward. Tightly he held the swirling thunder in his clouds, gathered the rays of his might in the thick mist. Anath's slanting wings were hidden within him. Silent he stood/ at the eastern horizon. Most heavy. I saw the edges of his feet sparkling like sapphires. Slow to anger, abounding in steadfast love, He will not remit all punishment. (translation mine)

It is important to keep in mind that Ratosh does not intend the speaker's vision to be taken literally. He is using cultic imagery to evoke the archaic cultural context the nativist wishes to revive without proposing a return to Baal worship. At the same time, applying to Baal phrases one associates with a long, continuous tradition of Jewish worship is a deliberately stinging rejection of Judaism.

The poem ends with a series of Biblical quotations recalling the consoling prophecies that alternate in the Hebrew Bible with rebukes and admonitions. From Isaiah 27:1, Ratosh quotes phrases evoking God's power over Leviathan, and from Psalms 126:2, its second phrase, "Our mouths shall be filled with laughter, our tongues, with songs of joy." The common reader in Israel would spontaneously call up the preceding phrase as well: "When the Lord restores the fortunes of Zion – we see it as in a dream –" To that reader the truncated citation unavoidably implies national renewal. In allowing the unmentioned context to shape the reader's response, Ratosh is using biblical citations as Hebrew poets have used them over the centuries, whether religious or secular. As with Zach and Amichai, the full connotative meaning of his borrowed lines can only be grasped if one brings to bear their original biblical context.

The poet's use of partial quotations and textual collage deserves a closer look, and the brief "Love" will serve this purpose well. Ratosh likes to make slight alterations in the quoted text, just enough to put his stamp on the words, while allowing them to remain recognizable to readers familiar with the original. For example, "Love" contains a slight change in the quotation from Psalm 24:7, "O gates, lift up your heads! Up high, you everlasting doors so the king of glory may come in." Here are the opening four lines of the poem:

> Lift yourselves up high, o everlasting gates, so the King of glory
> may come in:
> The monk's cloak is torn and a canopy of peace set up:
> Go forth, my beloved,
> And we will go down to the blossoming vineyards.
> (translation mine)

He also likes to juxtapose lines from different biblical texts, or, more rarely, to dovetail a biblical text with one from the traditional prayer book. In our example, brief phrases from The Song of Songs, chapter 2:15, are interwoven with the words of a sixteenth-century mystical Sabbath prayer, itself drawing upon The Song of Songs: "Come, my beloved, (from the mystical prayer in which the next phrase is "toward the Bride; let us welcome the Sabbath")/ Let us go forth (to the) vineyards blossoming (Song of Songs)."

To add to the shocking effect of the conjunction of eros and piety, the speaker in "Love" appears to be a temple prostitute, a woman with a prescribed sexual role within a pagan rite. She alternates between offering herself to the monk and to Baal. The poem includes the plea to God, "How long will you hide your face from me?" familiar to us from the Psalms. Ratosh juxtaposes this pious cry with another borrowing from The Song of Songs (5:3): "I had taken off my robe – was I to don it again?" He then adds a parallel structure of his own: "I had spread out my arms – was I to withhold them again?" (The parallel line in the Bible is "I had bathed my feet – was I to soil them again?"). When the speaker expresses longing for Baal, she uses familiar language from the Psalms, as exemplified above. This would constitute an affront to religious readers. Even quotations and allusions to The Song of Songs can be offensive to a religious Jewish reader. But Ratosh does not intend merely to offend. Rather he is making a claim for the new culture that he believes Israeli "Hebrews" should espouse in the land that links them to their Canaanite roots.

Not all of Ratosh's works are of the somber Canaanite cast of They Who Walk in Darkness." For example, his brief lyric "Strong Drink," perhaps in the tradition of medieval drinking songs, indulges in a humorous use of the Bible:

We've poured out the wine
And the barrel is
Empty. Let those who've a thirst
Take to water.
We've poured out the water,
The barrel's
Empty.
Let those who've a thirst
Take strong drink.

In the beginning God created
Strong drink
To separate the waters.
(trans. A.C. Jacobs)

Ratosh returns to Genesis 1 in a more somber poem ironically entitled "Light." Here the primal scene of creation is also birthplace of a fundamental conflict within human nature. This is a prose rendition of the poem's first two stanzas: "In the beginning was Woman and all her might, and all the Baalim arose from the sea. Therefore, was Man left alone on dry land? And the land was in chaos and darkness was over the abyss. In the beginning was Man, naked and enflamed, and the Ashtarot came down from the mountain. And therefore Man was a parched thing, poured out between the two waters. And God's spirit hovered and darkness was over the abyss. In the beginning was daylight separating darkness from darkness." Ratosh suggests that men and women are by their nature as distinct and obscure to one another as are the two kinds of darkness. Primal man and woman are at war, alienated from each other by the intervention of the divinities that seduce them. Note the repetition of the phrase "darkness was over the abyss." I translated Ratosh's "Elohim," as God, and this is accurate, if we read the passage as do most readers of Hebrew. However, the word Elohim can also be interpreted as referring to another Canaanite deity, on a par with the Baalim and Ashtarot of this poem.

I take us back momentarily to Natan Zach to compare his treatment of Genesis 1 with the above, in a poem written in colloquial language and a semi-serious mood. Zach, too, is using a passage from the creation story to contemplate human nature. Here is my prose translation of the entire poem, entitled "When God Said Let There Be Light":

When God said 'let there be light' for the first time, he meant that he shouldn't be in the dark. He wasn't thinking about the heavens at that moment, but the trees were already starting to fill up with water and birds were given air and bodies. It was then that the first wind blew toward our Lord and He saw it with the eyes of his very own glory and thought that it was good. He wasn't thinking at that moment about people, the great multitude of people. But they were already thinking about themselves, without leafy camouflage, and in their hearts were already dreaming up a scheme about pain. When our Lord thought first about night, he wasn't thinking about sleep. 'Thus, thus I will be happy,' the good Lord thought to Himself. But they were already a multitude. (translation mine)

Zach has transformed God into a being with all the psychological characteristics of humanity, a being who thinks of his creature comforts above all else and, like most of us, is able neither to foresee nor control the consequences of his purely practical, self-centered actions. The poet's tone is several (affectionate) steps down from the decorum with which Ratosh treats the creative actions of the deities.

* * *

Our last poet is T. Carmi, whose *The Brass Serpent*, a cycle of seven poems, exemplifies yet another manner of fusing traditional texts and twentieth century sensibilities. Carmi is a modernist poet of the generation of Zach and Amichai, and, not incidentally, a scholar of Hebrew poetry. His poetic voice ranges from sardonic self-criticism to lyrical emotional immediacy. Like Ratosh, Carmi configures the Bible within its early Near Eastern cultural context. He differs from Ratosh, however, in that he does not do so in order to promote a nativist ideology, but, instead, in order to delve into the mythic content of the Bible that rabbinic Judaism has shunned (for theological reasons) and uses it to express complex personal associations. Carmi integrates the sources into his elusively modern poetic diction with love for Jewish tradition and the Hebrew language that contains it. Perhaps more than other secular Israeli writers of his generation, it is important for Carmi to evoke and merge with what T. S. Eliot called "the vanished mind of which our mind is a continuation" (Eliot 451). He finds inspiration in the Talmud and other post-biblical rabbinic writings, including Jewish mystical texts, no less than in the Bible but remains, nonetheless, a distinctly secular poet.

The Brass Serpent has two epigraphs, one the passage from Numbers (21:8) that recounts the making of the brass serpent during the Israelite sojourn in the wilderness, the other a quotation from The Zohar (The Book of Splendor), a twelfth-century Jewish mystical text from the Iberian Peninsula. The passage from The Zohar reads as follows:

> Three voices are there which are never lost . . . the voice of a woman in labor, when she mounts the chair of pain: that voice floats from end to end of the world: the voice of a man when his soul departs from his body: the voice floats from end to end of the world: the voice of the serpent when he sheds his skin . . . (Carmi, 1966)

As the first two lines of the poem are from Genesis 3:15, "They shall strike at your head/ And you shall strike at their heel," the reader's associations have already encompassed, within an interval of a few seconds, the serpent of the Garden of Eden, the ambiguously magical serpent of the early Israelites, and the snake as conceived by the medieval mystical imagination. The poem's biblical amalgam includes allusions to Miriam's story, her role as chief musician, prophetess and leper; the Zoheleth stone, where serpent rituals took place (1Kings 1:9)[11]; poetry from the books Job and Isaiah, both of which link the serpent with the mythic sea monster Leviathan; The Song of Songs and the book of Joshua. There are also several phrases in *The Brass Serpent* strongly suggesting that Carmi has dipped into the Targum, the various translations of the Hebrew Bible into Aramaic, and used some of its narrative embellishments in his imagery.[12] Such, for example, is a scornful line about the sale of clothing made out of snakeskins. It is very likely that Carmi's image is inspired by the Targum version Genesis 3, according to which God made splendid clothes for Adam and Eve out of the serpent's skin. Perhaps more important is the straightforward narrative link the Targum creates between the serpent from Genesis and the seraphs of Numbers 21. I think it highly likely that Carmi was aware of this embellishment.[13]

In Carmi's hands, the serpent is a complex and enigmatic poetic trope capable of representing modernist explorations of human imperfection and the longing to be healed. As is appropriate for a work about a mythic creature that once symbolized wisdom, fertility and vitality and still represents the field of medicine, this cycle of seven poems captures the experiences the speaker undergoes as he moves from a state of diseased abjection to the attainment of recovery. Carmi constructs the poem around the ancient belief, reflected in Numbers 21, that the serpent is a cosmic power, both slayer and healer. God's command to fashion a serpent icon reflects magical thinking according to which one can neutralize the effects of a dangerous object by making an image of it. Despite the Targumist's efforts, the accretions of myth surrounding the serpent do not fit together neatly in the Bible, and thus it is fitting that the serpent is a composite figure in Carmi's poems as well. It is not an accident that in *The Brass Serpent*, the creature both crawls and takes to the air, in light of the Genesis serpent's mode of locomotion after the tempting of Adam and Eve and the evidence that winged serpents were common in Near Eastern mythology. No one is certain about the meaning of the word "seraph," synonymous with "serpent" in Numbers 21:6-8. The radical, consonants SRP, suggests that a seraph is a fiery creature. And Carmi alludes to other mysteries as well.[14]

Carmi finds in all of these layers of meaning and lacunae a rich context for the utterances of the poetic speaker, a conflicted, searching individual. For all his alluding to several layers of Jewish text, Carmi uses the biblical myths not to explore his identity as a modern Jew, but rather as objective correlatives for the pain of imperfection and longing for a return to wholeness that is common to all people. In the first poem, Carmi follows the form of Genesis 3:15, in which God addresses the serpent directly but reverses the addressee, so that the first lines of the poem read, "He will strike at your heel/ You will strike at his head." This is followed by "He will stay still, still without shame, / And you will rush like a lover." Carmi creates an incantatory rhythm by continuing the biblical pattern of alternating You/he statements. The second stanza reads as follows: "Silently he will nest in the heart/And whisper his truth/ You will seek him morning and night/ In all the caves of deceit" (translations mine).

In the second poem, the serpent and the poet/speaker merge. In it, the allusion to The Song of Songs 6:11-12 creates irony; the infected speaker in search if healing echoes the words of the intoxicated lovers: "I went down to the river bank to see if my flesh had blossomed, to see if my hands had put forth buds and my eyes regained their fire." This poem ends with the haunting words of the poet-snake: "O, I have made of my skin a dry channel and the waters have left for the sea; the snake has shed its skin and his voice wanders the world over." In the opening stanza of the fourth poem, Carmi quotes Numbers 21:8 in its entirety: "Make a seraph figure and mount it on a standard. And if anyone who is bitten looks at it, he shall recover." Carmi continues with his own words: "And if his heart is hollow and his world is in darkness, as he looks at the shining one, his own light will blaze and he shall live." Each stanza continues with a variation linked to the biblical text through the syntax of the final refrain, "And he shall live." The last stanza allows the secular theme to emerge most explicitly; man is the author of his own healing: "And he shall look at his own handiwork, see it and live (translations mine)."

In the fifth poem, it is the serpent of Genesis 3 who speaks: "They say I am the most devious of all creatures on earth. Look at me; I am revealed to you atop a standard, flesh of your pain, unfurled like the sun in its orbit." Each verse begins with the pattern, "They say that . . .," followed by yet another allusion to God's curses in Genesis 3 and the brass serpent's sly retorts, the latter being poet's own creations, of course. In the last poem, Carmi returns to the text of Numbers 21:8, this time breaking up the words so that each stanza opens with a biblical phrase, all phrases being in the proper order of the original text. This time, the speaker comments on the events in the life of Miriam and her deep connection with the serpent. Here, for example, is the second of three stanzas: "'And he placed it atop a tall standard.' Miriam, Miriam the prophetess, sister to murder, to the flower and the dragon, teach me to conceal, and to be revealed like the striking snake and to open my hands before the snow-white tabernacle" (translation mine). The last phrase contains a reference to Miriam's bout of skin-whitening leprosy, God's response to her rebellion against Him. Throughout *The Brass Serpent*, Carmi maintains a negative capability that allows him to convey both the anguish of the skeptical, self-loathing poet and the magical beliefs held by forgotten ancestors. Like T. S. Eliot before him, Carmi has used ancient fragments of myth, unmoored beliefs, to embody both the full and the hollow places within twentieth century experience. And like Eliot, Carmi leaves it to the reader to complete the poem as s/he weaves a tissue of interpretive associations between the imagistic fragments.

Carmi's Song of Degrees *Shir ha-ma'alot*, (also translated as *song of ascents* or *steps* but in modern Hebrew meaning *virtues* as well) is a love lyric that uses biblical quotation in an innocent, yet witty manner that is in harmony with the joyful mood of the poem. Carmi takes advantage of the uncertainty surrounding the word *ma'alot*, which appears in the superscription to fifteen of the psalms. In transferring words of praise from a religious to a secular context Carmi means to elevate the love experience, not to demean the religious, in contrast with Amichai in the love poem "If I Forget You, O Jerusalem," which I examined earlier. The love Carmi delights in is both spiritual and physical. The beloved, the "crown of the night," has rescued the speaker from a death of the spirit. Here is the poem, as translated by Dom Moraes:

> A song of degrees; in flight,
> To the head of my life you rise,
> Crown of the night,
> And they return, my eyes,
> So plagued with dust yesterday,
> And I recover my hands
> Which drifted away
> To the sand, and my voice
> Breaking free on its way to the dance,
> O yes
> I remember my name
> All the names your good silence bred,
> And to you, head
> Of my life, it will rise
> Explicit and bright at each step
> Of this song of degrees. (trans. Moraes)

The poem concludes with a reiteration of the phrase "song of degrees," which owes its playfulness to the simple fact that it does not stand as an isolated noun phrase, as it appears in the Bible and in the first line of the poem, but is instead embedded in a complete syntactic unit. Along with other flaws (failing to convey at least one important pun), the translator was not able to convey another association that Carmi exploits in linking his love poem with the biblical songs of thanksgiving, and that is the musical association. In the penultimate line, Carmi uses the word *sulamot*, which means both ladders and musical scales, but is translated by Moraes as *step*. Carmi has created a palimpsest of sorts; a paean to the woman who revived his spirit through love is etched over the fainter traces of a biblical hymn thanking God for his own kind of love. And I think this is not a bad place for us to end our exploration of secular uses of biblical text.

The ingenuity of Israeli poets and their openness to their biblical legacy have yielded, and continue to yield, a harvest of richly layered texts. It is not always easy to determine where reverence gives way to ironic distancing, but even where we have detected a respectful fondness for the biblical text, the God of Jewish tradition has been absent from the scene. This mixture of secularism and biblical inspiration is fairly representative of the culture of Israel as a whole, at least until the last two decades. When the Israelis deflate the grandeur of the Bible, they are at the same time mocking themselves and the ideological excesses that accompanied the Zionist search for links to the biblical past that was their claim to the land of Zion. The frequent debunking of the Bible is an act of rebellion. But beneath it, we discover the Israelis' melancholy consciousness of their diminished and morally ambiguous status in comparison with the mythic biblical figures and, more to the point, in comparison with the anonymous writers who created the masterful anthology. For the secularist Israeli poets, the Hebrew Bible remains a primary stratum, its sounds and rhythms never far from the music of their modernist poetry. It is beloved linguistic treasure that nonetheless arouses contradictory feelings. Ambivalence is the hallmark of modernism, and the Israeli modernist poets we have encountered fully exploit the words of the Bible to voice conflicted feelings about the text itself and what it represents, as well as the existential dilemmas they lived through in mid-twentieth- century Israel.

NOTES

1. Biblical Hebrew ceased to exist as a spoken language after the Babylonian exile, which occurred around 580 BCE ((Saenz-Badillos 166)

2. Chana Kronfeld's *On the Margins of Modernism* includes an instructive introduction to the subject of allusion in Israeli poetry. In her chapter "Theories of Allusion and Imagist Intertextuality," she provides some historical background to present day Israeli views of allusion, going back to the theories proposed in the rhetorical manuals of Spanish Hebrew poets, written in the period referred to as the Golden Age, the flowering of Jewish culture, and Hebrew verse, in the Iberian peninsula, between the ninth and twelfth centuries. These theories reflected poetic norms and practices based upon allusion, producing poems "in which the biblical text is a necessary component of any semantic construal and structural cohesion" (116). The manner in which biblical verses were interwoven within a poem became systematized, and labeled as *shibbuts* and *remizah*, literally, inlaying and hinting, respectively (116).

3. The book is *Al tishlach yadchah el ha-na'ar* [Do Not Raise Your Hand Against the Boy]. Ed. Aryeh Ben-Gurion. Jerusalem: Keter Publishing, 2002.

4. Shimon Sandbank. Shetei breichot ba-ya'ar: Kesharim u-makbilot ben ha-shira ha'-ivritve-shirat eropa [Two Pools in the Wood: Hebrew Poetry and the European Tradition: Influences and Parallels]. Tel-Aviv: Tel-Aviv UP, 1976.

5. The English renditions of the Hebrew throughout the essay are from the Jewish Publication Society's Hebrew and English Tanakh, second edition, 1999.

6. In the western portion of Jerusalem, about one mile from the walled Old City, there used to stand a Protestant missionary by the name Talitha Cumi, with those word carved over the stone doorway. It stood on a main thoroughfare, and Zach must have passed it often. This lovely late nineteenth century stone structure was torn down some years after Zach's poem was written, and only the stone doorway now remains standing.

7. In his article on Ratosh, Dan Laor notes that Julius Wellhausen's seminal work on the Hebrew Bible appeared in Hebrew in 1938.

8. In his essay "Psalms," Alter states, "The Hebrew poets did not hesitate to borrow images, phrase, or even whole sequences of lines from the Syro-Palestinian pagan
psalmodic   tradition" (1987, 244). For a fuller treatment of the relationship between Hebrew and Canaanite literature, please refer to "Hebrew Bible and Canaanite Literature" by Jonas C. Greenfield, in R. Alter and F. Kermode 1987.

9.   Since the beginning of the nineteenth century, gradual secularization was the dominant   cultural trend in Jewish life, and for all his non-conformism, Ratosh was no less secular than the typical twentieth century settler in Palestine/Israel. Prominent Israeli critic Baruch Kurzweil, wrote in the early nineteen-fifties that secularization was the cardinal feature of Israeli literature. He observed that "[T]he literature of the young, especially that written by the Israeli-born, Israeli-educated among them, differs radically from that written by previous generations, whether secularist, Zionist or otherwise.... The narrative of the young writer is evidence of the death throes of traditional Jewish values (Bein hazon le-vein absurdi, 1954; quoted in Laor 1983 230).

10. The letters YHWH are always printed without the diacritical marks representing the vowels and when encountered by a Jewish reader, YHWH will be decoded or uttered as Adonai (my Lord) or Ha-shem (the name).

11.   Entsiklopedyah mikra'it [Encyclopedia Biblica] 5, 827. Both articles, on Serpent and Nehushtan, contain valuable information on rituals and beliefs about this mythic creature.

12. Targum is the collective name for translations of the Bible into the Aramaic spoken by the Jews throughout the Near East for several centuries before and after the common era. During that period, the Bible was read aloud in both the original Hebrew and in the Targum during religious services. From time to time, the Targum weaves midrash, interpretive and embellishing passages, into the translations of obscure biblical passages, to enliven the text with lore, or when theological elaboration was deemed necessary. Later rabbis looked to Targum, especially Targum Onkelos, for help in interpreting ambiguous texts.

13. Targum Neofiti 1 interpolates a narrative within Numbers 21 that is meant to explain the sudden appearance of serpents in the midst of the Israelites. According to the story, the serpent of Genesis did not complain when God commanded him to "eat dust," whereas the Israelites "murmured" complaints although God provided them with quail and manna. For this reason God has sent serpents "to rule over the people which has murmured" (Targum Neofiti: Numbers 116); all of this embellishment in order to insert the word "Therefore" at the beginning of verse 6.

14. Other mysteries: there is an etymological link between the "whispering," rustling sound of the snake referred to in the Bible and the whispering of soothsayers; the verb *to guess* in Hebrew comes from the radical NHSh, also the root of the noun Neash, serpent. We know little about the nature of the Israelite worship of Nehushtan, the snake idol, also etymologically related to *nehoshet*, brass in biblical Hebrew and copper in the modern language. These worship practices, which Israel inherited from the Canaanites, were abolished during the reforms of King Hezekiah, as noted in 2 Kings, 18:4. (Entsiclopediya mikra'it [Biblical Encyclopedia]) 5 827).

Works Cited

Alter, Robert. *Canon and Creativity: Modern Writing and the Authority of Scripture.* New Haven: Yale UP, 2000.

———. *After the Tradition: Essays on Modern Jewish Writing.* New York: E. P. Dutton and Co., 1969.

———. "Psalms." *The Literary Guide to the Bible.* Eds. Robert Alter and Frank Kermode. Cambridge, MA: The Belknap Press of Harvard UP, 1987.

Amichai, Yehuda. "A Sort of Apocalypse." *The Selected Poetry of Yehuda Amichai.* Trans. Chanah Bloch and Stephen Mitchell. New York: Harper and Row, 1986.

———. "Ani rotseh levalbel et ha-tanach [I Want to Muddle the Bible]." *66 Meshorerim:_mivhar hamishim shenot shira ivrit hadashah.* [Sixty-six Poets: An Anthology of Fifty Years of New Poetry]. Ed. Zisi Stavi. Tel-Aviv: yedi'ot aharonot –sifrei-hemmed, 1996.

———. "If I Forget Thee, O Jerusalem." *Selected Poems: Yehuda Amichai.* Trans. Assia Gutmann and Harold Schimmel. Hammondsmith: Penguin Books, 1971.

"Like the Inner Wall of a House." Amen. Trans. Yehuda Amichai and Ted Hughes. New York: Harper and Row, 1977.

———. "Shelosha perushim [Three Exegeses]." *Ve-lo al menat lizkor* [And Not for Memory's Sake]. Tel-Aviv: Schocken, 1975.

————. "To the Full Extent of Mercy." Trans. Chana Kronfeld. *On the Margins of Modernity.* Berkeley: California UP, 1996.

Avidan, David. *Mashehu bishvil mishehu: mivhar shirim: 1952-1964* [Something for Someone: Selected Poems 1952-1964]. 1964. Tel Aviv: A. Levin-Epstein-Modan, 1975.

Carmi, T. *"Nehash ha-nehoshet* [The Brass Serpent]." *Shirim: Mivhar 1951-1993* [Selected Poems: 1951-1994]. Tel-Aviv: Dvir Publishing House, 1994.

————. "The Brass Serpent." *The Brass Serpent and Other Poems.* Trans. Dom Moraes. London: Andre Deutsch, 1971.

————. "A Song of Degrees." Trans. Dom Moraes. *The Brass Serpent and Other Poems.*

————. "Shir ha-ma'alot [A Song of Degrees]." *ha-Yam ha-aharon: shirim* [The Farthest Sea: Poems]. Merhavyah: Sifriyat po'alim, 1966.

————.*The Penguin Book of Hebrew Verse.* Ed and trans. T. Carmi. Hammondsmith: Penguin Books, 1981.

Cohen, Joseph. *Voices of Israel, Essays and Interviews with Yehuda Amichai, A. B. Yehoshua, T. Carmi, Aharon Appefeld and Amos Oz.* Albany: State University of New York P, 1990.

Eliot, T. S. "London Letter." *The Dial,* LXXI.4 (October,1921).

Entsiklopedyah mikra'it [Encyclopedia Biblica]. Jerusalem: Mosad Bialik, 1950-82.

JPS Hebrew English Tanakh: *The Traditional Hebrew Text and on. the New JPS Translation* Second Edition. Philadelphia: The Jewish Publication Society, 1999.

Kronfeld, Chana. *On the Margins of Modernity.* Berkeley: California UP, 1996.

Kushner, Lawrence. *Rivers of Light: Spirituality, Judaism and the Evolution of Consciousness.* San Francisco: Harper and Row, 1981.

Laor, Yizhak. "Ha-esh she-yats'ah min ha-atad [The Fire that Came Out of the Thornbush]." *Bikort u-farshanut* [Criticism and Interpretation] (1990) 27: 99-124.

————. "Bein ideologia le-estetikah [Between Ideology and Aesthetics]." *Siman Keri'ah* (1983) 16-17: 226-231.

Ratosh, Yonatan. "Ha-holchai ba-hoshech [They Who Walk in Darkness]." *Yalkut Shirim* [Selected Poems]. Ed. Aharon Amir.Tel-Aviv: Mahbarot le-sifrut-zmorah, 1991.

————. "Ahavah [Love]." *Yalkut Shirim* [Selected Poems]

————. "Strong Drink." Trans. A. C. Jacobs. Boas Evron. "Uriel Shelah and Yonatan Ratosh." *Modern Hebrew Literature* (1981-1982)7.1:37-40

————. "Or [Light]." *Yalkut Shirim* [Selected Poems]

Saenz-Badillos, Angel. *A History of the Hebrew Language.* Trans. John Eldwode. Cambridge,UK. Cambridge UP. 1993.

Targum *Neofiti and Targum Pseudo-Jonathan:* Numbers. Trans. Martin McNamara. Collegeville, MN: Liturgical Press, 1995.

Wellhausen, Julius. *Prolegomena to the History of Israel.* Edinburgh: A. & C. Black, 1885.

Yizhaki, Yedidyah. "Iyun ba-shir "ha-holchei bahoshech [A Study of the Poem "They Who Walk in Darkness"]. *Bikoret u-farshnut* [Criticism and Interpretation]. (January, 1978) 11-12: 193-223.

Zach, Natan. "Enosh kehatsir yamav [Man's Days are as the Grass]." *Shirim Shonim* [Miscellaneous Poems]. Tel-Aviv: Hakibbutz Ha-meuchad, 1966.

——. "Like Sand." Trans. Warren Bargad and Stanley F. Cheyet. *Israeli Poetry: A Contemporary Anthology.* Eds. Warren Bargad and Stanley F. Cheyet. Bloomington, IN: Indiana UP, 1986.

——. "Talitha Cumi." Trans. T Carmi. *The Penguin Book of Hebrew Verse.* Ed. and trans.T. Carmi. Hammondsmith: Penguin Books, 1981.

13   Justice and the Old/New Jewish Nation in Shulamith Hareven's *Thirst: The Desert Trilogy*
Ranen Omer-Sherman

Among contemporary Israeli writers, scripture is not explored simply for its own sake but also for its continuing impact. David Jacobson insists that the Bible's ancient stories must be retold "to emphasize possible connections between what went wrong with political sovereignty in biblical times and what [is] going wrong in modern times" (154). Because the impact of biblical materials on the contemporary condition of *all* of our lives has been made manifestly evident by the global repercussions of the conflict between Israel and Palestine, readers everywhere may be more interested than at any previous time in examining how such writers, working through a lens of constructive anachronism, are self-conscious about inhabiting a strange confluence of past and future, not to mention striking spatial congruencies. In this regard, the late Israeli novelist Shulamith Hareven's (1930-2003) *Thirst: The Desert Trilogy* (*Tsima'on: Shlishyat hamidbar* in Hebrew) offers readers an unprecedented exploration of ancient and contemporary understandings of justice and human liberation.

Encompassing "The Miracle Hater," "Prophet," and "After Childhood," *The Desert Trilogy* interrogates the archetypal desert experience as a story of nationalism and authority—as well as an encounter with the sacred—in ways that creatively trouble the present moment wherever (ideologically or geographically) the reader might be located. Yet there is a certain inevitable logic to this retelling. As Israeli sociologist Oz Almog observes of the Zionist pedagogy with which Hareven's generation was raised: "Educators used the Bible as a guidebook and described the landscape to their pupils in the context of Biblical stories. The landscape was mythologized and turned into a stage for a national historical pageant before the eyes of enchanted pupils, bringing home to them the richness of the nation's past that endowed...its spirit on the present" (Almog, 168). At the same time, the reborn Hebrew language would invariably carry with it the burden of ingrained palimpsests and archetypes of earlier conquests and victims.[1] Ostensibly set in the time of *Exodus*, *Joshua*, and *Judges*, the resolutely spare language of Hareven's three novellas offers a searingly "timeless" perspective on the Middle East's history of conquests and displacements.

Taken as a whole, *The Desert Trilogy* offers an exciting gateway into the role of the biblical narrative in the immediate context of the troubling ideological debates that fragment contemporary Israeli life. In Hareven's narrative of transiency, the comforts of home, unity, and dwelling are tested against the metaphoric spaciousness of a desert landscape with an endless horizon. For she is acutely aware that when it comes to imagining the austere wilderness, that richly disorderly space of exile and liberation that has both invigorated and troubled the integrity of the Jewish nation from its very beginnings, the Hebrew Bible's fraught relation to its disorderly wilderness offers the modern Israeli imagination a complex spatial poetics. In this regard, it is worth paying heed to Pardes' sense of the biblical desert as an indeterminate space of fissured identities, radical skepticism, and questioning of official narratives of the nation. Unlike their anointed patriarch, the desert wanderers of Exodus are "confused and fearful about homecoming," unsure about the binds of collective identity: "The wandering Israelites are skeptical about the very premise that Canaan is their homeland. The only land they wish to return to is Egypt. But they end up in the wilderness, between Egypt and the Promised Land, returning to neither" (104). It is not that wilderness skepticism is sanctified or well-rewarded by God. The desert generation, doubting God, is "doomed to remain forever in the arid land of the desert" (Pardes 50). At times it seems as if both their God and the desert gleefully collaborate in an inexplicable plot to destroy them. The people's complaints earn them only the threat of utter annihilation and oblivion:

> Say to them, 'As I live,' says the Lord, 'I will do to you just as you have urged Me. In this very wilderness shall your carcasses drop. Of all of you who were recorded in your various lists from the age of twenty years up, you who have muttered against Me, not one shall enter the land in which I swore to settle you—save Caleb son of Jephunneh and Joshua son of Nun. Your children who, you said, would be carried off—these will I allow to enter; they shall know the land that you have rejected. But your carcasses shall drop in this wilderness, while your children roam the wilderness for forty years, suffering for your faithlessness, until the last of your carcasses is down in the wilderness. (Numbers 14: 29-34)

Precisely because of such foreboding moments, for many Bible critics the wilderness signifies little more than a site where 'childhood' is enacted, where the people "moan and groan...unaware of God's providence" (Pardes 34). The Canaan that awaits them is too intangible to console the exiles of the "howling waste" (Deut. 32: 10). Here is where, as Hareven's retelling itself underscores, the triumphal God of monotheism seems little more than an ascendant Pharaoh, just as likely to exterminate the exiles as any other tyrant. In Exodus, Deuteronomy, and Numbers, the exilic sojourn in the desert is filled with death and tribal disorder but also blesses the people with God's undivided interest in their growth as a nation. Biblical scholar Athalya Brenner has noted that these books offer numerous variations on the related themes of liminality and "passage":

> A passage from loosely-defined population into ethnicity; a passage from a 'religion of the fathers'...to a communal covenant bound, legally grounded, exclusive monotheism; a passage from the axis of space, from one country (Egypt) to the threshold of another (Canaan); a passage through the axis of time, represented by the typological forty years in the (mythic) wilderness; a passage from disorganization and confusion into institutionalization. (Brenner 11)

Embracing this liminal space offered Hareven a way to write outside the Zionist metaplot of territorial redemption, even to mount a spirited critique of the nation—indeed   of the very idea of "nation"—through two temporal continuities.

As if imagining each of Brenner's phases of flux and transformation, Hareven provides a refreshing return to the earliest Hebrew literary relation to the wilderness by reading 'desert' as a geographic disjunction that urgently disrupts the clear continuity of national narratives in the Middle East even today, with its tensions between the unsettled and the settled, occupiers and occupied. Rather than repeat the conventional triumphalism of the preeminent biblical story of liberation, Hareven's bold intertexuality (containing traces of Exodus Numbers, Deuteronomy, Joshua, Judges) reveals the diminished ethics of contemporary nationalist politics. In many ways, *Desert Trilogy* is the preeminent example of how employing a desert aesthetic allows a shift from nation building, Zionist heroics, and the collective cause to an exploration of alternative, inclusive, and accommodating visions. Throughout, the desert is strategically deployed to suggest that neither Palestinian nor Israeli can truly be "at home" in the Land so long as racialized exclusions, violence, and dispossessions remain official policy. An eloquent humanist of the Israeli Left, Hareven casts her narratives on the side of the universal victims of conquest and war by invoking a new reading of one people's myth. As a cosmopolitan intellectual her thought reveals a certain debt to the nature of the exilic intellectual delineated in the work of the German theorist Theodor Adorno who, in *Minima Moralia*, asserts that "Dwelling, in the proper sense, is now impossible. The traditional residences we grew up in have grown intolerable. . . .

The house is past. . . .it is part of morality not to be at home in one's home" (87).

Alongside her critique of Zionism, Hareven presents a distinctly feminist intervention that provides a narrative focus that unmasks the women's and children's stories that are obscured by the patriarchal texts. Yael Feldman aptly portrays them as "these lean, poetic miniatures...nothing less than counterhistories" that present the biblical story of wandering "from a totally unfamiliar angle" (160).[2] Each of the three stories, revisiting some of the most charged dimensions of Hebraic myth, delineates different dimensions of a polytheistic desert tribe's struggle from murderous practices toward something resembling civilization. In Hareven's cultural imagination, this is by no means a triumphal or tidy evolution. Controversial aspects of nascent patriarchal leadership, the dangers of the core myths of monotheism, as well as treatment of cultural difference (just what to do with the Other?), are all part of Hareven's interpretive framework.

***

As numerous obituaries in the Hebrew and international press bore witness, Hareven was uniquely situated to address traumatic aspects of displacement. Though rarely drawing directly from her life experience as Holocaust survivor it certainly bears noting her origins and subsequent political activities. Born in Poland, she arrived in Palestine in 1940 and remained in Jerusalem for the rest of her life. After serving in the Hagana underground, she was a combat-medic in the 1947-48 siege of Jerusalem. During the fifties, Hareven worked with refugees from Arab countries in Israel's transit camps. The first female member elected to the Hebrew Language Academy, Hareven seemed prouder of her longtime membership in the Israeli Peace Now movement. The French magazine *L'Express* included Hareven on its list of 100 women "who move the world." A passionate critic of Israel's military rule over the territories, the late novelist spent time among Palestinians during the first Intifada (how the ever-mounting casualties of sucide bombers and helicopter gunships in the current conflict make the stones and broken bones of those days almost evoke nostalgia for those days!) and in her late career she remained committed to deconstructing the internal religious and ethnic divisions in Israeli life.

Accordingly, her trilogy, as it evolves, participates in the ancient Jewish midrashic tradition of retelling the sacred text in ways that creatively accommodate the shifting paradigms and perceptions of the present. In her rendering, the timeless desert becomes a fitting metaphor for human life, which is itself a hard land of exile. Hareven's richly meditative exploration of the dark and lingering power of ancient myth and language derives directly from her response to the urgent demands of the present. In the modern land of Israel/Palestine, the Hebrew Bible, much like the Koran, has been invoked to justify acts of murderous violence and dispossession, but also the dream of accommodation. Little wonder that, when alluding to Abraham, the father of

Middle-Eastern monotheism and Jewish wandering as well as the preeminent refuser of idolatry, Sidra DeKoven Ezrahi, one of Modern Hebrew literature's most innovative critics, cautions that "we dare not invest any place with absolute meaning or treat others' idols as targets for obliteration. Turning our iconoclastic hammers toward our own idols, as legend represents Abraham doing in his father's shop, may be the beginning of religious reformation; turning it towards the gods of others is the beginning of genocide" ("Sacred Space," 19-20). Hareven achieves that reconsideration of the totems of myth and history with irony, compassion, and humor without resorting to arid didacticism.

Just as it was with the Rabbi's midrashic response to the destruction of Jerusalem in the first century of the previous era, Hareven's insistence that the sacred text serve the urgent moral dilemmas of the present offers a bold response to the traumas of a reborn Jewish nation. Every Jewish child brought up with a modicum of Jewish literacy learns through the Passover liturgy that the Jews were condemned to wander the desert for forty years. Such readers will be alert to how the narrative's full title, *Thirst: A Desert Trilogy*—with its stark emphasis on the deprivation of the Jews' wilderness experience—insinuates that Hareven's ancient Hebrews live in a constant state of both physical and spiritual thirst. A disturbing exploration of the elusiveness of "Justice," *Desert Trilogy* is one of the most provocative examples of the modern Hebrew literary community's response to the troubling weight of the Bible as a living part of both the individual psyche and a collective sense of national belonging. As both Brenner and Pardes remind us, the desert of Exodus is often envisioned as the site of the Jewish people's birth as a national collective. Hareven's novel, however, seems to consider that fraught origin as a sentient landscape that wisely "teaches" a refusal of stasis, a strange realm shaping Judaism's future as a constant unfolding and adaptation to the new.

Examining her culture's conscience in "God is the Other Language," an essay of the 1990s, Hareven asserts that "There are people in this generation who have decided for some reason that the values of the Book of Joshua take precedence over the morals of Isaiah and the prophets; this is their order of primacy in keeping the commandments, and it is far from mine. In other words, their God is far from my God. According to their model, God is cruel and human beings even crueler. According to my model, very often human beings are better and have a greater sense of justice than does the God that people fashioned for themselves in ancient times" *(Vocabulary of Peace* 59). For Hareven, the Book of Joshua's grisly slaughters and conquests form the cynical palimpsest for present-day violence and the problem of the ever-threatening Other. Interestingly, Yerach Gover tells of an investigation by a social psychologist who determined that Israeli youth were so impacted by "uncritical" teachings of the Bible that they came to regard Joshua's destruction of the peoples of Jericho and Makkedah as "rationales" for the contemporary Israeli army to act vengefully against Arab villages in the aftermath of war.[3] Perhaps this is why Hareven is drawn to the open potentiality of the desert—as a blank space for meditating on the current plight of her society, indeed all "tribal" aspirations.

Hardly comfortable with the Bible's official version of events with its strong paternal images, Hareven's trilogy offers an elaborate counterhistory that nevertheless resonates with the sacred text's own representation of the friction between faith and doubt—an existential tale of the wilderness gesturing beyond temporal confines toward suppressed stories and repressed identities. Thus, far from adapting the reductive tendency of some feminist scholars—which first began to emerge in the late 1980s—to condemn the Hebrew Bible for everything from the invention of genocide to the "slaying of the goddess," Hareven proves at times a surprisingly conservative redactor, underscoring the universality of the text, especially insofar as the latter implicates injustices in the present. For here, in a highly suggestive passage from the introductory paragraphs of "The Miracle Hater," the situation presented is an unavoidable challenge to the Israeli reader:

> The Hebrews had multiplied greatly and not all of them could find work in and around Raamses. They descended on the province, innumerable flocks of men and women who stood long hours in the sun, or sat in the shade of the baked-brick walls, looking for work. The Egyptians would come, take the five or ten of them that they needed, and drive the rest off. For a while they would vanish; yet soon they were back again, mute in the fly-ridden sunlight, waiting, more of them every year. There was no getting rid of them. (*Desert Trilogy*, 7)

In this passage, Hareven's ancient Hebrews rapidly acquire a certain resemblance to the masses of the Palestinian day-workers who, in the pre-Intifada days of the trilogy's composition, would cross the Green Line daily in search of meager employment opportunities in Israel's building trades, constructing its modern pyramids in place of the Jewish labor that was no longer attracted to literally building the state. Invoking the archaic conflict over Canaan between colonizers from the desert and the colonized, Hareven reveals a pattern of disruption that hasn't changed over the centuries. Her historical perspective suggests that Zionism, whatever its moral strength and historical necessity, must be viewed as the blind reiteration of this conflict.

In her account of the functions of biblical allusions in modern Hebrew literature Smadar Shiffman argues for a hierarchy of intertextual achievement worthy of consideration here. Least of all in her rankings is the presence of biblical allusion in a way that grants "depth" but somehow diminishes the contemporary scene of the novel, "as if we and our deeds can hardly be of much significance when compared with our forefathers." Shiffman's next level of achievement identifies instances where the allusion not only "grants the novel depth and enriches it [but also] may shed a new or unexpected light upon the biblical origin." Finally, Shiffman extols those narratives in which "the biblical story could be read both as the original myth . . . and as a quite mundane human story, the regaining of which is not especially tempting" (86). Hareven provides us with a rich exemplar of this model. In *Thirst: The Desert Trilogy* she illuminates the alluding narrative, allowing this doubling to expose our own contradictory responses, whether as Israelis or others, to the pressing exiles and homelands, totalitarian deities and false prophets, which form the interwoven strata of the ancient past and our grim contemporary reality.

Hareven long perceived her culture's reliance on the reassuring category of eternal victimhood as profoundly inhibiting when it comes to cultivating empathy for Others. If one is "the sole and eternal victim," one invariably inhibits one's children from seeing "anyone who is not me" (*Vocabulary of Peace* 151). This perspective would explain her intentional ambivalence in the critical early passage of "The Miracle Hater" cited earlier. Inevitably, Hareven inhabits the unenviable position of the modern Hebrew writer who, as Eliezer Schweid contends, necessarily possesses "a double identity: identification with the Zionist realization and identification with its victims. The realization of Zionism was the hope, the salvation...the field of activity and creativity and self-realization. At the same time it was the source of injustice to the defeated-undefeated enemy, which continued to confront it" (39). The rift between divine law, the law of nature, the law of the state and the law of the individual (conscience) has of course served as an enduring provocation in world literature since at least the moment that Sophocles's *Antigone* first erupted on stage. Certainly the strain between law and justice has been a major modernist theme in Jewish literature, building on the foundations of Abraham's arguments with a wrathful God in Genesis: one thinks immediately of Franz Kafka's "The Penal Colony" and *The Trial* as well as recent works such as Philip Roth's provocative "American Trilogy." And with increasing emphasis, Israeli fiction (arguably more than any other recent national literature) has evolved as a corpus focused on the plight of the individual, caught between a dream of justice and the often draconian consequences of state law. For Hareven, even the triumph of Mosaic law over persecution is liable to succumb to a tyrannical dictatorship. Therefore, her feminist retelling of scripture affirms its universal dimensions of human liberation while at the same time, "the law" itself is unsparingly depicted as a rigid bureaucratic system, insensitive, arbitrary, often engendering injustice. The individual's conscience is trampled and ground to bits in the hands of external justice.

Throughout Hareven's three stories, the hapless individual gets into terrible trouble in the name of an established system's rules, power, and authority. In this regard her readers are confronted with something more far-reaching and enduring than a veiled meditation on the contemporary Middle-East. Feldman declares that "the damaging potential of myth had preoccupied Hareven" for many years (165). If the *Trilogy* sets forth a rewriting of the Bible, it must therefore critique some of the most central myths upon which Western culture, with all its attendant forms of cruelty and insanity, is founded. As Feldman emphasizes, readers should be aware that a short time following the appearance of "After Childhood," the conclusion to the trilogy, Hareven published an innovative critique of Freudian therapy, charging that Freud ignored a crucial patriarchal myth at the core of both culture and the individual's psyche (Feldman, 175). This of course is the *Akedah*, the Hebrew term for the near-sacrifice (and in some rabbinical sources even murder) of Isaac by Abraham.[4] Feldman refers to this as one of the central myths that "repeatedly preoccupied Hareven in her essays" (171). Considering such a forceful conviction that this is the fatal repetition of Western culture that extends into our own uncertain times, it does not seem a stretch to read Hareven's trilogy in the spirit of a challenge to that pernicious presence.[5] Indeed, a key thrust the miniature narratives share is a rigorous interrogation of the insidious ways that righteous myths, that rationalize violence, serve contemporary political realities. In this sense, Hareven is a 'traditional' modern Hebrew writer, for the metaphor of the akedah is a prominent feature of secularist Israeli literary culture. Indeed, Ruth Kartun-Blum claims that this motif "remains indisputably the most prominent and most powerful" biblical intertext of modern Hebrew literature" (20). Each generation of 20th-century Hebrew writers has told it anew. For instance, we have the Mandate-era poet Zelda (1914-1984), whose work appeals to messianic, nationalist, and liberal secular audiences alike, darkly juxtaposing the biblical nomad with her memories of a familial patriarch in "With My Grandfather": "Like our father Abraham/ who counted stars at night/who called out to his Creator/from the furnace./ who bound his own son/on the altar—/ so was my grandfather" (Schwartz 230). The poet Haim Gouri (b.1923), another foundation figure in the early years of Israeli poetry, penned a lyric "Isaac" (1960) describing Abraham's modern descendants as individuals "born with a slaughterer's knife in their heart."[6] And Aryeh Ben-Gurion, editor of a recent collection of poetry and essays on the binding of Isaac, writes "Our soul has been wearied by all those who have been killed."[7] As a whole, Hareven's work underscores that this inherent violence is the most promising—and threatening—feature of all three monotheistic religions: the father sacrificing his son (which of course includes the murder of Jesus by *his* father, God).[8]

In "The Miracle Hater," the first story of the series, we encounter the events of *Exodus* from the distant vantage of Eshkhar, a marginal shepherd who prefers the farthest outskirts of the wandering Israelites because of a fixed distrust of prophets and elders. Joining him, the reader meanders among the camps of the lesser families, suffering women, disconsolate worshippers of lost gods in the form of molten idols, and a variety of other transgressors. In Hareven's retelling it seems that their story, the "unofficial"l one, is central. The older narrative's focus on a variety of losses, the collective details of "frustration and death, thirst and hunger" (Pardes 57) is shifted to accommodate the individual's direct experience of the consequences of nation-building. Readers anticipating a loftier approach to nation building and Moses' leadership will be surprised. As a leader of the lowest classes of wanderers, Eshkar is a socially diminished, unhappy version of Moses (the latter is barely visible in this narrative). He even shares Moses' concern with justice. But here is the pivotal difference that Feldman observes: "Like Moses, Eshkhar is motivated by a quest for justice, except that in his case it is individual rather than national" (161).

Believing the woman he was destined to marry has been taken from him unjustly, Eshkar beseeches Joshua to overrule the calculating logic of arranged marriages and bride-prices.[9] But he is dismissed by the haughty leader who remarks that "We work miracles. Justice is not our concern." And that seems a succinct enough summary of the novel's own concerns. For apparently, the newly established code of abstract law is not equipped to take care of the existential fate of the alienated individual. So, not unlike a disaffected Jew of modernity, Eshkar's radically alienated wanderings take him "far" from the miraculous pillars of smoke and fire (negatively echoed and bitterly parodied as "from God there came no accounting, neither by day, nor by night, when the huge stars hung in their orbits overhead"). Wandering in solitude, his self-emancipation is slyly set against both the collective emancipatory rhetoric and the strangely prolonged epic of Exodus, Numbers, and Deuteronomy: "he knew things that they did not: that the desert was inhabited, that it had limits, that it could be crossed from end to end in a matter of weeks. The deception of miracles was keeping them purblind and lost" (51). Thinking about Eshkar, it helps to remember that in the Jewish Scriptures, the desert is a place of severe deprivation, but also a landscape of flux producing radical clarity and revelation; a formless but sublime expanse wherein the bold human imagination first conceives of divine intelligence, a revolutionary conception of a bodiless God that is without form, as this passage dating to the late seventh century B.C.E. asserts:

> The Lord spoke to you out of the fire; you heard the sound of words but perceived no shape—nothing but a voice. . ..Take care, then, not to forget the covenant that the Lord your God concluded with you and not to make for yourselves a sculptured image in any likeness, against which the Lord your God has enjoined you. For the Lord your God is a consuming fire, an impassioned God. (Deuteronomy 4:12-24)

In the penetratingly poetic language that has challenged the reach of centuries of Jewish imagination, the writer of Deuteronomy seems to proclaim that Absence is the realization of what can be.

With this paradigm of desert as site of revelation in mind, Hareven seems attentive to the fact that in later books of the Hebrew Bible the same prophet who might curse the people with the fate of the barrenness of the wilderness might also recognize it as a site of an exalted spiritual state and glance back enviously toward the forty years of wandering as a period in which the people shared a special intimacy with the deity who accompanied them. For Hareven too, the desert is a site critical to perception, distance, and imaginative change. The novelist's skepticism toward the viability of the nation-state simultaneously embraces the desert as a place where the lack of static demarcation engenders exciting readjustments and new interpretations of reality. To put it simply, her desert is where individual consciousness emerges.[10]

***

At times, Hareven's focus on her ancient characters seems complicated by her sense of the tragic dimensions of Jewish wandering in ensuing centuries. Throughout *Desert Trilogy*, the spectre of contingency and the acute vulnerability of human communities are underscored, particularly when urban space threatens to crumble into desert space. In her long unsparing view of human history, the present's complacent urban dwellers are the future's humiliated refugees: "The whole city became one great hunger of goats. . ...Soon the whole city will be a desert, cried the women. Soon it will be a wilderness. Come see the mighty citadel of Gibeon turn into a land of jackals" (77). The fated dissolution of a people in the maw of a surrounding wilderness is a tangible threat. Eventually, adding to Eshkar's own doubling of Moses, the shepherd and his fellows form what Feldman insightfully identifies as a parallel universe on the outskirts of the main camp: "complete with a popular leadership" and a sort of "mock shadow government" whose guiding principle seems to be the "avoidance of miracles" (*No Room of Their Own*, 161). At such moments, in imagining the existential exile of Eshkhar and his confederates, Hareven transports the reader via rueful, often darkly comic, reverberations of the biblical text, though as if through a distorted lens:

> Eshkhar asked what they would do if the people did not let them go. We shall have to wait and see what we do then, said Aviel uncertainly. Though Yakhin says that we will smite them. . ..If the people do not let us go, said his perfectly still eyes to Eshkhar, then they are a people of slaves and will be cut down just as he was. Did you not see for yourself how easy it was to kill? (45)

In her sly reversals and inversions of the Bible's liberatory rhetoric, Hareven casts the problem of the individual's role in a new light. The problem with divine miracles seems always that, for the sake of epic destiny, they ignore the lived experience of the first generation doomed to be killed off in the wilderness, particularly the quotidian plight of women.

In the original text, though a variety of women (midwives, wives, mothers, daughters) prove to be wise and resourceful agents whose humane interventions (disobeying Pharaoh's edict to slay all male babies) ensure that Moses will survive to liberate his people—these women's voices are almost obliterated from the text. In this regard, it is important to appreciate how, while reexamining the text's ethical potential to bear on present realities, Hareven's trilogy constitutes one of the boldest exemplars of a feminist critique of the Hebrew Bible's silencing of women. For example, as Brenner argues, in spite of the fact that the ancient text's androcentric ideology works "through the rationale that female nurturing capacities are indispensable to individuals, society and nation" after the domestic/reproductive agenda is fulfilled, the accompanying gender politics "wisk them off [the stage] at once in order to make place for the 'real' figures of *history*—the fathers" (13). Perhaps for that reason, Hareven's female characters have no consciousness of dwelling in an incomplete present, nor is the awaiting land their exclusive orientation.

An investigation of how Hareven's gender politics is formulated in relation to the biblical text may be further strengthened by considering Judith Butler's notion of the male body configured through its exclusions, which, not surprisingly, Butler derives from a similarly ancient Western discourse: "Plato's scenography of intelligibility depends upon the exclusion of women, slaves, children. . ..This domain of the less than rational human bounds the figure of human reason, producing that 'man'. . .This is a figure of disembodiment, but one which is nevertheless a figure of a body, a bodying forth of a masculinized rationality, the figure of a male body which is not a body. . ..This figuration of masculine reason as disembodied body is one whose imaginary morphology is crafted through the exclusion of other possible bodies" (*Bodies that Matter*, 48-49). When considering this ancient Greek/Hebraic topography of exclusions, one appreciates just what is gained by Hareven's dark recasting of the miraculous bringing forth of waters in Numbers 20:10.

> In all this commotion the two women were unable to reach it.
> Duress had overcome them and left them too weak to fight. In any
> case, their babies were no longer alive. Moses and his escort passed
> by without seeing them. Hopelessly, they stood staring at the wall of
> flowing water and at the hideous, fatal fracas taking place there. The
> infants' arms dangled earthward, obviously dead. (38)

Eventually, the two women join a nomadic group of those who feel their interests are neglected by the priestly officials, headed by Eshkhar and his friend Aviel and accompanied by Aviel's sister Yona whose leadership mirrors the official "Moses-Aharon-Miriam triad," which Feldman calls a "kind of mock shadow government."[11] In discerning an alternative story beneath the surface of the text, Hareven joins her characters' refusal to align themselves with the narratorial "we"—as if to provide a secure existential dwelling place for the disloyal and the "unfaithful" secular reader more at home with the unprecedented autonomy of the 21st century than with traditional obedience. Deeply mindful of having left the Egyptian "House of Bondage," the trio's mundane struggle toward independence from both the collective fate decreed by a vengeful desert deity and the cattle-like collectivity of "the people" ruefully echoes Moses' fiery rhetoric before Pharoah: "Eshkhar asked what they would do if the people did not let them go . . . Yakhin says that we will smite them . . . If the people do not let us go" (45). And so on.

Growing up in Israel, fully acquainted with the traditional Jewish canon, Hareven composed her narratives out of an acute awareness that Moses is not mentioned—except once in a very modest way—in the *Haggadah* that Jews read at the Passover celebration of the Exodus. Some rabbis have speculated that this omission discouraged hero worship. In this light it does seem significant that, rather than offer a legendary figure who would conform to a model of a Spielberg or De Mille epic-heroic scale, Hareven consciously strives to keep her Jewish hero within these perversely diminished proportions. It is exciting to explore how Hareven's distrust of the power guiding the patriarchal staff—quite congruent with Judaism's refusal to lionize Moses or any other human being—attains even greater significance when set against a feminist critique of Zionism she voiced elsewhere. Feldman describes how in Hareven's 1974 essay "Fraternal or Filial Society?" the author already expressed concern over the paternalistic role and greatly magnified status of Israel's political leaders, such as David Ben Gurion and Moshe Dayan (perhaps today one might add Ariel Sharon), claiming that their "big daddy image" conditions the "sons" to be dependent, thoughtless, and to shirk personal responsibility.[12] From the early pages of "The Miracle Hater," and throughout her *Trilogy*, Hareven strategically distances the reader from the consolation of fascism's 'great leader' paradigm—insinuating an ominous equation between the childlike people's reliance on the miraculous and the contemporary Israeli acquiescence to the violence of the state.[13] Though she never dwelled on it, the fact that the author arrived in Palestine as a child refugee from Poland sheds additional light on the issues of power and vulnerability that resonate in such a sustained way throughout her essays and fiction.

In spite of its trajectory of dissent, Hareven's reading of the biblical source is neither reductive nor consistently antagonistic. For in yet another essay, "Against Charisma," she warns that "the first things that get lost in charismatic leadership are facts," since the people are not interested in assessing reality but rather in achieving a "giddy symbiosis with their leader" such as occurred in Hitler's Germany (which created her own displacement as a child). Here she pays affectionate tribute to the biblical Moses as the archetypal anti-charismatic personality, "the most humble of men, a stutterer, inelegant of speech, who needed an interpreter; a man with whom the people were most certainly not enthralled, calling him 'that man Moses,' barely accepting his rule over them" (*Vocabulary of Peace* 201). Hareven notices that Moses' thankless task is to wean the people away from their yearnings for the idolatrous past to embrace historically revolutionary ethics. As biblical scholars such as Pardes aptly observe of Deuteronomy, "the entire period of wandering" is "an initiatory voyage" into true individualism. The latter is a condition that transforms slaves into "active participants who. . .may fashion new social models while questioning the validity of the sacred corpus that is passed down to them" (Pardes, 68-69). In a highly compatible spirit, Hareven asserts that "the charismatic leader destroys the boundaries of the ego in his mythic relationship with the public: I am you and you are me" until "norms vanish and obedience to the law becomes unimportant. . . .the charismatic leader trades in amorphous myths, before the existence of law and democratic organization" (*Vocabulary of Peace*, 204). The lesson to be gleaned for all societies in crisis is that "mythology prevents real confrontation with the regime because it creates a situation of no doubts." And, since left alone, "myths inhibit change" (204), the artist's vigilant re-creation and retelling are required in each generation.

In his innovative study of the controversial "Post-Zionist" debates that have flared in Israel in recent years (its voices have subsided somewhat since the outbreak of the Al-Aqsa Intifada), Laurence Silberstein argues that "the binarism of homeland/exile is central to Zionism" (20). He argues that this stark opposition has engendered further ostensibly irreconcilable (and stagnating) polarities:

> Homeland as a source of security, stability, refuge, nurturing, safety/exile as site of danger, insecurity, instability, threat, anxiety; *heimlich/unheimlich*; homeland is good/exile is bad; homeland is productive/exile is parasitic; homeland is conducive/exile is not conducive to redemption through labor; homeland is welcoming/exile is hostile; homeland is life-giving/exile is life-threatening; homeland is creative/exile is stultifying; homeland is nurturing to Jewish national culture/exile is destructive; homeland is unifying/exile is fragmenting. (22-23)

Well aware of the intrinsic contribution this series makes to her nation's myths and identity, Hareven writes as if the desert, as both diaspora space and corridor toward reterritorialization, fatally scrambles and disrupts the certitude of the binary oppositions Silberstein describes. Even her Moses embodies the author's paradigmatic indifference to national coherence, inhabiting a divided consciousness, a torn ego haplessly divided against itself: "Some said that he had two hearts in his breast, one Hebrew and one Egyptian, and that he had murdered the Egyptian one so as to leave no trace of it" (11).[14] And for his pragmatic followers, it is telling that they know *nothing* of a divinely sanctioned "Promised Land," and strive only to return to an "ancestral" haven or refuge. One of the most provocative of her polemics, which addresses the contemporary resonance of the Mosaic laws, asks rhetorically:

> To which commandments would I give primacy today? What oppressed us in previous generations and threatens to oppress us today is the patriarchal establishment, which contains hierarchies,

holds ceremonies, and sanctifies the past. Like every patriarchal establishment, it foments feelings of ownership, of nationalism, of condescension toward anyone who is not like me, as well as fanaticism. I prefer the commandments that are based on personal righteousness and doing justice—that is, everything concerning the dynamic between people—over every commandment dealing with place and land and ownership. Every time the group that calls itself 'The Temple Mount Faithful'—the very designation smacks of idol worship—goes up to rant and rave on the mount, to pray there and to fan the flames of hostility and discord and hatred, I want to shout in their ears: "When ye come to appear in my presence—who hath required this of ye, to tread down my courts?. . .incense of abomination it is unto me. . . . Yea, when ye make many prayers, I will not hear; your hands are full of blood. . ..Cease to do evil; learn to do well; seek justice, relieve the oppressed, do justice for the fatherless, plead for the widow.' Are any words clearer than these? 'Do justice for the fatherless and plead for the widow,' even if they are not of the people of Israel. One justice for the stranger and the dweller. (*Vocabulary of Peace* 59)

Outraged by Jewish fundamentalism's failure to understand the revolutionary spirit of the prophetic text, Hareven's insistence on a just Middle-East has a rich corollary in her backward glance at the ancient Hebrews.

"Prophet," the second novella, revisits the sanctified violence of Joshua 9. Hareven craftily places readers this time in the walled city of Gibeon (rather than the camps of the Hebrews), where they experience events through the woeful perspective of Hivai, a Gibeonite seer staggered by the apocalyptic events that engulf him and his society. Feldman declares that "For the Hebrew, or any biblically literate reader, the crucial reversal of narrative perspective is signaled by the mournful Gibeonites' dire phrase 'It was from the east, from the desert, that evil would come' (Feldman, 163, Hareven 66) which reads as a direct inversion of Jeremiah's famous prophetic dictum in Jeremiah 1:14: "From north evil shall come." In this regard, Stanley Nash's view is useful: Hareven consistently "stresses the need for anthropological breadth to endow . . . Israeli[s] with 'the primary capability of accepting [that] which is different from [them] as a fundamental equal'" (223).[15] Even more to the point, Feldman asserts that, beyond merely thinking about the Semitic Other in the abstract, Hareven effectively places the Israeli reader "in the uncomfortable position of reading about *themselves* (at least in the generic sense—biblical ancestry being an integral part of Israeli identity) as the *Other* (164). Feldman further explains that it is intrinsic to Hareven's narrative strategy that "readers are expected to constantly shift perspectives if they want to 'get into' the narrative. This is especially true of the second novella. While in the first we are still within the Israelite camp...in ["Prophet"] we are asked to step into the shoes of an utterly other" (*No Room of Their Own*, 161). Moreover, as a particularly menacing, threatening entity, the very rumor of whose approach is capable of annihilating everything sacred to a once-complacent people, whose city has not seen war "since the days of their great-grandfathers" (73). The narrative's tone grows ominous in just a few deft phrases: "the ways of the world began to turn upside down about one hour after sunrise," and the "whole apprehensively lowing swarm of life" flees its proper dwelling place in the countryside for the habitation of humans. This was once a haughty site of security: "No one had threatened Gibeon for ages. It was a city as large as a royal capital and it had forgotten what fear was like" (66-67). But now it is stricken by dread. Hareven's apocalyptic imagery of the material privations and cultural decline endured by the Gibeonites dexterously draws the reader into a scene of desolation whose timeless and melancholy resonance rings all too universally:

> Longingly they watched the fruit in the valley rot on the trees, dropping to be eaten by great clouds of raucous birds that arrived with the eastward-racing clouds...With the autumn breeze came the smell of rotted grapes, as heady as wine, and the fierce, sweet, cloying odor of ripe figs. Summer was over. The city was barricaded tight. Large jars of olive oil stood against the walls and all the storerooms were full of lentils and beans. And yet people stared at the full jars and sacks as if looking right through them. There will be hunger, they said, it isn't far off. (76)

Provoked by fear of a future that Hivai can no longer prophesy, the community's widening existential crisis ironically resembles the condition, and self-perpetuating rationales, of a certain embattled middle-eastern state: "Of course there was no justice in the city. How could justice be dispensed when the enemy was at the gate?" (79).

***

With much justification, Israelis and other readers attuned to the problem of nationalist violence are likely to read the Book of Joshua as a disturbingly affirmative representation of the execution of an ancient program of ethnic cleansing, which appears to be prescribed by divine agency. The program is accomplished through a war of conquest, in which difference of religion and ethnicity seem to constitute a sanction for annihilation. For many readers after a century of violence sanctified by state, ethnicity, or religion, Joshua is a grim tale that would seem to have little consolation to offer the present (excepting for the messianic politics of the Right). It might profitably be read as a mirror of our own atrocities. The story seems as relentlessly ugly and violent as the latest headlines from the Palestinian-Israeli conflagration. Yet as Hareven is clearly aware, Joshua is also a text configured by contradiction and ambivalence in ways that might just as easily inspire the writer's ethical response to contemporary crisis. "Prophet" gestures especially to the campaigns conducted in Jericho, Ai, and against the five kings at Gibeon. In the stories of Rahab and the Gibeonites, Israel not only accommodates outsiders but punishes an insider for the crime of appropriating Canaanite plunder. What Hareven undoubtedly noticed about these transformations is that they seem to undermine or blur the boundaries articulated by the Deuteronomic code: the stories of Rahab and the Gibeonites argue for flexibility in the determination of Israel's internal boundaries. "Prophet" imaginatively draws from the Scripture's commemoration of singular moments in which the inhabitants of Canaan approach Israelites and succeed in securing an exemption from destruction.

Ostensibly, the scriptural text is preoccupied with group survival, which requires the coherence and maintenance of internal boundaries at any cost. A careful reading reveals another current, one that seems to argue for moderation, seeing Israel as only one of several disparate peoples who inhabit the land ostensibly reserved for them. It is as if the ancient narrative energy of the Biblical text itself resists the imposition of inflexible idealism, so that we are not only left with a certain ambivalence regarding Israel's identity and relationship to other peoples of Canaan but also what we might call a resistance to the official narrative of Deuteronomy. Perhaps the most representative example of the latter's teleological thrust is articulated in these stark terms: *when you have driven them out and settled in their land, and after they have been destroyed before you, be careful not to be ensnared by inquiring about their gods* (Deut. 12:29-31).

In various ways, the Deuteronomic Code prescribes the preservation of the boundaries that distinguish Israel from the other peoples of Canaan. The social environment encoded in Deuteronomy clearly reflects a great deal of internal anxiety and vulnerability. The *b'nei Yisrael* will certainly enter a land inhabited by others more numerous and powerful than themselves. However, the true threat posed by the indigenous inhabitants is not their imposing cities or great stature (which can be neutralized by divine might) but rather through their *difference*. Israel's perceived vulnerability to the power of difference finds expression in Moses' directives: the people of Israel must vanquish and overcome the "seven nations," while ensuring that they do not associate or intermarry with them in the process.

So if the Book of Joshua may be read as Israel's evolving confrontation with difference, it is interesting that one of the key retellings in Hareven's narrative concerns the *bnei Yisrael's* encounter with the Gibeonites, no doubt because it *reverses* certain aspects of the conventional scheme I just outlined. Now in his mid-forties, Hivai, the failed prophet (or rather seer in the Hebraic sense, since he merely predicts the future rather than critiques society [Feldman, 159]), enjoys a few brilliant but ultimately ephemeral flashes of insight. Ruefully pondering his four past it seems that "his life had the plodding gait of an ox that walks the straight furrow of time from the Was to the Will-be" (69) and sees in his waning powers of prophecy and his culture's impending catastrophe an opportunity for self-liberation. After making one final futile gesture to his old belief system, the sacrifice of "a small slave child," Hivai fatally misreads the future in the child's entrails, later discovering to his horror that he has inadvertently caused the destruction of his own beloved daughter as well. Intriguingly, Feldman considers the grotesque consequences of Hivai's "prophet's block" (163), as a likely reverberation of the novelist's indictment of the moral paralysis of her own culture. Through such devices Hareven boldly underscores her timeless message that the mythic template that still underlies human belief systems remains a dangerously pernicious presence.

Weary of failure, the hapless seer abandons his people to dwell among the Hebrews. Newly arrived from the desert flatlands, the latter are a strangely uncultivated people who seem to dwell in the future, so ill-equipped to cope with their new surroundings that at first Hivai is persuaded that they will soon disappear from the landscape:

> Why, they were like newborn babes in this mountain land, they
> and their god together. . .Their god was not of this country, neither
> bone of its bone nor flesh of its flesh...soon the Hebrew god would
> flee back to the desert he had come from and show his face no more
> in the land of men. And the invaders would flee with him, like chaff
> before the wind: from the desert they had come and to the desert they
> would return. No one would remember them or their god. (96)

But as time passes the strangers remain an obdurate presence and Hivai reluctantly elects to sojourn among them: "He knew he could not stay in this place, yet he had nowhere to go. He was neither Gibeonite nor Hebrew...an outcast in the mountains, with nowhere to return to, no people, no city, no god" (119). For their part, Hivai's acquired hybridity troubles the Hebrews. Is the seer a "convert" or is he merely Other, and hence a polluting presence? Hareven is clearly fascinated by the Torah's infatuation with the fraught relation between the unassimilated Other and the threshold of national adulthood as the Hebrews inherit Canaan. Is it possible to accommodate the alien and still serve God by "dwelling apart"?

Besides succeeding as a profoundly moving meditation on the nature of insider-outsider consciousness as an ancient, rather than exclusively modern, phenomenon, "Prophet" responds to another pressing dynamic that, though unspoken, nevertheless haunts the original text. It is as though, as long as the people of the land remain faceless or voiceless, the ethic of extermination may be fulfilled without compunction. The Book of Joshua, though, underscores the danger involved in intimate, quotidian contact with the people of the land, for recognizing the humanity of others would appear to make killing them a more dismal prospect. Hareven reads her desert sojourners through Exodus and Deuteronomy's representations of the unsettling transformation of Canaanites from Others into marginal Israelites in ways that trouble the present. "Prophet" challenges the exclusivistic boundaries set out in Deuteronomy, ultimately expanding those boundaries to address the current tensions between contemporary claimants to the land of Israel/Palestine as well as such ambivalences as the "Arab-Israeli" vs. the "Palestinian" or the Jewish Arab vs. the dominant culture. As a whole, her project provokes as a reexamination of Zionist ethics. For instance, though the Hebrews tolerate Hivai, who labors tirelessly for the strangers from the eastern deserts, it is a utilitarian relation at best:

> They thanked him with a rough pat on the shoulder and forgot
> him the moment they left him, as though he himself were but another
> of their tools... Not once had he failed them, not for a moment had he
> left the camp or stopped cutting wood, fetching water, and faithfully
> doing his chores. And still he was as much an outsider as ever. (109)

At such temporally ambiguous moments as this, it seems clear that the wilderness, the most liminal geography on the Jewish map of the world, remains the most apt landscape for a Hebrew writer who, without betraying the justice of the Zionist cause, to plead for the rights of minorities.[16] Perhaps it may *also* be the best way of addressing the exilic or liminal condition of being a Jewish woman in a martial state. In the end it is perhaps less ironic than fitting that Hareven employs the Exodus narrative, the Bible's greatest argument for freedom and liberation, to question the modern assumption of the power of territorial redemption. Hareven's ambivalence in relation to Exodus's official narrative of homecomings, indeed the prospects for reading *Trilogy* as an allegorical commentary on contemporary Israeli society, seems linked to her sober awareness of her culture's deep melancholy: "A recent study that examined the causes of emigration came up with a finding that surprised many Israelis, particularly those who perfunctorily cite 'security, army, reserve duty' as the prime causes of tension. It emerged that so-called security tension was very low on the scale of the causes of emigration. The highest places were occupied by feelings of disappointment and frustration, defined as dissatisfaction with and a sense of not belonging to Israeli society, a feeling that they had not found their place, an inability to influence events—all social causes par excellence" (*Vocabulary of Peace* 123). Throughout her writings Hareven is mindful of the unfortunate divide that often prevents the individual from identifying with the wish-fulfillment of the mythic collective.

Hareven's bold narrative focus on the marginal affairs of women or the otherwise powerless within the grand design of a mass movement orchestrated by a remote God seems to put into question the prospect of a genuine homecoming for those forced to linger on the margins of the official story. Moreover, the very prospect of arrival seems to be greeted with a marked degree of ambivalence by Hareven's Hebrews: "Some said it was foolish to work the land. They were a people of shepherds, and shepherds they would always be, wandering untrammeled from place to place with their flocks. . . . Their birthplace was the desert, stone houses were not for them; they and their children were meant for mats and booths, free to come and go as they pleased" (107). Hareven's portrayal of the lingering traces of a desert zeitgeist in her characters is usefully compared to Berger's speculation that, in encountering permanent (which he calls "customary" nomads, the Israelites might have seen the "ideal condition" strived for by those "who wish to avoid being taken over by the land they take over" ("The Lie of the Land" 135). For Hareven, Mosaic wandering inhabits a liminal space between the triumphal fulfillment of conquest and the painful deferment of a dream.

Perhaps such precarious habitation is as William Pinar suggests: "Living on the margins may be dangerous but at least you can breathe there" (28). For in "Prophet," though years after their arrival in the destined homeland, having reluctantly begun to move into crude stone shelters and perhaps somewhat saddened to find themselves suddenly bound to agricultural and natural cycles, the people remain as existentially unsettled as dry leaves, for "sometimes hot and fierce, a desert wind blew through the camp, they would stand for a moment gazing silently eastward, breathing the wind in deeply, with endless longing" (108). At such moments, one senses an unsettled undercurrent of melancholy diasporism in *Desert Trilogy*, a nostalgia for a morally unblemished exile that resists the triumphal Zionist assumptions about destined homeland and territory that continue to underscore the works of many of her literary peers even on the Zionist left.

Hivai, now an old man with a hard-won share of modest wisdom, no longer bears the burden of prognosticating the national destiny of the Gibeonites, remains content that his prophetic powers, though rejuventated, are limited to the quotidian and daily practical exigency rather than the collective, or epic: "He knew when it would rain on the mountains...he knew which date palm would would bear the first fruit, and what he would find when he opened his traps, a lizard, mouse, or jackal cub. They pleased him, these prophecies, like small, humble blessings" (126). In a similar spirit both the title and spare plot of "After Childhood," the conclusion to the trilogy, suggests a plea for a transcendence of the violent biblical reality, urgently underscoring the need to discover post-exilic arts of living in the present that transcend all forms of violent martyrdom.

Both textually and geographically, Hareven's vision embodies Trinh Min-ha's evocative call for a postcolonial feminism that serves as "a permanent sojourner walking bare-footed on multiply de/re-territorialized land" (334). The quiet community depicted in "Prophet" seems committed to remain on the outskirts of the violent nationalist conquest of the Land which Joshua undertakes, content to eke out a quiet existence in the dry lands of the Negev, a quotidian preoccupation with goats and desert wells, as if yearning to preserve something of the pristine wilderness experience.

In the final story, "After Childhood," Salu, a youth from the remote settlement grows up with the grim knowledge that his father tried to sacrifice him to settle accounts with God: "ever since then his eyes blinked rapidly, as if fending off a strong light" (131). Again Hareven riffs on the persistent mythic wound of the *Akedah* to great effect. The villagers are embarrassed by the atavistic presence among them, by the living parody of the old stories: "A mad dog, a dreamer, they said about Salu's father, today every flea says I'm Abraham...They spat as if to get rid of an unclean taste" (134). Eventually, Salu's narrative reverses that of Hivai's position in "Prophet," for, as an adult, his father's madness causes his tribe to shun him.

A wayfarer for many years, Salu eventually settles among a community of other Semites, the Hittites, who, as he learns their language and ways, tolerate his alterity: "The blinkard, they called him. As if his twitch had made him tribeless, they had long ago stopped thinking of him as a Hebrew" (158). Thus, *Trilogy* concludes much as it began, with a peripatetic character lingering just outside of the nation, on the margins of the official story of homecoming. As an adult (embodying Hareven's sense of these recalcitrant Hebrews' enlarged consciousness), the desert dweller marries Moran, a visionary woman from the mountains who insists that they live out their lives on the fringes of the power-struggles of pre-monarchical Israel. Consoled by the enigmatic but inveterate voice of the desert, Moran savors "the warm air stroking her face as if the whole strong wilderness were breathing close to her, quiet and warm" (186). Hareven's desert, not unlike her sense of the Bible itself, always teases the individual toward eternal paradigms beyond the false gods of their cultures, though sometimes that beckoning leaves them stranded in cultural isolation.

***

For some readers, undoubtedly the question still begs: just why should this particular ancient, hoary story disturb those who inhabit redeemed space? Why recycle it? Perhaps Hareven's motives become clearest when juxtaposed with a striking statement made in the conclusion of a lecture she delivered to graduates of the Hebrew University in June of 1990:

> All of us in all generations were, are, and will be present at Mount Sinai—not Sinai as a sound-and-light production or a single pyrotechnical happening, a spiritual stock exchange in which those who were present gained and those who were absent, or not yet born, lost. Not even Sinai as territory, which may be ours today and under the rule of others tomorrow. In the Sinai of knowledge there is room for all of us, friends and enemies, opponents and admirers, all of us who populate the earth, without any limitation at all, in a different ecology yet unknown to us in most other fields. Perhaps, very slowly, we shall come to know it. (*Vocabulary of Peace*, 78)

Inhabiting the fraught contemporary world of identity politics—rightly recognizing that we define ourselves not only by virtue of who we are, but by who we are not—biblical scholars and readers have been forced to grapple in recent years with the troubling dimensions (with their contemporary resonances) of becoming Hebrews and not Egyptians; Israelites and not Canaanites; the destiny of *am-segulah*, the "chosen people," vs. the *goyim asher lo-y'da-ucha*, "those people who do not know you," the one, true God. In our age of unredeemed territorial conflict, many somberly conclude that this post-desert legacy has led to exclusive claims to land, to boundaries drawn in blood, and even to sanctioned acts of violence, including genocide, against the Other. In her controversial study, *The Curse of Cain*, Regina Schwartz bleakly concludes that the ideology that predominates the ancient text is "agonistic," one in which a sense of unique identity or social memory is consistently developed against or antagonistic to another person or religion or nation.[17]

Hareven's view embraces this troubled reading while at the same time manages to offer a more nuanced view. Her stories affirm that few paradigms are ever exclusively or intrinsically adhered to in the Hebrew Bible, a corpus woven from many different sources and periods.[18] Too, it is worth remembering that Hareven's trilogy is creatively bound up as much with the biblical language of origins as it is with a daily language increasingly inflected by violent realities. For if *Thirst: The Desert Trilogy* is a cautionary tale of the dangers present when we create identities agonistically, by violently stressing the difference between ourselves and those we label as the "other," the *Trilogy* also succeeds by offering a generous reading of the Hebrew Bible's own complex ethical currents. Hareven seems to demand that contemporary readers recognize that postmodern ambivalences over identity, the coherence of the nation, the sanctity of territory vs. human life, are already woven into the strangely rich fabric of the ancient Bible. As Pardes has long argued, while patriarchy reigns in many of its individual texts, the Hebrew Bible also contains significant counter-traditions that do not support the "monotheistic repression of femininity" (Reinhartz, 47). Knowing that she inherits the Bible's weighty burden of language, Hareven is never free "intertextually"—she can never invent a new liberatory language out of nothing. Instead, she toils, patching together fragments of the Bible's contradictory and multiple strands to respond to the urgent needs of the present. In developing these stories, Hareven strived to ameliorate the encoded tribalism of liberation, to ensure that the prophetic message of the sacred texts was restated in the most inclusive terms possible. Ultimately however, it is the desert vision of Numbers itself, promising a just allocation of territory for the land's inhabitants, that provides the foundation for her own vision: "Unto these the land shall be divided for an inheritance according to the number of names. To many thou shalt give the less inheritance: to every one shall his inheritance be given according to those that were numbered of him" (Num. 26: 53-54). A peaceful and just dwelling is prescribed here. Yet, embracing a skeptical perspective on the national narrative, embracing transience over stasis, Hareven participates in a global feminist literary paradigm of doubt.

Kerstin Shands evocatively describes such an ethos as a "hypertransgressive contemporary feminism" in which "stillness, home, rest, and refuge...are left behind by impatient and incessant movement" (10). Dispersal from the linear absolutes of the male canon of conquest into the nude and forlorn landscape reveals more fully both contemporary reality and what we might still aspire to become.

Demonstrating how an Israeli novelist might combine an unequivocal commitment to the Jewish State with a prophetic zeal for peace and social justice, Hareven nevertheless occupied a challenging position in a deeply threatening Middle East beset by dangerous fundamentalisms on all sides. Throughout her life, her work expressed the spirit of the renowned cultural historian Yael Zerubavel's view that "the collapse of historical time into a mythical temporal framework . . . poses its own danger of obscuring historical distinctions and the need for a more critical attitude toward the examination of current historical developments." (128). For the Israeli concerned with the ethically fraught nexus of national space and peoplehood, the Hebrew Bible, particularly Exodus with its epic narrative of exile and homecoming, will always cast its shadow over the present conflict. But the sacred text also offers a rich language for narrating the dilemmas and uncertainties of dwelling in a contemporary space that is also an ancient site of painfully similar conflicts.

Hareven's three desert meditations, bridging past and present, remind us that those who wandered out of Egypt, including Moses, perished in the desert ("For the Lord had said of them, They shall surely die in the wilderness" [Num. 26: 65]) and it was a new generation born in the wilderness who God deemed worthy to enter the land. Each story offers a synecdochic portrait of the national scene, and the news is in many ways grim. One can only hope that those of us shattered by the despair of appalling violence, the desolate wilderness of inhumane relations between Israelis and Palestinians, will somehow endure long enough to emerge blinking from our age's idolatrous territorial fantasies and witness a new generation come forth to deliver a fresh beginning and open up all of our horizons once again. I suspect that for many readers, Hareven's indirect biblical commentary—juxtaposing exilic ambivalence with a feminist reading strategy—will emerge as a benevolent alternative to losses incurred by Zionist "security" on Jews and Palestinians alike.

In the contemporary situation of Israel and Palestine one might wonder about a modern Hebrew text that so stresses the desert experience as the necessary narrative of the moment, antithetical to myths of territorial possessiveness. Still, while Hareven's novel clearly appeals directly to contemporary Israelis, who may still be "purblind and lost"—whether haplessly intoxicated with the imperative of regained soil and place or simply benumbed after the centuries of wandering that culminated in the European Holocaust—her work may be profitably read by all readers not to endow any place or "truth" with a value that obscures the sanctity of human life.

NOTES

    1. This creative and spiritual problem was anticipated as early as 1926. In Gershom Scholem's darkly candid assessment in a letter to Franz Rosenzweig regarding the renewal and secularization of Hebrew: "The Land is a volcano, and it hosts the language...[But] what will be the result of updating the Hebrew language? Is not the holy language, which we have planted among our children, an abyss that must open up? People here do not know the meaning of what they have done. They think they have made Hebrew into a secular language and that they have removed its apocalyptic sting, but it is not so...All those words which were not created arbitrarily...but were taken from the good old lexicon, are filled to the brim with explosive meaning...God cannot remain silent in a language in which He has been evoked thousands of times to return to our life....Would that the lightness of mind which guided us on this apocalyptic path not lead us to destruction" ("Reflections on Our Language" 27-29).

    2. This discussion is greatly indebted to many of the insights Yael Feldman develops in her rich reading of the "psychopolitics" of *Thirst: The Desert Trilogy* which appears in her groundbreaking study, *No Room of Their Own: Gender and Nation in Israeli Women's Fiction* (Columbia UP, 1999): 159-176. Her discussion is the most comprehensive of this and other Hareven works to date, especially valuable for its analysis of Hareven's critical reception in Israel as well as the novelist's early career. Feldman, whose work has guided me a great deal, tells me that she feels that Hareven saw herself as staunchly "Zionist"; nevertheless my own discussion emphasizes the ways her narrative might be put in dialogue with post-Zionism's questionings of identity and territorial justice.

    3. One of the questions of the study reads as follows "Suppose that the Israeli army conquers an Arab village in battle. Do you think it would be good or bad to act toward the inhabitants as Joshua did toward the people of Jericho and Makkedah?" Among other conclusions, the study noted that "the overestimation of statehood as a supreme value and the idea that assimilation is the greatest evil, and the influences of militaristic values in ideological education, are further sources of discriminatory tendencies." See Yerach Gover, *Zionism: the Limits of Moral Discourse*, 5-6.

    4. See Feldman's analysis of the trope of the akedah as it evolved in both Hareven's oeuvre and Israeli culture, 170-76.

    5. For a recent novelistic retelling whose vision often seems commensurate with Hareven's sense of Abraham's family as a paradigm of spiritual and political dysfunction, see the Cambridge-based author Jenny Diski's *After These Things* (Little Brown, 2004).

    6. The final two stanzas read:

Isaac, as the story goes, was not sacrificed
He had a long life, saw what pleasure had to offer,
until his eyes went dark.

But that hour
he bequeathed to his descendants
who are born

with a knife
in the heart.

My translation is a reworking of Naomi Tauber and Howard Schwartz's version in *Voices Within the Ark: The Modern Jewish Poets*, edited by Howard Schwartz and Anthony Rudolf (New York: Avon Books, 1980), 98.

      7. In *Al tishlakh yadkha el hanaar: Shirim vedivrei hagut al haakeda* (Lay not thine hand upon the lad: poetry and essays on the binding of Isaac), edited by Aryeh Ben-Gurion. Tel Aviv: Keter Publishing House, 2002. The anthology opens with Haim Be'er's essay "The Fire and the Wood" which describes the *akedah* as the deepest infrastructural paradigm of life and literature in Israel, illuminating its resonance through echoing traces of phrases such as "Lay not thine hand upon..." and "the fire and the wood." Be'er characterizes these as the akedah's "eternal DNA coils."

      8. Another memorable re-creation of the Genesis tale of the Binding of Isaac may be found in Amos Oz's early short story about a passionate kibbutz patriarch and a son whose eagerness to satisfy his father's ambitious plans for the Day of Independence leads to his spectacularly horrific demise. "The Way of the Wind," *Where the Jackals Howl and Other Stories*. Trans. Nicholas de Lange and Philip Simpson (New York: Harcourt, 1981).

      9. Later succeeding Moses as the leader of the people, Joshua, together with Caleb, is the only leader out of the twelve representatives sent by Moses to explore the Promised Land, to advocate the conquest of the land. See Num. 13.

      10. Though I am speaking here of contemporary Hebrew literature, it is noteworthy that in other noteworthy novels, such as Paul Bowles' *The Sheltering Sky* or Michael Ondaatje's *The English Patient*, the desert landscape is subject to continual change, flux, and erosion in ways that urgently underscore their characters' inner revelations and adjustments to new realities.
Notably, these texts share the anti-nationalistic tendencies of Hareven's politically inflected midrash.

      11. In contrasting a feminist perspective on the biblical text Hareven is undoubtedly thinking of the harsh treatment of Moses' sister-prophetess. In Exodus, God punishes Miriam with leprosy for challenging her brother's authority, leading to her being quarantined outside the official camp of the Israelites. For many feminist biblical readers this is highly suggestive of an inherently androcentric ideology, where
"Women are at the boundary of the symbolic order, the border between men and chaos. As borderline figures, women partake of the properties of a border: they are neither inside nor outside" (Brenner 86). I would also argue that it is precisely such indeterminacy that inspires Hareven to articulate a feminist politics/poetics of wandering, and insider-outsider dwelling; these sustain a critique of both the origins of her tradition's gender biases and the symbolic male order of the violent present.

      12. It is surprisingly useful to consider Hareven alongside Gertrude Stein who, after returning from her thirty-one year sojourn in France, thought she recognized the germ of European-style dictatorship tactics in the America of the Depression: "There is too much fathering going on now...Everybody nowadays is a father, there is father Mussolini and father Hitler and father Roosevelt and father Stalin and father Lewis and father Blum and father Franco is just commencing now and there are ever so many more ready to be one. Fathers are depressing....I say fathers are depressing any father who is a father and there are far too many fathers now existing. The periods of the world's history

that have always been most dismal ones are the ones where fathers were looming and filling up everything" (quoted in Carson, 53).

13.	Hareven's critique might be considered alongside Amos Oz's troubled reflections some years ago on the legendary Moshe Dayan: "the charms of death inspire Dayan....one glimpses a poetical, romantic lust for death which I would gladly accept in a poet or author, but which inspires dread in me when it is expressed by a man who makes decisions concerning the lives and deaths of many people" (*Under this Blazing Light*, 28-29).

14.	I am grateful to an anonymous reader of an early draft of this essay for bringing to my attention the resounding echo of Freud's *Moses and Monotheism* at this intriguing moment in Hareven's novella.

15.	Nash insightfully addresses the way Hareven's work encodes the word *aharayut* (responsibility) which itself contains the word *aher* (other), demanding concern for Other persons. See "Character Portrayal and Cultural Critique in Shulamith Hareven's Work" (224).

16.	Interestingly, Israel's Supreme Court Justice Edmond Levy recently declared that "An entire population has been designated as hewers of wood and bearers of water," in response to a report criticizing the country's insitutions of higher learning for discriminating against minority groups, including Israeli Arabs. See Haim Watzman, "Israeli Supreme Court Declines to Intervene in Case Over University Admissions," *Chronicle of Higher Education* (February 11, 2004).

17.	See Regina M. Schwartz, *The Curse of Cain: The Violent Legacy of Monotheism*.

18.	Certain recent trends in feminist biblical scholarship tend to support the notion of a biblical text that contains multiplicity. For example, *A Feminist Companion to Genesis* (Continuum, 1993) contains nine articles on the Creation stories alone.

New History, New Language –
Dimensions of Biblical Intertextuality
In Rachel's Poetry
Yehudit Ben-Zvi Heller

The past leaves within us multiple traces, and each one of us makes sense of them to create history. This is precisely the process that the Israeli poet Raḥel (Rachel) Bluvshtein-Sela (1890-1931), undergoes in her poetry as she employs Biblical allusions and their connection to the land to claim her own identity and language. Her poetry becomes an intermediary space between linguistic cultures and ideological views. My paper explores several poems by Raḥel including "From Across," "Rachel," and "Day of Tidings," examining how Raḥel draws upon Biblical allusions, which reflect and connect into a historic memory, and then uses those allusions to express intensely personal experiences in the present. Raḥel reinserts these deeply personal experiences into a new collectivity. By reclaiming the Hebrew language, which until then, was primarily relegated to the religious sphere, this pioneering intellectual integrates the practicality of everyday life into her poetics. "From Across" relates the last scene of Moses on Mt. Nebo – a wide reaching vision that Raḥel uses to explore the personal relationship between a man and a woman. "Rachel" exhibits a similar movement. This poem about both the poet and the Biblical mother subjectively reclaims a new identity in the old land. In "Day of Tidings," Raḥel takes a Biblical event as a fable reflecting on current day issues.

The poet's life story itself looks as if it was taken out of a folk legend in order to construct a cultural icon. Raḥel Bluvshtein was a beautiful and gloomy woman, who lost her mother in the course of her childhood and in her late teens, left her country. She gave up the comfort of her home in Russia and immigrated to the land of Israel, to participate in the vision of rebirth of a land. In the *Eretz*[1], Rahel chose and dedicated herself to hard physical labor. When Rahel arrived in Palestine in 1909, she hardly knew Hebrew. She made a vow of silence, and soon after her arrival, she started taking Hebrew lessons. Yet reading books, especially the Hebrew Bible, was not enough for her; she regularly visited a children's nursery in order to learn the "idiom that is naïve as a baby, unpretentious as the soil is" (Rahel, *Shirat Rahel* 52), from the children themselves. She was captivated by the landscape of the new homeland, and when Chana Maizel, "the mother of the female workers" in the courtyard of Kvutzat Kineret[2], wanted to send her away to study Agronomy in France, Rahel tried to escape the mission, "as it is common in stories of folk saints," ("Rahel's Grave – The Secular Version" 3).[3] After all her deliberations, she did go, and enrolled in the agricultural academy in Toulouse, France, where she was the only woman in her department. Her years of exile extended beyond her plan. Because of WWI she was forced to return to Russia, where she contracted tuberculosis. In 1919, Rahel finally returned to *Eretz Israel*, and like many tortured legendary saints, she denied her serious health condition. When her condition worsened, and her sickness was exposed, her friends from Kineret, who had already settled in Deganya,[4] turned their backs on her and left her alone. Her brother and sister-in-law from Tel Aviv did not give her a home. "Even the abandonment by friends and family is also a reoccurring element in lives of the saints," says Sered (3). The admirers of her poetry did not help her. In their eyes, her suffering nurtured her creativity. True love she never found; the accessible, beloved poet Rahel was completely alone in her life and in her death. Dr. Uri Milshtein, an Army historian, whose grandmother was a sister of Rahel, claims "that in the story of the poet's life, there are all the motifs of Aristotelian tragedy, as he describes it, "a tragedy that leads to catharsis"'(3).[5] As Milshtein notes, "People love pleasant tragedy, aesthetic tragedy, and here they have a rich Russian daughter who ended her life in terrible despair on a rooftop in Tel Aviv. This tragedy turned into pleasant music in her poems" (3).[6]

Academic researchers who have discussed Rahel focus on her personality and life story, not her poetry. The ones who attempt to refer to the poems, quote a line here and there; literary analysis and its requisite research have seemed unnecessary in her case. "It is common to think that a visit in Kineret is enough to understand her poetry," wrote Sered (4).[7] In 1969, Dr. Reuven Kritz tried to right this. In his book, *On Rahel's Poetry*, Kritz analyzed each one of her 144 poems. "I tried to show the impression that Rahel's poems are simple is only the surface of things. In deeper reading, you can tell that there are many layers and dimensions in her poems," he says (4).[8] After Kritz came, others, some who relate to Rahel's poetry in a literary personal connection like Uri Milshtein's *Rahel's Poems – the Secret of their Charm* in 1993, place Rahel in a wider context of women's poetry, as did Dan Miron in his 1991 book *Founding Mothers, Step-sisters*.

I complement this recent research with analysis, which explores the rich Biblical allusions in Rahel's work, examining these allusions in the process I outlined: the appropriation of mythic allusions to understand her personal present, than using them to reinsert herself into a contemporary collectivity. For Rahel, poetry is like Moses' *Nebo*, that elevated dimension of reflection and manifestation: where ends meet, where times and events shift, where the particular and the universal merge and make new meanings.

Mineged is the title of the second volume of Rahel's poetry, and also of the poem below. The scene and the expression came from the Deuteronomy, as God says to Moses: "Yet, you will see the Land from across [mineged], but you will not enter there!" (32:52). Nebo[9] is the name of the mountain upon which Moses climbed to view the Promised Land that he could never enter. From that mountain he looked out over the land whose vision had carried him for the forty years during which he led the people of Israel through the desert. Atop Mount Nebo, Moses could see far into the distance. Beneath him was the Jordan River, across from him lain the Land. And there, he died.

> "Go up this Mount of Avarim, Mount Nebo, in Mo'ab, which is facing Jericho, and behold the land of Canaan that I am giving to the people of Israel for a possession, and die in the mount into which thou goest up, and be gathered to thy people!" (32: 49-50)

The mountain's name – *Nebo*, holds multiple meanings: it is the location where Moses went up to have his last look and to die, it is also a place of vision and transition, a metaphor.[10] The word Nebo, in Hebrew *Nevo*, relates to the word *nevu'ah* which means in Hebrew prophesy, seeing ahead to the future; *Navi* in Hebrew is the word for a prophet, a seer. Also, the verb *la'vo* in Hebrew means to come, to enter. The latter adds an opposite dimension to the mountain's name and its biblical reputation - Moses did not come in, did not enter the Promised Eretz Israel. *Nevo* literally becomes a metaphoric concept, a carrying across, by the implications of the biblical scene. Such connotation is also hinted through the name *Avarim* (quote above), which in Hebrew evokes the meanings: sides, passing, and passages. The combination of both Hebrew concepts *Nevo* and *Mineged* (Nebo and From Across), make the meaningful connection of transitions and realizations of endings and death an integral part of life cycle in the particular Deuteronomy setting just as much as they do for Rahel 3000 years later.

Mineged[11]   מנגד

kashuv halev. ha'ozen kashevet!   קשוב הלב. האוזן קשבת!
Ha'va? ha'yavo?   הבא? היבוא?
be-khol tzipiyah   בכל ציפייה

yesh etzev nevo.   יש עצב נבו.

ze mul ze – ha'khofim hashna'yim   זה מול זה – החופים השניים
shel nakhal ekhd.   של נחל אחד.
tzur hagzera: צור הגזרה:
rekhokim la-ad.   רחוקים לעד.

paros kapayim. Ra'oh mineged.   פרוש כפיים.ראוה מנגד.
shama – en ba.   שמה – אין בא.
ish u'nevo lo   איש ונבו לו
al eretz raba.   על ארץ רבה.

From Across
The heart listens. The ear listens.
Has he already come? Will he come?
In every anticipation
4.   there is the sadness of Nebo.

One across from the other - the two banks
of one stream.
God's order:
8.   distant forever.
Spread out hands. Behold from across.
Over there - no entrance.
Each man and his Nebo
12.   Upon great land.

In the first verse of this poem, Raḥel establishes both its focus and its message, or lesson: "In every anticipation there is the sadness of Nebo." The atmosphere is one of anticipation (for the beloved) but, what kind of anticipation? Within the excitement of waiting, there is also the recognition of fear. The awaiting lover is not pacing from the window to the door; she is not looking at her watch or in the mirror. Instead, it is the pacing between the body and the mind. There is heaviness and a sense of being torn and divided. "The heart listens. The ear listens" — Two entities, physical and emotional, are expressed. She moves from the inside (the feelings of the one who is waiting), outward (to the two banks of the river); and then she moves across and above, to the general, Nebo. These transitions represent three stages: the individual (the narrator) who is the waiting lover, the two of them together and the whole, the general collective.

In the middle verse, she expands the idea. Facing each other, the two banks of one river, which by the very nature of things by the rule of reality, will never meet, will always be apart. Here, she is not the only one divided between the love and the recognition of reality; two different people feel the division.

The third verse, the conclusion, seems to return to the opening verse. Yet, this transition that takes place between the first verse and the last, makes a small significant difference. The difference lies in the wording. At the beginning of the poem, it is "In every anticipation there is the sadness of Nebo;" the focus is on the present situation – anticipation. The shifting takes place in the middle, as a result of recognition and realization of a situation: "One across from the other - the two banks/ of one stream. / God's decree: distant forever" (5-8). The third and final verse admits the change - "Nebo" becomes an integral part of a personality: "each person and his Nebo —!" Every person carries an experience of yearning; therefore, every person carries the knowledge of sadness, of a void. Every person has something that he or she longs to reach, or to overcome, to enter. Yet, that thing is not always ultimately reachable. By framing this conclusion with the association of Nebo, Rahel takes it beyond the subjective, only- personal level. Relying on the historic and Biblical dimension, she conceptualizes a new term, by using the name/place and the word, by giving it a historic and Biblical dimension. By doing this, she elevates the poem to yet another level. The philosophical scope is where the meaning of Nebo assumes a wider circle, a circle that can include everyone's possible loss, pain and hidden disappointment, as part of the living passage. The experience of Nebo elevates like Moses', whose *"Nevo"* was not only the climb to the peak of the mountain.

Rahel   רחל

hen dama bedami zorem,   הן דמה בדמי זורם,
hen kola bi ran –   הן קולה בי רן –
Rahel haro'ah tzon Lavan,   רחל הרועה צאן לבן,
Rahel – em ha'em.   רחל – אם האם.

ve'al ken ha'bayit li tzar   ועל כן הבית לי צר
ve'ha'ir – zarah,   והעיר – זרה,
ki hayah mitnofef sudarah   כי היה מתנופף סודרה
lerukhot hamidbar;   לרוחות המדבר;

ve'al ken et darki okhaz   ועל כן את דרכי אוחז
bevitkha kazot,   בבטחה כזאת,
ki shmurim beraglai zikhronot   כי שמורים ברגלי זכרונות
mini az, mini az.   מני אז, מני אז.

Rachel
For her blood flows in my blood,
For her voice croons in me -
Rachel the shepherdess of Laban's flock,
4.   Rachel - the mother of mothers.

And so, the house is confining for me
and the city - foreign,
for her shawl had been fluttering
8.   in the desert winds.

And so I'll hold on to my way
with such certainty,
for in my feet memories are kept
12.   since then, since then.

Rahel the poet returns and refers to the biblical scene where Rachel the
shepherd enters history (Genesis 29:6-10).   For Rahel, the image of the
shepherdess ("Rachel", 3) who is approaching at dusk from the distance,
accompanied by a cloud of desert dust lifted by the herd, is a breathtaking scene
in her "here and now," just as much as it impressed Jacob then in Biblical days.
Jacob, taken by the vision of Rachel, rises to roll the stone off the well, an act
that led him to his future, made a new connection, family, gave him his new
identity – Israel.   For the poet too, that ancient image is a revelation.   She
identifies with the Biblical Rachel who left her home for love.   She too left
behind the city[12], so young, yet sure of her way (9-10).   Now, in the present,
being in the same land, wandering the same landscapes, the bonds between past
and future become meaningful for her (11-12).

Here, in the poem, the connection between the two Rahels, the biblical and
the poet, is made by the word *hen*, which means (in Hebrew) for, since, yes,
obviously, connecting between times and combining the two women.   It is a
word that distinguishes presence, awareness.   The word *hen* is derived from the
word *hi'ne*, which means: here, still, yet, behold, (Genesis 29:7).   The point of
the poem is the notion of duality.   Here the double is about wholeness,
completion; the two Rahels are in one – "her blood flows in my blood"
("Rachel", 1), unlike the lovers in the poem "Mineged" where the two can never
meet, forever looking from across, split eternally by the land (river).   Here, in
this poem, through the land, both Rahels are united – "for in my feet memories
are kept " (11) - finding meaning and a sense of identity, also "Rachel - the
mother of mother" (4), a family reunion.   The merging of the two is conveyed
through the repetition of words and sounds, for example: "her blood in my
blood" (1), "Rachel" (3,4), "mother" (4), "her voice that sings" (in Hebrew:
"ran") (2) with "flocks of Laban" (3); In Hebrew, the word for flow (the blood)
- *zorem* (1) and the words for mother of mother- *em ha'em* (4) rhyme.   The
repetition here creates a circular movement, as if the poem started from its end
and its end is its beginning: it is because of those ancient days of "since then"
(12), that the bond between the two Rahels exists.   The repetition is not only the
aesthetic strength of the poem, but its idea, as well.   Indeed, the principle of
repetition is about words and sounds that reappear, return and through this,
connect.   Rahel uses this structural connecter as an overtone to make an

additional meaningful link, a correspondence that goes from the very beginning
of the poem (and history): "For her blood flows in my . . . " (1), all through to its
last line: "since then, since then" (12). By paralleling language, meanings and
time, a sense of the biblical parallelism is recaptured, portraying the return of a
daughter, a reconnection with the land, reflecting on the old (ancient Raḥel)
reborn and become new through the poet and pioneer Raḥel.

Still linking between the biblical to the present, still staying within the name
itself, I want to examine the meaning of the name Raḥel, (in English Rachel),
and how it applies to both, the biblical and the poet. *Raḥel* means ewe, a mature
full-grown sheep: "These twenty years have I been with thee, thy ewes and thy
she-goats have not cast their young. . . ."(Genesis 31:38). The biblical references
all lead and connect to the shepherd stories. It is sheep that constitute Jacob's
reward for his "free" work for Laban[13]: both the woman for whom he stays to
work and to whom he wishes to prove himself, and the actual sheep he cares for
and from which he makes a fortune for himself. The biblical Raḥel is a risk-
taker. She marries and follows a man from nowhere to a promised place, carried
by the vision of her love. She is named the "Mother of Mothers" ("Rachel" 1),
although she only had two sons and died giving birth on the road. Perhaps she
earned that title because of the extraordinary love story (Genesis 29:20), and the
ultimate woman-mother motif - dying while giving birth. The poet (who also
died young), who also leaves one life behind following her love and vision of a
new life in the same promised land, recognized these similarities, and derived
from them her new vision and identity – "for her blood is the soul"
(Deuteronomy 12:23).

Kan Al Pney Ha'adamah	**כאן על פני האדמה**

Kan al pney ha'adama – lo be'avim, me'al –	כאן על פני האדמה – לא בעבים, מעל –
al pnei ha'adamah hakrovah, ha'em;	על פני האדמה הקרובה, האם;
le'he'atzev be'otzbah velagil begilah hadal	להעצב בעצבה ולגיל בגילה הדל
hayode'a kol kakh lenakhem.	היודע כל כך לנחם.
lo arpiley makhar – hayom hamumash bayad,	לא ערפילי מחר – היום המומש ביד,
hayom hamutzak, hakham, ha'etan:	היום המוצק, החם, האיתן:
lirvot et hayom haze, hakatzar, ha'ekhad,	לרוות את היום הזה, הקצר, האחד,
al pney admate'nu kan.	על פני אדמתנו כאן.

beterem ata haleyl – bo'u, bo'u hakol!   בטרם אתא הלַיל – בואו, בואו הכל!

ma'amatz me'ukhad, akshani ve'er   מאמץ מאוחד, עקשני ועֵר

shel elef zro'ot. ha'omnam yibatzer   של אלף זרועות. האומנם יִבָּצֵר לגול
lagol

et ha'even mipi ha'be'er?   את האבן מפי הבְּאֵר?

Here On Earth

Here on earth - not in the clouds, above –
on earth that is so close, the mother earth;
to sorrow in her sadness, and to exult in her
             meager joy

4   that knows so well how to console.

Not the misty tomorrow – but the today that materializes in
the hand,
the solid, warm, firm today;
drink deep, of this single, short day

8.   here on our own land.

Before night falls – oh, come all!
A unified effort, stubborn and awake
with thousand hands. Is it really impossible to
             roll

12   off the stone from the mouth of the well?

The first verse introduces the physical, geographical location as the framework for the poem's idea: Here on earth – location as direction. Let us note two meanings: a. Here on earth, that which is near and can be felt, that to which one can relate; b. this earth that is so close, the mother earth - a relative, both physically and emotionally nearby. The double meaning is in the intertwining of associations, by the pointed directions (the earth down here versus the clouds above - often the sky is what is wished to be reached, and the ground is the limit). This is further emphasized by the expansion to the specifics in the second verse. Here, the repetition of the "here" versus "above" particularizes the concept of the general meaning of "clouds" to the specifics of "misty tomorrow," as opposed to the "here on earth" as the solid and evolving today. By this type of repetition with only a slight change, B (the clouds) takes the place of A (the "here") (5). A sense of movement and development is created to reflect and to credit the value of the present in light of these very special happenings - the rebirth of the homeland (5, 8). "The today that materializes in the hand, and can be sensed by the hand —here on our own land" is a new paradigm whose essence hugs within itself the concepts of tomorrow and yesterday - and therefore why should it be "impossible to roll the stone from the mouth of the well?" (11-12).

The reference to the well couples the past with the future. The well's memory conceptualizes the Israelite heritage and the biblical telling of history — it is about the land of promises. The notion of the well as the future, fresh water from the depth of earth, represents a birth, a new beginning. All that merges with that previous Beginning, of biblical ancestors who dug those wells (Genesis 26:18-33) .[14] They, too, understood the significance of the well - making that abstract vision of promise (12:1-2)[15] into a premise of continuity (the misty tomorrow - verses today that materializes in the hand ("Here" 5)).

Rahel's choice of the word *lagol,* which means to roll (11), over other choices (such as: *le'hasir*: to remove, to uncover, or *lakhasof:* *t*o revile, and *lidkhof* :to push), achieves at once a few goals or meanings that are joined to reflect the motion of a spirited vision. By using *lagol* (to roll), we can grasp beyond the obvious significance of the biblical associations. The well connects the present shepherds with their ancient forefathers. The well is a meeting place, an intersection between indoors and outdoors. It is the point were distances meet and combine, linking the far away with the nearby. The well is where connections are being made - exchanges of news, social and romantic interactions (Genesis 29). It is a place where the tired and the wanderer rest, and where herds would overcome their thirst. It is a sign that civilization is nearby, a sign of life - both heaven and a haven.

Isaac, the middle forefather, as I have mentioned, was known as a well digger (26:18-33). Rebecca, his wife, made her entrance to history at the well, where she shares her water not only with people but also gives the tired Camels to drink (24:15-67). So does another significant foremother, Rahel (29). This is where her future husband, Jacob, meets her. Jacob, too, rolls off the stone from the mouth of the well and acquires his future as a man and a leader. In Genesis 29, a great importance is attributed to the well, and to the act of rolling the stone off the mouth of the well. In that chapter alone, that act is mentioned three times. The size of the stone is mentioned there as well (29:2-3). In Rahel's poem the act of moving the stone shifts from an individual act to a communal one, ("Here" 10-11), suggesting the importance of working together to the building of the new community. The act of rolling the stone from the mouth of the well fulfills the role of foretelling the upcoming, and reflects strength and inner energy. Also, within the concept of the well is a symbol of incubation, like a womb that is linked to futility and continuity, serving as another tie to the motherland (2). The well is the "eye" the vision, and also the feeling of the land that is the solid and firm — the "here" (6,8).

An additional aspect of the word *lagol* (to roll), related to that mentioned above, is the roundness found in the movement and meaning of the word, again hinting at the idea of a cycle. The word *gilgul* (a turn, rolling, metamorphosis) is derived from the same root as the word *galgal* (wheel). These are all connected and are considered in Rahel's choice of this word. By rolling the stone off the well, a link would be made, a connection between past and future; by the physical act, a rebirth by the common and so powerful effort of hands, more and farther will be reached.

In her poem, Raḥel says:". . .lagol et ha'even mipi hab'er" - to roll off the stone from the mouth of the well, whereas in Genesis the phrase is: "me'al pi ha'ber" (11-12) - which means, in general, the same. Yet, the word *me'al* means above, so the wording literally is: to roll the stone that is above, or over the opening of the well. Both are linguistically correct, however these differences are deliberate. In the biblical text, the focus is on the physical effort, to emphasize Jacob's bodily strength and the immediate attraction and special connection that are about to emerge. First, we hear about the size of the stone (Genesis 29:2-3) [16] and the gathering of the shepherds who are waiting for each other in order to roll the stone of the well (29:8).[17] Then, when Raḥel the shepherd appears, it is only Jacob who gets to remove the stone and water the herds of his uncle (29:10).[18] Raḥel the poetess, three thousands years later, uses this memory to make a point by phrasing it slightly differently - there is no need to "manipulate" the situation, the connection was already made for us then. This is why the land is a "here" - a sure and clear thing - a concept of "back to the roots." The word *mipi* (from the mouth) points in a direction, a direct action relationship: straight from the mouth versus off the mouth.

Another significant aspect on the use of language in this poem has to do with the framework and the rhythm. The rhyming AB-AB, runs through it and becomes the overall framework, which Raḥel never chooses only for the sound or rhyme. The interconnections, and relationships among meanings between the A and the B are important additions to the poem:

> A-(1) **me'al**/above **ha'dal**/meager (3) above-clouds, fogginess and uncertainties which rhyme with small, insignificant and poor.
> B-(2) **ha'em**/the mother **le'nakhem**/to console (4) mother/real comfort and consolation.
> A-(5) **bayad**/by hand **ha'echad**/the one (7) the hand can put together, create does, the hand of god. The one here is the hand. by putting hands together one becomes (as in verse 3, the unified - *me'ukhad* effort of the hands is the call).
> B-(6) **ha'eytan**/ firm **kan** here(8)   strong, reliable, steadiness of the now-here that is close and can be touched.
> A-(9) **hakol**/everyone, everything **lagol** (11) everything to be discovered, to be continued.
> B-(10)**va'er**/awake **hab'er** the well(12) freshness, energy, awakeness

The repetition in the poem is one more noticeable structural factor that frames and adds range to its ideas. It appears as a figura etymalagica as in line 3: "le'he'atzev be'otzbah velagil begilah hadal – to sorrow in her sadness, and to exult in her meager joy", as a way of sound and visual emphasis. It also appears as a chiasm in the use and placement of the word *here - kan*. This starts the whole poem, and it is the last word of the second verse (8). The first *kan* (here) is pointing to the place as the right direction on earth. The second *kan* (here) is on our land/earth. Here Rahel exhibits the use of structure to reveal an evolution of idea from the more general to the specific, from the ideal to the practicality of the present reality.

As in the previous poems, Rahel works here as well with the paralleling of duality: one across from the other, opposites – "Here on earth - not in the clouds above" (1). The sense of duality, of "two banks/of one stream" ("From Across" 5-6), is used as an instrumental tool in her love poems, to reflect on the conflicting identity, feelings, and the double reality of a secret love. In her poem, "Rahel," "since her blood flows in my blood"(Rachel 1), the biblical foremother Rahel, and the poet merge into one, and in this poem the element of "two" acts as an anchor of the present as the path to a future. The presentation of two worlds reflects the quality of complete clarity, here the choice has been made clearly and the world of clouds above is mentioned only to strengthen the value of the earth below. The poem is a sensible reflection of the new present – pioneering, as a concrete ideology that dominated the horizon of tomorrow and made it the very present reality.

Yom Besorah   יום בשורה

וארבעה אנשים היו מצורעים פתח השער - -
ויאמרו איש אל רעהו: - - הזה יום בשורה
הוא. (מלכים ב', 9-3 :7)

beshekvar hayamim ha'oyev hanora	בשכבר הימים האויב הנורא
et shomron hevi bematzor;	את שומרון הביא במצור;
arba'a metzora'im la bisru bsorah.	ארבעה מצורעים לה בישרו בשורה.
La bisru besorat hadror.	לה בשרו בשורת הדרור.
keshomron bamatzor – kol ha'aretz kulah,	כשומרון במצור – כל הארץ כולה,
vekaved hara'av mineso.	וכבד הרעב מנשוא.
akh ani lo oveh besorat ge'ulah,	אך אני לא אובה בשורת גאולה,
im mipi metzora hi tavo.	אם מפי מצורע היא תבוא.
hatahor yevaser vega'al hatahor,	הטהור יבשר וגאל הטהור,
ve'im yado lo timtza lig'ol –	ואם ידו לא תמצא לגאול –
az nivkhar li linpol mimtzukat	אז נבחר לי לנפול ממצוקת המצור

190   Yehudit Heller

hamatzor
or leyom besorah hagadol.   אור ליום בשורה הגדול.

Day of Tidings
"And there were four lepers
at the entrance of the gate – – and they said to one another: – –
this day is a day of good tidings... ." (Kings II 7:3-9).

                    In bygone days the terrible enemy
                    laid siege to Samaria;
                    four lepers brought her good tidings.
        4.   Brought to the city the tiding of liberation.

                    Like besieged Samaria - so even is the whole
                        country,
                    and the burden of famine is unbearable.
                    But I would reject tidings of redemption,
        8.   if it should come from a leper's mouth.

                    He who is pure will declare, and only he will
                        redeem,
                    and if his hand cannot redeem –
                    then I prefer to die from the hardship of siege
        12.   at the break of the great day of tidings.

In order to comprehend this complicated poem and the issues it presents, it
is important to go verse by verse, and figure out the contents and their
connection to Biblical references.

                    In bygone days the terrible enemy
                    laid a siege to Samaria;
                    four lepers brought her good tidings.
        4.   Brought to the city the tiding of liberation.

Here is an ancient story laying the substructure of the poem. At a time
when the kingdom of Aram fought the kingdom of Israel and laid siege to its
capital, Samaria, four lepers were outside at the gates of the city (6-8:24-25).
Their reason for being there, according to the Torah is that lepers should not be
in the company of others (the healthy). The siege was so strong, and the famine
so great, that one woman chased the other, saying, "give me thy son and we will
eat him today and we will eat my son tomorrow!" (6:26-29). Because the lepers
were stationed beyond the city's gate, they were the first to see that the enemy
was gone and to bring the city the good news of liberation.

The second verse is where the biblical event becomes an allegory shifting between the biblical story and the poet's present linking meanings, which rely on the old text, yet move onto the new reality (of the poet).

> Like besieged Samaria - so even is the whole
>   country,
> and the burden of famine is unbearable.
> But I would reject tidings of redemption,
> 8.   if it should come from a leper's mouth.

Now the particular becomes the universal: Samaria under siege as a metaphor, a microcosm of the country, or even the entire world (5) that is in distress and trouble, that is besieged (6). The word "but" (7) is the turning point where the balance of the poem changes and creates a disturbance. The voice of the poet comes through clearly and announces: "But I would reject tidings of redemption, if it should come from a leper's mouth." What kind of an announcement is this? It is a statement of the absolute, which Rahel introduces in the third verse. :

> He who is pure will declare, and only he will
>   redeem,
> and if his hand cannot redeem -
> then I prefer to die from the hardship of siege
> 12.   at the break of the great day of tidings.

At this point, the poem develops to its climax (9): "He who is pure will declare, and only he will redeem." Only the pure can bring the good message. This purity is such a central concept that Rahel repeats it twice in the same sentence that only the pure can redeem. Reinforcing the absurdity is Rahel's choice to die rather than be saved by a leper (10-12).

Rahel declares in these lines a strong, merciless statement. Isn't redemption for all? They are lepers, why reject them even more? Perhaps, in order to get an answer, one must examine what Rahel means by her use of *lepers*. Who are they? Does she refer to lepers in body or lepers in soul and mind? There is not much information about them in the Biblical reference at the opening of the poem, only a sense that directs us to revisit the ancient text. According to the story in Kings II, the four lepers went down to the enemy camp out of desperation, deciding they had nothing to lose. When they reached the camp of Aram they realized the place was empty. They initially went in, taking everything they could put their hands on for themselves, instead of running back to let the rest of the city know the war was over. They immersed themselves in robbing and stealing and fulfilling their own needs, postponing the news while the city remained in fear and tremendous hunger:

> "They went into one tent, and did eat and drink, and carried from
> there silver and gold and raiment, and went and hid it; then came

> back and entered into another tent and carried from there also, and
> went and hid it." (7:3-10).

Suddenly the fear of punishment awakened the lepers and reminded them to stop
their own "celebration" and not to delay bringing the news to the city until the
next morning. (7:9). Rahel refers to the absolute symbol of physical impurity
and contamination (leprosy), refocusing the story by looking at traits and
behavior characteristics. Her use of the biblical event centers on choices people
making; she speaks about those who are self-serving and corrupt in their nature.
Rahel presents the question of absolute morality – Who is *pure*? Who is the
leper? [19]

In her "Day of Tidings" Rahel, gives an idealistic prophet-like moral
message. Hers is the kind of message reminiscent, in a way, of the Ten
Commandments. Practically speaking, perhaps the poem would not stop actions
of violence, dishonesty and corruption. But nevertheless, it poses the never-
ending question of "Good and Evil" in a new light, positioning a noble boundary
between right and wrong. As in "From Across" here too, the biblical context
becomes a fable reflecting on current day issues. By doing such, Rahel inserts
the Hebrew language with new connotations. She makes the ancient story
accessible in a new and everyday way.

Rahel's words continue to be essential to the Hebrew language today. In his
editorial entitled "Enlightened Minority Government" (Maariv , 11/21/02),[20] the
journalist Menahem Ben relates the implications of Rahel's "Day of Tidings" to
his current reality in the same way she applied the biblical significance to hers.
In his distress with a specific [right wing] religious party in the Israeli
government and its approach to the Middle East peace process, he states that "an
[Israeli] government that would rely on Arabs, and exclude that [other] party of
'corrupted peacocks', will be cleaner, more harmonious. . . . Perhaps by getting
rid of that *party of lepers* peace would become a practical possibility, as the
public will object to peace that such a party is involved in creating, for 'I would
reject tidings of redemption, / if it should come from a leper's mouth'" (2). The
initial story of *Samaria* and its *lepers* was drawn upon by Rahel, yet became
visual and flexible with fresh applications, a new fable, and language relevant to
a daily evolving reality.

Conclusion

Generally speaking, the idea of pioneering expresses a sense of
reconnection and return to land. Rahel returns not only to the land, but also to
the language. These two elements of pioneering form the core of her poetic
work, which reflects the sense of ideological connection between individual and
collective, land and language. She, furthermore, searches for a way to connect
her private exile to the collective experience. Rahel reworks the language of the
Bible to reflect her "Genesis," her struggle between tradition and assimilation,
and to find a way of using Hebrew to express that reality. Her poetry becomes

the site at which these tensions are worked out and connections are created, a "third space" where all these strands can meet. The poems indeed become her way of connecting and reflecting, of making sense and meanings, as well as pointing and paving new directions. She uses the poetry to constitute her own subjectivity. Her poetry becomes her borderland, her special in-between space.

In the passages between the different dimensions and layers of her poems (as in her life), a dramatic turnabout is formed, transforming the poems from "flat figures" to "round figures." They become multi-dimensional not only via the varying inter-conversations that occur in each poem, but also by the interconnections among the poems by means of ideas, landscapes and time periods. The simple poems "have become a splendid necklace of words" (Shirat Rahel, 77) on the neck of Rahel, who too transforms, from the naïve poet to a self aware and forceful poet that moves in between the personal and the general subject and integrates them to a whole. Thus, the divided nature of her poetry allows two simultaneous readings. The uniqueness and the sense of fierceness of her poetry derive from their potential to be read in different ways. The wholeness of this poetry is derived from the joined forces of these readings.

For Rahel, poetry becomes like Moses' *Nebo*, that lofty "space" of mirroring and engagement: where fragments fuse and the periphery becomes the main focus, where periods and events are transformed, where the personal and the collective merge and connect with new relevance through a new language. The two sides within her correspond in a tongue of contradictions and unsettled tensions, and turn pain to pane, and a past into a future. "The artist doesn't want any other paradise but existence itself," said Osip Mendelstam in his 1919 Acmeist[21] manifest, (*Modernism's Manifests,* 33).[22] Indeed, Rahel succeeds in entering the artist's "paradise;" she eternally exists through the language she revived.

Notes

1. *Eretz* literally means in Hebrew *land/country*, is a common name, used as a nickname, among Jewish people for The Land of Israel.

2. Kvutzat Kineret the first kibbutz established in 1913 in (those days – Palestine), located by the Sea of Galilee near the city Tiberya, nowadays consists of 850 people including 390 members.

3. My translation for the purpose of the article – Professor Susan Sered's article (in *Nashim*'s first issue, 1998, Hebrew) quoted in Vered Kelner article, which was published in Maariv Newspaper literary page, 11/21/02 (Hebrew).

4. Deganya - a kibbutz by the Sea of Galilee.

5. My translation for the purpose of this article.

6. My translation for the purpose of this article.

7. My translation for the purpose of the article.

8. My translation for the purpose of the article.

9. In Hebrew – Nevo.

10. Metaphor – in the original Greek sense of a crossing over in as well as its contemporary sense.

11. I translated all translations and transliterations of Rahel's work for the purpose of the article.

12. She leaves her home in Russia, and she leaves Rishon-Letzion her first home in the Land of Israel. Also important to remember that she wrote most of her poems in Tel-Aviv while the practice of physical work was only in her heart, for she was already quite sick, alone and away from her beloved fields of Kineret.

13. Laban is the Father of Rechel and Lea. Genesis 29-31.

14 . " - - And Isaac dug again the wells of water, which they had dug in the days of Abraham his father – and he called their names after the names by which his father had called them. - - And he called the name of it [the well] Rehobot – for now the Lord has made room for us, and we shall be fruitful in the land —."

15. "Get thee out of thy country — and go to the land that I will show you, — and I'll bless thee and make thy name great."

16. "…and a great stone was upon the well's mouth."

17. "…[you should] water the sheep, and go feed them. And they [the shepherds] said, we can not, until all the flocks are gathered together, and till they roll the stone from the well's mouth; then we may water the sheep."

18. "And it came to pass, when Jacob saw Rahel … Jacob went near and rolled the stone from the well's mouth, and watered the flock of Laban … ."

19. Albert Camus asks a similar question through Rieux, the doctor of the city Oran in his book, "The Plague".

20. My own translation from Hebrew for this article. From Maariv Newspaper, November 21 2002, in the Art and Literature addition (2).

21. Poetic Stream in Russia, following and rejecting the symbolism movement. Its ideas strived for more balance and precise knowledge of the relation between the subject and the object.

22. Editor: Benjamin Harshav. My translation from the Hebrew.

Works Cited

Alter, Robert. *Hebrew Modernity*. Bloomington: Indiana U Press, 1994.
———. *Canon and Creativity: Modern Writing and the Authority of Scripture*. New Haven: Yale U Press, 2000.
———. *The Art Of Biblical Poetry*. New York: Basic Books, 1985.
Bar-Yosef, Hamutal. *Symbolism Bashirah hamodernit (Symbolism in Modern Poetry)*. Tel-Aviv: Ha'kibbutz Hame'ukhad, 2000. Hebrew.
Bar, Amos. *Sipurah Shel Rachel (Rachel's Story)*. Tel-Aviv: Am-Oved P, 1998. Hebrew.

Ben, Menahem. "Enlightened Minority Government." *Maarive Newspaper* 11/21/02, Hebrew.

Berlin, Adele. *The Dynamics of Biblical Parallelism*. Bloomington: Indiana UP, 1985.

Bloch Chana. *Spelling the Word, George Herbert and the Bible*. Los Angeles: U C P, 1985.

Bhabha, Homi. *The Location of Culture*. London: Routledge, 1994.

Carmi, T., ed. and trans. *Hebrew Verse*. New York: Penguin Books, 1981.

Chertock, Haim. *We are All Close: Conversations with Israeli Writers*. New York: Fordham U P, 1981.

Chomsky, William. *Hebrew: the Eternal Language*. Philadelphia: The Jewish Publication Society of America, 1957.

Cohen, Israel. "Shirat Rahel (Rachel's Poetry)."*Image to Image*. Tel-Aviv: Dvir, 1949. 246-249. Hebrew.

Domb, Risa ed. *New Women's Writing From Israel*. Portland: Vallentine Mitchel, 1996.

Even-Shoshan, Avraham. *The New Hebrew Dictionary*. Jerusalem: Kiryat Sefer Publishers, 1967.

———. ed. *Concordantzia Hadashah Latanakh (A New Concordance of the Bible)*. Jerusalem: Kiryat Sefer Publishers, 1996.

Ezrahi, Sidra Dekoven. *Booking Passage*. U of California P, 2000.

———. *Modernism and Postmodernism in the Hebrew Narrative*. Jerusalem: Hebrew University P, 1994.

Feldman, Yael S.. *Gender and Nation in No Room of Their Own: Israeli Women's Fiction*. New York: Columbia U P, 1999.

Feingold, Ben-Ami. *Lilmod Rahel (Teaching and Studying Rachel's Poetry)*. Tel-Aviv: Ramot, Tel-Aviv U P, 1996. Hebrew.

Harshav, Benjamin. *Language in the Time of Revolution*. Berkeley: U of California P, 1993.

———. ed. *Manifestim shel modernism (Modernist's Manifests)*. Jerusalem: Carmel Publishers,2001. Hebrew.

———. *Omanut Hashira (The Art of Poetry)*. Jerusalem: Karmel Publishers,2000. Vo. 2, Hebrew.

———. *Antologia Historit Bikortit (hebrew Renaissance Poetry – A Historical-Critical Anthology)*. Jerusalem: Biyalik Ist. P, 2000. Vol. 1, 10-30.

Henderson, Mae, ed. *Borders, Boundaries, and Frames*. New York: Routledge, 1995.

Govrin, Nurit. *Ktivat Haaretz (Literary Giography)*. Jerusalem: Carmel P, 1998. Hebrew.

Hooks, bell. "Language, a Place of Struggle." *Between Language and Culture*.
    Dingwaney, Anuradha and Maier, Carol eds. U of Pittsburgh P, 1995.
    295 – 301.
Jerusalem Bible. Jerusalem: Koren Publishers, 1977.
Kartun-Blum, Ruth. *Profane Scriptures: Reflections of the Dialogue with the
    Bible in Modern Hebrew Poetry*. Cincinnati: Hebrew Union College
    Press,1999. 6.
Kelner, Vered. "Rahel's Grave – The Secular Version." Maariv Newspaper
    11/21/02, Hebrew.
Klauzner, Yosef. *Yotsrim U-Vonim: Maamare Bikoret (Creators and Builders:
    LiteraryCriticism Assays)*. Tel-Aviv: Dvir P, 1929. Hebrew.
Kristeva, Julia. *Nations Without Nationalism*. Trans. Leon S. Roudiez. New
    York: Columbia UP, 1993.
Kritz, Re'uven. *Al shirat Rahel (On Rahel's Poetry)*. Haifa: Pure P, 1969.
    Hebrew.
Kugel, James. The Idea of Biblical Poetry – Parallelism and Its History. New
    Haven: Yele UP, 1981.
Kushnir, Shimon and Snir, Mordekai, eds. *Rahel Ve'shiratah (Rachel and her
    poetry)*. Tel-Aviv: Davar P, 1971. Hebrew.
Lieblich, Amia. *Conversations with Devora: An Experimental Biography of the
    First Modern Hebrew Woman Writer*. Trans. Naomi Seidman. Eds.
    Chana Kronfeld and Naomi Seidman. Berkeley: U of California P,
    1997.
Milshtein, Uri ed. *Shirey Rahel U'mikhtave'ah Bikhtav Yada (Rahel's Poems,
    and Her Letters in Her Hand Writing)*. Kineret P, 1969. Hebrew.
Milshtein, Uri ed. *Shirey Rahel – Sod Kismam (Rahel's Poems - the Secret of
    their Charm)*. Ramt-Efal: Sridut P, 1993. Hebrew.
Miron, Dan. *Imahot Meyasdot Akhayot Khorgot (Founding Mothers
    Stepsisters)*. Tel-Aviv: Hakibbutz-Hame'ukhad P, 1991. Hebrew.
Mintz, Ruth Finer. *Modern Hebrew Poetry: A Bilingual Anthology*. Berkeley:
    U of California Press, 1966.
Pardes, Ilana. *The Biography of Ancient Israel*. Berkeley: U C P, 2000.
——. *Habriah Lefi Havah (Countertraditions in the Bible: A Feminist
    Approach)*. Tel-Aviv: Hakibbutz Hameuchad P, 1996. Hebrew.
Rahel. *Shirat Rachel*. Tel-Aviv: Davar Publishers, 1949. Hebrew.
Said, Edward. "Mind of Winter: Reflections on Life in Ex*ile*." *Harper's
    Magazine*. September, 1984. 54.
Schiff, Alvin I. *The Mystique of Hebrew: an Ancient Language in the New
    World*. New York: Shengold P, 1996.
Schwartz, Howard & Anthony, Rudolf eds. *Voices Within the Ark, The Modern
    Jewish Poets*. Rudolph, Avon Books, 1980.
Seidman, Naomi. *A Marriage Made in Heaven: The Sexual Politics of Hebrew
    and Yiddish*. Berkeley: U of California P, 1997.
Shahar, Eyal. "Uri Mesaper al Rachel" (Uri talks about Rachel, an interview).

Davar li'yeladim. Tel-Aviv: Davar, 1969. Hebrew.

Shavid, Eli. *Shirat hayahid be'ma'agal ha'rabim (the Singular Poetry in the Collective Circle- on Rachel's poetry and their link to the Bible)*. Tel-Aviv: Am-Oved, 1964. Hebrew.

Sokoloff, Naomi B., Lapidus Lerner,Anne & Norich, Anita eds. *Gender and Text in Modern Hebrew and Yiddish Literature*. Cambridge: Harvard U P, 1992.

Sontag, Susan. *Illness as Metaphor*. New York: Farrar, Straus and Giroux, 1978.

15   Postcoloniality, Feminism
and the Bible in Ngũgĩ's a *A Grain of Wheat*
Peter W. Mwikisa

Christianity is not only a salvation religion, it is a confessional religion: it imposes strict obligations of truth, dogma and canon. . . . Christianity requires yet another form of truth obligation different from faith. Each person has the duty to know who he is, that is to try to know what is happening inside him, to acknowledge faults, to recognise temptations , to locate desires: and every one is obliged to disclose these things either to God or to others in the community and, hence , to bear public or private witness against oneself.
—-Michel Foucault, *Religion and Culture*

-I-

The accretion of biblical themes and allusions in Ngũgĩ's work provides a way of evaluating his decolonizing project from an alternative perspective to the radical Marxist aesthetics that so far have been dominant in appreciations of his work. As a self-proclaimed Marxist revolutionary, Ngũgĩ shed his Christian name "James" to suggest that he had divested himself of the faith and the colonial mentality he believes it engenders. His revolutionary credentials cemented by his incarceration by the Kenyan Government in 1978, Ngũgĩ has been lionized as the leading revolutionary writer in Africa, eclipsing writers that come from countries such as South Africa, Mozambique and Angola that have traditions of Marxist inspired liberation struggles. However, since the collapse of the Soviet Union and the decline in the ideological appeal of socialism, Marxism itself has come under siege. In literature works, such as Ngũgĩ's, that draw their appeal on the basis of Marxist revolutionary aesthetics have come to seem increasingly anachronistic and in need of alternative and broader grounds of critical appeal. The aim of the present discussion of Ngũgĩ's deployment of biblical signifiers is to offer such an opportunity for an alternative appreciation of his work. The paper sees A Grain of Wheat as substantially a discourse on the Bible and postcolonial Christianity.

The argument in the paper is that although Ngũgĩ appears to reject the Bible and Christianity as hallmarks of the colonization of the mind, his views about how to decolonize the African mind may owe a more deeply ingrained debt to the Bible, particularly to the New Testament and to the Christianity of his early mission school education, than to *Das Kapital* or *The Communist Manifesto*. So Ngũgĩ's oppositional stance towards Christianity and the Bible as instruments of cultural imperialism should not be thought of exclusively in terms of an invasive decolonization strategy launched from the standpoint of a secular ideology, i.e. Marxism. His strictures against Christianity and the Bible may, instead, be seen also as a product of internal dynamics within the Christian faith in the postcolonial context that lead believers to reflect anew on the relevance of the major tenets of their faith without necessarily rejecting it. In fact, Peter Nazareth is probably right to suggest that Ngũgĩ is the most Christian African writer (13).

Relocating Ngũgĩ's work from the secular to the religious in the way suggested above does not, of course, detract from the potency of his anti-imperialist critique. On the contrary, such an approach brings out the strengths of Ngũgĩ's critique of imperialism because it highlights the connection, made by postcolonial critics, between colonial racism and Christianity in the propagation of imperialism. In explaining the connection, Spivak states, for instance, that colonial racism inscribed women as bearers of racialized bodies on the one hand, while Christianity, on the other, contributed towards imperial production of colonial subjectivity as of universalized souls (Spivak 291). Ngũgĩ's work, particularly *A Grain of Wheat,* explores the connection. It is an exploration that while it does not necessarily divest Ngũgĩ of his revolutionary mantle, adds to it an aspect of heresy. I use the word 'heresy' decidedly in a positive sense to suggest that despite the Marxist label that has stuck on to him, Ngũgĩ is a Christian who does not reject Christianity completely but simply questions its prevailing orthodoxy. His *A Grain of Wheat,* does not only exhibit a masterly familiarity with the Bible and Christian discourses, but it is also a carefully elaborated expression of dissent from within against Christian orthodoxy and established authority.

The argument presented here is in two parts as is suggested by the Foucauldian epigram at the head of the paper. In the first part of the epigram Foucault refers to Christianity as a religion that imposes "strict obligations of truth, dogma and canon" (169). The first part of the paper therefore examines the way in which Ngũgĩ deals with the issue of the canonicity of the Bible, i.e. the fact that Christianity makes it an obligation for believers to hold the Bible, as the exclusive word of God and permanent source of truth. In dealing with this issue, Ngũgĩ contributes to the postcolonial debate about whether it is possible to accept the Bible as the exclusive word of God while at the same time acknowledging its complicity in the seamier aspects of European colonialism in Africa. He asks the question whether the Bible has a revolutionary potential that could be harnessed in the process of the struggle to decolonize the African mind, even though it is a colonial text that is heavily implicated in the dissemination of colonial culture.

The second part of the argument is based on Foucault's other assertion in the epigram, namely that Christianity is a "confessional religion" that "requires" of its believers the processes of self-examination and confession (167). The paper argues that Ngũgĩ's vision of decolonization is closer in ideology to Christianity than to Marxism because he attaches great importance in his work to what Foucault calls "acts of self examination and confession" (169). Christian salvation and Marxist-style freedom from necessity are similar because they are both utopian goals whose attainment depends on faith. In addition, a dualistic language dominates both and ultimately collapses all difference into binaries (good and evil, in the former, and labour and capital, in the latter) that lead to a marginalization of other concerns, such as women's issues, race and ethnicity. Nevertheless, there is a basic difference between them. There is nothing in Marxism that corresponds to the Christian truth obligation to practice self-examination and confession. Therefore the paper examines the manner in which the emphasis on the practice of self examination and confession influences Ngũgĩ's depiction of female characters. Ngũgĩ's women characters, particularly Mumbi in *A Grain of Wheat,* come across less as Marxist revolutionary fighters than as catalysts and agents of the Christian practice of self- examination and confession.

-II-

I shall deal first with Ngũgĩ's contribution to the discourse about the canonicity of the Bible as a postcolonial problematic. A self-proclaimed Marxist who adopts a historical materialist approach to African social realities, he nevertheless uses the New Testament themes of sacrifice, betrayal, confession, atonement and redemption in his most celebrated novel, *A Grain of Wheat.* In addition, he draws on the New Testament for his characterisation. His leading characters in the novel allude to biblical characters, e.g. Kihika is a Christ-like figure; Mumbi is reminiscent of Mary, the mother of Jesus; Karanja and Mugo turn their backs on the liberation struggle and echo the betrayal of Judas Iscariot. The use of Biblical characters as models is also evident in Ngũgĩ's post colonial works, written after *A Grain of Wheat.* The hero of the eponymous *Matigari* is a Christ-like figure even more so than Kihika. The play that landed Ngũgĩ into trouble and led to his incarceration in 1978, *I Will Mary When I Want,* is shot through with the Christian binaries of good and evil even though it is couched in the Marxist language of class.

A strong rhetorical reliance on the Bible, a text often inveighed against for its role in facilitating the imposition and later the perpetuation of the very colonial mentality that he seeks to dispel, is a delectable irony that even Ngũgĩ himself has felt the need to explain. In an interview with Jane Wilkinson he tries to dispose of the contradiction with the explanation that for historical reasons the Bible had become part and parcel of the African heritage, and when he uses it, Ngũgĩ merely draws on a body of knowledge that he can assume he shares with his audience (qtd. in Wilkinson 130):

> I use the Bible quite a lot, or biblical sayings, not because I share in any belief in the Bible, or in the sanctity of the Bible. It is just simply a common body of knowledge I can share with my audience. (130)

This rather bland statement sounds like an effort by a professing scientific socialist to dispose of an embarrassing but persistent irritant. Later on in the course of the same interview, however, he suggests that there is a weightier issue behind his insistent use of biblical themes and allusions. In a point that gets an ample elaboration in the play *I Will Marry When I Want*, Ngũgĩ equates Christianity and the Bible with alcohol. "Even today in many neo-colonial regimes as in Kenya," he explains, "the Church and the bar are the only two venues available for people's entertainment, particularly on Sundays" (130). Surely, Ngũgĩ goes beyond seeing the Bible as merely a readily available term of reference. These lines from *I Will Marry When I Want* hint at the sinister role Ngũgĩ thinks the Bible plays in the stupefaction of the Africans:

> We cannot end poverty by erecting a hundred churches in the village;
> We cannot end poverty by erecting a hundred beer halls in the village;
> Ending up with two alcoholics.
> The alcoholic of hard liquor,
> The alcoholic of the rosary. (114)

The lines are an unmistakable allusion to the Marxian equation of religion, in this case Christianity, with the opium of the people.

Furthermore, in *Decolonising the Mind*, Ngũgĩ castigates African writers and intellectuals of his generation who continue to write in English instead of indigenous languages. He asserts that by so doing the writers and intellectuals cut themselves off from empowering contacts with the peasants and workers of their societies. He laments most of all the fact that the African intelligentsia by continuing to write in English instead of indigenous languages recklessly leaves the African masses exposed to the onslaught from imperial culture and the propaganda of the maligned ruling elites in Africa who have a field day of unimpeded communication with the masses in African languages (26). "For example," he says, "The Bible is available in unlimited quantities in even the tiniest African language" (26). The Bible is presented as a central text of the imperial culture from which the African mind is in dire need of liberation.

Ngũgĩ is not by any means alone in his indictment of the Bible for its complicity in the colonial conquest of Africa. An apocryphal story generally passed on by word of mouth and rehashed in various written versions wherever the Christian mission was established in Africa goes: "When the white man came to our country, he had the Bible and we had the land. The white man said to us 'Let us pray.' After the prayer the white man had the land and we had the Bible" The same idea is reiterated by Ali Mazrui in *Cultural Forces in World Politics* (14). Mazrui asserts that of the three imperatives behind European imperialism, namely: God, the Bible, and Glor and Gold, all stand for God. Ngũgĩ himself laments the fact that for most Africans during the colonial period and for many years afterwards, the Bible provided the main literary experience. He says:

> African children who encountered literature in colonial schools and universities were made to experience the world as defined and reflected in the European experience of history. (*Decolonizing* 93)

Clearly Ngũgĩ is deeply troubled by the fact that the Bible is implicated in facilitating Western imperialism both in the past and in the present.

Musa Dube, who describes the Bible as a "cultural text of imperialism" (Dube 15), talks about the connection between the Bible, its readers and the institutions of Western imperialism in terms that resonate with the fundamental tenets of Ngũgĩ's decolonizing politics She argues that the Bible, as part of the imperialist culture that was rammed down the throats of subjugated peoples, is "implicated in the colonization and alienation of subject people from their own languages, religions, environments and culture" (Dube 15). Dube's statement is entirely consistent with Ngũgĩ's view that decolonizing the African mind means both a radical reversal of the effects of colonialism and a restoring of Africa's cultural integrity through the revival of indigenous languages, religions, environments and cultures. It is precisely to such a revival that Ngũgĩ harks when, in *I Will Marry When I Want,* Kiguunda blames his wife, Wangeci, of having talked him into doing something foolish when he had agreed to undergo a Christian marriage ceremony long after the two of them had been living together as husband and wife after their traditional African marriage. Kiguunda says:

> Who wanted a church wedding?
> You an old woman
> Wanting to go through a humiliating ceremony?
> And all because of looking down on our culture!
> You saw fools going for foreign customs
> And you followed in their footsteps.

> Do you think it is only foreign things
> Which are blessed? (*I Will Marry* 109)

In other words, when it comes to the issue of the role of the Bible in facilitating European imperialism and the concomitant colonization of the mind, the evidence, as Dube asserts, "is overwhelmingly damning" (15). Ngũgĩ would concur whole-heartedly.

The crucial problem that the Bible raises for Ngũgĩ as a writer with a Christian background, struggling, nevertheless, for the emancipation of the continent from mental colonization, is perhaps best summed up in a statement by the similarly placed Dube who explains,

> Those of us who grew up professing the Christian faith in the age
> of the armed struggle for liberation, from World War I to the South
> African independence (sic) in 1994, were never left to occupy our
> places comfortably...We were called upon to explain the ethics of our
> religion, to justify its practice, its practitioners and institutions [...] how
> could we as black Africans justify our faith in a religion that has betrayed
> us – a religion of the enemy, so to speak. (4)

The problem stems directly from Christianity's truth obligations, which include the obligation for all believers to hold the Bible, as a permanent source of truth (Foucault 170) and to regard the scriptures of other religions as falsehoods.

Ngũgĩ's treatment of the issue of the canonicity of the bible is best illustrated by an incident towards the beginning *A Grain of Wheat*. In the incident, the young Kihika rejects his teacher's assertion that female circumcision was an abomination: and "as Christians we are forbidden to carry on such practices (85)." He points out that Jesus himself had undergone a circumcision rite. He says:

> It's just the white people say so. The Bible does not talk about
> circumcising women. (86)

When the teacher decides to punish him for this 'blasphemy', Kihika refuses to submit to the punishment and demands that the teacher first cite a scripture that proved him wrong. "You will hit me only after you have told me the wrong I have done," Kihika said trembling with anger (86). Although he is unable to provide such a scripture, the teacher nevertheless insists on meting out the punishment, upon which Kihika bolts out of the classroom, never to return.

Eventually, Kihika joins the Mau-Mau guerrilla movement to fight against British colonial rule.

What is interesting about the incident described above is that at the same time as it re-affirms the validity of the Bible as the source of permanent truth, it also makes the Bible itself also affirm the validity of the practices of other religions. If the Bible is the source of permanent truth, in Ngũgĩ's novel part of the truth it reveals is that the religious texts and practices of other faiths are equally valid before God.

Ngũgĩ thus reveals the Bible as a site of contestation between Kihika, on the one hand, and the teacher, on the other. The teacher tries to use the Bible to suppress indigenous ritual practices in the interest of the spread of Christianity, while Kihika invokes the authority of the Bible to defend non-Christian religious practices against a rampantly hegemonizing Christianity. The teacher loses the contest because the verse from the Bible that he cites as proof that female circumcision is wrong, embarrassingly, fails to support his case. Not only does the verse not mention female circumcision, but also "circumcision of the flesh was not even specifically condemned" (86). Kihika, on his part, is vindicated in his defiance. He has scored an important moral victory on behalf of pre-Christian indigenous religions using the authority of the Bible itself. In other words, the Bible can be read in such a way that its canonical status in Christianity does not necessarily work to suppress indigenous religions, but to endorse their validity.

Such instances of Christianity's central text being turned against it are not mere imaginative whims of an eccentric revolutionary writer. John Karanja, in an article on the establishment of mission stations in Kenya, gives accounts of how biblical authority was invoked during the colonial period to support observance of non-Christian religious practices among Christian converts (254 – 84). Thus, forms of circumcision, bride-price and polygamy were often tolerated among converts because it was pointed out by them that they were not specifically condemned in the Bible.

Invoking biblical authority to circumvent Christian suppression of traditional African religious practices is a potent weapon in Ngũgĩ's decolonizing cultural politics. If he can use the Bible to show that pre-Christian African religious practices were valid proof of knowledge of God then it would follow, to paraphrase as Chinua Achebe's famous phrase, Africans knew about God and did not hear of him for the first time from European missionaries. The argument used by Christian missionaries that European expansion of their culture and religion to Africa was justified because it introduced the benefits of civilization and knowledge of God to backward and Godless peoples would all of a sudden fall away.

Christianity's radical potential from Ngũgĩ's point of view then clearly lies in the extent to which it is able to admit that African knowledge of God predates Christian missiology, thus opening the possibility for Christians to read the Bible in a way that urges them to accept the validity of other faiths and to co-existence with them. Such a sentiment was generally absent among the of proselytizing discourses of the missionaries. Ngũgĩ implies that the Christian truth obligation to hold certain books as a source of permanent truth must be extended to include the religious narratives of faiths other than Biblical ones.

In the above view Ngũgĩ concurs with leading African biblical scholars, among them Musa Dube and Canaan Banana, who argue that the Bible has no role in the decolonization process unless it were re-written so that it includes the sacred narratives of cultures other than those of the biblical holy lands.

> Religious shrines and traditions of the peoples of Asia, Africa, Latin America, Europe and the Caribbean must surely be important sources of God's revelation. (Banana 30)

Musa Dube sees evidence of God's self-revelation in the widespread phenomenon of "*Semoya*" in southern Africa. Semoya, "Spirit," is a notion that refers to the idea of an ever-present agent of God among all the believers (116). Through it men and women receive powers of prophecy, and truth, which on occasion supersede that from the Bible. A case in point is that of Virginia Lucas, a woman possessed by the spirit who was repeatedly asked, "Why are you a female church leader when the Bible seems to forbid it," and she replies, "I have been asked this question several times before. I always tell people that God spoke to me through the Spirit, God never opened the Bible to me, God's spirit told me to open a church and heal God's people, which is what I am doing now" (Dube 42).

In the above discussion I have tried to demonstrate an often-overlooked aspect of Ngũgĩ's use of biblical themes and allusions, namely: the fact Ngũgĩ uses biblical themes and allusions in order to find grounds in the Bible itself to defend the integrity of pre-Christian African beliefs and practices. It is important for him to do this because he is anxious to show that Africans also draw inspiration from sources other than the Bible. The following speech by Kihika in response to Karanja's criticism that he contradicts himself when at one point he says Jesus had failed and, at another, that Kenyan's need a Christ.

> Yes – I said he had failed because his death did not change anything, it did not make his people find a centre in the cross. All oppressed people have a cross to bear ... In Kenya we want deaths that will change things, that is to say, we want true sacrifice. But first we have to be ready to bear the cross. I die for you, you die for me, we become a sacrifice for one another. So that I can say that you, Karanja, are Christ. I am Christ. Everybody who takes the oath of Unity to change things in Kenya is Christ. Christ then is not one person. All those who take up the cross liberating Kenya are true Christs for us Kenyan people. (*A Grain* 95)

The above passage when read in conjunction with Kihika's own subsequent death in the novel, described as a "crucifixion by General R., suggests that Ngũgĩ uses Kihika as a Christ-figure, to prove that the Bible provided inspiration as well as heroic figures who were adopted as role models by freedom fighters" (26). This is indeed supported further by the fact that Kihika himself "read the Bible everyday, and took it with him wherever he went" (22).

However, what is often overlooked is the fact that juxtaposed with all these references to the Bible and the need for oppressed people to carry their own crosses refer to the pre-Christian practice of oath taking—"Everybody who takes the oath of unity to change things in Kenya is Christ" (95). This is sleight of hand by Ngũgĩ because while disclosing the fact that Jesus was an inspirational figure to the Mau mau fighters, he also succeeds in showing that the Bible endorses the non-Christian practice of "oath-taking." It is possible, in fact, of the two sources of inspiration the force of the oath of unity that swore the Kenyans to secrecy and readiness to die for their country, rather than the example of a self-sacrificing Christ, urging his fellow sufferers to turn the other cheek, made the Mau mau the dreaded organization that the colonial regime in Kenya sought to suppress by a brutal state of emergency. Ngũgĩ has cleverly used the Bible to show that people can draw inspiration from non-biblical faiths in ways that are identical and complementary to the way they can from the Bible.

The validity of traditional African faith is starkly contrasted with the sham and hypocrisy of post-colonial Kenya's Christianity in *I Will Marry When I Want*. Gicaamba is distressed by the way the neo-colonial elite in post-colonial Kenya use Christianity to "shut the eyes of the poor/ the peasants and all the workers/ the masses as a whole/ ensure that they never wake up and open their eyes/ to see what we are really doing to them" (113). As if in search of an alternative source of spiritual renewal, he harks back to the power of the pre-Christian practice of oath taking which in the past powered the Mau mau struggle for independence

> When we took the Mau mau oath,
> We used to make this vow:
> I'll always help this organization
> With all my strength and property
> I'll always aid members of this organization
> If a bean falls to the ground
> We shall split it equally among us
> If I fail to do so
> May this, the people's oath destroys me.
> And the blood of the masses turn against me. (*I Will Marry* 113)

This recognition that traditional African belief systems and practices are as valid sources of inspiration as those described in the Bible is not unique to Kenya. The Chimurenga liberation war that brought about majority rule in Zimbabwe gained some of its impetus as much to Christianity as to the spirit of a woman called Ambuya Nehanda (Banana 30). Nehanda was a spirit medium that inspired the Shona rebellion against the imposition of colonial rule in the 1890's. When finally she was arrested, the colonial regime executed her by public hanging. Yvonne Vera's eponymous novel re-enacts her story (1993).

The suggestion of a degree of harmonious co-existence between biblical beliefs and traditional African beliefs is only odd from the point of view of proselytizing mission Christianity, which emphasises a radical rupture between pre-conversion and post conversion religious states, a radical discontinuity between the world of the "saved" and "unsaved" Africans. However, as Karanja has shown, conversion in Kenya, and arguably elsewhere in Africa, occurred on the large scale it did because the converts did not perceive a radical discontinuity between biblical beliefs and practices on the one hand and traditional African beliefs and practices on the other (Karanja 269). Conversion may not have been as fundamental a break with pre-biblical religions and faiths as the missionary proselytisers would have wished; on the contrary, it may have been possible because in Christianity and the Bible Africans found ways of legitimating and preserving their own pre-Christian beliefs and practices. This is, I suggest, at the heart of Karanja's suggestion that in Kenya the African church acquired a distinctly Kikũyũ character because:

> It was important for mission Christianity to accommodate itself to the realities of Kikũyũ culture if it was to survive, let alone make an impact. (269)

It was an accommodation in which the missionaries followed a Kikũyũ lead rather than exercise their authority (269).

Ngũgĩ's deployment of biblical signifiers needs to be grasped, neither as a primarily Marxist-inspired attempt to expose the complicity of the Bible in the perpetuation of the infamies of colonialism in Africa, nor as an endorsement of the Bible's canonical status in Christian dogma as a timeless and placeless Word of God. Rather Ngũgĩ beckons us towards readings of the Bible that deconstruct its own claim to be the sole source of permanent truth for believers.

In fairness to the Christian Mission Societies who are in some respects the butt of Ngũgĩ's most barbed attacks, it is only right to point out that what Ngũgĩ is doing here is to problematize, from an African nationalist perspective, an issue that the mission societies themselves anticipated and had been grappling with as far back as the 1920's. According to D'Costa there were three major positions in the debate on the issue of the relationship between Christianity and other faiths. The "exclusivists" maintained that other faiths are marked by humankind's fundamental sinfulness and are therefore erroneous, and that Christianity offers the only valid path to salvation. Then there were the "inclusivists" who affirmed the salvific presence of god in non-Christian religions, but maintained that Christianity was the definitive and authoritative relation of God. Finally, there were the "pluralists" who argued that other faiths are equally salvific paths to the one God who is not exclusively Christian and that Christianity's claim that it is the only path to God should be rejected. These paradigms are a useful grid for the general mapping of the post-colonial manifestation of the problematic (D'Çosta 22, 52 80). Ngũgĩ, Dube and Banana are perhaps latter day pluralists.

-III-

I wish now to turn to the second part of my argument, namely; that Ngũgĩ's concern with the Christian practice of self-examination and confession leads to a depiction of women characters, particularly Mumbi in *A Grain of Wheat,* that may be best understood not as revolutionaries in a Marxist struggle, but as inspirational religious icons that serve as catalysts and agents of the Christian practices of self-examination and confession. The theme of *A Grain of Wheat* is encapsulated in the scene towards the end of the story when, upon hearing that Mugo had confessed his role as the betrayer of Kihika, Gikonyo says:

> He was a brave man... He stood before much honour, praises were heaped upon him. He would have become a chief. Tell me another person who would have exposed his soul for all the eyes to pick at...Remember that few in that meeting are fit to lift a stone against that man. Not unless I – we- too in turn open our hearts naked for the world to look at. (235)

Gikonyo's words above signal to the reader Ngũgĩ's preoccupation with self-examination and confession and bring to mind Foucault,s characterization of Christianity as a confessional religion. Foucault states:

> Each person has the duty to who he is, that is to try to know what is happening inside him, to acknowledge faults, to recognize temptations , to locate desires: and every one is obliged to disclose these things either to God or to others in the community and, hence, to bear public or private witness against oneself. (Foucault 170)

It is precisely because of the emphasis on confession and self-examination in the novel that Mugo has our sympathies even though he betrays Kihika, the revolutionary hero. Mumbi, too, retains our respect, even though in a moment of uncharacteristic weakness, she sleeps with Karanja while her husband is in detention and conceives the former's child. Karanja, on the contrary, remains the arch-villain in the novel because he never carries out the obligatory self-examination and confession that redeems the other characters.

From the point of view of radical feminist politics, there is not much to choose from in the positions that orthodox Marxism and Christianity ,as ideologies, assign to women. As stated earlier on in this paper Christianity and Marxism are utopian ideologies whose respective languages are dominated by binary oppositions which tend to collapse all differences in a manner that subordinates women's issues to male privileging issues of the conflict between "good" and "evil" or the class struggle. Christianity and Marxism both have what Jocelyn Murray calls, "an essentially virile profile"(68). Ngũgĩ's tendency to portray women as junior partners in revolutions in which men are invariably the leaders may be explained as the result of the influence of either revolutionary Marxism or Christianity. However, the fact that he uses women as catalysts and agents in acts of self-examination and confession which are important to Christianity but not to Marxism, makes Ngũgĩ ideologically closer to Christianity than to Marxism. This contention is made, not in order to downplay the significance of Ngũgĩ's revolutionary politics, but to suggest that his work does repay critical attention on the basis of approaches other than the overtly political.

The fact that there is only one major woman character in the *A Grain of Wheat* does not necessarily compromise Ngũgĩ's radical decolonizing politics even from a feminist perspective. What is disturbing is the range of virtues that Ngũgĩ draws upon or highlights in women in his attempt to create the character of Mumbi.

By his own admission Ngũgĩ began writing under the literary influence of the oral traditions of his native Kikũyũ culture, the Christian literature of his early mission school education and the English Literature masters of his secondary and university education curricula, particularly, Shakespeare, Conrad and D.H Lawrence and it seems that it is to these influences that Ngũgĩ looks for virtuous femininity in his characterization of Mumbi. Consequently, Mumbi comes across as a woman in a man's world and the feminine virtues that she embodies seem to be a projection of male desires as women's virtues generally are in Conrad, Lawrence and Shakespeare.

Let us begin with Ngũgĩ's depiction of Mumbi's childhood and early youth. Ngũgĩ seems anxious to hold her up as a model girl-child. While the boys, like Kihika, Gikonyo, Karanja and others engage in heated discussions about colonial rule and the need for the struggle, Mumbi is the apple of her parent's eyes and her destiny seems focussed on making some man a good wife when she grows up. She is modelled too closely on the sort of girl that the missionaries would have liked their converts to believe was Mary, the immaculate would-be mother of Jesus. She also recalls Miranda, Prospero's dutiful daughter, whose perfect childhood makes her the appropriate future bride to the man from the brave new world, Ferdinand, in Shakespeare's *The Tempest*. Mumbi is to Gikonyo as Miranda is to Ferdinand. Both women are embodiments of their respective societies' projections of male desires and are offered to men that are considered to deserve them best of all because they (the men) in turn embody society's ideal manhood.

Further on in his depiction of Mumbi as a young woman, it is to D.H.Lawrence to whom Ngũgĩ turns for the attributes that would supposedly endear her to both male and female readers. There is clearly something Lawrentian about descriptions of Mumbi in *A Grain of Wheat*. The sexual act between Mumbi and Gikonyo puts one in mind of both Miriam and Paul of *Sons and Lovers* and Mellors and Constance Chatterley in *Lady Chatterley's Lover*:

> "Let us explore the wood," Gikonyo suggested in a voice vibrant with subdued emotion. They came to an open space at the centre of the forest. . . . He stood facing Mumbi and surrendered himself to a power he knew drew them together. He held her hands and his fingers were full, so sensitive. (91)

Anyone with a mere acquaintance with Lawrence would not fail to recognize echoes of the Lawrentian male-dominated eroticism that finds its fullest expression in the sexual act in the woods. The trembling woman that sends a quiver of fear and joy trilling in his blood is perhaps as close as Ngũgĩ as a writer can get to Mellors and Constance without courting accusations of plagiarism.

> She lay against his breast, their hearts beat each to each … Mumbi was trembling, and this sent a quiver of fear and joy trilling in his blood. Gradually, he pulled her to the ground, the long grass covered them. Mumbi breathed hard, but could not, dared not, speak. One by one Gikonyo removed her clothes as if performing a dark ritual in the wood. (91)

It is in the climax of the sexual act that Mumbi can be read as Ngũgĩ's pretext to celebrate with D. H. Lawrence, the mysterious male potency embodied in the phallus, which achieves some sort of apotheosis in the eyes of women, smitten by a Freudian primeval penis envy. In the sex scene between Gikonyo and Mumbi, as in Lawrence's sex scenes, it is the man's sexual agency that is celebrated, as is clear from the fact that the penis is presented as an instrument for prising the female spirit open and eliciting the involuntary moan (92).

> Gikonyo found himself suspended in a void, he was near breaking point and as he swooned into the dark depth, he heard a moan escape Mumbi's parted lips. (*A Grain* 92)

It is as if Mumbi's sexual organs, and Mumbi herself, had no existence except as sources of the pleasure Gikonyo, had by right, as a man.

The next key moment in Mumbi's life is her marriage, which, in a Nelson and Winnie Mandela-like fashion, is cut short when Gikonyo is arrested and sent into detention for being a member of the Mau mau, leaving her to fend for herself throughout the hard years of the state of emergency. Ngũgĩ portrays her as a strong woman who endures with fortitude and supports her own and her husband's parents.

> Mumbi was depressed because there was no man in the house. In the end

> She tied a belt round her waist and took on a man's work. (141)

In an attitude reminiscent of the apartheid regime's towards Winnie Mandela in South Africa, the colonial regime, taunts and harasses Mumbi and banishes her from her home. The regime sends her to a regrouped village over which Karanja is the chief appointed by the regime. She steadfastly rebuffs Karanja's advances and stays loyal to her husband for seven long years, a worthy object of her warrior husband's love. Her loyalty to her husband is even more remarkable because Karanja whose favours she spurns is chief of the village and has power of life and death over her. She is aware of the danger she is in as she states:

> Karanja always pointed out to me that my faithfulness was in vain...He did not humble himself in front of me as he used to do. In stead he laughed to hurt me, and I hung on to Gikonyo with all my heart. I would wait for him, my husband, even if I was fated to rejoin him in the grave. (*A Grain* 149)

Gikonyo, on his part, survives the trials of detention because his spirits are buoyed by the cherished hope that his wife remains true to him and he would one day see her again. Ironically, it is the desire to see his wife again which becomes his undoing. Unable to hold on any longer, he confesses to having taken the Mau-mau oath to the colonial authorities in order to obtain his release and realize his hope of being with his beloved wife again. However, when Mumbi learns from Karanja of her husband's imminent release, she is so overwhelmed with joy and gratitude that she allows Karanja to make love to her. It is a weakness she regrets immediately when she collects her thoughts, but as luck would have it, she conceives. So when Gikonyo returns home he finds his wife nursing another man's child. A woman whose image was his source of hope and strength becomes the object of destructive, self-righteous indignation. In a reaction not too dissimilar to Othello's when he contemplates his supposed betrayal by Desdemona —

> Was this fair paper, this most godly book,
> Made to write whore on? (IV.ii.69)

Gikonyo's thoughts are wracked by imaginings of Mumbi's fall from grace:

> The image of Mumbi moaning with pleasure as her naked body bore Karanja's weight corroded him everywhere. He recreated the scene in its sordid details: the creaking bed, Karanja's fingers touching Mumbi everywhere etc., (*A Grain* 120)

At this point Gikonyo seems completely oblivious to the fact that he is himself guilty of betrayal since he confessed to having taken the oath to escape detention. Perhaps he could see his betrayal as mitigated by the fact that it had served the greater cause of reuniting them. But this only serves to intensify his sense of injury, for he finds his wife "begrimed," to borrow Othello's term, for no higher purpose than wanton lasciviousness.

The unfairness of Gikonyo's judgement and Mumbi's patient acceptance of his reaction suggests that Ngũgĩ is at pains here to show that women played an important role in the struggle for independence. Yet no matter how much sympathy the reader may feel for Mumbi, she hardly comes across as a revolutionary in a sense that would commend itself to the women's struggles in a Marxist tradition. The Setswana word for woman, "Mosadi," means " one who stays home and waits, " because women traditionally were the home-keepers and stayed home while the men were out hunting or at war. There is too much of a "mosadi" in Mumbi to make her a credible Marxist revolutionary.

Conrad, too, leaves his mark on the Ngũgĩan woman. Later in the novel Mumbi is cast in the role of Conrad's "Intended" in *Heart of Darkness*. Like Kurtz's intended who waits patiently for the protagonist of her ideals to return from Africa, Mumbi waits patiently for the return of her husband and protagonist of her freedom ideals to return from detention. And like Kurtz in *Heart of Darkness* who experiences a disintegration of the idealism that had inspired him, Gikonyo too, because he can not withstand loneliness and isolation in prison, and pining for the company of his wife, betrays the ideals that Mumbi, in her perfection, embodies and which had led him to join the Mau-mau.

In casting Mumbi in the mould of the Conradian woman who embodies illusory ideals which idealistic men pursue at their own peril, Ngũgĩ may have been a more profound critic of his own revolutionary idealism than he probably intended. A conventional practice in literature is to make the man whose attitudes to life the writer approves of generally win the favours of the virtuous heroine of the story. A possible explanation of the incredible sexual scene between Mumbi and Karanja could be that Ngũgĩ may thus be commending Karanja's cynicism and refusal to be taken in by the ideals of the struggle. Such cynicism seems vindicated by the fact that the putative heroes of the struggle betray the ideals for which other people sacrificed their lives and make   a sham of the struggle even in the midst of preparations to celebrate its supposed success. The fact that Ngũgĩ depicts Karanja successfully seducing Mumbi seems to revise the significance of the earlier scene in which it is Gikonyo rather than Karanja who wins Mumbi's favours during the race to the train, which appears to be a commendation of Gikonyo's loyalty to Kihika and an indictment of Karanja's cynicism.

Furthermore, Mumbi's sexual encounter with Karanja, the struggle's arch enemy and the arch-traitor of the revolution results in a child. Ngũgĩ could as easily have made Mumbi make love and have a child with any one of the unsullied, self-proclaimed revolutionaries that worship at Kihika's shrine. The fact that he does not may be a grudging commendation of Karanja's refusal to be taken in by the utopian ideals of the struggle that led many a naïve person to death or incarceration. Ngũgĩ may be grudgingly conceding that the idealism that drives the struggle may be fundamentally flawed and to be less preferable to Karanja's sceptical cynicism that makes him invest in the tangible and immediate benefits of siding with the might of the colonial regime.

The aspect of Ngũgĩ's attempt to delineate of Mumbi's character in a way that does not make her a mere projection of patriarchal desires occurs towards the end of the story in the aftermath of the struggle. The end of the struggle in the novel is a moment of stock- taking and every body is required to undertake the introspection to enable them to come to terms with their roles in the struggle. Mumbi is among the first to do this. Her acceptance of the child she has with Karanja, despite the loathing she felt for Karanja, suggests that the struggle has left every one "holding the baby," so to speak. She leads the way in dealing with the seamy but inalienable aspects of their history that the child represents. Hence, her jubilation when her husband, Gikonyo, in the end deals with the betrayal and accepts the child. Furthermore, not only does she bare her own soul to Mugo when she explains the circumstances of her seduction by Karanja, but she in turn listens to Mugo's confession without passing judgement on him, even though the person Mugo betrayed was her own brother Kihika. Similarly, she does not pass judgement and seek revenge against Karanja for his role as a member of the colonial regimes home-guard or for the strain in her marriage.

Mumbi's attitude is completely at odds with that of the self-appointed high-priest of the revolution, General R., who advocates a witch-hunt against those who betrayed the revolution would be judged and condemned "by their actions" (*A Grain* 238). Mumbi is an embodiment of nation-building attributes which recall both the creator in the sense that Ngũgĩ explains in the remarks cited above, and the divine grace by which Mary becomes the most blessed among all women. In other words, Ngũgĩ's Mumbi is not so much the Marxist freedom fighter but the pious receptacle of the divine grace through which society is saved.

In *Penpoints, Gunpoints and Dreams*, Ngũgĩ draws on his traditional Kikũyũ cultural background and explains that his inspiration for the image of Mumbi is, in fact, the traditional Kikũyũ culture in which the name 'Mumbi' means "one who moulds" and is used to refer to the creator or God.

> There are various kinds of creatorship that are recognised in Gikũyũ culture: There is *mumbi wa iguru na thi;* the creator of heaven and earth. There is *mumbi wa nyungu*; maker of pots . . . *mumbi wa mihianamo*; maker of images. (10)

Ngũgĩ states that in the Gikũyũ culture, "Mumbi" is generally a girl's name and implies an association of women and the Godhead or creatorship. It seems reasonable therefore to assume that in his depiction of Mumbi in *A Grain of Wheat* Ngũgĩ makes the association of women as bearers of nation-building qualities with the godhead or the creator in order to highlight the role of women in his view of revolutionary struggle.

Ngũgĩ's depiction of Mumbi as a bearer of socially-constructive attributes, owes as much to traditional African culture as to Christianity but not much to Marxism. Mumbi is a rather idealized apparition constructed also from the attributes of biblical women. The attributes ascribed to her are not those of a woman who would fight for women's issues and represent the aspirations of women in a secular revolutionary struggle. Mumbi is an obvious allusion. is to Mary, the mother of Jesus in the Bible The fact that Mumbi is a Mary-like figure is clear from the fact that descriptions of her childhood share a pedigree with those to be found in mission school readers intended to inculcate Christian values among female converts who often bore local variations of the name Mary, e.g., Maliya, Meli, Mariya etc. Like Mary in the Bible, Mumbi is presented as a paragon of her culture's feminine virtues. Subtle correspondences are disclosed as the story progresses: despite her premarital sexual encounter with Gikonyo, she is nevertheless presented as a virtuous woman fit to be the mother of the Jesus-like child that would embody the troubled land's future. Furthermore, like Mary who is betrothed to be married to a carpenter, Mumbi is betrothed and eventually marries Gikonyo, a wood carver (i.e., like Mary in the Bible, Mumbi marries a man who works with wood). Both Mary and Mumbi bear children who are not biologically sired by their husbands, and both husbands have excruciating psychological problems coming to terms with the fact.

As with the New Testament in which Mary is primarily the bearer of the Christ-child through whom society finds its redemption from an unwholesome past, Mumbi is a conduit for bringing into the world the child that embodies both the idealism that drives the struggle and the human weaknesses that lead people to betrayal it. "We want a Kenya built on the heroic tradition of resistance of our people," (*A Grain* 221), General R. tells the party at the Uhuru celebrations. But the child's conflicted parentage reminds us that General R. is wrong. It is not through the search for heroes to revere and traitors to punish, as General R. suggests when he says: "We must revere our heroes and punish the traitors and collaborators with the colonial enemy" (221) that a viable future will be secured. For the truth is that such a clear-cut division between the sheep and the goats is not possible because "all have sinned and fallen short of the glory of God."

Mumbi is aware of the need for every one that was involved in the struggle to examine his or her heart so that when reconciliation and forgiveness finally come they are not a mere sweeping of the dirt under the carpet. When her husband offers reconciliation and forgiveness before they had together carried out the introspection that she believes should come first, she stops him, saying:

> No! Not to-day. People try to rub out things, but they cannot. Things are not easy. What has passed between us is too much to be passed over in a

> sentence. We need to talk, to open our hearts to one another, examine
> them, and then together plan the future we want. (*A Grain* 246)

And, as if to underscore the indelibility of the history she talks about, she
concludes, "But now, I must go for the child is ill" (*A Grain* 246).

Towards the end Gikonyo comes round to Mumbi's way of thinking, when
overawed by Mugo's confession of his role in the betrayal of Kihika, he rejects
General R's retributive justice. He says of Mugo:

> He was a brave man... He stood before much honour, praises were heaped
> upon him. He would have become a chief. Tell me another person who
> would have exposed his soul for all the eyes to pick at...Remember that
> few in that meeting are fit to lift a stone against that man. Not unless I –
> we- too in turn open our hearts naked for the world to look at. (*A Grain*
> 235)

Hearing Gikonyo speak this way, Mumbi "felt herself lifted to the clouds" (234).

However, the virtues with which Ngũgĩ invests Mumbi in order to enable
her to fit this role are incongruous with the rough and tumble of the struggle for
power and resources. They produce a woman perched upon a pedestal, shrouded
in oracular mystique, high above the day-to-day rough and tumble of social
struggles for power and resources. Her role in the novel seems be to facilitate as
well as to exemplify the practice of self-examination and confession which,
according to Michel Foucault, is one of the truth obligations of the Christian
faith.

Ngũgĩ may have intended Mumbi to come across to the reader as a
revolutionary activist in the Marxist sense of the word but the attributes that he
has thus assigned to her move him closer to Christian than to Marxist
revolutionary ideals. The fact that Mumbi has virtually no agency in the novel
would dismay many women readers—Mugo, Mohanty, Spivak—who would
prefer to see a more positive positioning of the function of female wombs and
bodies (Spivak 291). Mumbi comes across as the long suffering woman whose
suffering confers upon her redeeming insights or graces – redeeming, not to her
and other women as such, but to men otherwise bent on a self-destruction. In
this way, she is cast in the same mould as Achebe's Beatrice in *Anthills of the
Savannah* whose suffering and loss of a lover are the price she pays for the role
of the high-priestess who acts as the midwife at the rebirth of the nation
destroyed by misguided ambitions of self-seeking men. It also earns Mumbi the
role of the novels oracular mouthpiece. In other words, Mumbi is an idealised
paragon of a virtuous African womanhood, and like Mary in the New Testament
whose virtues are intended to make her a fitting object of the immaculate
conception, Mumbi is carefully drawn so that she becomes an appropriate
mouthpiece for the author's ethical insights in the novel and bears the child who
embodies the society's future hopes. Above all, Mumbi's role is to be catalyst

and agent the act of self-examination and confession that give *A Grain of Wheat* its moral force and makes it a profoundly religious work.

Ngũgĩ may owe his decolonizing vision to Edward Said or Franz Fanon's cultural politics, but the latter two ignore or subsume women's issues within the anti-imperialist struggle and have little to say about the role of religion in revolutionary struggles. In Ngũgĩ women and religion are not ignored. On the evidence of *A Grain of Wheat* Ngũgĩ seeks to satisfy women's aspirations in quasi-religious roles as facilitators and practitioners of the processes of introspection and confession. Such a role for women may not intersect too happily with the demands of a secular revolutionary anti-imperialism but does not detract from the validity of his decolonizing project, especially if Ngũgĩ's decolonizing vision is understood as addressing the religious inflection in the imperial production of human subjects.

Works Cited

Achebe, Chinua. *Anthills of the Savannah.* London: Heinemann, 1987.

Banana, Canaan. "The Case for a New Bible." In *'Re-Writing' the Bible: The Real Issues.* Ed. John L.Cox, Isobel Mukonyora, and F.J. Vestraelen. Gweru: Mambo P,1993.

Conrad, Joseph. *Heart of Darkness.* Hammondsworth: Penguin, 1983.

Dube, Musa. *Postcolonial Feminist Interpretation of the Bible.* St.Louis, Chalice P, 2000.

D'Costa, G. *Theology and Religious Pluralism.* Oxford: Basil Blackwell, 1986.
  The Church Mission Society and World Christianity. Studies in the History of Christian Missions. Ed. Ward Kevin Ward and Brian Stanley. Cambridge: Ferdmans and Richmond, Surrey: Curzon P, 2000, fn.

Foucault, Michel. *Religion and Culture.* Selected and ed. Jeremy Carrette. New York: Routledge, 1999

James, Adeola. "Writing and Gender: Micere Mugo Interviewed by Adeola James." *In Their Own Voices: African Women Writers Talk.* London: James Currey, 1990. 93-101.

Karanja, J. "The Role of Kikũyũ Christians in Developing a self-conscious African Anglicanism." *The Church Mission Society and World Christianity.* Studies in the History of Christian Missions. Ed. Kevin Ward and Brian Stanley. Cambridge: William B. Ferdmans and Richmond, Surrey: Curzon, 2000 254-284.

Lawrence, D.H. *Lady Chatterley's Lover.* Hammondsworth: Penguin, 1993
———. *Sons and Lovers.* Hammondsworth: Penguin, 1987.

Kings, Gavin. "Mission and the Meeting of Faiths." *The Church Mission Society and World Christianity.* Studies in the History of Christian Missions. Ed. Kevin Ward and Brian Stanley. Cambridge: William B. Ferdmans and Richmond, Surrey: Curzon P, 2000. 66-90.

Mazrui, Ali. *Cultural Forces in World Politics*. London: James Currey, 1990.

Mohanty, Chandra T., Ann Russo, and Lourdes Torres, eds. *Third World Women and the Politics of Feminism*. Bloomington: Indiana UP, 1991.

Murray, J. "The Role of Women in the Church Missionary Society." *The Church Mission Society and World Christianity*. Studies in the History of Christianity. Ed. Kevin Ward and Brian Stanley. Cambridge: William B. Ferdmans and Richmond, Surrey: Curzon, 2000. 66-90.

Mwikisa, P.W. "Rearticulation of Difference: Ngũgĩ's Redeployment of Biblical Signifiers in *A Grain of Wheat* and *I Will Marry When I Want.*" *Journal of Theology for Southern Africa*. Spec. Issue: Reading the Bible in Africa 108 (2000): 95-113.

Nazareth, Peter. Ed. *Critical Essays on* Ngũgĩ *wa Thiongó*. New York: Twayne. 2000. 15-16

Ngũgĩ wa Thiong'o. *A Grain of Wheat*. Rev.ed. Oxford: Heinemann, 1986.

———. *Decolonizing the Mind: The Politics of Language in African Literature*. London: James Currey, 1986.

———. *Penpoints, Gunpoints and Dreams: Towards A Critical Theory of the Arts. and the State in Africa*. Clarendon Lectures in English Literature. 1996. Oxford: Clarendon P, 1998

Ngũgĩ wa Mirii and Ngũgĩ wa Thiongo. *I Will Marry When I Want*. Trans. From Kikũyũ by authors. London: Heinemann, 1982.

Williams, Peter. "'Not Transplanting' Henry Venn's Strategic Vision." *The Church Mission Society and World Christianity*. Studies in the History of Christianity. Ed. Kevin Ward and Brian Stanley. Cambridge: William B. Ferdmans and Richmond, Surrey: Curzon . 2000.147-172.

Wilkinson, Jane. Ed. *Talking with African Writers: Interviews with African Poets, Playwrights and Novelists*. London: James Currey, 1992.

Shakespeare, W. *Othello*. Edited by A. Walker and John Dover Wilson. London: Cambridge UP, 1969.

———. *The Tempest*. Ed. C. Dymkowski. New York: CUP, 2000.

Spivak, G. "Three Women's Texts and a Critique of Imperialism." *Critical Inquiry*, (1985): 262-280.

Usry, Glen and Craig S. Keener. *Blackman's Religion: Can Christianity Be Afrocentric?* Downers Grove: Intervarsity P, 1966.

Vera, Yvonne. *Nehanda*. Harare: Baobab Books, 1993.

Missionary Movements, Imperialism & Christianity
Danielle Melvin

> Now it is not good for the Christian's health to hustle the Aryan brown,
> For the Christian riles and the Aryan smiles, And it weareth the Christian down. And the end of the fight is a tombstone white with the name of the late deceased And the epitaph drear: "A fool lies here who tried to hustle the East.
> —Rudyard Kipling and Wolcott Balestier, heading to Chapter V of *The Naulahka: a story of West and East*

There are many connecting threads in the motifs that I have encountered in reading African, Caribbean, Indian, and Latino postcolonial literature. Displacement, marginalization, exploitation, mimicry, isolationism, and imperialism are a few, but none are as reactionary to me as the thread of Christianity. Whether in Soyinka's *Death and the King's Horseman* (1976), Ngũgĩ's *Matagari* (1980), Rushdie's *Midnight Children* (1980), Dangarembga's *Nervous Conditions* (1988), or Edgell's *Beka Lamb* (1986), the influence of Christianity is revealed, whether syncretistically, overtly, satirically, or symbolically. It seemed as if every oppressed character that I was introduced to in my readings had somehow confronted the Christian religion in some form or fashion whether through Catholic or Protestant missionary schools and churches, or by assimilating Christian practices and beliefs within their own traditional practices. Christianity's resiliency to survive in postcolonial literature even under unfavorable conditions reveals two major ideas. First, the role of Christianity in shaping the cultural environment of many postcolonial regions cannot and should not be undermined. Secondly, groups colonized under the auspices of Christianity have proven to be as equally as resilient as Christianity in surviving under adverse conditions forming a knotted relationship between Christianity and those groups affected by Christian ideology which is often seen in syncretistic practices. These ideas are most important to me in my attempts to explain the relationship between Christianity and colonialism within postcolonial texts. However this task demands more than my individual undertaking, although I believe regardless of the size, any undertaking in this initiative is worthwhile.

Even though a generous amount of literature has already been devoted to the double theme of Christianity and colonialism, Christianity and colonialism are themes too personal, too profound, and too impacting upon the 21st century to ignore. Colonialism in practice may be over, but its form has transfigured throughout the ages, and although the practice of Christianity has continued throughout a considerable portion of the history of the world, its form has experienced considerable changes as well.

To promote colonization of the African countries, I believe that colonial settlers and colonizers used Christian missionaries knowingly and unknowingly as assistants, but I do not believe that the promotion of colonization was also the aim of all Christian missionaries. In this chapter I consider some of the portrayals of missionaries and churches as represented by characters from *Things Fall Apart* and *Devil on the Cross*. First I discuss how these portrayals are used by the authors, and the effects these portrayals have upon the relationship between colonization and Christianity as represented primarily through missionaries. I also discuss the similarities and differences between the aims of the colonizer and the missionary. Secondly, I suggest a critique that is derived from the portrayals depicted by Achebe and Ngũgĩ, de-centering. Thirdly, I consider the affects of writings that deal with colonial issues in a postcolonial setting, and I end with concluding thoughts for this chapter.

Missionaries' widespread influence within Africa is reflected in the literature of postcolonial Africa. Achebe and Ngũgĩ are no exceptions. Achebe's *Things Fall Apart* considered one of the most important novels in portraying the influence of colonization upon Africa from an African perspective is an example. Note Achebe's description of Mr. Brown, a fictional missionary in the epic novel *Things Fall Apart*: "In this way Mr. Brown learned a good deal about the religion of the clan and he came to the conclusion that a frontal attack on it would not succeed. And so he built a school and a little hospital in Umofia" (166). Later on, Mr. Brown who brings considerable peaceful change to the village not only through conversion but medicinal and educational practices, becomes stricken with bad health and was forced to leave. His successor, Mr. Smith is quite the contrary to peaceful and gentle Mr. Brown: "[Mr. Smith] condemned openly Mr. Brown's policy of compromise and accommodation. He saw things as black and white. And black was evil" (169).

Mr. Brown and Mr. Smith were both missionary preachers who helped establish a Christian church in the village of Umofia. Their modes of establishment were vastly different however, in that Mr. Brown was more cooperative with the Ibo people of Umofia while Mr. Smith was less cooperative and highly intolerant of the traditional religious practices: "Within a few weeks of his arrival in Umofia Mr. Smith suspended a young woman from the church for pouring new wine into old bottles. This woman had allowed her heathen husband to mutilate her dead child" (170). With these portrayals, Achebe depicts the two most familiar personalities of the missionary leaders. One personality, Mr. Smith, connotes a taskmaster, while the other personality, Mr. Brown, depicts a Livingstone figure. These prototype-missionaries, paved the way for the impressions that would be left behind long after colonialism had ended. Interestingly, *Things Fall Apart* is one of the most widely taught novels throughout high schools and institutions of higher learning and could be the first introduction to traditional African themes for many of its readers. The potential influence of these types of portrayals cannot be ignored in creating un-receptiveness toward Christianity. Readers that are already empathetic with the stories of those oppressed, generally become apathetic to those using oppressive tactics. By creating missionary characters that depict a rigid and unaffectionate system of Christian thought, readers in turn may become hostile not just to the Christian practices but Christianity itself.

Although Ngũgĩ's popularity within the United States may not be as recognizable, he is one of the premier voices of African thought and prose. Ngũgĩ has created a seemingly negative impression of the effects of missionary activity as described in his work, *Devil on the Cross* by the rambunctious character, Kĩhaahu. In *Devil on the Cross*, one of the testifiers, Kĩhaahu wa Gatheeca, declares the usefulness of Christianity for marginalizing indigenous people:

> Better meanness that is covert: better a system of theft that is disguised by lies. Or why do you think that our imperialist friends brought us the Bible? Do you think that they were being foolish when they urged workers and peasants to close their eyes in prayer and told them that earthly things were vain? Why do you think I go to all the church fund-raising Haraambe meetings? (123)

Before I discuss the actual missionary interactions with the native people of Kenya and Nigeria as represented in the texts, I would like to draw attention to the language used by Ngũgĩ's and Achebe's narrators. Achebe uses the phrase "frontal attack" (166) while Ngũgĩ's lively character, Kĩhaahu, begins his harangue with the phrases, "meanness that is covert," "system of theft disguised by lies" (123). These descriptive adjectives and phrases evoke pictures of militarism, and create an imperialistic attitude of dividing the tribe and in the aftermath of the division, conquering the land, an idea that missionary activities should not totally be exonerated from. Yet, I believe that the usage of this language sets up a preconceived idea about missionary movements being more closely related to the exploits of colonialism than the Biblical-aims of evangelism, and the outcome of these preconceptions largely depend on whether "Mr. Smith" or "Mr. Brown" is portrayed.

As the language suggests, missionary movements and colonialism often appeared to work simultaneously, linking the religious movements of the colonizing nations with the political movements. The linkage of religion and politics or in this case, Christianity and colonialism seems difficult to untangle, and this is not surprising when religion and politics are involved. Missionary movements did influence the spread of Imperialism in Africa, yet not all the aims of missionary movements were to continue the spread of Imperialism in Africa. The validity of Kĩhaahu's comments about Imperialism and the Bible are valid for Kĩhaahu's agenda, and it must be evaluated upon the basis of this agenda, which I believe is to exploit his own country and people for profit and gain. Kĩhaahu is representative of not only the neo-colonizer but also the post-colonizer of colonial times. As Kĩhaahu reminds the listeners of his testimony, "Why do you think that our imperialist friends brought us the Bible?" (123). He is merely an echo of former times, and as Ngũgĩ depicts in Kĩhaahu, a time that continues to influence Kenya. But are the missionaries to blame? Did the imperialist friends really just bring the Bible to help divide and conquer the people of Africa? Frantz Fanon author of *The Wretched of the Earth* believes so and likens the Christian religion to parasites that need to be destroyed:

> That is why we must put the DDT which destroys parasites, the bearers of disease, on the same level as the Christian religion which wages war on embryonic heresies and instincts, and on evil as yet unborn. The recession of yellow fever and the advance of evangelization form part of the same balance-sheet [...]. I speak of the Christian religion, and no one need be astonished. The Church in the colonies is the white people's Church, the foreigner's Church. She [church] does not call the native to God's ways but to the ways of the white man, of the master, of the oppressor. And as we know, in this matter many are called but few chosen. (34)

Fanon's position on Christianity and what Christianity represents through the church echoes Ngũgĩ's character, Kĩhaahu, and this is not coincidental. Ngũgĩ was deeply influenced by Fanon, as well as Marx and Engels (Lovesey). Fanon's position as echoed by the character Kĩhaahu brings up a significant point. Christianity was often used not to teach the precepts found within the pages of the Bible, but to reemphasize the precepts of the colonizers and the system of colonialism. Fanon's description is an example of Imperialism at work through the vehicle of missionaries. Missionaries may have employed the tactics of imperialism at times, but all missionaries were not imperialists governed by their desires for land and wealth. Kīhaahu supports the fraudulent practices of Christians who have replaced the precepts of the Bible with their own agendas and objectives. Kīhaahu asks why the imperialists brought the Bible, and now the question must be raised, why do postcolonial works such as *Things Fall Apart* and *Devil on the Cross* bring us portrayals of the Bible in their writings? What should we gather?

Fragmentation and displacement. These words are commonly used in postcolonial studies. Both terms indicate separation or a breaking apart, but when discussing the people who were oppressed by colonialism, fragmentation and displacement describe the mental shifting between two worlds—the world of the colonizer, and the world of the colonized. The colonized must not only evaluate their own thinking patterns as they relate to the traditions of their native homelands, but also decide what traditions if any from the colonizers they will discard or continue. These traditions included education practices introduced through mission schools, commerce and business practices introduced through colonialism, and finally the religion introduced through colonialism. Missionaries during the colonial era potentially had to make similar decisions with their treatment of Christian apparatus especially the Bible in determining which portions of the Bible would be discarded or adapted to fend off or assimilate into the native religious practices of the regions. For example, notice Mr. Brown's description of God to one of the great elders in the village, Akunna: "You should not think of Him [God] as a person [...]. It is because you do so that you imagine He must need helpers. And the worst thing about it is that you give all the worship to the false gods you have created" (165). Mr. Brown's explanation of God lacks an integral premise of Christianity. This is the belief in the Trinity, God the father, God the son in the person of Jesus Christ, and God the Holy Spirit. Akuuna's perception of God as a person has credibility when the Trinity is examined, but Mr. Brown eliminates this point. Mr. Brown's theology is an example of what Wilbert Shenk refers to as "Christendom":

> Christendom insisted that an entire population or society was Christian. No place was given to mission or evangelization. "Christianization" was a one-time step. Subsequently, the essential task was to maintain the religiopolitical status quo [...]. Religiously, Christendom was maintained through a sacerdotal-sacramental system that was subject to various abuses. From time to time there were appeals for reform and renewal of the church. Important as these reforms were, they largely failed to challenge and overcome Christendom's deeply non-missionary understanding of the church [...]. The solution to this was to encourage the formation of missionary societies, patterned after the trading companies and newly emerging voluntary societies. (6)

Writers such as V.S. Naipaul in his novel *Mimic Men*, often portray characters that seem to be de-centered from both their indigenous environment and the foreign environment that they traveled to. Likewise, missionaries and their portrayals of Christianity became de-centered from their own foundational beliefs fostered in the classrooms of seminaries and sanctuaries of churches thousands of miles away, but not practiced until arrival in their targeted areas. The results of this de-centering from their home environment, is the same for both the missionary and the post-colonized. These results were the creation of a new identity due to the deletions and additions made necessary to adapt to their new environments. For the previous colonized mind such as Naipaul's character, Ralph Singh, it became easy to lose one's identity in a place that was void of any reminders of home. What was lost for the missionary removed from their home environment, in most cases was their identity in the Bible. De-centering the Biblical message from the actual Bible is probably one of the most under-studied concepts in the study of relationships between Christianity and African regions, but arguably one of the most important. What I mean by this is that I believe most missionaries referred to by authors such as Ngũgĩ and Achebe were actually so far removed from the Biblical premises of evangelism, that what most people received as the gospel of Christ, was only a poor imitation of Christianity and rather the Christendom Shenk refers to. And since these imitations were derived from some of the methods used in the prestigious churches and seminaries back in Europe, it is not surprising that "Europe itself is now a post-Christian society where religion is essentially an identity tag" (Woodward 46). One would laugh at any student who attempted to write a dissertation on Shakespeare's tragedies after having read only a single copy of the cliff notes of *Romeo and Juliet*. It is just as absurd to consider Biblical perspectives from people who have never studied the Bible. Jesus Christ, the central figure of Christianity and evangelism, says the second greatest commandment after loving God is to "love thy neighbor as thyself" (Matt. 22:37). Yet the neighbors of the missionary settlements as portrayed in the works of Achebe and Ngũgĩ were often treated in a way altogether foreign to the concept of love. Missionaries whose aims were never Biblically based set the standard, or rather lowered the bar for missionaries whose pursuits were actually Bible-centered. A narration like Kĩhaahu's set the standard for misinterpreting Christianity because the church that Kĩhaahu calls to the reader's attention was flawed as well. Notice Gatuĩria's father's comments to Gatuĩria after he learns Gatuĩria will teach music and culture at the university:

> How can you strip me naked before the whole church congregation
> [...]? Remember the Ham of old, who saw Noah's nakedness and refused
> to do anything about it [...]. He was cursed to sire the children of darkness
> forever. If God had not later had mercy on him and sent the children of
> Shem to our Africa, where would we, the children of Ham, now be? (135)

Unbeknownst to Gatuĩria's father neither Ham, nor Ham's children are cursed. According to the actual Bible passage that Gatuĩria's father makes reference to, only one of Ham's sons were cursed, Canaan (Genesis 9:25).

When postcolonial works revisit colonial themes such as missionary involvements during colonization, one or two things happen. First, the post-modern writer can create what I like to call a new variety of history. By variety I mean a type of writing that includes past historical facts with facts or incidents that were often eliminated or reduced in order to maintain certain ideologies within an environment. For example, consider the collapse of communism in Eastern Europe in the late 1980's. History books that were issued under communist regimes to support communist beliefs had to be revised to include eras and people that were eliminated due to their anti-communist positions. African postcolonial writers have the same responsibility, which is to reintroduce to the world themes and notion that were excluded from literary works by those in support of the colonial system and imperialistic rule. Thus, Achebe and Ngũgĩ have the ability to provide a new version of an old argument, which is the question of the role of Christianity during the colonial period.

Secondly, rather than create a new version, the post- modern writer can fall into the trap of reiterating the same themes and notions that they so vehemently resist. All that is in the past is not useless to the present, and all that is in the present is not useless to the past. Both past and present learn from each other, and the writer who recognizes this and interweaves their writing with subject matter that pulls from the past and present has learned to portray in their writings a more stable picture where no one particular group is either deified or defamed. In response to an interview question, Derek Walcott, reemphasizes this point: "The whole process of civilization is cyclical. The good civilization absorbs a certain amount, like the Greeks. Empires are smart enough to steal from the people they conquer. They steal the best things. And the people who have been conquered should have enough sense to steal back" (75).

In response to the question I raise earlier, I believe that Achebe and Ngũgĩ have brought us the Bible in their works in an attempt to interpret the role of Christianity during colonization, but have done so by merely cutting and pasting certain premises of Christianity from Christianity's overall foundation based on the Bible. Thus, rather than de-colonizing Christianity within their texts, they mimic the same practices of the missionaries' de-centering style of Christianity. As Chinweizu et al. suggests in Toward the Decolonization of African Literature: "If decolonization is the aim, such synthesis must be within the parameters of the African tradition rather than outside it. It should expand and renew the tradition through new syntheses and breakthroughs rather than leave it unchanged and in moribund stasis" (239).

The African tradition remains solidified in Achebe and Ngũgĩ's works, but it is the new syntheses and breakthroughs that are lacking, or in Walcott's opinion, the stealing back. Theoretical and narrative interpretations of the Bible are necessary and vital to understanding post-colonial texts that have been so riveted socially and religiously by Christianity. However, these interpretations must include more balanced portrayals of Christianity derived from current and past analysis of Biblical themes.

Works Cited

Achebe, Chinua. *Things Fall Apart.* New York: Ballantine Books, 1959.

Chinweizu, Onwuchekwa Jemie, and Ihechukwu Madubuike. *Toward the*
       Decolonization of African Literature. Washington, D.C.: Howard
       UP, 1983.

Fanon, Frantz._*The Wretched Of The Earth.* New York: Grove Press, 1963.

Kipling, Rudyard and Wolcott Bailstier. Introduction. *The Naulahka: a*
       story of West and East. London: Macmillan, 1925.

Lovesey, Oliver. Ngũgĩ *wa Thiong'o.* New York: Twayne, 2000.

Milne, Anthony. "This Country Is a Very Small Place." Conversations with
       Derek Walcott. Ed.William Baer. Jackson, MI: University Press of
       Mississippi, 1996. 70-78.

Thiong'o, Ngũgĩ wa. *Devil on the Cross.* Oxford: Heinemann, 1987.

Starkloff, Carl. *A Theology of The In-Between.* Milwaukee: Marquette UP,
       2002.

Woodward, Kenneth L., et.al. "The Changing Face of the Church." *Newsweek*
       16 Apr. 2001: 46+.

17   The Theology and Poetics of Sin and Punishment in *Go Tell it on the Mountain*

Babacar M'Baye

This paper explores the ways in which James Baldwin's 1953 novel *Go Tell it on the Mountain* reflects a diversity of religious cultural elements that have parallels in European-American and African religious worldviews and poetic traditions. On the one hand, the paper will discuss how the cultural elements in the book reflect traits that are traceable to Biblical and Puritanical interpretation of sin and divine punishment. Second, the paper will describe how the Biblical and Puritanical ideas about sin and punishment that Baldwin uses are blended with patterns from a diversity of African cultures.

The outline of the paper is as follows. First, this paper will describe the plot and historical context of *Go Tell it on the Mountain*. Second, the paper will identify the elements from Biblical and Puritanical theology of Sin that Baldwin appropriates in order to discuss his childhood and race relations in the United States during the early part of the twentieth century. Third, this paper will analyze Baldwin's use of a Biblical theology of sin through a language that recalls the worldview of a diversity of traditional West-African Islamic societies. Finally, this paper will examine the Biblical sermons that Gabriel Grimes, one of the major characters in *Mountain*, delivers in a manner that is quite similar to how the *griot* [African traditional poet and historian] tells an epic.

Go Tell it on the Mountain emerged out of a turbulent social and political context. In *Mountain*, Baldwin represents the racial violence and lynching cycles that tore apart the American nation in the first half of the twentieth century. This violence is suggested in the scene in which Gabriel walks the empty streets of Harlem and bumps suddenly into the dead body of a Black man: "There had been found that morning, just outside of town, the dead body of a soldier, his uniform shredded where he had been flogged, and, turned upward through the black skin, raw, red meat. He lay face downward at the base of a tree, his fingernails digging into the scuffed earth" (142). This quotation reflects the terror of racial violence in the America of the 1910s, 20s, and 30s that Baldwin wanted to condemn.

In the recent biography "James Baldwin," David Van Leer said that James Arthur Baldwin was born on August 2, 1924 in Harlem, New York [perhaps out of wedlock] (2). In 1927, Emma Berdis Jones, Baldwin's mother, married David Baldwin, a strict preacher who was embittered by what he viewed as "the tyranny of 'white devils'"(2). David projected his anger on Baldwin by calling him "the ugliest child ever seen" and "the Devil's son."[1] David's abuse led Baldwin to seek a way out of oppression through reading and inquiry. As David Leeming wrote: "By the fifth grade, it became clear that he [Baldwin] had a talent for research and writing. At home he read and reread *Uncle Tom's Cabin* until his mother, fearing for his eyes, hid it from him" (13). Emma was proud of her precocious son, "but her husband said he wanted the boy to be a preacher of the gospel" (13).

In *Go Tell it on the Mountain*, Baldwin tells his own story through the voice of John Grimes, a fourteen-year-old boy, who struggles with his repressive stepfather Gabriel and with religious conversion. In the first part of the book, John is anxious as he realizes that the freedom and education that he wants to have are in the White world, outside the religion and the preachhood that his parents expect him to uphold when he becomes an adult. "Everyone had always said that John would be a preacher when he grew up, just like his father" (11). In the second part of *Mountain*, the narrator takes us back and forth to the South and up North in Harlem where most of the story takes place. The flashbacks allow the reader to see the dualism that overwhelmed John's father Gabriel, his mother, Elizabeth, and his aunt Florence before and after they migrated North in the early part of the twentieth century.

John's story begins to unfold in the city of Harlem on his fourteenth birthday as he also wrestles to come to terms with his own sexuality and his complex relationships with his family. The image of a "yellow stain on the ceiling transforming itself into a woman's nakedness" (18) and the reminiscence of a moment when "in the school lavatory," he was "alone, thinking if the boys, older, bigger, braver, who made bets with each other as to whose urine could arch higher" (19) leads John to believe that he has sinned. His father's wrathful condemnation of sin reinforces John's guilt-ridden conscience, forcing him to seek spiritual repentance and salvation in the Temple of the Fire Baptized where Gabriel serves as deacon and caretaker. Later, John experiences religious conversion when he falls on the "threshing floor" of the church and discovers his intricate relationships with God and his family.

The influence of European-American Theology of Sin in *Go Tell it on the Mountain*

Go Tell it on the Mountain discusses the cultural intimacies and ideological conflicts between Blacks and Whites in the United States. On the one hand, *Mountain* reflects traits that have parallels in Puritan theology. On the other hand, the book shows the influence of European-American culture on John, who is the major character of *Mountain*. In the novel, Baldwin explores issues of racial conflicts between Blacks and Whites as well as ideas of cross-cultural and cross-racial unity that he considers very important in the relationships between African-Americans and European-Americans.

In *Mountain*, the influence of Euro-American culture is visible in the religious discourse that Baldwin's characters develop in order to define their identity in relation to White culture and the West. Early in the book, Gabriel develops a Puritanical theology of terror and damnation against his adoptive son John and his biological offspring, Royal. Gabriel's theology is rooted in a traditional European Christian worldview that interpreted Black suffering as part of a divine course of Justice resulting from Noah's curse of his son Ham.[2] As told in the Bible, Ham, who was one of the sons of Noah, saw his father lying in his tent drunk and naked. Knowing that Ham did not look away when he saw him, Noah got angry and cursed Canaan, the son of Ham.[3] The story of Noah influences the manner in which John and Gabriel explain their relationships with each other. John believes that he sinned by imagining his father's nakedness. The narrator describes:

> Yes, he [John] had sinned: one morning, alone, in the dirty bathroom, in the square, dirt-gray cupboard room that was filled with the stink of his father. Sometimes, leaning over the cracked, "tattle-tale gray" bathtub, he scrubbed his father's back; and looked, as the accursed son of Noah had looked, slimy, like the serpent, and heavy, like the rod. Then he hated his father, and longed for the power to cut his father down.
> Was this why he lay there, thrust out from all human or heavenly help tonight? This, and not that other, his deadly sin, having looked on his father's nakedness and mocked and cursed him in his heart? Ah, that son of Noah had been cursed, down to the present groaning generation: *A servant of servants shall he be unto his brethren.* (197)

As this statement suggests, John believes that his predicament derives from the curse that Noah made against his son Ham. John makes a connection between Noah's naked body—that Ham stared at and the bare torso of Gabriel that he [John] saw. John's belief that he has sinned against his father and his conviction that this act is connected with Ham is a product of his European Christian upbringing. Intrinsic in Christian theology is the idea that Blacks are a cursed people who are suffering since the time of Ham's damnation. As Susan Gubar argues in *Racechanges: White Skin, Black Face in American Culture*, this theology has been used to pathologize Black people on both sides of the Atlantic and justify their economic and social exploitation.[4] This theology of damnation permeates the worldview of Gabriel Grimes who uses it in his sermons. In the middle of *Mountain*, Gabriel delivers a speech to a congregation led by a group of preachers called the Twenty Four Elders. Gabriel's lecture is as follows:

> For let us remember that the wages of sin is death; that it is written, and cannot fail, the soul that sinneth, it shall die. Let us remember that we are born in sin, in sin did our mothers conceive us—sin reigns in all our members, sin is the foul heart's natural liquid, sin looks out of the eye, amen, and leads to lust, sin is in the hearing of the ear, and leads to folly, sin sits on the tongue, and leads to murder. Yes! Sin is the only heritage of the natural man, sin bequeathed us by our natural father, that fallen Adam, whose apple sickens and will sicken all generations living, and generations unborn! (103-104)

Gabriel's representation of sin as an intrinsic part of human nature is traceable to Puritan theology in which sin is represented as an element that permeates life. Gabriel's imagery of sin as an organism that grows into human beings permanently is analogous to Thomas Hooker's description of evil as a part of life. In *The American Puritans: Their Prose and Poetry*, Perry Miller has an essay entitled "A True Sight of Sin," in which Thomas Hooker, a late sixteenth and early seventeenth-century Puritan leader and Philosopher, wrote: "We are all sinners, it is my infirmity, I cannot help it; my weakness, I cannot be rid of it" (153). Hooker also said that sin was "a desperate malignity in the temper of the stomach that should turn our meat and diet into diseases, the best cordials and preservatives into poisons, so that what in reason is appointed to nourish a man should kill him" (162). Like Gabriel, Hooker uses a biological language in which the female stomach is represented as the birthplace of sin. In addition, like Gabriel, Hooker believes that sin permeates human existence.

Another parallel between Gabriel's and Hooker's theology is their representation of sin as a sign of divine punishment. Hooker said that sin was "the greatest evil in the world, or indeed that can be. For that which separates the soul from God, that which brings evils of punishment and makes all evils truly evil, and spoils all good things to us, that most needs be the greatest evil" (162). This fundamentalist vision of sin and punishment is the source of the theology in *Mountain*. In his reminiscence of his past life, Gabriel describes his relationships with the outside world in a language that draws heavily on orthodox notions of sin, damnation, and fear. Gabriel is always anxious and guilt-ridden when he imagines his adulterous affair with Esther, the mother of his deceased son Royal, as an act that has brought a curse in his life. While praying in the Temple, Gabriel remembers "the curse repeated, so far, so long resounding, that the mother of his first son had uttered as she thrust the infant from her—herself immediately departing, this curse yet on her lips, into eternity" (114).   Gabriel believes that Esther cursed him when she was delivering Royal, reminding the preacher of his sin and cruelty toward a woman he did not support.   This belief in a predestined omen shreds Gabriel's life, leading him to imagine what the other churchgoers would say about him if only they knew that he was an adulterer and a sinner, not a saint.   When he prays, Gabriel imagines that "They [the congregation] seemed suddenly to mock him, to stand in judgment on him; he saw his guilt in everybody's eyes.   When he stood in the pulpit to preach they looked at him, he felt, as though he had no right to be there, as though they condemned him" (135-136).

Gabriel's confusion impels him to seek refuge in faith.   He stands near the altar and prays for forgiveness and rebirth: "Have your way, Lord / Have your way" (113) and "I'll obey, Lord / I'll obey" (114).   This prayer helps Gabriel regain his faith and begin to believe that he can prevent others from sinning.   He promises to save the soul of his wife Elizabeth—whom he married when he moved to New York to live with Florence.   At this point, Gabriel can remember the words he had told Elizabeth the day when he proposed to her: "Sister Elizabeth," he said, "the Lord's been speaking to my heart, and I believe it's His will that you and me should be man and wife . . . I done been down the line, . . . and maybe I can keep you from making some of my mistakes, bless the Lord . . . maybe I can help keep your foot from stumbling . . . again" (187).   Gabriel's belief that the Lord spoke to him and gave him power to keep people from sinning convinced Elizabeth to surrender to his authority.   Elizabeth agreed to the marriage and saw a sign of God's presence in Gabriel, "a sign that He is mighty to save" (188).

The theology of sin and suffering that Gabriel develops has negative effects on the lives of the Grimes family.   The effects are visible in how Gabriel attempts to make John hate White people and surrender to a fundamentalist psychology of terror.   In "Everybody's Protest Novel," Baldwin defines this psychology as "the terror of domination" of "medieval times, which sought to exorcize evil by burning witches," (13).   One example of terror is when Gabriel attempts to make John fear White people by telling him that they do not like Black people.   When Roy is brought home after he has been stabbed by a White gang, Gabriel tells John "You see? . . . It was white folks, some of them white folks *you* like so much tried to cut your brother's throat" (45).   This statement shows how Gabriel uses John as a scapegoat for his own powerlessness toward White oppression.   Because he is unable to deal with racial subjugation, Gabriel ends up projecting his fear and weakness on John whom he perceives as both an accomplice and a victim in the evildoing of Whites.   "With the air of one forcing the sinner to look down into the pit that is to be his portion" Gabriel "moved away slightly so that John could see Roy's wound" (45).

Later, when standing near Roy, Gabriel tells Elizabeth: "You can tell that foolish *son* of yours something, . . . him standing there with them big buckeyes. You can tell him to take this like a warning from the Lord. *This* is what white folks does to niggers. I been telling you, now you see" (46). As this quotation suggests, Gabriel perceives himself as victim of a destructive "White evil" in which he sees John as a participant. Gabriel's representation of Whiteness in negative terms is an irrational sentiment that is rooted in the fear that centuries of violence, discrimination, and injustices on Black people trigger in his consciousness. Discussing Gabriel's attitude toward John, Fern Marja Eckman argues in *The Furious Passage of James Baldwin* that it invokes the terror that David Baldwin, Baldwin's stepfather, created in his son's consciousness by making him feel that he could not succeed in the White man's world.[5]

Yet Gabriel's fear cannot be dismissed as an irrational sentiment since it is an effect of White-on-Black violence. Gabriel's response derives from what Baldwin describes in *Rap on Race* as "the fears of white people" to recognize that "Blacks are involved with the American people and in American life" (3). As Margaret Mead argues in *Rap on Race*, this is the fear of admitting that Blacks and Whites have a blood relationship and a common experience (6). The paradox that Baldwin and Mead perceive in American culture comes from the history of racism and discrimination that Blacks have endured in the United States. The history creates a dilemma and powerlessness that the African-American feels for being socially alienated. Baldwin described this feeling in "The American Dream," a speech that he gave in Oxford, England in 1965:

> It comes as a great shock to discover that the country, which is your birthplace, and to which you owe your life and identity has not, in its whole system of reality, evolved any place for you. The disaffection and the gap between people, only on the basis of their skins, begins there and accelerates throughout your whole lifetime. You realize that you are 30 and you are having a terrible time. You have been through a certain kind of mill and the most serious effect is again not the catalogue of disaster—the policeman, the taxi driver, the waiters, the landlady, the banks, the insurance companies, the millions of details 24 hours of every day which spell out to you that you are a worthless human being. It is not that. By that time, you have begun to see it happening in your daughter, your son or your niece or your nephew. You are 30 by now and nothing you have done has helped you to escape the trap. But what is worse is that nothing you have done, and as far as you can tell nothing you *can* do, will save your son or your daughter from having the same disaster and from coming to the same end. (32-33)

Baldwin's argument that alienation in Black life was a result of White denial came at a point when he wanted to take his stepfather's rhetoric of terror and use it to resist oppression. Like John, Baldwin grew to accept his father's idea that the Whites will not allow Blacks to succeed. Gabriel's anti-White rhetoric, which echoes that of David Baldwin, was a conservative and fatalistic theology that Baldwin often used to criticize European-Americans. As Fern Marja Eckman explains, by the end of the 1960s, Baldwin began to accept hesitantly his father's idea that Blacks were victims of "the economic and social ramifications of the white man's theory" and became "the guardian of David Baldwin's anger" which "burns steadily, like a sacred flame" (27). The power of David Baldwin's ideology on James Baldwin is visible in how John, Baldwin's persona, wants to use his father's anger and crush the people and lights of New York City. Like John, Baldwin, at one point, wanted to use David Baldwin's "sacred flame" as a weapon against White America. These sentiments of death wish and apocalypse towards White people identify the stage when Baldwin was angry the most about his conditions of being a Black man in America. In *Notes of Native Son*, Baldwin writes:

> This was the time of what was called the "brownouts," when the lights in all American cities were very dim. When we re-entered the streets something happened to me, which had the force of an optical illusion, or a nightmare. The streets were very crowded and I was facing north. People were moving in every direction but it seemed to me, in that instant, that all of the people I could see, and many more than that, were moving toward me, against me, and that everyone was white. I remember how their faces gleamed. And I felt, like a physical sensation, a *click* at the nape of my neck as though some interior string connecting my head to my body had been cut. I began to walk. I heard my friend call after me, but I ignored him. Heaven only knows what was going on in his mind, but he had the good sense not to touch me—I don't know what would have happened if he had—and to keep me in sight. I certainly had no conscious plan. I wanted to do something to crush these white faces, which were crushing me. I walked for perhaps a block or two until I came to an enormous, glittering, and fashionable restaurant in which I knew not even the intercession of the Virgin would cause me to be served. I pushed through the doors and took the first vacant seat I saw, at a table for two, and waited. (80)

This statement suggests the analogy between Baldwin and John, which is their nervousness and alienation in the White world. Like Baldwin, John feels as if he were the only Black man in a world dominated by Whites. Yet, John's feeling about Whites is rarely consistent. John's journey in White culture begins in the morning of his fourteenth birthday when he goes downtown and spends a few coins that his mother gave him as a present. On his way to the movie theatre, where he intends to spend the money, John goes to the top of a hill situated in the middle of Central Park, New York, and observes the city in all its dimensions with a full sense of the power and privilege that he [John] can have in America and in the West. The narrator describes in the scene as follows:

> In Central Park, the snow had not yet melted on his favorite hill. This hill was in the center of the park, after he had left the circle of the reservoir, where he always found, outside the high wall of crossed wire, ladies, white, in fur coats, walking their great dogs, or old, white gentlemen with canes. At a point that he knew by instinct and by the shape of the buildings surrounding the park, he struck out on a steep path overgrown with trees, and climbed a short distance until he reached the clearing that led to the hill. Before him, then, the slope stretched upward, and above it the brilliant sky, and beyond it, cloudy, and far away, he saw the skyline of New York. He did not know why, but there arose in him exultation and a sense of power, and he ran up the hill like an engine, or a madman, willing to throw himself headlong into the city that glowed before him. (33)

This passage suggests John's ambivalent attitude about White culture. On the one hand, John is attracted to White culture. He is thrilled to discern the wealth and elegance of rich White women and men who walk in Central Park, wrapped in "fur," holding "canes," or walking their dogs. John's fascination with the attire and leisure of the White promenaders reflects his desire to be associated with a European culture in which he sees himself as a participant. As visible in his position on top of the hill, John perceives himself as an insider who knows the secret of the West and who is aware of the education and higher possibilities that the city can give him. In this sense, John is the persona of Baldwin who was in love with the city for the discovery and adventure that it gives to the soul-searching individual. In his essay "Black City Lights: Baldwin's City of the Just," James M. Hughes describes Baldwin as a cosmopolitan intellectual who, like Henry James and Walt Whitman, found the American city as "a bridge to the European city" (234-235). Hughes' statement gives the impression that the American city gave Baldwin the means to transcend racism and celebrate universalism in Europe. Although it is fair to say that Baldwin used New York as a passage to Europe, one must admit that the city was, for him, more a site where the dilemma of race was acute than anything else. The city is the place where Baldwin became aware of injustice and dualisms. Baldwin's ambivalence is visible in John's attitude toward the city. Although he is attracted to the wealth and leisure in Central Park, as Baldwin was to the city, John realizes that the overseeing position that he occupies on top of the hill is hardly comfortable since it makes him feel angry with White people. John's anger at Whites is visible in the narrator's description of how "he [John] ran up the hill like an engine, or a madman, willing to throw himself headlong into the city that glowed before him" (33). Later, a sudden force makes John want to destroy the city and its people. The narrator describes the scene as follows:

> When he reached the summit he paused; he stood on the crest of
> the hill, hands clasped beneath his chin, looking down. Then he,
> John, felt like a giant who might crumble this city with his anger; he
> felt like a tyrant who might crush this city beneath his heel; he felt
> like a long-awaited conqueror at whose feet flowers would be strewn,
> and before whom multitudes cried, Hosanna! (33)

John's violent urge to crush the city of New York expresses his hatred of Whites for keeping Blacks in poverty. John blames Whites for expecting him to live and work in the *Broadway*, "where the houses did not rise" and "where the streets and the hallways and the rooms were dark, and where the unconquerable odor of dust, and sweat, and urine, and homemade gin" polluted the atmosphere (34). This gloomy picture of a poor and unclean *Broadway* gives John a sense of legitimacy for wanting to kill White people. John's death wish comes from his dissatisfaction with the discrimination and unemployment that he notes in the lives of Blacks in Harlem. When he thinks about Gabriel's economic life, John sees it a "narrow way" where "he would grow old and black with hunger and toil" (34).

John's realization of the predicament that he could face in the future is rooted in the history of economic and social injustice that besieged Harlem in the middle of the twentieth century. The Harlem of the 1950s and 60s in which John would have become an adult was terribly poor. In *Harlem: The Making of a Ghetto*, Gilbert Osofsky describes this Harlem as a neighborhood where 91 percent of homes were classified as slums (193). As Osofsky has argued, about half of the Harlem youngsters who went to high school during the 1950s and 60s dropped out before completing their degrees (200).

In *Dark Ghetto: Dilemmas of Social Power*, Kenneth B. Clark gave more startling statistics. According to Clark, the median income of Blacks in Harlem between 1940 and 1960 was $3, 480 compared to $5, 103 for White residents of New York City (35). Half the families in Harlem had incomes under $4000, while 75 percent of all New York City residents earned more than $4,000 (35). As Clark argued, only one in twenty-five Black families in Harlem had an income above $10,000, while more than four in twenty-five of the White families did (35). These statistics show that "the Negro in Harlem found himself increasingly isolated culturally, socially, and economically by a wall of racial prejudice and discrimination" (26).

The racism that Clark described is the root of the fear and double consciousness that Black people experience in the United States. Continuous injustice is the major factor that leads John to want to "throw himself headlong into the city that glowed before him" (33). The desperation and violent urge that John and Baldwin experience in the White world is reminiscent of that "peculiar sensation" that W.E.B. Du Bois described in *The Souls of Black Folk* as "this sense of always looking at one's self through the eyes of the others, of measuring one's soul by the tape of a world that looks on in amused contempt and pity" (5). From this "peculiar sensation" of invisibility and vulnerability toward an "amused contempt and pity" of Whites, there emerges in the Black psyche a desire to take action in self-expression and in thought, a process that Du Bois and Cornel West called "strivings." These "strivings" identify "the quasi-mystical" power to reinvent oneself that African-Americans have developed in order to resist oppression. As Eric J. Sundquist points out in *To Wake The Nations: Race in the Making of American Literature*, Du Bois' notion of "Black Strivings" elaborates "on his view that the racist denial of opportunity to blacks in America has allowed 'the power of body and mind' to be 'wasted and dispersed'" (486). In this sense, "Black Strivings" is a dormant power of self-transformation and self-preservation lying beneath the ambiguous double-consciousness of the African-American. As Du Bois wrote:

> Here in America, in the few days since Emancipation, the black man's turning hither and thither in hesitant and doubtful striving has often made his very strength to lose effectiveness, to seem like absence of power, like weakness. And yet it is not weakness—it is the contradiction of double aims. The double-aimed struggle of the black artisan—on the one hand to escape white contempt for a nation of mere hewers of wood and drawers of water, and on the other hand to plough and nail and dig for a poverty-stricken horde—could only result in making him a poor craftsman, for he had but half a heart in either cause. (5-6)

This statement stresses the regenerative skill that African-Americans acquire from the experience of longing for cultural identity and economic advancement in America. Du Bois, then, like Baldwin, recognizes the capacity of African-Americans to revive their unearthed energy and reconstruct their dislocated selves in order to conquer injustice. Cornel West discusses this regenerating force in Black consciousness when he states in *The Future of the Race*: "Black strivings are the creative and complex products of the terrifying African encounter with the absurd *in* America—and the absurd *as* America. Like any other group of human beings, black people forged ways of life and ways of struggle under circumstances not of their own choosing" (79). West's concept of "Black Strivings" as a creative way of struggle under an absurd existence is consistent with Du Bois's representation of "strivings" as a resistance against oppression in a context of dispersed Black selves.

The African Religious and Cultural influences in *Go Tell it on the Mountain*

Despite its centeredness on the Christian heritage of African-Americans, *Go Tell it on the Mountain* has salient cultural patterns that have parallels in West African Muslim societies such as Mali and Senegal. In *Mountain*, the African traits are blended with Christian patterns and are visible in the rhetorical strategies that Baldwin uses when he describes how Gabriel, the deacon of The Temple of the Fire Baptized, interacts with his congregation. In his sermons, Gabriel uses rhetorical strategies that are similar to those of the African *griot* [poet and historian]. [6] The oratory devices that Gabriel uses include dramatic description of characters, emphasis on actions and time, and repetition of names.[7] These standards are included in the following passage:

> He [Gabriel] took his text from the eighteenth chapter of the second book of Samuel, the story of the young Ahimaaz who ran too soon to bring the tidings of battle to King David. For, before he ran, he was asked by Joab: "Wherefore wilt thou run, my son, seeing that thou hast no tidings ready?" And when Ahimaaz reached King David, who yearned to know the fate of his headlong son, Absalom, he could only say: "I saw a great tumult but I knew not what it was."
>
> And this was the story of all those who failed to wait on the counsel of the Lord; who made themselves wise in their own conceit and ran before they had the tidings ready. This was the story of innumerable shepherds who failed, in their arrogance, to feed the hungry sheep; of many a father and mother who gave to their children not bread but a stone, who offered not the truth of God but the tinsel of this world. This was not belief but unbelief, not humility but pride: there worked in the heart of such a one the same desire that had hurled the son of the morning from Heaven to the depths of Hell, the desire to overturn the appointed times of God, and to wrest from Him who held all power in His hands powers not meet for men . . . Oh, yes, they had seen it, each brother and sister beneath the sound of his voice tonight, and they had seen the destruction caused by a so lamentable unripeness! Babies, bawling, fatherless, for bread, and girls in the gutters, sick with sin, and young men bleeding in the frosty fields. Yes, and there were those who cried—they had heard it, in their homes, and on the street corner, and from the very pulpit— that they should wait no longer, despised and rejected and spat on as they were. (119)

Gabriel's sermon is consistent with the African-American preacher's storytelling strategy. The relationships are visible, first, in Gabriel's act of warning sinners against the hellish life that awaits them if they do not change their ways, which is a parable and a rhetorical technique that is traceable to the oral performance of the Black preacher. As James Weldon Johnson describes in his introduction to *God's Trombones: Seven Negro Sermons in Verse*, the African-American preacher usually ends a sermon by invoking "the Judgment Day" or by warning or exhorting the sinners (2). According to Johnson, the use of admonition is the last stage of the preacher's sermon, following a long process during which the orator represented "the Creation, went on to the fall of man, rambled through the trials and tribulations of the Hebrew Children, [and] came down to the redemption of Christ" (1-2).

Another connection between Gabriel's sermon and Johnson's poem is the function as conveyor of the message of God that the two Gabriel characters play. The sermon "The Judgment Day," which is the last oration in *God's Trombones*, has a scene in which God asks the angel Gabriel to go blow "the silver trumpet" and "wake the nations underground" (54). The angel took God's message to the sinners:

> Oh-o-oh, sinner,
> Where will you stand,
> In that great day when God's a-going to rain down fire?
> Oh, you gambling man—where will you stand?
> You whore-mongering man—where will you stand?
> Liars and backsliders—where will you stand,
> In that great day when God's a-going to rain down fire? (55)

The function of whistle-blower and invoker of divine punishment that the angel Gabriel plays in "The Judgment Day" is analogous to that which Baldwin's Gabriel plays in *Mountain*. Like Johnson's Gabriel, Baldwin's Gabriel is a counselor to the Lord whose mission is to wake the sinners and urge them to leave their secular and epicurean ways, repent, and walk in the holy path before the Judgment Day comes. This profound message, which underlies both orations, suggests the wisdom, inventiveness, and emotional intensity of the African-American religious folklore and theology from which *Mountain* was crafted.

Yet, Baldwin's literature, including his sermons, is not comparable to African-American oration only. For example, Baldwin's Biblical narrative can be interpreted as a story about the frustration that King David felt when he found out that his son Ab'salom had plotted to kill him.[8] Gabriel's tirade suggests that King David interpreted Absalom's act as a thoughtless act of pride and vanity. Despite its Biblical origin, Gabriel's sermon reflects the African *griot*'s way of narrating an epic. This similarity is visible in how Gabriel tells the story about King David in a dramatic manner that allows the reader to see the correspondence between the lives of the two characters. Like an African *griot*, Gabriel impersonates the character of the epic that is being told. Gabriel's use of impersonation is noticeable in how he creates a parallelism between King David and himself. In this sense, the tension between King David and Absalom alludes to the conflict that occurs between Gabriel and his son Royal. When he walks in Harlem during a race riot, Gabriel imagines Royal's body "sprawled heavy and unmoving forever against the earth, and tears blinded his eyes" (143). In Harlem, Gabriel met Royal in the streets and saw "a blank hostility" in his eyes and "a burning cigarette [hanging] from between his lips" (142). From Gabriel's point of view, Royal's deportment is, like Absalom's, a defiance of divine law that can lead to destruction.

In addition, Gabriel's sermon refers to many names, such as Ahimaaz, King David, and Joab. This use of names in oratory is common in African epic poetry. One example is the passage in the legend of Sundjata Keita, [9] told by Guinean historian Djeli Mamadou Kuyate, where the character of Sumanguru Kante talks with his *griot* Bala Faasege. The conversation, which is taken from Ralph Austen's *In Search of Sunjata: The Mmande Oral Epic as History, Literature and Performance* is as follows:

> What is your name?
> The griot replied, "My name is Nyankuma Dookha."
> Sumanguru said, "I am going to take your name from you;
> And apart from those with special knowledge,
> No one will know your name any more.
> I shall name you after my xylophone.
> What I am going to do to you,
> That is what I shall make your name.
> The third will be your surname
> Your first name is Balo;
> I will cut your Achilles tendons;
> Your surname is Kuyate."
> They call him Bala Faasege Kuyate.[10] (36-37)

The *griot*'s reference to names such as Nyankuma Dookha, Sumanguru, Balo, and Kuyate is consistent with Baldwin's allusion to Ahimaaz, King David, and Joab, revealing the importance of names in African poetry on both sides of the Atlantic Ocean.[11]

Moreover, Badwin's sermon and the African epic share the use of actualization, which is the storyteller's representation of the past in a vivid, theatrical, and life-like manner.[12] One example of actualization is in the sermon above where Baldwin describes the destruction that King David saw looming towards the unbelievers (119). Gabriel's apocalyptic vision of people who fall in the "gutters" of pride shows his ability to create graphic words and images that can frighten the believers and bring them to repent for their sins. The use of this apocalyptic quality in Gabriel's sermon is traceable to African epic poetry where the speaker's ability to create graphic images is vital. For example, in the legend of Sunjata Keita, Sumanguru tells Bala Faasege "I will cut your Achilles tendons; / Your surname is Kuyate" (37). The statement suggests Sumanguru's intent to make Bala his lifetime poet and historian, deceiving the image of dismemberment that the *griot* uses for a theatrical purpose only.[13]

Another parallel in Gabriel's sermon is in the way in which the preacher interacts with the audience. A patient narrator, Gabriel tells the story of King David gradually, reminding the audience that the story is unique because it describes the fate of "all those who failed to wait on the counsel of the Lord." In this statement, Gabriel creates a time and setting for the particular story that he is about to tell. Later, he invites his audience to show interest in his story by asking, "Is there a soul here tonight?" to which the congregation responds by saying, "Yes!" "Tell it!" "Amen! You preach it, boy" (103-105). The call-and-answer exchange in the Temple of the Fire Baptized is identical to those of the Wolof people of West Africa. When Wolof listeners want to show interest in the performance of the *griot* artist such as the musician Youssou Ndour,[14] they say, "*waaw waaw!*" [Yes, indeed!], "*eskeey!*" [Tell it!], or "*deug-la!*" [That is so true!].

The African presence in *Mountain* is also visible in the possession rituals in the book. When he goes to church, John Grimes, the central character, participates in a series of possession rites. Baldwin describes: "On this threshing-floor the child was the soul that struggled to the light, and it was the church that was in labor, that did not cease to push and pull, calling on the name of Jesus" (113). The trance that John experiences is traceable to the series of intense spiritual and emotional revivals that occurred in American churches during The Great Awakening. As suggested in William D. Piersen's *Black Yankees: The Development of an Afro-American Subculture in Eighteenth-Century New England*, the Great Awakening started in New England in the 1730s and 1740s when preachers of the New Light such as Jonathan Edwards and George Whitefield began to manifest their faith in "overt physical responses such as screeching, fainting, convulsions, visions, and possession by the holy pulpit" (67). The Awakening was an important moment in the history of American Christianity since, as Piersen pointed out, it weakened "the cold, inhibited Yankee style of religion" and emphasized "felt religion," opening "the possibility of conversion without so much attention to doctrinal niceties or closely scrutinized preparation" (67-68). The Awakening was also important since it allowed the Africans to participate in the series of possession and emotional downpouring despite their limited knowledge of the Biblical texts (68).[15]

Yet, although it is traceable to American Protestant tradition, the trance that John experiences on the floor is analogous to the possession that takes over the participants in West-African Islamic Sufi night-chants known as *Jaang*. These night-chants are centuries-old rituals in which Muslim congregations in Africa are joined in sequences of singing, crying, worshipping, and dancing that may last all night long.[16] The revivals are similar to the ones in which Gabriel and his parishioners participate in a series of songs, dance, trance, and rituals.

More evidence of the similarity between West African Islamic rituals and the Christian performance in *Mountain* is visible in the praise singing and spirit worshipping that characterizes both of them. Baldwin represents praise singing and spirit worshipping in the scene where John is on the threshing floor. Baldwin describes:

> The silence in the church ended when Brother Elisha, kneeling
> near the piano, cried out and fell backward under the power of the

Lord. Immediately, two or three others cried out also, and a wind, a foretaste of that great downpouring they awaited, swept the church. With this cry, and the echoing cries, the tarry service moved from its first stage of steady murmuring, broken by moans and now again an isolated cry, into that stage of tears and groaning, of calling aloud and singing, which was like the labor of a woman about to be delivered of her child.   On this threshing-floor the child was the soul that struggled to the light, and it was the church that was in labor, that did not cease to push and pull, calling on the name of Jesus.   When Brother Elisha cried out and fell back, crying, Sister McCandless rose and stood over him to help him pray.   For the rebirth of the soul was perpetual; only rebirth every hour could stay the hand of Satan.

Sister Price began to sing:

"I want to go through, Lord,
I want to go through.
Take me through, Lord,
Take me through." (113)

The scene reflects the influence of African-American Christianity on *Go Tell it on the Mountain*. The actions described in the passage are examples of the African-American religious and vernacular tradition known as "testifying." From a religious sense, "testifying" is a moment of spiritual awakening in which the African-American worshipper enters into a state of trance or possession, expressing his / her true belief in God and his / her strong desire to have privileged relationships with Him. As visible in Brother Elisha's act of falling "under the power of the Lord," the person who testifies conveys through words or action his / her beliefs in the omnipotence of God. In *Talkin and Testifyin: The Language of Black America*, Geneva Smitherman writes: "To testify is to tell the truth through 'story.' In the sacred context, the subject of testifying includes such matters as visions, prophetic experiences, the experience of being saved, and testimony to the power and goodness of God" (150). In this sense, the series of wailing, moaning, calling, singing, and dancing in which the worshippers in *Mountain* participate is a form of "testifying" since it bears witness to their strong belief in God. Likewise, the hymn "I want to go through, Lord" that Sister Price sings is a form of "testifying," since it shows her desire to become united with God.

Yet Sister Price's song also reflects elements that are similar to those in African Islamic praise singing and spirit worshipping. The series of emotional downpouring, isolated wailing, and testimonials, singing, and dancing in which the congregation in *Mountain* participates is similar to those in the Wolof *Jaang*. Like the spiritual and physical performance in *Mountain*, the Senegalese *Jaang* is a ritual in which the participants sing, wail, worship, and dance together for hours. The rituals in the Wolof *Jaang* and those in the church in *Mountain* create social unity, respect for the ancestors, and faith in God.

An additional parallel between the performance in *Mountain* and that of the Wolof Muslim ritual is in the songs. Like Sister Price's song, which is polyphonic in structure, the songs in the Wolof *Jaang* are often composed of two melodies sounded together. In Sister price's song, an accented line "I want to go through, Lord" is juxtaposed to an unaccented verse "I want to go through." In a similar way, the Wolof *Jaang* song tends to juxtapose two or more independent musical phrases that are sung in the style of a call-and-response verbal exchange. One example is the song "Mame Malick Sy" of the Senegalese band Toure Kunda:[17]

> YA ILAHI
> . . . .
> Coming through from God
> Passing through from the Prophet
> Going through to Cheikh
> Passing through to Malick (Touré).[18]

Like Sister's Price's stanza, the four verses of "Mame Malick Sy" juxtapose a series of accented and unaccented phrases that form a harmonious unit. In the Senegalese song, the first two lines of the verse "Coming through from God" and "Passing through from the Prophet" are sung in a highly pitched voice in contrast with the last two lines that are chanted in a low pitch. The first line of "YA ILAHI" is a condensed form of "La I laha, Ila laha," which is an Arabic phrase that translates as "there is no God but Allah." This line may have influenced slave culture in the New World. In *Black Music of Two Worlds*, John Storm Roberts notes:

> Some Jamaican hymn-singing occupies a position halfway between the British and black U.S. styles. However, a host of differences are there all the same: vocal tone, fractions of timing, backing—a whole developing tradition. Also, some African singing, especially Muslim prayer songs such as the Guinean "La Illah Ila Allah," available on Vogue Esoteric, makes equally striking use of long, highly decorated notes. (163)

Robert's argument that Muslim prayer singing and spirituals have structural similarities can be corroborated when one analyzes a slave song that Michael E. Gomez documented in *Exchanging Our Country Marks: The Transformation of African Identities in the Colonial and Antebellum South*. According to Gomez, the following song was chanted by Tony William Delegal, a hundred-year-old African who lived in Currytown, Savannah, in the 1930s (174). The song goes:

> Wa kum kum munin
> Kum baba yano
> Lai lai tembe

Ashi boong a nomo
Sha wali go
Ashi quank
Kum baba yano
Lai lai tambe
Ashi lai lai lai
Shi wali go Dhun. (174)

Delegal's song is proof that the free slaves did not forget the traditional songs of their homeland. As Gomez argued, "The fact that Delegal (a form of Senegal?) could remember these words is itself testimony that African languages were kept alive by the African-born and passed on to descendants in certain instances" (174). As Sterling Stuckey suggested in *Going Through The Storm: The Influence of African American Art in History*, one factor that eased the survival of African languages in slave culture was that the African slaves used them to send "unspoken" information safely in songs, tales, and conversation while avoiding the reprisals of the planter (71-72).

In addition, one may argue that Delegal's song might have come from an African Sufi psalmody. Delegal's verse repeats the words "Lai lai lai" which is similar to the Muslim invocation "La I Laha I la Laha." This Muslim verse is commonly heard in the religious revivals of the Senegalese Islamic sect known as the *Layenne*. In this sense, the expression "lai lai lai" that Delegal repeats could have from Senegal or from any parts of Africa where Islamic Sufi culture was influential during the slave trade.[19]

Go Tell it on the Mountain is a great contribution in the study of African-American literature. First, the book has sermons and worldviews that help us understand the relations between African-American culture and a diversity of traditions in the West and in Africa. The sermons and rituals in *Mountain* are a few of the numerous examples where one can find affinities between African-American and African cultures. In reflecting cultural forms that have parallels in Africa, the three books show that African-American literature is a medium that suggests the influence of African traditions in Black-American culture. In this sense, *Mountain* contributes to the studies of the African retentions in African-American culture by providing literary examples that either corroborate or dispute the theories that scholars from the disciplines of folklore, history, and literary criticism have developed on the subject. The ways in which the book reveals Africanisms that can be unnoticeable when they are described in abstract forms show that African-American literature is a medium that can help understand the African continuities in Black-American culture.

In *Mountain*, the African elements are visible in the scenes where Gabriel Grimes delivers a sermon in a manner that is similar to how the African *griot* [poet and historian] tells an epic. Like the African *griot*, Gabriel uses oral strategies such as the dramatic representation of characters; emphases on names, time, and action; and a continuous interaction with the audience. The African traits in *Mountain* are also visible in the series of dance, songs, trance, and intercessions in which the parishioners in The Temple of the Fire Baptized participate as they rescue John Grimes when the latter falls on the "threshing floor" of the church (113).   The forms of worshipping and intercession in *Mountain* have parallels in the Wolof cultural therapeutic ceremony called *Ndoep* and in the West-African Islamic singing rituals known as *Jaang*.

Additionally, *Mountain* interrogates relations between Blacks and Whites in American society and culture.   Through the voice of Gabriel Grimes, James Baldwin suggests the impact of Puritanical representation of sin and punishment in the theology in which his stepfather David Baldwin immersed him when he was a child in Harlem in the 1920s.   Baldwin criticizes Gabriel Grimes for developing a European-influenced theology of terror, fear, and divine punishment that reinforces racism, exploitation, and divisions between Blacks and Whites in America.   James Baldwin was a brave intellectual who spoke about race relations honestly at any cost.   As one reviewer observed in Shari Dorantes Hatch's *African-American Writers: A Dictionary*: "Never one to shy away from lashing out at European Americans for their racist practices, Baldwin also never hesitated to express his views when they conflicted with the views being touted by African Americans of his day" (13). This statement shows that Baldwin was able to get his point across with honesty without fearing retaliation.

This cross-cultural and transnational reading of *Go Tell it on the Mountain* recognizes that the cultures of the Black Diaspora are vast and need to be explored further through comparative and interdisciplinary methods.   My analysis of sermons, worldviews, and ideologies in *Mountain* seeks to show the importance of African-American literature in the study of African and Diaspora currents in American culture.   In the near future, I would like to explore the historical circumstances, such as the trans-Atlantic slavery and migrations, which have allowed the patterns discussed in this study to permeate American culture and become so resilient in twentieth-century African-American literature.   I would also like to study the ways in which African cultures are brought to the United States and the Black Diaspora where they intermingle with various traditions.   Evidently, this research will present enormous challenges since tracing African cultures to the exact places where they were brought in the Diaspora requires new definitions of the concepts of "African" and "Diaspora" histories.   As Paul Lovejoy argued, "'African history' not only followed the slave route to the Americas and the Islamic world, but 'Diaspora history' came back to Africa with the repatriates, thereby complicating the African component in the evolution of the Diaspora. The African Diaspora came to embrace Africa itself" (*The African Diaspora* 1-2).   Following Lovejoy, this paper recognizes that the history of the African Diaspora is complex, and that the relations between the peoples in the Diaspora and in Africa are ambiguous despite the resilience of
Africanisms in the cultures of the Blacks in the New World.

NOTES

1. See Fern Marja Eckman, *The Furious Passage of James Baldwin* (New York: Popular Library, 1966) 36.

2. See Susan Gubar, *Racechanges: White Skin, Black Face in American Culture* (New York: Oxford UP, 1997) 127; Winthrop D Jordan, *White Over Black*, 56; Stanley Elkin's *Slavery: A Problem in American Institutional and Intellectual Life* (Chicago: U of Chicago P, 1976) 38; and Suniti Humar Chatterji, *Africanism: The African Personality* (Bankim Chatterji Street, Calcutta: Bengal Publishing P, 1960) 1.

3. (Gen 9, 25-27)

4. Gubar, *Racechanges*, 15, 128.

5. See Fern Marja Eckman, *The Furious Passage of James Baldwin* (New York: Popular Library, 1967) 27; and James Baldwin, *The Fire Next Time* (New York: Dell Book, 1963) 41-42.

6. For a study of the rhetorical strategies of the African *griot*, see Isidore Okpewho, *African Oral Literature: Backgrounds, Character, and Continuity*, 26.

7. For a study of oral devices in African traditional poetry see Donald Cosentino's *Defiant Maid and Stubborn Farmers: Tradition and Invention in Mende Story Performance* (London, New York, Sydney: Cambridge UP, 1982) 5; Mohamadou Kane, *Essai* 97; Samba Diop, *The Oral History and Literature of the Wolof People of Waalo, Northern Senegal: The Master of the Word (Griot) in the Wolof Tradition* (Ontario, Canada: Edwin Mellen P, 1995) 107-108; and Isidore Okpewho's *The Epic in Africa: Towards a Poetics of the Oral Performance*, 161.

8. See Gen (2:18). Taken from the sixteenth, seventeenth and eighteenth chapters of *The Second Book of Samuel*, Baldwin's and Gabriel's story is about the blend of love and aversion that King David felt when he was told by Ahim'a-az that his son Absalom had conspired against him (2:18).

9. The epic describes the life of the king Sunjata Keita of former Malian Empire. The epic of Sunjata is told in many books including Djibril Tamsir Niane, *Sunjata: An Epic of Old Mali*, trans. G.D.Pickett (London: Longman, 1965); Ralph A. Austen, *In Search of Sunjata: The Mande Oral Epic as History, Literature and Performance* (Bloomington: Indiana UP, 1999) 36-37; and Thomas A. Hale's *Oral Epics from Africa: Vibrant Voices from a Vast Continent* (Bloomington: Indiana UP, 1997) 11

10. Austen, *In Search of Sunjata*, (37)

11. See John S. Mbiti, *Introduction to African Religion* (London: Heinemann, 1982) 25-6, 42-3, 87-90, 125, 127, 131. Also see John S. Mbiti, *African Religions and Philosophies*, 39, 45, 79, 82; Elliot P. Skinner, *Peoples and Cultures of Africa: An Anthropological Reader* (Garden City, New York: Natural History P, 1973) 125, 267-68, 270-271, 562-63.

12. This device is similar to the narrative strategy that Anthony Graham-White described as the storyteller's impersonation of the character of the epic "as dramatically as possible" (27). See Anthony Graham White, *The Drama of Black Africa* (New York: Samuel French, Inc, 1974) 27.

13. In *Defiant Maids*, Donald Consentino wrote: "The images that he [the *griot*] chooses from his vast, but finite, repertoire are unconstrained by prior thematic import and, for the most part, undetermined in narrative surface. He is thus free to modify these images according to his specifications, and to arrange them according to his wit, his will, and his intelligence" (55). See Donald Cosentino, *Defiant Maid and Stubborn Farmers: Tradition and Invention in Mende Story Performance* (London: Cambridge UP, 1982) 55.

14. For a discussion of Ndour's performance strategies, see Richard Gehr, "Neo-Griot: Youssou Goes One Step Beyond" *Rock & Roll Quarterly* (Winter 1991): 19.

15. The Great Awakening did not occur in the Northeast only. As William D. Piersen, Mechal Sobel, and LeRoy Moore Jr., pointed out, the Great Awakening also developed in the South, probably from the mid-eighteenth through the nineteenth century, where Blacks and Whites participated in revivals in which possession, ecstatic experience, emotional intensity, fervid stirrings, and vivid feelings were more attractive than the "Puritan" inhibitions in religious worship. See William D. Piersen, *Black Yankees: The Development of an Afro-American Subculture in Eighteenth-Century New England* (Amherst: The U of Massachusetts P, 1988) 68-69; Mechal Sobel, *The World They Made Together: Black and White Values in Eighteenth-Century Virginia* (Princeton, NJ: Princeton UP, 1987) 3, 67; LeRoy Moore Jr., "The Spiritual: Soul of Black Religion," *American Quarterly* 23 (December 1971): 658-659.

16. *Jaang* is the Wolof term for Islamic singing ritual. The word also means "to sing," "to study" or "to worship."

17. Toure Kunda (the Kunda family in Manding) is one of the most prominent Senegalese music groups. The band was founded in the 1977 by the Amadou Tilo Toure and his brothers Ismaïla and Sixu Tidjane Toure. The Toure Kunda is one of the first bands to export African traditional music to the arena of world music in Europe. The band draws from the traditional rhythms of the Mandingo, the Wolof, and the Arab-Sufi to the modern African-American sounds of James Brown and Aretha Franklin.

18. See Islmaila Touré and Sixu Tidiane Toure, "Mame Malick Sy," *Mouslaï*, cd, WEA / ATLANTIC, Paris, 1996. The stanza quoted from the song is:

YA ILAHI

....

DIOGHU TCHI YALLA
DIAR TCHI YONENTE
DIAR TCHI MALICK
INEU LEUHOU MAODOK
KHALIFA MALICK AMO MOROME

19. For a discussion of the relationships between West African Islamic culture and African-American culture, see Sylviane Diouf, *Servants of Allah: African Muslims Enslaved in the Americas* (New York and London: New York UP, 1998) 5, 45, 46; Aminah Beverly McCloud, *African American Islam* (New York and London: Routledge, 1995) 1; Allan D. Austin, *African Muslims in Antebellum America* (1984) 29-36; and Mattias Gardell, *In the Name of Elijah Muhammad, Louis Farrakhan, and the Nation of Islam* (Durham: Duke UP, 1996) 32.

Works Cited

Austen, Ralph A. *In Search of Sunjata: The Mande Oral Epic as History, Literature and Performance.* Bloomington: Indiana UP, 1999.

Baldwin, James. *Go tell it on the Mountain.* New York: Laurel, 1985.

———. "Everybody's Protest Novel." *Notes of a Native Son.* New York: Bantam, 1955.

———. "The American Dream." *The New York Times Magazine.* 7 Mar. 1965: 33-36.

———. *Notes of a Native Son.* New York: Bantam Book, 1955.

Clark, Kenneth B. *Dark Ghetto: Dilemmas of Social Power.* New York and Evanston: Harper Torchbooks, 1965.

Eckman, Fern Marja. *The Furious Passage of James Baldwin.* New York: Popular Library, 1967.

Gomez, Michael A. *Exchanging Our Country Marks: The Transformation of African Identities in the Colonial and Antebellum South.* Chapel Hill: U of North Carolina P. 1998.

Gubar, Susan. *Racechanges: White Skin, Black Face in American Culture.* New York: Oxford UP, 1997.

Hatch, Shari Dorantes and Michael R. Strickland, eds., *African-American Writers: A   Dictionary.* Oxford and Denver: ABC-CLIO, 2000.

Hughes, James M. "Black City Lights: Baldwin's City of the Just." *Journal of Black Studies* 18 (1987): 230-241.

Johnson, James Weldon. *God's Trombones: Seven Negro Sermons in Verse.* New York: The Viking P, 1927.

Leer, David Van. "James Baldwin." *African American Writers.* Vol 1. Ed. Valerie Smith. New York: Scribner's, 2001. 1-13.

Lovejoy, Paul. "The African Diaspora: Revisionist Interpretations of Ethnicity, Culture and Religion under Slavery." *Studies in the World History of Slavery,Abolition and Emancipation*, II, 1 (1997). <www2.h-net.msu.edu/~slavery/>

Mead, Margaret and Baldwin, James. *A Rap on Race.* Philadelphia: J.B. Lippincott, 1971.

Miller, Perry. *The American Puritans: Their Prose and Poetry.* Garden City, NY: Doubleday Anchor Books, 1956.

Osofsky, Gilbert. *Harlem: The Making of a Ghetto: Negro New York, 1890-1930.* New York: Harper Torchbooks, 1971.

Piersen, William D. *Black Yankees: The Development of an Afro-American Subculture in Eighteenth-Century New England.* Amherst, MA: The U of Massachusetts P, 1988.

Roberts, John Storm. *Black Music of Two Worlds.* Trivoli, NY: Original Music, 1972.

Smitherman, Geneva. *Talking and Testifying: The Language of Black America.*
    Boston, Mass: Houghton Mifflin Company, 1977.
Stuckey, Sterling. *Going Through the Storm: The Influence of African-*
    American Art in History. New York: Oxford UP, 1994
West, Cornel and Henry Louis Gates, Jr., eds. *The Future of the Race.* New
    York: Knopf. 1996.

18 Growing Up Black and Gay in the Heart of the Bible Belt: Randall Kenan's Perspective on Fundamentalist Religion in *A Visitation of Spirits*

Dr. Marie T. Farr

For both blacks and whites, the American South has a tradition of "old-time" Bible-based religion, especially Southern Baptist. For black Americans, religion often became, especially during slavery and, later, the Civil Rights movement of the 1960s, inextricably bound up with the search for freedom and equality. In *A Visitation of Spirits*, his first novel, published in 1989, Randall Kenan both celebrates the strength of Old Testament-based religion and critiques the devastating effects of its inflexibility on the two main characters, a gay 16 year old high school student, Horace Cross; and his minister and cousin, Jimmy Green. Lindsey Tucker calls the novel "an inverted vision quest where, instead of the usual assistance from benign tutelary spirits, he is visited instead by a punishing presence" (313). Kenan also examines several wives—Ruth, Anne— and mothers—Jimmy's mother Rose, Horace's mother Aretha— who were victimized by the misogyny of a largely patriarchal religion and culture. Like many postmodern authors, Kenan experiments both with narrative point of view and time sequence: he counterpoints Jimmy's experiences and memories a year after Horace's death with the events leading up to Horace's suicide. The narrative shifts from the first to the third person and from December 8, 1985 to April 30, 1984 and back again.

Raised by his great-aunt within a largely black community in Chinquapin, North Carolina (the original of the novel's Tims Creek setting), Randall Kenan recognizes how religion is inextricably tied to race, class, gender, and—most important—sexual orientation.   Sometimes religion fosters self-worth—the Cross family saw themselves above the rest of the community—but more often it forms barriers to people's development, as it does to Jimmy, who fails Horace by dismissing his questions about his attraction to men.   As Eve Kosofsky Sedgwick points out, "The ability of anyone in the culture to support and honour gay kids may depend on an ability to name them as such, notwithstanding that many gay adults may never have been gay kids and some gay kids may not turn into gay adults" (from "Axiomatic" in Epistemology of the Closet, rept. in *The Cultural Studies Reader*, ed. Simon During [London: Routledge, 1993: 259). Jimmy admits to having "experimented" with men in his past, but he refuses to name Horace as gay; he insists, instead "You're perfectly normal" and tells him to pray to "God to give you strength and in no time . . ." (*Visitation* 113-114). But Kenan slyly and ironically includes Horace's biology science project on tropism, which Horace defines as "An orientation of an organism, usually by growth rather than by movement, in response to an external stimulus" (155). Men's bodies had attracted Horace since he was a child and the intensity of his attraction to men grows as he develops into adolescence.

Religion also fails Jimmy's great-aunt Ruth, who, like her biblical namesake, follows the one she loves, her husband Jethro, into the Cross family but is treated like an outsider by its members, especially Zeke, and blamed for Jethro's drinking.   And, most importantly, religion fails Horace, who feels ostracized by his sexuality.   In the church scene his demon leads him to revisit, he queries "his folk, his kin. Did he know them? Had they known him? It was from them he was running. Why?" (73) The refusal of church as well as family and school to recognize part of Horace's essential nature—and religion's making homosexuality a sin—meant that no one actually knew him.

Kenan, who has been termed a magic realist, acknowledged in an interview with Michelle Orecklin, that "'One of the things I have always taken issue with in Southern literature is that it is almost all rooted in social realism. . ..I grew up around people who took the Bible literally, and still do.' So [she continues] in college, when Kenan first read such South American authors as Gabriel Garcia Marquez, he abandoned his plans to be a physicist and turned to writing. 'When I encountered writers who wrote about spirits like they would changing a carburetor, I realized you can come at this form from an entirely different vantage point.'"   What Kenan does, then, is to present demons, ghosts, and goblins as "real," leaving it to the reader to decide whether they come from Horace's mind or the Bible, comic books, and medieval texts on black magic. Unlike most "coming out" narratives, this novel is permeated by religious references, from the author's acknowledgment of *"the inscrutable grace of the Host of Hosts"* to epigraphs for the section titles; from the characters' Old-Testament prophets' names to references to the Middle Passage and allusions to biblical verses.   In the theater scene the tone shifts to that of prophesy, the language of black oratory, and Kenan's prose captures the cadence of biblical phrasing.

The novel's title suggests a paradox, for "visitation" refers positively to the visit of the Virgin Mary to her cousin Elizabeth—and thus of comfort— and negatively to the appearance of a supernatural being, for Horace, demons, satyrs, and other apparitions conjured up from comic books, medieval texts and the Old Testament, who are supposed to turn him into a bird so he can escape the ravages of his lust for men. "Visitation" suggests the imposition of the will of a higher being upon a mortal. The section titles, as well as the epigraphs, also reflect this merger of religion and the occult: White Sorcery, Black Necromancy, Holy Science, Old Demonology, and Old Gods, New Demons.

Religion is also tied to class.   Members of the Cross family hold themselves as better than both whites and other blacks, not only because of their name (the white line of Crosses has nearly died out) and property, but because of their church: "Old man Thomas Cross was the second chairman of the deacon board of First Baptist of Tims Creek, and his father Ezra, who got so much land from the old Cross family, so the saying goes, in the 1870s, once slavery was over, was the first—he even donated the land the church stands on" (51) Both Horace and Jimmy benefit from this class-consciousness—Horace, for example, when his aunts come to his rescue after he's been in a fight with a white boy, and Jimmy as pastor of the church and first black principal of the Tims Creek Elementary School. However, both suffer from it as well. Horace's homosexuality conflicts with his family's religious view that only heterosexuality is normal. And Jimmy, Horace's foil, suffers from trying to minister to those who either do not believe or who dismiss him as the boy they knew and do not listen.

The family names seem deliberately to be drawn directly from the Old Testament, with all the strictness that implies. In addition to Ezra, the founder, the Cross family includes Thomas, Zeke's (Ezekiel's) father; Sammy, Zeke's son, Retha, Zeke's wife; and Horace, Zeke's grandson. (53-55). Jonnie Mae, Jethro, Zelia and Agnes are Zeke's siblings. Like the prophet for whom he was named, Ezekiel lost his wife through death and feels called upon to lead the congregation. As the head deacon after his father, Ezekial (Zeke) tried to emulate his father, who was "a solemn man" (53). His Old Testament rigidity is reflected when Horace noticed—but could not reach a conclusion about the fact—- that most of those weary souls who came to Zeke, his grandfather, for counseling entered "his room of confession, repentance, and rebirth" but "left as somber as they had entered" (71).

Both Horace (whose name after the Roman poet is most obviously <u>not</u> biblical) and James Greene (named from the New Testament, not the Old) are exceptions to this Old Testament naming. Both have at times succumbed to their sexuality, Horace with Gideon Stone and the gay theater people, Jimmy with a variety of women while at divinity school. But James follows an acceptable path. He loves and marries Anne; his mistake is his desire to possess her. She resists: "You've got my body, Goddamn it. You have my friendship. Leave my fucking soul alone!" (176) Jimmy cannot leave her soul or those of his conventional parishioners alone. He longs to change their expectations: "I want to introduce a new way of approaching Christian faith, a way of caring for people" (110). Yet at the gravesite of his grandmother, Jimmy, who has rejected his mother Rose who left home when her sisters treated her like a servant, recognizes "the magnitude of my crime" but remains "unrepentant". Horace falls in love with another "out" gay boy, Gideon Stone, but having given in to his desires feels revulsion and later hits Gideon. Both Horace and Jimmy fail and feel guilt for that failure.

The family's founder Ezra Cross had a "dream that one of his own progeny would stand before the altar as His, and his, minister"—and Jimmy, whose middle name Malachai refers to a messenger sent to chastise Israel for its corruption, is destined to be the fulfillment of that dream (115). The Old Testament chapters in Malachi say that "men should seek instruction from his mouth, for he is the messenger of the Lord of hosts"(2:7). But there are difficulties preaching to those who knew you as a child, as Jimmy realizes:

> A preacher. A minister. A man of God. In the book of Luke the apostle writes that Jesus returns to Nazareth and reads from the Scriptures during
> the services, saying that he has come to fulfill them. He tells us that the people in the synagogue were then 'filled with wrath, and rose up, and thrust him out of the city, and led him unto the brow of the hill whereon their city was built, that they might cast him down headlong. . ..' [I]t's commonly known among Southern Baptists that it's hard to preach to people you know and who've known you all your life and most of your family's life. It is formidable. (114)

Whereas Jimmy's problem is coping with the rigid expectations of his religious congregation, Horace's problem is in a sense created by his religion: he is caught between two worlds, that described by his religion and that described by science and mathematics. Only in medieval tomes and popular culture's heroes like Batman, the Hulk, and the Conjurer does he discover a world of magic—of spirits and demons. When he questions his own sanity in devising a spell to change himself into a bird and thus lose his homosexual urges, he thinks "Of course he was not crazy, he told himself; his was a very rational mind, acquainted with sciences and mathematics. But he was also a believer in an unseen world full of archangels and prophets and folk rising from the dead, a world preached to him from the cradle on, and a world he was powerless not to believe in as firmly as he believed in gravity and the times table" (16). The world of magic called to him from books like *Magicians of the Bible* and *Essays on the Dark Arts*, and through them he hoped to perform his own spell—his own miracle.

Kenan underscores Horace's belief by dividing the novel into "White Sorcery," "Black Necromancy," "Holy Science," "Old Demonology," and "Old Gods, New Demons". And he uses as epigraphs to the novel a quotation from Charles Dickens' *A Christmas Carol,* emphasizing the shortness of a spirit's time, and fittingly, a modern science fiction allusion from William Gibson's *Neuromancer:* "To call up a demon you must learn its name. Men dreamed that, once, but now it is real in another way . . ." (243). Horace hopes to call up a demon but instead surrenders to a voice in his head that impels him to irrational acts.

Under "White Sorcery," the opening chapter which deals with an aged Zeke and an even more aged Ruth, widow of his brother Jethro, the epigraph from *Habakkuk* 2:20 begins "The Lord is in his Holy Temple; let all the earth keep silent before him". As we later learn, Ruth will not keep silent about all the wrongs the supposedly Christian Cross family has done to her. She and Zeke have a running feud which they settle peaceably only in the fourth section, "Old Demonology". The first words of the chapter are both an exclamation and a prayer: "Lord, Lord, Lord" as Ruth slips and falls due to her age. Almost immediately following this scene, the process of hog killing is described by a third-person narrator, with the title "Advent (or The Beginning of the End)," suggesting that the ritual of hog-killing which once unified the community, like the labor-intensive tobacco harvest eulogized in the final chapter, no longer are workable. The rest of the opening section details Horace's dreams and plans, as well as the ritual he follows. . After the ritual, at the end of the section, Horace marches, "surrounded by hobgoblins and sprites and evil faeries and wargs—aberrations like himself. . .and he was happy, O so happy, as he cradled the gun in his hand like a cool phallus. . . ." For he believes "this was his salvation, the way to final peace. . ."(28). This sense of his being an "aberration" from his family and religion leads, not to peace but to his death.

The epigraph to the second section, "Black Necromancy," is a short invitation: "Whosoever will, let him come . . ."(29). The first chapter, entitled "James Malachai Greene: Confessions" reveals Jimmy's life in Durham, while he was working for his theology degree. One of his professors, "a Christian Jew," (31) predicted that Jimmy would make a "great theologian" because of his curiosity to *"know God"* "in the Old Testament way. Like some of the prophets or David or Joseph" (33). But Jimmy does not seem to know himself, much less God. Jimmy sees Horace as a romantic, and quickly dismisses his sense of guilt as his own romanticism. He says:

> I keep dreaming about him, about that morning. Keep thinking there was something I could have done said. If not that morning then before, long before . . . but that's just me being a romantic. (36)

Jimmy's thoughts turn to his personal triumphs —being the first black principal of his school—and then to his year ago encounter with his nearly naked cousin, who had "*a strange, almost clownlike smile on his face.*" But it was too late for Jimmy to reach Horace; he's only told by the demon "Horace ain't home" (41).

For Horace, designated the "chosen nigger" by his family (or so his cousin tells him), the black church provides both strength and guilt. At first, led by the demon voice to his old church, reliving the scene of his baptism provides comfort and security, as he sees his kinfolk and dead community members listening to his dead pastor, the Reverend Hezekiah Barden. But the text of Paul to the Romans which Barden cites accuses men who lie with men of being "'Unclean. . .'"(79). Both comfort and security are destroyed by Horace's sense of sin for his homosexuality, which makes him outcast, excluded from the congregation. Nevertheless, he refuses the demon's demands to lop off the head of the old parson, just as he later refuses to attack the chicken truck coming at him down the highway or to shoot his cousin Jimmy.

Twice Horace has encounters with what might be his salvation—first with the angel and next with his doppelganger in whiteface. The first, at the football field, is where Horace almost is saved:

> There through the bleachers he could see it, standing in the middle of the field. It was obscured by shadows, but it clearly was a manlike figure, dark, clad in what appeared to be thick, black robes. On its head was a helmet that shone silver, and it carried a huge scimitar that carried the faint glint of moonlight. And the wings. . . . The hand that did not grip the sword beckoned to Horace, Come, come. Horace could hear the whispers of many voices in his ear, whispers whispering, *For behold, the day cometh, that shall scorch as an oven; . . . and all the proud, yea, and all that do wickedly, shall be stubble. . . . (165)*

Horace begins to step forward toward the voice. But hearing a car door slam, and white men coming, the angel disappears and Horace flees after hearing the demon voice say "The gun, fool. Use the fucking gun" (167). The next encounter Horace has with the possibility of salvation is at the Crosstown theater, where he meets "a black man, dressed in a sun-bright costume, orange and green and blue and red, like a harlequin's" (219) and discovers the man is him in whiteface, a not-so-subtle reference to Horace's attempt to have white friends and, perhaps, live as white. Gradually, as he reviews his orgiastic career at the summer theater and his crush on Everett Church Harrington IV, he begins to see the attraction of suicide: "life beneath the ground had a certain appeal it had never had before. . . . No more, no more ghosts, no more sin, no more, no more" (231).

It is not until near the novel's end, in the graveyard to which his ghostly doppelganger has led him, Horace finally "saw what he had led himself to see, the reason, the logic, the point" (232):

> *Your sons and your daughters shall prophesy,* said the prophet Joel, *your old men shall dream dreams, your young men shall see visions.* (Joel 2:28)

He sees his people in the past, present, and the future. He sees the Middle Passage, with Africans "shackled up and loaded onto ships like barrels of syrup and made to sit there crouched in chains, to defecate and urinate and choke on their own vomit, in the heat, in the stench of day and weeks and months, and they will bring forth children who will die, who should die, rather than be born into this wicked world" (232). He sees war and poverty, and above all, he sees the failure of God's promise to Noah, the rainbow sign.

> And the bow shall be in the cloud; and I will look upon it, that I may remember the ever-lasting covenant between God and every living creature of all flesh that is upon the earth. (Genesis 9: 13-14, 16)

The questions, "Who will be the savior? Where is the rain?" (234) as he looks at the plight of his people, give him insight. Kenan uses I Corinthians 13:12 (For now we see through a glass, darkly; but then face to face: now I know in part; but then shall I know even as also I am known.): Horace saw clearly through a glass darkly and understood where he fit. Understood what was asked of him (234). He was asked to be the savior of his people, as his family and community had expected. But "Horace shook his head. No" (234).

He refuses to be the savior, perhaps because he does not want to be known, as the passage suggests. More likely, such a choice to become their savior would mean giving up an essential part of himself.

The final section, "Old Gods, New Demons" has as its epigraph the definition of the grammatical term "subjunctive" as used for "doubtful" or "hypothetical" statements. And that is how we are to understand the chapter entitled "Horace Thomas Cross: Confessions". Although we are told Horace burned his autobiography, we get Horace's memories in the voice of a child: of the chocolate chip cookies he loved, the television and comic book monsters like Dracula and Frankenstein, the way he felt when "touching a man, finally kissing him" and afterwards "regretting that it was such a sin" (250). The memories conclude with the final realization:

> Then I remember the day I realized that I was probably not going to go home to heaven, cause the rules were too hard for me to keep. That I was too weak. I remember me. (251)

> The last encounter Jimmy has with Horace is in the demon's voice, whose crude language is very different from either biblical or rhetorical language: "He [Horace] don't like life, see. Too many fucking rules. Too many unanswered questions. Too many loose ends. You see, life the way Horace wants it ain't condoned, you know what I mean? : And condonation—if that's what you call it—is what he wants. : So—" (252-253)

Instead of shooting Jimmy, Horace shoots himself, just as he had shot his double in the theater, thereby demonstrating how much he hated himself.

> Jimmy sums up Horace's plight by blaming the community: He, just like me, had been created by this society. . . . His reason for existing, it would seem was for the salvation of his people. But he was flawed as far as the community was concerned. First, he loved men; a simple, normal deviation, but a deviation his community would never accept. And second, he didn't quite know who he was. (188)

But Jimmy also is unsure about who he is, despite his divinity degree, his pastorship, and his principal's position. He rested his belief in his wife Anne, but her cancer that spreads in her until it kills her symbolizes her unfaithfulness. Jimmy mourns her loss. But Tucker, following Freud, sees Jimmy as a melancholic, "as one who suffers the loss of a beloved object in such a way that, instead of undergoing the normative processes of grief. . .the subject incorporates the object. . .. rather than deflecting desire onto another object, the melancholic personality refuses the loss, surrenders desire and. . ..attempts to maintain the lost object as a living presence" (323). Certainly Jimmy remains in his unchanged house and in his job three years after Anne's death.

But Jimmy also has failed his mother, who was treated like a servant by her sisters because of her out of wedlock children, until she left again. As the minister at her father's funeral reads from Paul to the Corinthians, Jimmy sees his mother Rose's "lonely, lovely, scorned eyes" (121). And still he refuses to offer the charity he owes her, so that he becomes as "sounding brass, or a tinkling cymbal" (1 Corinthians 13:1). Jimmy remains unrepentant and unforgiving, though "the magnitude of my crime washed over me" (121).

But as Lindsey Tucker points out, using Diana Fuss's concept of "'outside'" as "'a consequence of a lack internal to the system it supplements'" "it would seem that it is the heterosexual Jimmy rather than the gay Horace who most embodies loss and sexual ambiguity" (309). Sexual ambiguity extends to most of the members of the Cross family, from Zeke who wonders whether his dead wife was ever happy with him, to Jethro, whom Tucker identifies as possibly gay.

Critics have noted that transgressions of the norm, in the novel as in life, mean ostracism from the family and the community. When Kenan was asked whether the black community was more homophobic or "about the same as the rest of America" he responded:

> . . . I think the truth is a lot of it has to do with the strength of the African-American church. Whether or not people are going to church doesn't matter. The church and its teachings ruled their early thinking. With alot of African-American men, and this is true all

over the country, machismo is very important in term of identity.
Homophobia is a direct result of that.   We're talking about the
military, we're talking about the labor force, and in most blue-collar
situations in this country. . . ..And I don't think it is more marked with
blacks than with white folk.   But black communities are a bit more
vocal (in their homophobia), I would say, and guilty of a lack of
support. (The Solon Interview)

It is precisely this lack of support—and its relation to religion—that Kenan
depicts in *A Visitation of Spirits*.   And as Adam Baron comments, Kenan
"demonstrates the blind alleys which certain attitudes lead people down,
especially when the world has moved on from those attitudes."   But, he says,
Kenan does this "with frankness and compassion". As Kenan himself declared:
"I don't like fiction that is polemical, that tries to prove or solve something in a
political arena" (*Salon*).   And in *A Visitation of Spirits* he writes, not with
criticism but with sympathy. Anyone who has transgressed a communal, and
especially a religious, norm can identify with the guilt and oppression felt by the
characters in this novel.

Works Cited

Baron, Adam. Rev. of *A Visitation of Spirits*. *The Richmond Review*.
        http://www.richmondreview.co.uk/books/visitati.html. 10/3/2001.
Gibson, William. *Neuromancer*. New York: Ace Science Fiction, 1984.
Kenan, Randall. *A Visitation of Spirits*. Anchor Books. NY: Doubleday, 1989.
Kenan, Randall. Interview with Fetzer Mills, Jr. "Journey to the Center of a
        Race." *Salon*. 1999. <http://archive.salon.com/books/int/1999/02/cov-
        _24int.html>
Kenan, Randall. Interview with Michelle Orecklin. "A Twist on Tradition."
        Time. <http://www.time.com/time/reports/mississippi/literature.html>
        Accessed 10/3/2001.
Kenan, Randall. The Solon Interview. . [possibly from Amazon.com]
        www.queertheory.com/histories/k/kenan_randall.htm. Accessed
        10/3/2001.
Sedgwick, Eve Kosofsky. "Axiomatic," *Epistemology of the Closet*. Rptd. In
        The Cultural Studies Reader. Ed. Simon During. London: Routledge,
        1993. 259
Tucker, Lindsey. "Gay Identity, Conjure, and the Uses of Postmodern
        Ethnography in the Fictions of Randall Kenan." *Modern Fiction
        Studies* 49.2 (2003) 306-331.
        <http://jproxy.lib.ecu.edu:2130/journals/modern_fiction_studies/v04>
The Holy Bible. Authorized or King James Version. Philadelphia: The John
        C. Winston Company, n.d. [1948]

19   She Had No Self Left: The Sacrificial Love of Miriam in D. H. Larence's *Sons and Lovers* and Hagar in Toni Morson's *Song of Solomon*

Sharon Raynor

She could easily sacrifice herself
But dare she assert herself?
-Miriam, *Sons and Lovers*-

When you know your name, you should hang on to it,
For unless it is noted down and remembered, it will die when you do.
-*Song of Solomon*-

As scholars, we are often faced with the challenge of teaching canonical works, non-canonical works, or both. In a classroom setting ". . . texts could be chosen to generate interesting conceptual problems, each of which moves the class along in its study of central terms" (Schlib 65). In this study, I have juxtaposed a canonical novel by a white male author with a non-canonical novel by a black female author that deal with the same subject or theme. This teaching style would provide students with the best of both worlds, without upsetting the "preservers" and/or "dismantlers" of the Western canon. This pairing of non-canonical and canonical works can lead "students to ponder how gender, ethnicity, and other factors have produced different works with different fates, even if they deal with similar topics" (66). This comparative analysis will focus on the double bildungsroman genre as it relates to both male and female characters and how this genre becomes restructured when taken out of the traditional European context.

A comparative analysis of D. H. Lawrence's *Sons and Lovers* and Toni Morrison's *Song of Solomon* reveals several striking similarities, from the influence of Lawrence upon Morrison, the male-female double bildungsroman that represents both the male and his female counterpart, the similarities between characters, the underlying Biblical tradition from which both novels evolve to the insightful non-canonical/canonical teaching of two well-known literary texts.

The main focus of this comparative analysis is not on the male protagonists, Paul in *Sons and Lovers* or Milkman in *Song of Solomon*, but on their female counterparts, Miriam and Hagar, respectively. These two female characters are appealing because they, too, are searching for their own identities while facing obstacles far different than those endured by men. They could be sister-figures, both becoming victims of sacrificial love. Miriam and Hagar seem to mirror each other exactly but in very different cultural circumstances. Even though Lawrence is writing out of the English cultural tradition during the early 1900s and Morrison out of the Black cultural tradition spanning decades in the 1900s, the two female characters seem to have an intended purpose once introduced into the novels. Unlike most secondary characters, Miriam and Hagar represent Paul and Milkman's counterparts and they have a significant impact on the protagonists. They both render the ultimate sacrifice for the men they so desperately try to love. I contend that it was Lawrence and Morrison's authorial intentions to write Miriam and Hagar as "sacrificeable" characters who evolve from a Biblical tradition of women who were destined to play a certain role, so when they sacrificed their moral values and dignity so Paul and Milkman could "come of age" we, as readers, would not displace our sympathies from the protagonists to these two characters.

The underlying premise for this contention is the Biblical tradition into which Miriam and Hagar are born. These characters have self-fulfilling prophecies that resonate through their names and play out throughout the novels. "Women in Biblical times were shaped by their patriarchal race, class, and social location, just as women today. Biblical women who were at the lowest stratum of society helped us to understand the multiple oppression of women in a most vivid way" (Fiorenza 105). By knowing the tradition, readers will assume they know Miriam and Hagar's destinies before completing the novels and therefore not sympathize with them when they attempt "to consume" the souls of Paul and Milkman and antagonize the existing mother-son relationship. The manner in which they are sacrificed and what happens to them by the end of the novels in their "coming of age" process becomes very significant to the *Bildung* of Paul and Milkman. Miriam and Hagar make very strong statements about their own search for identity and how this is shaped and formed in a male-dominated world by both male and female authors writing out of very distinct cultural traditions. In spite of the Biblical connotations, the gender and the cultural traditions of Lawrence and Morrison will have a dramatic impact on the fates of Miriam and Hagar.

According to Charlotte Goodman in "The Lost Brother, the Twin: Women Novelists and the Male –Female Double Bildungsroman," the genre is defined as follows:

> The design of the male-female *Bildungsroman* is circular;
> tripartite in structure, it describes the shared childhood experience of
> a male and female protagonist who inhabit a place somewhat

> reminiscent of a perlapsarian garden world where the male and
> female once existed as equals; then such novels dramatize the
> separation of the male and the female character in adolescence and
> young adulthood as the male, like hero of the typical male
> Bildungroman, journeys forth to seek his fortune, while the female is
> left behind; and finally, the novels conclude with a reunion of the
> male and the female protagonist. (30)

The construct of the *Bildung* will take on different forms for the various characters. First, the characters in this study are separated by race and gender. Secondly, the place and time affect their process. Thirdly, the circumstances that they must face are very different. Fourth, the histories in which they are born into direct their searches for identity. But most importantly, the reasons for which they seek this process are vastly different and so are their individual outcomes. In the male-female double bildungsroman, the evolution of both the male and female characters is traced. "Though female characters sometimes play an important role in male *Bildungsroman* by helping the hero to define his own identity as they do in *Sons and Lovers* and *The Portrait of an Artist as a Young Man*, for example, there is no question who the real hero is" (Goodman 30). But for the purpose of this study, certain patterns that are unique to the double bildungsroman will be touched upon in order to place more emphasis on "how" Miriam and Hagar were sacrificed by Paul and Milkman, since we know "why."

In *Sons and Lovers*, Lawrence introduces the readers to Miriam Leviers at the end of Part I in the novel. She is described as a woman who "was inclined to be mystical" who believed that "Christ and God made one great figure, which she loved tremblingly and passionately" (143) and possessing all her life within her eyes, "which were usually dark as a dark church, but could flame with light like a conflagration. She might had been the one of the women who went with Mary when Jesus was dead" (154). In the Biblical tradition, Miriam was the older sister of Moses. She becomes responsible for him when she finds him floating in a basket on the river. Miriam made sure that their mother raised Moses, and she was there with Moses throughout the nine plagues and came out of Egypt with him. The Biblical Miriam is a woman of God and a prophet herself, but she had to play a less prominent role because Moses was a more important prophet. Miriam not only refused to recognize Moses as a prophet of God, but she also criticized his marriage to an Ethiopian woman. She becomes jealous over Moses' relationship with God and is punished for her behavior. She was punished to become "leprous" (white as snow) and sent from the camp for seven days. God soon restores her after Moses pleads for her. In the Biblical sense, Miriam is restored because of the very person she envies. From another perspective, Miriam can be read as a woman of liberation, as a leader, and as one of the women who was privileged to know the things that men did not. The parallels between this tradition and Lawrence's Miriam will evolve throughout her bildung.

At the time before Paul Morel endures the death of his older brother, William, and has to become a lot more for his mother than just her "new" oldest son, he meets Miriam when he visits her family at Willey Farm. Miriam was at first weary of Paul because he looked like a "Walter Scott hero, could paint and speak French, knew what algebra meant, and who rode the train to Nottingham every day" (143). Miriam and Paul begin a very antagonizing courtship. Miriam is portrayed as being discontent in her position as a girl. "She wanted to learn, thinking if she could read, as Paul said he could read. The world would have a different face for her and a deepened respect" (144). She starts to envy Paul from the beginning. Miriam's "beauty—that of a shy, wild quivering sensitive thing—seemed nothing to her. Even her soul, so strong for rhapsody, was not enough. She must have something to reinforce her pride, because she felt different from other people" (144). Even though "she scorned the male sex" (144), she sees Paul as weak so now would be her opportunity to be stronger than he. "Then she could love him. If she could be mistress of him in his weakness, take care of him, if he could depend on her, if she could, as it were, have him in her arms, how she would love him" (144)! In the Biblical tradition, Miriam was used to Moses being depended on her. She was responsible, so to speak, for his growth from a baby found on a river to becoming the prophet of God. Lawrence's Miriam wants Paul to need her. Now that Paul's brother has died, he seems very vulnerable to not only Miriam but to his mother as well.

This new relationship with Miriam threatens his old relationship with his mother. Paul's attachment stems from his younger years. He "suffered very much from the first contact with anything. When he was seven, the starting school had been a nightmare and a torture to him. But afterwards he liked it. And now that he felt he had to go out into life, he went through agonies of shrinking self-consciousness" (Lawrence 88). Even before William's death, Paul becomes an attachment for his mother, Mrs. Morel, as well as her replacement for William after he dies. "Mrs. Morel clung to Paul. He was quiet and not brilliant . . . and still he stuck to his mother. Everything he did was for her. She waited for his coming home in the evening, and then she unburdened herself of all she had pondered, or all that had occurred to her during the day. He sat and listened with earnestness. The two shared lives" (114). This relationship with Mrs. Morel evolves into something more than the typical mother-son relationship. As Paul's courtship with Miriam evolves, the relationship with his mother becomes even more strained. According to Daniel R. Schwarz, "As Paul becomes dependent on Miriam for aesthetic stimulation and for bringing out his spiritual aspect, he almost gives her the status of his mother and creates competition between the two women within his psyche" (89). Paul is able to project cruelty upon Miriam because of his mother's influence.

Paul notices that Miriam seems bitter about being a girl and her responsibility as a girl. "But Miriam almost fiercely wished she were a man.

And yet she hated men at the same time" (155). The parallels between the Biblical character and the novel character are becoming more evident as we see Miriam's apparent jealousy over Paul. Lawrence, still drawing upon Biblical connotations, places this obvious hostility between Paul and Miriam in an Edenic garden environment. The "communions" between the characters were always in the midst of "honeysuckle . . . [with] streaming scent, bosses of ivory, and roses gleam[ing] on the darkness of foliage and stems and grass" (160). In Miriam's garden of roses with "a white, virgin scent," she succeeded in making Paul feel "anxious and imprisoned" (160-6). Her passion for flowers is almost more intimate than her feelings for Paul.

When Miriam gains a spiritual possession of Paul, this infuriates Mrs. Morel. She believes that Miriam "is one of those who will want to suck a man's soul out till he has none of his own left. She will never let him become a man; she never will" (161). Mrs. Morel knew that Paul would let himself be absorbed by Miriam.

At the moment Miriam discovers that she loves Paul, she also realizes the complete control his mother has over him. Miriam prays instantly for the Lord not to let her love Paul but then reflects upon this request. This signifies the first sign of the role Miriam is going to play in Paul's development:

> Something anomalous in the prayer arrested her. She lifted her head and pondered. How could it be wrong to love him? Love was God's gift. And yet it caused her shame. That was because of him, Paul Morel. But, then, it was not his affair, it was her own, between herself and God. She was to be a sacrifice. But it was God's sacrifice, not Paul Morel's or her own. (172)

Since prayer is essential, Miriam begins to pray once again. "But, Lord, if it is Thy will that I should love him, make me love him—as Christ would, who died for the souls of men. Make me love him splendidly, because he is Thy son. Then she fell into that rapture of self-sacrifice, identifying herself with a God who was sacrificed, which gives to so many human souls their deepest bliss"(172). Miriam is willing to sacrifice herself for the love of Paul. The intimacy between Paul and Miriam evolves spiritually through their many conversations about religion and spirituality. Even though Paul realizes this, he still has passionate tendencies toward Miriam, but neither can overcome the barriers of spirituality and passion that keep them apart. Paul "could not bear to look at Miriam. She seemed to want him, and he resisted. He resisted all the time. He wanted now to give her passion and tenderness, and could not" (193). Paul is struggling with a constant inner conflict. He wants Miriam sexually and spiritually, but he realizes that this will cause his mother great pain. Paul believes, as his mother once thought, that Miriam would consume his soul. "He felt that she wanted the soul out of his body, and not him. All his strength and energy she drew into herself through some channel that united them. She did not want to meet him, so that there were two of them, man and woman together. She wanted to draw all of him into her. It urged him to an intensity like madness, which fascinated him, as drug-taking might" (193-9). Miriam not only endures the flirtatious moments Paul has with other women but she also puts up with the Paul's cruelty when his mother becomes jealous and resentful of the relationship. He projects his hatred and frustration toward Miriam instead of his mother:

> It was all weird and dreadful. Why was he torn so, almost bewildered, and unable to move? Why did his mother sit at home and suffer? He knew she
> suffered badly. But why should she? And why did he hate Miriam, and feel so cruel towards her, at the thought of his mother. If Miriam caused his mother suffering, then he hated her—and he easily hated her. Why did she make him feel as if he were uncertain of himself, insecure ... How he hated her! (193)

Paul and Miriam only share a brief kiss before his mother falls sick and he realizes that he loves his mother more than anyone else in the world. But Miriam is still willing to sacrifice herself for Paul's passionate love but Paul realizes that her love is too good for him. They seem to have to purge themselves before they can become intimate.

At this point, Paul and Miriam both realize that their relationship is hopeless and their lives grow apart. Paul becomes even more torn between his love for his mother and his need to be with Miriam.

> Paul was dissatisfied with himself and with everything. The deepest of his love belonged to his mother. When he felt he had hurt her, or wounded his love for her, he could not bear it. Now it was spring, and there was battle between him and Miriam. This year he had a good deal against her. She was vaguely aware of it. The old feeling that she was to be a sacrifice to this love, which she had had when she prayed, was mingled in all her emotions (215).

Miriam, like Paul, is struggling to resolve her feelings. She did realize that she could not have a life with Paul. "She saw tragedy, sorrow, and sacrifice ahead. And in sacrifice she was proud, in renunciation she was strong, for she did not trust herself to support everyday life" (215). Their relationship becomes more intense but their sexual intimacy is inhibited and Paul continues to scorn Miriam for not practicing more restraint. He retorts that she "wheedle[s] the soul out of things and begs things to love [her]." He claims that she doesn't want to love; she is positive and not negative. As time yields itself to Miriam and Paul, they ponder the thought of marriage but Paul is still agonizing with his deep love for his mother. Miriam decides "to relinquish herself to him, but it was a sacrifice in which she felt something of horror. This thick-voiced, oblivious man was a stranger to her" (284). Paul realizes that during their moments of passion, Miriam's "soul stood apart in horror" and that he became "very dreary at heart, very sad" (285). Since their love is a failure and Paul never wants to marry, they end their relationship.

Miriam and Paul remain friends throughout his turbulent affair with another woman, whom Miriam criticizes because she knows that their relationship was not of God. In the meantime Paul is still trying to make his mother happy. But once his mother is diagnosed with terminal cancer, Paul can no longer find comfort in this other woman. He misses Miriam's spirituality. Its only when his mother dies that he knows that his soul will always be a part of hers. Even though his mother has released him, Paul could not release her. The possible reunion between him and Miriam would not work because "she could not take him and relieve him of the responsibility of himself. She could only sacrifice herself to him—sacrifice herself every day" (414). Paul also refuses to give Miriam life by denying himself his own life. But for Miriam, "how unutterably bitter, it made her that he rejected her sacrifice! Life ahead looked dead, as if the glow were gone out . . . without him her life would trail on lifeless" (415). The novel ends with the notion that Paul, even through all of his childish behavior, is just beginning his bildung, while Miriam's has ended on a spiritually dead and lifeless note. "Paul's final failure with Miriam—he can't take her even after his mother's death—is the last scene of the novel. Throughout, this fatal inability to come to terms with Miriam as a person, has been the indicator of Paul's immaturity and narcissism" (Pullin 71).

Lawrence's Miriam and the Biblical Miriam are not very different characters. They both are spiritual beings that are envious of the men in their lives. They are also both punished for their deviance, so to speak. Lawrence's Miriam sacrifices herself and her moral values because she wanted to please Paul passionately and sexually. She loses herself through this sacrifice. Unlike in the Biblical tradition when Moses came to his sister's rescue even after her jealousy and criticism in order for her to be restored, readers will not know if Lawrence's Miriam is restored. But we can assume that it will not be by Paul since he has more to gain from Miriam's lifelessness than her restoration. Miriam is manipulated "in Paul's painful effort at self-identification, the effort to become himself" (49). But Paul fears Miriam because "she has forced him into the realization of "hate and misery of another failure" (72). Lawrence's writing of Miriam as a sacrificeable character distorts her image as a spiritual being. Before discussing the significance of Miriam's bildung, let's examine Hagar's in *Song of Solomon*.

Morrison's novel celebrates Milkman Dead's archetypal journey across ancestral terrain to discover his family heritage and identity—his *Bildung*. Upon this journey, he becomes acquainted with several characters that have a direct affect on his "coming of age" process and he upon theirs. The one character who finds herself in the search for her own identity while also trying to love

Milkman is his cousin, Hagar. She appears early in the novel and at age ten or eleven instantly "pulled him like a carpet tack under the influence of a magnet" (29). Her grandmother, Pilate, who is also Milkman's aunt, introduces Hagar to Milkman. "She was, it seemed to him, as pretty a girl as he'd ever seen. She was much much older than he was. . . maybe even seventeen. She was as strong and muscular as he was" (45). Milkman feels elated in her presence. "He seemed to be floating. More alive than he'd ever been, and floating" (45). Very early, Milkman finds himself in love. When she sang the song of their ancestors, her voice "scooped up what little pieces of heart he had left to call his own" (49). Hagar "was just fine, but still, she wasn't regular. She had some queer ways"(76). Milkman finds himself being rebellious against his father and spending more time with Hagar and Pilate because his mother and father seem to possess so many secrets.

Hagar, in the Biblical tradition, carries the burden of her name. She is an Egyptian slave girl of Abraham and Sara. Her story is often read as one that "show[s] the intersection of racism, classism, and sexism by women of color in different continents" (Fiorenza 105). In one regard, she is seen as "the concubine to patriarchal Abraham, mother to outcast Ishmael, and handmaiden to jealous Sara" (Brenner 119). "Her body was sexually exploited, and she was humiliated and ridiculed by her mistress" (Fiorenza 105). In another sense, Hagar can be viewed as a character that "God instilled hope in" and the slave woman who gave God a name, the God who sees" despite her conditions of "extreme poverty [that] cause her to be sold into slavery, of being "a single mother abandoned by her husband," and being used by Sara "as an instrument for meeting her needs" exposes "the many hidden scars and memories of the history" of slavery and "a powerful people around her [that] tried to erase her from historical memory" (105). The new cultural identity that is imposed upon Hagar exposes the plight of women who live under multiple oppression. She can be read as a positive character whose life was "denied and demeaned by [the] scriptural presentations." Her life "had a reality and meaning including ritual practices and spiritual experiences quite unlike that given it by the patriarchal tradition in which [her story was] set in scripture" (143). Morrison's Hagar is born out of a rich and complex Biblical tradition that guides her life in the novel.

The novel progresses rather quickly, and several intimacies are revealed about both Milkman and Hagar. Milkman is nursed by his mother, Ruth, "a pale but complicated woman given to deviousness and ultra-fine manners," (75) when he "was old enough to talk, stand up, and wear knickers. She seemed to know a lot and understand very little. Never had he thought of his mother as a person, a separate individual, with a life apart from allowing or interfering with his own" (78). And she despised his relationship with his own cousin, Hagar. Ruth knew there "was something truly askew in this girl. That here was the wildness of the Southside . . . . the absence of control" (138). She believed that Hagar was capable of doing anything because she lived in a world that had no order. But after twelve years of "going with" Hagar, Milkman was growing bored with her.

> Everybody knew about Hagar, but she was considered his private honey pot, not a real or legitimate girl friend—not someone he might marry. Now, after more than a dozen years, he was getting tired of her. Her eccentricities were no longer provocative and the stupefying ease which he had gotten and stayed between her legs had changed from the great good fortune he'd considered it, to annoyance at her refusal to make him hustle for it, work for it, do something difficult for it. He didn't even have to pay for it. It was free, so abundant, it had lost its fervor. There was no excitement; no galloping of blood in his neck or his heart at the thought of her. She was the third beer. Not the first one, which the throat receives with almost tearful gratitude; nor the second, that confirms and extends the pleasure of the first. But the third, the one you drink because it's there, because it can't hurt, and because what difference does it make? (91)

Morrison illustrates Milkman's commodication of Hagar. His relationship with her was making him lazy, so he felt it best if he ended things.

He decides to buy her something for Christmas because "the end of the year was a good time to call it off" (91). He has fond memories of their time together. He wants to remember her as the "vain and distant creature that he took in his arms" (92). He was in love with her from the moment they first met. "She became a quasi-secret but permanent fixture in his life. Very much a tease, sometimes accommodating his appetites, sometimes refusing" (98). Milkman "was delighted to be sleeping with her and she was odd, funny, quirky company, spoiled, but artlessly so and therefore more refreshing than most of the girls his own age. There were months when Hagar would not see him, and then he'd appear one day and she was all smiles" (98). After a few years of seeing each other, Milkman became more involved in his own life and abandoned Hagar for his own interests. She would pout and sulk and claim that he did not love her as he once did. At age thirty-one, he decides to tell Hagar, who was thirty-six, that their nineteen year relationship would have to end because they were cousins and "he was not what she needed. She needed a steady man who could marry her. He was standing in her way. And since they were related and all, she should start looking for someone else" (98). After "stretching his carefree boyhood out for thirty-one years" he decides that he is doing this for Hagar because he loves her and "you couldn't be selfish with somebody you love" (98). He assumes that Hagar will accept "his" decision and will be able to continue her live as usual. He writes her a note that ended: "Also, I wanted to thank you. Thank you for all you have meant to me. For making me happy all these years. I am signing this letter with love, of course, but more than that, with gratitude" (99). Hagar's reaction stemmed from the "flat-out coldness" of the words "gratitude" and "thank you." These very words sent Hagar's world "spinning into a bright blue place where the air was thin and it was silent all the time, and where people spoke in whispers or did not make sounds at all, and where everything was frozen except for an occasional burst of fire inside her chest that crackled away until she ran out into the streets to find Milkman Dead" (99).

Hagar spends her days trying to kill Milkman, while he becomes more involved with searching for his family's heritage and discovering their secrets. For Milkman, this was the key to his identity but for Hagar, Milkman consumed her identity. His mother wondered how "had that chubby little girl weighed down with hair become a knife-wielding would-be killer out to get her son" (135). Ruth becomes more involved with this situation. She finally confronts Hagar who was overwhelmed in "the presence of *his* mother" that she "let a morbid pleasure spread across her face in a smile." Unimpressed because, according to Ruth, "death always smiled. And breathed. And looked helpless." She threatened to cut Hagar's throat out if she touched one hair upon Milkman's head. This threat shocked Hagar because "she loved nothing in the world except this woman's son, wanted him alive more than anybody, but hadn't the least bit of control over the predator that lived inside her. Totally taken over by her anaconda love, *she had no self left*, no fears, no wants, no intelligence that was her own" (136-7 emphasis mine). She told Ruth that she would try to restrain from killing Milkman but she could not make her any promises. Hagar views Ruth through her jealous frustration as

> the woman who had been a silhouette to her, who slept in the same house with him, and who could call him home and he would come, who knew the mystery of his flesh, had memory of him as long as his life. The woman who knew him . . . cleaned is behind, Vaselined his penis . . . fed him from her own nipples, carried him close and warm and safe under her heart, and who had opened her legs far far wider than she herself ever had for him. (137)

Hagar thought it was Ruth that she should kill instead of Milkman and then maybe Milkman would come to her. He tells Ruth that Milkman "is her home in this world" and Ruth tells her the same. At this moment, Hagar and Ruth become the same in their intentions toward Milkman and "he wouldn't give a pile of swans shit for either one" (137). They are both ready to kill each other because they both want Milkman out of the other's life. Pilate informs them both that Milkman will only die by his own ignorance and a woman will probably be the one to save him rather than killed him.

Milkman's life dilemma escalates as his father wants him to be more like him and hate his mother; his mother wants him to hate his father like she does; his sisters will not speak to him; and Hagar wants him dead. His search for identity takes him on trips and through different initiations but also leads him back to Hagar for closure. He realizes that he used her and "she stood there like a puppet strung up by a puppet master who had gone off to some other hobby" (301). But little did he know that Hagar's demise was inevitable. Hagar was a "pretty little black-skinned woman who wanted to kill for love, die for love. She needed what most colored girls needed: a chorus of mamas, grandmamas, aunts, cousins, sisters, neighbors, Sunday school teachers, best girl friends, and what all to give her the strength life demanded of her—and the humor with which to live it" (306-7). After this realization and a brief glimpse in the mirror, Hagar engages in a wild shopping spree because she needed to fix herself up for Milkman. She does not realize how she looked until she presents herself to her mother and grandmother: "the wet ripped hose, the soiled white dress, the sticky, lumpy face powder, the streaked rouge, and the wild wet shoals of hair" (314). Upon this realization and with tears in her tears, Hagar collapses with a fever and soon dies whispering and wondering why Milkman never liked her hair. According to bell hooks in *Black Looks: Race and Representation*:

> For black people, the pain of learning that we cannot control our images, how we see ourselves (if our vision is not colonized), or how we are seen is so intense that it rends us. It rips and tears at the seams of our efforts to construct self and identity. Often it leaves us ravaged by repressed rage, feeling weary, dispirited, and sometimes just plain old brokenhearted. These are the gaps in our psyche that are the spaces of mindless complicity, self-destructive rage, hatred, and paralyzing despair. (3-4)

Hagar never established her own identity as a woman or developed any ideas or values about her life. She instantly becomes Milkman's sacrifice, being used, abused, and abandoned before her self-discovery. Very similar to the Biblical Hagar, Morrison's Hagar also suffers but she also leaves behind her name and legacy. She forces her family, community, and even Milkman to question what happens to a person when they love someone else more than they love themselves—the ultimate sacrifice.

While Hagar dies, Milkman is embarking upon a quest that leads him to his ancestors. He learns the legend about the song of his ancestors: the Song of Solomon, the African slave who flew away and left his wife and children behind. Milkman is discovering his identity through the legends and songs of his ancestors but also realizes that "while he dreamt of flying, Hagar was dying. He had hurt her, left her, and now she was dead—he was certain of it" (332). As the novel nears the end, Milkman realizes the consequences of his stupidity and that his regret would stay with him forever and "always outweigh the things he was proud of having done. Hagar was dead and he had not loved her one bit" (335). Milkman is about to take flight. Because of the sacrifices of others, he learns how to return live to those who gave it to him (Holloway 113).

Hagar's reaction to rejection has been very different than that of Miriam. The similar circumstances do not produce the same bildung for the two characters. According to Stephanie A. Demetrakopoulos, "Hagar's feminine typology needed a traditional community of women to help her reach adulthood. Hagar does not want to be unattached and floating . . . She has grown up completely surrounded by a chaotically feminine yet providing world. She never had to strive for anything" (97). Her mother and grandmother's "totally uncontingent and supportive love may have taken from her the development of the strength she needed to survive Milkman's abandoning her" (97).

In the novel we see Hagar being ruled by the moon, thus suggesting a cyclical pattern for her bildung. She tries to kill Milkman on the thirtieth day of each menstrual cycle. She is still a girl at age thirty-six when she dies. Pilate gives Milkman Hagar's hair so he could carry his guilt. Hagar's bildung can be viewed as "commercial enslavement" (Brenner 122). Morrison emphasizes that men and women undergo different life stages and development on their quest for maturation. "It is as if the *birth* of the feminine ego begins the mid-life, or second stage of life, for a woman. But Milkman needs to undergo the *death* of the masculine ego to become a complete person at age thirty-one" (Demetrakopoulos 93). Morrison makes a very distinct point in her writing of Hagar. Many Black female characters share some of the same situations faced by their white sisters and often seen as victims, sex objects, mother haters, little mammies and rebellious outsiders. Often they are seeking a new, viable existence distinct from their historically and culturally predetermined roles, and thus seek transformations that are often unachievable or disrupted" (LeSeur 102). Miriam's *Bildung* does not end as the typical male-female double bildungsroman. "Morrison uses life-stage boundaries to delineate character change and growth. [Hagar] explodes out of the niches others have made for [her], individuating in bent and killing ways, but nevertheless insisting on change" (98). She experiences a circular pattern in which she does not move forward but return to her origins and physically dies because, in a patriarchal society, Hagar cannot find her place. She dies surrounded by the women who could have possibly given her the strength to survive such male manipulation. This ending distinguishes itself from Lawrence's ending of his novel. Morrison is a valuable writer because she is a woman, and women have special knowledge about certain things that come from the way they view the world and from their imagination (Harding and Martin 61). Just because Milkman is the one to explore "the Ulysses theme-the leaving home," he is not more important than Hagar because she stays at home.

For Miriam, her *Bildung* ends more similar to the typical male-female double bildungsroman with the suggestion of a reunion between her and Paul. However, Lawrence hinders Miriam from fully developing. Typically, "each character is intensely involved in the psychic life of his or her counterpart. Each character also embody a separate aspect of the author's own psychic life, the female character representing the author's identification with those women who have been forced to conform to traditional female gender roles, the male character, the author's desire for learning, power, mobility, and autonomy" (Goodman 31). Lawrence does not allow Miriam to fully develop, which emphasizes her place in a patriarchal society. Though not in complete collapse, Miriam does experience a spiritual death—the very change that allowed her to sacrifice herself for Paul's love. Even though, Miriam feels spiritually dead and lifeless after the final departure from Paul, she was the one who liberated him from her hold, as the Biblical tradition suggests. She could not free Paul from the responsibility of himself. She was willing, even after sacrificing herself and spirituality, to allow him to complete his process of growing up. "In many ways, Miriam appears to be a strong figure with a secure sense of herself and of superiority to her surroundings. But in this, she is merely being manipulated as a mirror image of Paul. Lawrence's method, whenever Miriam as a character becomes real in any sense, is reduce her to size, destroy her before she becomes too much of a threat" (Pullin 61-6). In the Biblical sense, this pattern is also recognizable between Moses and Miriam. Whereas Moses liberates Miriam, Lawrence's Miriam liberates Paul.

Both Lawrence and Morrison have written novels that are very similar in nature. Morrison takes the genre one step further because of the cultural tradition from which she is writing. She is able to explore how death impedes the narrative for her female character. She expands on the sentiment of "loving someone too much." Morrison's Hagar must die in order for Milkman to live and come into his manhood. Lawrence's Miriam does not die a physical death but a spiritual one. Given the time period, she was expected not to grow old alone. Because of her unstable love for Paul, she faces this dilemma. The Biblical tradition has an underlying significance for each novel, depending upon the manner in which one chooses to read Miriam and Hagar's characters. This reading allows the female characters their individuality and a place to reach a level of maturation that is unique to their culture and growth. The level of maturation for each depended solely on that of another. Their willingness to sacrifice themselves and their development for the men they loved has become a relatively familiar theme in many literary works, a theme that carries an undaunted truth.

Works Cited

Brenner, Gerry. "*Song of Solomon*: Rejecting Rank's Monomyth and
    Feminism."*Critical Essays on Toni Morrison*. Ed. Nellie McKay.
    Boston: G.K. Hall & Co., 1988. 114-24.
Demetrakopoulos, Stephanie A. "The Interdependence of Men's and Women's
    Individuation." *New Dimensions of Spirituality: A Biracial and*

Bicultural Reading of the Novels of Toni Morrison. Ed. Karla F.C.
   Holloway and Stephanie A. Demetrakopoulos. Connecticut:
   Greenwood P, 1987. 85-100.

Fiorenza, Elisabeth Schussler. *Searching the Scriptures: A Feminist Perspective,
   Volume One.* New York: Crossroad, 1993.

Goodman, Charlotte. "The Lost Brother, The Twin: Women Novelists and the
   Male—Female Double Bildungsroman." *Novel: A Forum on Fiction*
   Fall 1993: 28-43.

Harding, Wendy and Jacky Martin. *A World of Difference: An Inter-cultural
   Study of Toni Morrison's Novels.* Connecticut: Greenwood P, 1994.

Holloway, Karla F.C. "The Lyrics of Salvation." *New Dimensions of
   Spirituality: A Biracial and Bicultural Reading of the Novels of Toni
   Morrison.* Ed. Karla F.C. Holloway and Stephanie A.
   Demetrakopoulos. Connecticut: Greenwood P, 1987. 101-14.

Hooks, bell. *Black Looks: Race and Representation.* Boston: South End Press,
   1991.

Lawrence, D. H. *Sons and Lovers.* New York: Bantam, 1985.

LeSeur, Geta. *Ten is the Age of Darkness: The Black Bildungsroman.* Columbia:
   U Missouri P, 1995.

Morrison, Toni. *Song of Solomon.* New York: Penguin, 1977.

Pullin, Faith. "Lawrence's Treatment of Women in *Sons and Lovers.*"
   Lawrence and Women. New York: Barnes and Noble, 1978. 49-74.

Schlib, John. "Text," "Reader," "Author," and "History" in the Introduction to
   Literature Course." *Practicing Theory in Introductory College
   Literature Course.* Ed. James Cahalan and David Downing. Illinois:
   National Council of Teachers of English, 1991. 59-75.

Schwarz, Daniel R. "Speaking of Paul Morel: Voice, Unity, and Meaning in
   Sons and Lovers." *D.H. Lawrence's Sons and Lovers.* Ed. Harold
   Bloom. New York: Chelsea House, 1988. 79-102.

20 Demonizing the Devil: the Postlapserian World of Zora Neal Hurston's *Sweat*

Fred M. Fetrow

When she died in 1958 Zora Neale Hurston was reportedly working on a novel with a Biblical setting.[1] If so, that would have been her second major work based in scriptural lore, since she had presented much of the social satire in *Moses, Man of the Mountain* (1939) through parallels among contemporary African Americans and the Jews of the *Old Testament*.[2] The final unfinished novel would have also closed the loop begun in 1926 when her early short story, "Sweat," appeared in *Fire!!*, in its premier issue "Devoted to Younger Negro Artists," and edited by Wallace Thurman, one of the main instigators of the Harlem Renaissance of the 1920s and 1930s.[3]

Closing the loop refers to the Biblical basis implicit in the structure, characterization, and thematic concerns of "Sweat," a story often cited as characteristic of Hurston's "emphases of her work: skill in presenting the picturesque idiom of Southern Negroes, credible characterization, and her absorption with love and hatred in intrafamilial relationships."[4] More recent commentaries tend to focus on a rediscovered Hurston now as important as a feminist as a folklorist.[5] But somewhere between initial discovery and the revisionary version of this important African American artist, appropriate attention to her artistry too often has been neglected or inadequate. A brief analysis of technique, with attention to "setting" beyond cultural atmosphere, characterization with regard to allegory, and thematic reconstruction, allows the reader of "Sweat" more fully to appreciate Hurston's careful workwomanship and to apprehend the consequent merger of form and meaning.

Since she begins at least figuratively at the beginning through broad allusion to the story of man's (and woman's) fall in the Eden episode, one perhaps should also start with the title of this latter day allegory. "Sweat" in the context of the storyline obviously connotes the labor inherent in Delia's efforts to be self-sustaining, but the plot complication and the Biblical reference cannot be overlooked. First, her meager existence, earned through the sweat of her laundry labor, is continually threatened by Sykes' exploitation of her work and the lack of any similar effort on his part. So much for the scriptural injunction imposed as the original couple were cast out of Paradise: here in a modern update, Delia literally sweats for her bread, while her barren marriage obviates any productive pain/labor associated with child bearing, and while her mate avoids the Biblical curse of labor by letting his wife bear that burden.

Lest these analogues seem contrived, or more a product of a critic's mind than of the author's imagination, consider how early in the story that Hurston makes clear how the reader should view the main characters and their plot situation. Note that Delia is introduced on the Sabbath, in the Spring, content with her laundry chores; it is Sykes, her husband, who intrudes upon her revery, dropping his snake-like whip over her shoulders. Her announced fear of snakes, and his pleasure in her fear sets the tone of their troubled marriage and anticipates the coming conflict. Delia's manner of characterizing his "assault" directly links their story to that played out in the Garden of Eden, as she says of his behavior, "Gawd knows it's a sin" ("Sweat," *Fire*, 40).

The ensuing narrative/dialogue is almost heavy-handed with repeated references to spiritual matters: he is *praying* (italicized emphasis is Hurston's) for an argument; she has "just come from taking sacrament at the church house"; he accuses her of hypocrisy for working on the Sabbath, having "done promised Gawd and a couple of other men" that he will no longer allow her to wash white folks' clothes. She defies him with language that pointedly summarizes her life: "Sweat, sweat, sweat! Work and sweat, cry and sweat, pray and sweat" (40).

All of the above strongly suggests but does not impose a Biblical parallel unless one perceives the story in its inverted version: it is Delia who bears the brunt of their fallen status, providing their living through the sweat of her labor; Sykes seems to represent the demonic re-introduction of evil into their post-lapserian world. Hurston reshapes the original "fall-of-man" story by recasting the male lead as the continuing presence of evil in the world, an evil that exacerbates the already cruelly difficult world of the other gender. By the end of this new story, the cost of this new knowledge is clarified: ultimately, men who victimize women will pay the price—the tables will be turned on those who continue such folly. As Delia assures herself, "Oh well, whatever goes over the Devil's back, is got to come under his belly. Sometime or ruther, Sykes, like everybody else, is gointer reap his sowing" (41).

Just as Sykes if punished by the very agency of hatred he arranges, he must also be made to realize that he has done it to himself. Apparently, Man (men) must relearn that lesson of the knowledge of good and evil in order to see the evil of their ways, as it were. Eve was originally cast as the culprit; influenced by Satan and the serpent, she instigated the rebellion in which both she and Adam were willing co-conspirators; in the retelling, Delia becomes the innocent victim of male obstinacy, and Sykes' identification with both the rattlesnake and Satan himself shows who is currently to blame for the battle of the sexes and the suffering of mankind.

That battle heats up in the story with the hot summer days of late July-early August. Introduced through the conversation of the town's male "sages," who comment on and condemn Sykes' immoral behavior, but who also do little more than talk, the confrontation is prefaced by a narrative announcement of Sykes' intention (or at least promise) to evict Delia from her own house, to dispossess her literally. Hurston portrays Delia during these months of her husband's blatant infidelity as Christ-like in her martyrdom: "Delia's work-worn knees crawled over the earth in Gethsemane and up the rocks of Calvary . . . ." The author's exaggerated description of the "Dog days" of August evokes another, earlier, Biblical garden in its ruined condition: "The heat streamed down like a million hot arrows, smiting all things living upon the earth. Grass withered, leaves browned, snakes went blind in shedding and men and dogs went mad" (42).

At this juncture in the story and in the lives of the principals, Hurston introduces the rattlesnake Sykes brings to Delia's house to torment her. Loading the language to exploit the irony of situation, Hurston reaches forward with foreshadowing and back to the origins with a clear increment in her Edenic premise. Sykes' refusal to take the snake away emphasizes his myopic view of free will (" . . . fact is Ah aint got tuh do nothin' but die") and prepares the reader for an ironic twist to come (43). Hoping to prompt her to move out of her own house out of fear of the six-foot rattler, Sykes instead provokes her into open rebellion, as she takes a stand against his oppressive presence in her life. We learn from their dialogue that it is she who has moved her church membership to avoid his spiritual company, just as it is she who orders him from *her* house. Ironically, and appropriately, given his demonic behavior, he expresses his mutual contempt for her by insulting her appearance, likening her to the devil's playmate: "You looks jes' lak de devvul's doll-baby tu *me*" (43).

Not surprisingly, by then the story reaches its awful climax on the same day of the week that it began—a Sunday. Returning late Saturday night from the "night service," a "love feast" at her new church, Delia addresses the unseen rattlesnake, ostensibly still in his soapbox on the front porch, as she returns from the barn to her kitchen door: "Whut's de mattah, ol' *satan* (my italics), you aint kickin' up yo' racket?" (44). The "Complete silence" from the snake's box prompts in her some wishful thinking about Sykes' reform, but the reader has already read the signals Delia misses. Her subsequent discovery of the snake in her laundry basket as she sings a familiar spiritual (ironically) about a peaceful death is not just an affront to her peace of mind—the reader processes immediately the symbolic import of this invasion. Sykes has introduced evil into their relationship; Delia's marriage bed has been corrupted by the snake's presence in it; her labor in cleansing the corruption of others is violated by the snake in the laundry basket; and, of course, the darkness of the night as she flees her own house, her only haven, suggests the previous banishment from Eden also prompted by a serpent. Hurston here provides Delia with a pronouncement that applies not just to the current crisis or her faltering marriage, but also to the recurrent warfare of the sexes: "Well, Ah done de bes' Ah could. If things aint right, Gawd knows taint mah fault" (44).

The author also arranges poetic justice in the small detail of the empty matchbox (safe). Because Sykes took all the matches, save the one Delia struck to light the lamp the night before, he cannot illuminate the shades-drawn bedroom early the next morning. His limited vision, like his prideful false notions of self-sufficiency, proves his undoing. Again, evil operates in the darkness—light brings awareness and knowledge. Note, however, how deftly Hurston merges reality, symbolism, and theme.

Observing Sykes' early-morning arrival as she hides "beneath the low bedroom window," Delia hears the snake before he does. She silently muses, "Dat ol' scratch is woke up now" (44). No doubt here referring to the snake as "ol' scratch," a common folk idiom for Satan, she could just as easily be naming her husband, and the reader is quick to note the implicit merger of Sykes, snake, and Satan. We can even forgive Hurston the intrusive editorial blurb about "The rattler is a ventriloquist . . .etc.," because we just *know* Sykes has to end up in the bedroom with his demonic Doppelganger ("in bed with the devil" is another folk aphorism that comes to mind here). Sykes' instinctive leap ("primitive instinct" Hurston calls it) into the company he seeks to avoid, his cry when bitten by the snake ("a cry that might have come from a maddened chimpanzee, a stricken gorilla"), followed by "another series of animal screams" all combine clearly (over-clearly, one could say) to show what Hurston has in mind.

The denouement completes the cycle of violence and the inverted Biblical allegory. With the resumption of daylight's warmth come clarity of vision and the recognition of awful truths. First, Sykes must acknowledge his sin and humble himself before God, which he does even before he realizes Delia is on the scene: "'Mah Gawd!' She heard him moan, 'Mah Gawd faum Heben!'" (45). As he crawls out the front door on his knees (a posture both realistically plausible and symbolically appropriate), he sees Delia watching him, but he must also ". . . see the tubs. He would see the lamp" (45). The awful truth comes to him as "she waited in the growing heat," as he "must know by now that she knew" (45).

In the limited sense that he dies in full realization of the extent to which he is responsible for his own death, Sykes seems almost tragic in his demise. And in the extended sense of the story's point, that tragedy includes Delia as well. Both finally are victims, but only he is culprit. Hurston's retelling of the Paradise Lost myth shifts the blame from the female temptress in league with the serpent to the oppressive male who would use the snake for his own evil purposes. Not much perception is required to recognize the thematic point in these reversals: Sykes becomes Satan just as surely as the snake is relegated to a supporting role; Delia as victim-heroine prevails because of her refusal to return evil in kind.

This story thus can be "enjoyed" for its plausible plot and believable characters, whether viewed in terms of rustic folklore or contemporary psychology, but the ultimate artistry and Hurston's thematic agenda depend upon a more time-honored, "conventional" use of Biblical allusion bordering upon allegory. Within that frame, Zora Neale Hurston belabors the self-evident with impunity because she "merely" demonizes the devil. Within the artistic terms of her creation, she cannot justly be accused of distorting the story; she simply "adjusts" an ancient myth to accommodate modern reality, and isn't that what all great storytellers do? "Sweat" *does* show that the line between love and hate is a tenuous border often breached, but Hurston advocates love in spite of hate, even as she acknowledges that hatred of hate is still hate. She seems to say that both sexes are guilty of cruelty to the other, but men have more power to be cruel and therefore are more guilty by default.

By giving Biblical authority to her sociological thesis, she can have it both ways—she can protest the traditional notion of female subservience with her own slightly amended version of an older precedent, one originally set in the garden of shame and now revitalized to reawaken us to a new knowledge of the proper relationship of men and women. Even without the Biblical reference points, an astute reader can easily (maybe uneasily?) understand "Sweat" as a modern parable for direct application. The allusive inversions make that application more compelling and the story more meaningful. Thanks to Zora Hurston's own artistic "sweat," medium becomes message in the fullest sense of that tired, but tried and true equation.

NOTES

1. See, for example, Robert Hemenway's "Zora Neale Hurston and the Eatonville Anthropology" in *The Harlem Renaissance Remembered*, ed. Arna Bontemps, Dodd Mead (1972), pp. 191-192. Hemenway quotes in his article an excerpt from a letter from Hurston to Harper and Brothers regarding "'the book I am laboring upon at present—a life of Herod the Great.'"

2. Hurston, *Moses, Man of the Mountain*, Lippincott, Philadelphia (1939).

3. *Fire!!*, 1 (November, 1926). For a full account of the genesis and demise of this publication, see Arnold Rampersad's summary in *The Life of Langston Hughes, Vol. 1: 1902-1941, I, Too, Sing America*, Oxford University Press, New York (1986), pp. 135-139.

4. From Darwin T. Turner's introduction to "Sweat," reprinted in *Black American Literature: Essays, Poetry, Fiction, Drama*, Merrill, Columbus, Ohio (1970), p. 340.

5. Noted novelist and feminist Alice Walker perhaps best exemplifies a current view/presentation of Hurston as a neglected, pioneering feminist. Consult, for example, Walker's "Zora Neale Hurston Reader," notably including Mary Helen Washington's introduction (pp. 7-25) and Walker's afterword, "Looking for Zora" (pp. 297-313). Not entirely coincidentally, the Hurston reader, formally titled *I Love Myself When I am Laughing . . .*, is published by The Feminist Press, City University of New York (1979).

21   **Materialism and Colonialism are Two Good Companions: 'The Love of Money is the Root of All Evil' in Jean Rhys' *Wide Sargasso Sea***

Seodial Frank H. Deena

According to Randy Alcorn, money has two faces. It is used to feed, clothe, house, build churches, spread the gospel, alleviate suffering, and provide betterment for people. Money is a tool to facilitate and expedite trade. It allows flexibility and convenience. God encouraged the people of Israel to make use of the convenience of money. Because of distance, he told them to exchange the tithes (crops and livestock) for silver (money), then convert it back to the goods of their choice once they arrived at the place of worship (Duet. 14:24-26). But it is also used to buy a slave, swindle a widow's land, purchase sexual favors, bribe a judge, and peddle drugs (33-37). Paul warns about the other side of money: "People who want to get rich fall into temptation and a trap and into many foolish and harmful desires that plunge men into ruin and destruction. For the love of money is a root of all kinds of evil" (1 Tim. 6:9-10). Numerous biblical incidents and characters warn against the danger of loving money. Achan's lust for materialism brought death to himself, family, and other men in battle (Josh. 7), the Prophet Balaam would have cursed God's people for payment from Balak (Num. 22:4-35), Delilah betrayed Samson to the Philistines for a fee (Judg. 16), Solomon's lust for more wealth led him to disobey the prohibitions of God's law concerning the accumulation of large amount of gold, silver, horses, and wives (Duet. 17:16-17), Gehazi lied to Naaman and then to Elisha, in order to gain wealth, for which he was punished with leprosy (2 Kings 5 20-27), Ananias and Sapphira withheld money they said was given to the Lord and were struck dead for it (Acts 5:1-11), the materialist Judas asked the chief priests, "What are you willing to give me if I hand him over to you?" then betrayed the Son of God for thirty pieces of silver (Matt. 26:14-16, 47-50; 27:3-

10), and Jesus warned against any form of excessive love for money: "Watch out! Be on your guard against all kinds of greed; a man's life does not consist in the abundance of his possessions" (Luke 12:15).

For Karl Marx, in a colonial society, capitalism, exploitation, and alienation are interwoven in their web-like destructive force. Marx took an economic approach to alienation, concerning "himself with the workers of the world: labor and its economic powerlessness" (Joseph 7). Alienation from self, for Marx, means,

> 'estrangement from the things,' which means the alienation of the worker from the product of his labor—that is, the alienation of that which mediates his relation to the 'sensual external world' and hence to the objects of nature. What the worker produces is not his own, but rather someone else's; it meets not his own needs; it is a commodity he sells to eke out a bare existence. The more he produces, the more his product and hence the objects of nature stand opposed to him. (Bulhan 186)

Marx's influence can be traced in Fanon's concurrence that alienation is primarily economic: "If there is an inferiority complex, it is the outcome of a double process:—primarily, economic;—subsequently, the internalization—or, better, the epidermalization—of this inferiority" (Fanon, Introduction to *Black Skin*, 11).

Economics, according to Rodney and Memmi, is at the center of colonization.[1] It is also the core of Antoinette Cosway/Mason/Rochester's tragedy. Margaret Paul Joseph's study of the importance of mirror as a reflection of otherness alludes to economic exploitation. Joseph argues that "the basis of the whole story is again a matter of economics . . . but wealth is turned into a major symbol of evil. Money is a corrupting influence and is linked to betrayal, revenge, and power." Continuing to illustrate how the power of money becomes the greatest evil, since money can ruin people's lives, Joseph advocates that "Annette Mason and Antoinette Cosway are both victims of Englishmen who, like countless others before them, went to the colonies to make money with no regard for the consequences on the lives of the people who lived there" (33-34). This paper demonstrates the role the love of money plays in Antoinette's tragedy.

Gossiping ex-slaves perceptively point out that Mr. Mason "didn't come to the West Indies to dance—he came to make money as they all do. Some of the big estates are going cheap, and one unfortunate's loss is always a clever man's gain" (29-30).[2] As one of Antoinette's colonizer/Prospero, Mr. Mason's marriage to Annette sparks hostility from the ex-slaves. The marriage also leads to Antoinette's tragedy and alienation. Joseph explains that "the rich Mr. Mason (so sure of himself, so English in his confidence, thinks Antoinette) marries Mrs. Cosway and saves the estate they all love; but in true Prospero fashion he is insensitive to the mood of the laborers on the island and this brings tragedy to his wife and her children" (34). Failing to discern the ex-slaves' changing attitude, Mason assures Annette: "You were the widow of a slave-owner, the daughter of a slave-owner, and you had been living here alone, with two children, for nearly five years," but Annette perceptively points out her new economic status' influence on the ex-slaves: "We were so poor then . . . we were something to laugh at. But we are not poor now. . . . You are not a poor man. Do you suppose that they don't know all about your estate in Trinidad? And the Antigua property?" (32). Later, Antoinette interprets economics as the basis of her alienation: "The black people did not hate us quite so much when we were poor. We were white but we had not escaped and soon we would be dead for we had no money left. What was there to hate?" (34). Howells summarizes that Annette's "alliance with the new colonialism" sparks new implications (110), and Emery concurs that "Annette's marriage solidifies the power of the neocolonialists; it also intensifies the conflict between blacks and whites. The Blacks call them "white Cockroach," but the whites call them "white niggers" (102, 100). Whites alienate Annette's family on the basis of her low economic status, while blacks alienate them on the basis of her high economic status. Howells sums up this tragedy: "Hated by the blacks and despised for their poverty by both blacks and other whites, Antoinette and her mother are the victims of a system the collapse of which has not only dispossessed them as a class but also deprived them as individuals of any means of independent survival" (110).

Steeped in typical colonizer's overconfidence and arrogance, Mason's late-rescue-attempt is futile. Coulibri has been set on fire, Pierre, Antoinette's little retarded brother, is killed, Antoinette is hurt, and Annette goes mad. "Indirectly, Mason is the cause of her madness," claims Joseph, but he also causes Antoinette's displacement and alienation (35). Robbed of her mother, brother, stepfather, Tia, Christophine, and Coulibri, Antoinette is placeless. After her recuperation at Aunt Cora's house, Antoinette is placed in a convent, "a place of . . . death" (56), where she prays "for a long time to be dead" (57).

Unaware of and unconcerned about his role in Annette's tragedy, Mason, "grinning hypocrite" and "coward" (40,47), blindly lays the foundation for Antoinette's tragedy by means of an arranged marriage. He supplies the dowery and arranges the marriage: "I want you to be happy, Antoinette, secure, I've tried to arrange. . . . I have asked some English friends to spend next winter here. You won't be dull" (59). Ironically, just the announcement of this colonial/patriarchal news produces "a feeling of dismay, sadness," and "loss," leading to the second dream which expands the first and foreshadows the colonial and patriarchal oppression and exploitation. The first dream occurs at Coulibri (26-27), and it is repeated two times (59-60, 187-90), each time with "more clarity and detail" (Olaussen 70). It also suggests Antoinette's "fear of sexual violation" (70). The second dream, like the first, precedes Antoinette's tragedy. It prophesies her marriage and so-called madness, links with Mason's manipulating role in marriages, and leaves Antoinette in loneliness. It also foreshadows "Antoinette's departure from the primeval forest of the West Indies to the imprisoning, enclosed garden that is England" (Friedman 125).

Where Mr. Mason's colonizing/patriarchal work ends, his son from a previous marriage, Richard Mason, commences. Richard is at the center of Antoinette's arranged marriage. He panics at Antoinette's reluctance to go through with the marriage (78-79) and gives Antoinette strong "arguments, threats probably," forcing her to keep the arrangement (90-91). Rochester distrusts him (91), and Christophine "is right to blame Richard Mason for his stepsister's affairs" (Le Gallez 143). Christophine echoes Richard's dark side: "Law! The Mason boy fix it, that boy worse than Satan and he burn in hell one of these fine nights" (110). Aunt Cora's argument with Richard Mason also illuminates his corruption: "You are handing over everything the child owns to a perfect stranger" (114).

From Mr. Mason to Richard Mason to Edward Rochester, their economic exploitation of Antoinette fosters her alienation. Rochester's, Antoinette's greatest colonizer, "moral decline of a 'gentle, generous' and 'brave' soul . . . may be traced to his materialism" (Le Gallez 141). Fragmented and exploited by his wealthy father willing all the family money to the older brother, "Edward is expected to contribute further to that status by taking part in an arranged marriage with a wealthy heiress" in order not to weaken the family status (141). Thus, his hypocritical playacting before the marriage is "a faultless performance," filled with "effort of will," rather than love, leaves Antoinette's hand "cold as ice in the hot sun," and deludes all except the blacks (76-77).

In typical colonial-imposing fashion, Rochester sweeps over Antoinette's fear, concern, and reluctance in preference for his "sad heart," the arrangement, and the "role of rejected suitor jilted by this creole girl" (78-79), because of the strong economic motivation and dictation. The colonizer/Rochester's main objective in a/the relationship with the colony/Antoinette is to 'rape' her and extract all her wealth. Rochester admits his quest for exploitation: "I didn't love her. I was thirsty for her, but that is not love. I felt very little tenderness for her, she was a stranger to me, a stranger who did not think or feel as I did" (93). And "the lack of any 'married woman's property act' ensures that Antoinette's money, on her marriage to Edward, becomes absorbed into his own estate" (Le Gellez 142). Even in the penultimate paragraph of Rochester's narration, as he prepares to return to England, he is obsessed with Antoinette's money: "I'd sell the place for what it would fetch. I had meant to give it back to her. Now—what's the use?" (173). But his letters to his greedy, exploitative father have already provided insights into this economic transaction which leaves Antoinette "a displaced person in her own country" (Howells 111). The letters authenticate that "thirty thousand pounds have been paid to me [Rochester] without question or condition," and that "no provision" has been "made for her" [Antoinette] (70).

Antoinette's money, now in the greedy, grasping hands of Rochester, drives the swindler Daniel Cosway to blackmail for a share of it. Cosway's revengeful exploitation climaxes Rochester's final stranglehold on Antoinette.   Daniel Cosway's eurocentric, epistolary method of communication to Rochester parallels Rochester's letters to his father, since both emerge out of a deep fragmented psyche and both seek to extract different measures of recompense. Furthermore, "Rochester, like Cosway, turns hate for his father into hate for Antoinette," claims Angier.   She further compares: "Cosway and Rochester share similar characters—even to their ultimate greed, which each gives rein to through a self-righteous desire for vengeance" (162).   Cosway's first letter to Rochester alludes to money several times and to the revenge motif: "My momma die when I was quite small and my godmother take care of me. The old mister [Antoinette's father] hand out some money for that though he don't like me. No, that old devil don't like me at all, and when I grow older I see it and I think, Let him wait my day will come" (96). But Antoinette's father and mother are deceased, thereby aborting his plans for revenge.   However, Antoinette remains his target, and he, like his namesake, Esau, believes that "vengeance is mine" (122). Cosway also knows that Mr. Mason has given Antoinette half of his money when he died (97). Cosway wants some of that money, so he mixes facts and fiction to extract money from Rochester, and in the process he further destroys Antoinette's life, love, and marriage. His second letter not only reveals his wickedness, but also his coerciveness: "You want me to come to your house and bawl out your business before everybody? You come to me or I come" (119). Moreover, Amélie confirms Daniel Cosway's imitation of white people and his mysterious life (120-21), while Cosway himself displays his blackmail: "'But if I keep my mouth shut it seems to me you owe me something. What is five hundred pounds to you. To me it's my life. . . . And if I don't have the money I want you will see what I can do'" (126).

Immediately after reading Cosway's letter, Rochester crushes the flower, foreshadowing his crushing of Antoinette's spirit. He sweats, trembles, sees the day as "far too hot" (99), looks like he has seen a zombie (100), gets lost and becomes afraid (105), and tightens his grip of alienation on Antoinette. He has bound her into economic dependence, rendering her unable to initiate or execute escape. Antoinette explains her economic bondage: "He would never give me any money to go away and he would be furious if I asked him. There would be a scandal if I left him and he hates scandal. Even if I got away (and how?) he would force me back. So would Richard. So would everybody else. Running away from him, from this island, is the lie" (113).

Antoinette, like Jesus, has been betrayed. Judas, the treasurer, loved money so much that he sold his master for thirty pieces of silver. In Antoinette's case there is much buying, selling, and betrayal. Rochester has sold his soul for thirty thousand pounds (70), but in so doing he has aided and abetted the selling of Antoinette's body, soul, and spirit for minus thirty thousand pounds and property.   Such grave devaluation and dehumanization of Antoinette results from the colonizers' (Mason, Richard, Rochester, and his father) love for money.   Christophine perceptively informs Antoinette about Rochester's love for money: "'Your husband certainly love money. . . . That is no lie. Money have pretty face for everybody, but for that man money pretty like pretty self, he can't see nothing else'" (114).   Indeed, Rochester's excessive and compulsive love for money, a colonialistic feature, blinds his moral and spiritual eyes. Rochester cannot see Antoinette's beauty and tragedy, the landscape's beauty, nor his action's corruption.   For the wounded and fragmented Rochester, "everything is too much. . . . Too much blue, too much purple, too much green. The flowers are too red, the mountains are too high, the hills too near. And the woman is a stranger" (70).   Coming from a cold and corrupted culture, Rochester fails to love Antoinette and cannot understand and appreciate her love.   Staley enlightens that "Edward comes from another world and cannot fathom the life of the passions; everything in the natural surroundings which epitomizes sensuous beauty tells him that this is Antoinette's world, and this is why he fears it from the beginning" (114-15). He wants an object and a passive partner, but his failure to control and dominate the landscape renders him powerless: "I wanted to say something reassuring but the scent of the river flowers was overpoweringly strong. I felt giddy" (83), and it also symbolizes his inability to celebrate the colorful and passionate personality and sexuality of his wife. Threatened and terrified by the landscape, a fearful Rochester "broke a spray off and trampled it into the mud" (99), and his cold and callous way of destroying the landscape symbolizes the way he destroys Antoinette in order to control her.   His greedy thirst/lust cannot be satisfied because his colonial perspective associates his hatred to Antoinette and her landscape:

> I hated the mountains and the hills, the rivers and the rain. I hated the sunsets of whatever color, I hated its beauty and its magic and the secret I would never know. I hated its indifference and the cruelty which was part of its loveliness. Above all I hated her. For she belonged to the magic and the loveliness. She had left me thirsty and all my life would be thirst and longing for what I had lost before I found it. (172)

This heavenly place where Antoinette belongs and where she wishes to stay (108), has been made into a hell by Rochester: "But I loved this place and you have made it into a place I hate. I used to think that if everything else went out of my life I would still have this, and now you have spoilt it. It's just somewhere else where I have been unhappy, and the other things are nothing to what has happened here" (147).

Rochester makes love to the rebellious, Amélie, next to his wife's room, and forms another economic exploitative union: "'But she love money like you love money—must be why you come together. Like goes to like'" (149), insinuates Christophine. And Antoinette rebukes Rochester's hypocrisy by comparing him to slave masters: "'You abused the planters and made up stories about them, but you do the same thing. You send the girl away quicker, and with no money or less money, and that's all the difference'" (146). And his monetary present ushers the girl into a life of prostitution to satisfy her love for money (140-41). Additionally, Rochester is willing to pay double and even triple to alienate Antoinette in his frigid attic and to maintain absolute silence (177-78). And Mrs. Eff and Grace Poole serve the devil for money because service to Rochester parallels service to the devil (177). Thus, by the end of the novel, the colonized, Antoinette, remains free from the clutches of the love of money, but the colonizer, Rochester, becomes possessed with money. His cold, callous heart would not allow him to leave Antoinette in the Caribbean, nor would it allow him to give her any of her own money. Rather, one form of corruption breeds another, and the more money he gets, the more dissatisfied he is. Despite his profession of religion (127), he has forgotten biblical warnings, stated earlier. He is also too blind to see truth in the testimonies of some of the world's wealthiest men. John D. Rockefeller postulates: "I have made many millions, but they have brought me no happiness," W. H. Vanderbilt agrees that "the care of $200,000,000 is enough to kill anyone. There is no pleasure in it," John Jacob Astor confesses: "I am the most miserable man on earth," and Andrew Carnegie acknowledges that "millions seldom smile" (qtd. in Alcorn 69). Furthermore, his secular religion fails to adhere to Christ's warning against laying up treasures on earth, and worrying about material things (Matt. 6:25-34), and it refuses to learn from Solomon's observation that "the sleep of the laborer is sweet, whether he eats little or much, but the abundance of a rich man permits him no sleep" (Eccles. 5:12).

Rochester has now inherited all Antoinette's money and "everything" from his family (177), yet he spends extravagantly on the marginalization of Antoinette, but not on her therapy, or freedom. But Antoinette, stripped once in her own country and now in England, the "cardboard world" where there is no mirror, only wants her red dress. This becomes culturally significant, since it links her with the Caribbean landscape (fire, sun, flowers)), the meaning of time, passionate memory with Sandi (183), and recognition (184). In her final effort to discover and define her cultural identity, she recreates the Caribbean culture, and fire and the red dress become significant symbols in this recreation: "I let the dress fall on the floor, and looked from the fire to the dress and from the dress to the fire" (186). In this symbolic connection, fire becomes the method by which she defines her cultural identity, while the red dress becomes the message of her Caribbean cultural definition. Angier concludes that Antoinette's "obsession with the red dress" becomes "a symbol of another reality, another time, and another place" (153).

NOTES

1. Memmi's statement reinforces the point that "colonization is, above all, economic and political exploitation" (149).

2. The ex-slaves also allude that Mr. Cosway's, Antoinette's father, degenerated economy, resulting from emancipation, has caused his death (28).

Works Cited

Alcorn, Randy. *Money, Possessions and Eternity.* Wheaton: Tyndale House, 1989.

Angier, Carole. *Jean Rhys: Life and Work.* London: Andre Deutsch, 1990.

Bulhan, Hussein Abdilahi. *Frantz Fanon and the Psychology of Oppression.* New York: Plenum Press, 1985.

Fanon, Frantz. *Black Skin White Masks.* Trans. Charles Lam Markmann. New York: Grove Press, 1967.

———. *The Wretched of the Earth.* Trans. Constance Farrington. New York: Grove Press, 1966.

Friedman, Ellen G. "Breaking the Master Narrative: Jean Rhys' *Wide Sargasso Sea.*" *Breaking the Sequence.* Eds. Ellen G. Friedman and Miriam Fuchs. Princeton: Princeton UP, 1989. 117-28.

Howells, Coral Ann. *Jean Rhys.* New York: St. Martin's Press, 1991.

Joseph, Margaret Paul. *Caliban in Exile: The Outsider in Caribbean Fiction.* New York: Greenwood Press, 1992.

Le Gallez, Paula. *The Rhys Woman.* New York: St. Martin's Press, 1990.

Memmi, Albert. *The Colonizer and the Colonized.* New York: Orion Press, 1965.

Olaussen, Maria. "Jean Rhys' Construction of Blackness as Escape from White Femininity in *Wide Sargasso Sea.*" *ARIEL* 24.2 (April 1993): 65-82.

Rhys, Jean. *Wide Sargasso Sea.* New York: W. W. Norton, 1982. (All subsequent citations are from this edition and by page number only).

Rodney, Walter. *How Europe Underdeveloped Africa.* Washington: Howard UP, 1974.

Staley, Thomas F. *Jean Rhys: A Critical Study.* Austin: University of Texas Press, 1979.

'What else God make women for?': Subverting the Politics and Spirituality of the Patriarchs in *The Hills of Hebron*

Maude Adjarian

In the Caribbean as elsewhere in the Americas, the colonial project initiated by Columbus in 1492 derived its authority and legitimacy from the Bible, a text that celebrates the works of fathers both earthly and divine. Judeo-Christian patriarchs are incarnated in God and in His sons, who are themselves descendants of God's own first-created son, Adam. Christian European (and later, North American) men thus sought to carry out the Columbian father's will which itself mirrored a divine one. In this way, these "modern Adams" imposed Western values and beliefs on the island populations who, like Eve, were seen as the dark-skinned servants of white males.

What the conqueror-settler fathers did to those they colonized, the colonized — in particular, colonized males — visited upon their own people and especially their women. Within the context of a fictional Jamaican revivalist Christian community, Sylvia Wynter's *The Hills of Hebron* (1962) subtly subverts the authority of both biblical and black colonial patriarchs. To work towards this end, the writer gestures towards another female never mentioned by name in the Bible, Lilith, who represents possibilities for a social and spiritual egalitarianism Wynter believes is essential to Jamaican national survival and progress. According to Talmudic legend, Lilith was the first wife of Adam; according to some Biblical commentators, she is also the woman figured in Genesis 1:26: that is, the daughter whom God made "in His image" alongside his son Adam.[1] Shortly after their creation, Lilith left Adam to live in the Red Sea because her husband did not treat her as an equal.[2] Eve was the second wife whom God made for Adam from Adam's rib. Thus reproduced from

Adam, Eve unlike Lilith, had an existence and spirituality permanently mediated by men.

Set between approximately 1920 and the late 1930s, a time when Jamaica, still under British colonial rule, was beginning to more consciously struggle with issue pertaining to its own national identity, *The Hills of Hebron* appears at first to center around three black colonial males—Moses Barton, his son Isaac and Obadiah Brown—who are the "fathers" or "father-designates" of a spiritual group called the New Believers. Yet analysis of each member of this male black Israelite trinity, especially in relation to specific women in the community— Kate Lansing, Gatha Randall Barton and her adopted daughter Rose—reveals how each man's authority, like that of the respective Old Testament patriarch he represents, rests upon the suppression and exploitation of females. With the exception of Obadiah,[3] these men do not question Biblical pronouncements: if anything, these men use Scripture for their own ends. The divinity they worship, though superficially transformed from white to black, still closely resembles the same Father God of the Judeo-Christian tradition. It is the women who, in seeing past scriptural writings and transcending the subordination of Eve become the catalysts of social change.

Moses Barton, founder of the Believers in the Kingdom of Heaven Now, later known as the New Believers, is "a prophet of the castaways, a cavalier of the impossible" (106). His dreams of gathering together spiritually elect men and women to accompany him to heaven stir Cockpit Center, the rural town where he begins his ministry, out of its apathy, resignation and despair. His blue turban and long white robe make him as farcical figure as that other "cavalier of the impossible," Don Quixote. His self-proclaimed divinity and priestly garb also bring to mind the Jamaican historical figure upon whom Wynter bases Moses, Alexander Bedward, who in 1894 established the Jamaica Baptist Church.[4] Like Moses, Bedward referred to himself as the Messiah and claimed that God had revealed to him that he would ascend to heaven on December 31st—the same day that Moses tells his followers he will return to his Father and "send back golden chariots" (110) for his followers. For his "prophesying," Bedward was institutionalized twice; Moses, too, gets sent to an insane asylum. Just as Bedward was branded by the British authorities as both madman and political propagandist for the strongly anti-colonial rhetoric that imbued his religious discourse, so too is Moses, who promises his impoverished followers that in heaven "the masters would be slaves and the slaves masters" and their subjects would be angels white angels" (110). Life in the hereafter is no different from life on earth: only social and racial power paradigms are reversed to favor the meek who never inherited the earth.

What transforms Moses from carnival charlatan into revered patriarch is the fervent belief he rouses in his first convert, a land-owning peasant woman named Liza Edwards. In the story Moses tells Liza of how God first spoke to him from a flaming rhododendron, he recalls the biblical vision his own parallels:

> The bush flamed orange and green fire. The Presence of God was all around me. I fall on my knees, I bow my head to the earth. [. . .] I remain there, I wait and I watch. The moon start to fall quickly towards the north. The Voice of the Lord was loud in my heart. "Moses, run and catch the moon," He said, "Moses, run and catch Me!" (108)

What is interesting about this particular passage is the way that God is associated with the moon, symbol of the feminine. It is as though Moses unconsciously realizes that in order to ascend to any kind of godhood, he must harness female energy—what Mary Daly, quoting Emily Culpepper, might call "gynergy."[5] When Moses confers the title "holy mother" on Liza (who in her deluded simplicity rejoices at being "summoned" to assume a place among God's chosen), what he really offers Liza is an empty token of exchange. For her newly "divine" status, Liza gives Moses land on which to build his temple and "as much money as she could spare to help him in his proselytizing mission" (109).

If Liza helps to establish Moses in Cockpit Center though her generosity and motherly ministrations, she is also the one who becomes the keeper of Moses's memory and vision after he is arrested and institutionalized. As divine carrier, she becomes the one who "infects" two other women in the town with religious fervor for Moses: Kate Lansing and Gatha Randall, both of whom eventually become mothers of two of Moses's many children. Like the Old Testament patriarchs before him who had multiple wives and concubines, Moses freely exercises biblical male privilege, only in his case, to at times comic extremes. Soon after he returns from the insane asylum, marries the wealthy Gatha and begins rebuilding his congregation with her money, he sates his lust with a parishioner named Sue. He justifies his actions by implicitly appealing to God's plan for the other followers. As he tells her, "the sacrifice of her virginity was necessary to their [the congregationalists'] successful exodus" (10) into the hills of Hebron where the New Believers would create a Heaven on earth. To Gatha, who gets locked outside the room where the "ritual" occurs, he calls out that he is "praying for the soul of a young Sister" (11). With the patriarchal traditions of the Bible to justify him, Moses exploits his position to gratify his own selfish desires for power and female flesh.

Moses's polygamous behavior and his assumption of the naturally inferior position of women further indicate how Moses figures in a general way the attitudes of males belonging to another of Jamaica's religious groups, the Rastafarians. The Rastafarian movement began in the 1930s and has its roots in Marcus Garvey's "Back to Africa" movement which started around the same time. While Garvey preached repatriation to Africa as the only solution to the plight of black people in white-dominated societies, Haile Selassie was crowned emperor in Ethiopia. For the Jamaican theologians who became the founders of Rastafarianism, Selassie represented the fulfillment of Garvey's prophetic 1916 statement that Africa would be the birthplace of "the Redeemer."[6] As a sect that celebrates a (black) Father-God, women are handmaidens to men. In *RastafarI Women* (1998), Obiagele Lake states that Rastafarian men see women as little more than children. They often use the phrase "to grow a dawta" to reveal the inherent female need for male guidance in all matters pertaining to Rastafarian life and spirituality (59). Ivor Morrish further suggests that, given the political origins of Rastafarianism and its vigorously anti-colonial stance, the movement could also be seen as a reaction against the matriarchal structure of black Jamaican family life, which came about through the workings of the slave system.[7] In other words, to be black and powerful meant either subordinating or doing away entirely with all possible "impurities" of race or gender.

However patriarchal its ideology, Rastafarianism is also a manifestation of the emerging Jamaican folk tradition that Wynter valorizes. Rural peasants of the kind she depicts in *The Hills of Hebron* are the very people who can create the folk culture that is the basis of "the only living tradition in the Caribbean.[8] For a nation like Jamaica just coming into political independence (which the island achieved in 1962, the same year Wynter published her novel), the establishment of such cultural foundations was critical to achieving national identity. But as Wynter also shows, Rastafarianism and other Jamaican religious cults, often do little to truly liberate believers and still less for the greater cause of national liberation. Indeed, many religious groups merely repeated the mistakes of those that came before. When Alexander Bedward claimed he would gather up "the elect" for a triumphant return to God's kingdom, thousands of his (impoverished) followers, sold everything they owned to follow him. When his ascension to heaven did not occur, they were left even worse off than before. In the 1930s, Leonard Howell (who like Bedward, was also eventually institutionalized for claiming divinity) founded one of the first Rastafarian communities at Pinnacle in St. Catherine's parish.[9] The principles of the Howell group echo those of Moses Barton and include the idea that blacks were the superior race. But Pinnacle Rastafarians went still further, advocating what Leonard Barrett has called "the negation, persecution and humiliation of the government and legal bodies of Jamaica."[10]

Needless to say, the Pinnacle attitude, though admirable in a Calibanesque way, did nothing for the greater cause of Jamaican independence. As Wynter suggests in the quietly desperate picture she portrays at the start of the novel of a socially and economically desperate New Hebron, the separation of communities from each other creates far more problems than it solves. Escapism in any form does little for those who attempt to flee or those who remain. When, in 1959, Claudius Henry, another Rastafarian leader, promised to lead his followers Moses-like into the promised land of Ethiopia, no ship came to Kingston harbor to carry the hundreds ready to sail away to a mythical black Eden.[11]   Like the disappointed and deceived Bedwardites, Henry's believers had been willing to believe that a better life and the manna of Heaven could be theirs through faith and acts that were either impossible or impractical.

In "The Hills of Hebron", Wynter uses incidents from the lives ofprominent women characters to illustrate the plight of the Jamaican masses who become too attached to religious monomaniacs. While Moses lives, Gatha, who before her marriage to the New Hebron Prophet was an independent and successful businesswoman, becomes little more than "a spectre at a feast" (13). It is only after his death that she (re-)emerges from Moses's shadow to take command of a community in shambles and implement her ideas for self-governance. That Moses must die in order for Gatha return to life suggests that true Jamaican emancipation can take place only after the belief in savior-figures is eradicated. In much the same way that Kate Lansing dreams of herself struggling against Gatha's husband like the biblical Jacob wrestles with the angel of God, so too, must the people resist easy solutions proffered by men like Moses Barton. Where her status as a female in a patriarchal order is concerned, Kate's vision further suggests a second level of struggle that she, like all the other females in her community must face: that of being dominated by men who empower themselves through female subjection.

While Gatha finds release from gender-bondage only after Moses dies, Kate finds hers earlier through the madness that comes upon her after Maverlyn, the child she has with the Prophet, drowns. Isaac, Moses's son by Gatha and Maverlyn's playmate, is the one who first suggests to Kate that her daughter "sleeps" in the spring where she loses her life, perhaps to defuse any anger she may feel towards him regarding Maverlyn's death. Indeed, Wynter suggests that Kate, who gladly accepts Isaac's story and stands "waiting for him to tell her what to do" (102), is just like her fellow New Hebronites in how both desire that someone—a man—lead them. However, Kate takes Isaac's suggestion to an extreme and ends up using it as an excuse to isolate herself from everyone in the community. Other congregationalists find Kate's psychological and social disconnection lamentable. But what they do not see is that her psychosis frees her from believing in the "rites . . . others used to assure (their) reality" (2). When, for example, community members try to bring Kate "back to earth "by bringing her to the church meeting that opens the novel, she rests secure that her reality is the true one and "accept[s] that she . . . [has] to pretend" (2) with fellow parishioners that they are right and she is wrong. Kate thereby demonstrates a female subversion of male mastery represented by Isaac.

That Kate implicitly sets the dead Maverlyn sets above the (black father) God Moses Barton claims for his people makes Kate a kind of gender heretic. For in "worshipping" her daughter, she also worships what the child represents: the feminine, and especially, motherhood. As a symbol, the dead Maverlyn signifies a past that is both personal (belonging to Kate) and communal (belonging to New Hebron).   Just as Kate remains trapped in the past by rejecting her daughter's death, so too does the congregation remain similarly entrapped by repeating isolationist/separatist behaviors that will ultimately get them nowhere near the "paradise" they seek.   More importantly, though, Maverlyn also represents the way in which women in the community are kept children forever by being "drowned" in religious ideologies hostile to female existence.

The rituals in which Kate engages as part of her daughter-worshipping are also significant in that they offer a clue to the nature of female spirituality that Wynter delineates in her novel.   She returns to Maverlyn's watery grave, positions her body and arms as though she were holding a baby and rocks her imaginary child to sleep.   Her "hymns" are the lullabies she croons to her daughter to which nature joins its voice.   During one such episode — which, interestingly enough, precedes one that takes place within the walls of Moses's church —, Wynter describes how "the clear water (of the spring) murmur[s] an accompaniment" (2) to Kate's song.   For the writer, female spirituality is of a piece with the natural world and has no architectural boundaries.   It is also intimately bound up with female embodiment, specifically, with the feminine ability to create life and nurture it.

Further evidence of this last point can be found in Wynter's depiction of the mother of another New Hebronite, Obadiah Brown.   May-May never joins Moses's congregation; rather, she is a member of another revivalist group, the Pukkuminans.   The Pukkumina cult, unlike Moses's fictional Christian one (and the Jamaican religious groups the New Believers represent), is based primarily in what Ivor Morrish states are "the magical beliefs and trance techniques of African religion."[12]   Its heavy emphasis on rhythmic singing, clapping, stamping to achieve communion with the spirit world recall Haitian *vodou* practices.   Within the contested Christian context of the novel, Pukkumina represents the pagan and the taboo.   May-May herself is a dancer and medium, known for becoming "the most completely possessed" (60) of all Cockpit Center Pukkuminans.   The intensity of her spiritual communion manifests dramatically on May-May's body, which becomes a "spinning, whirling, leaping" instrument with "breasts erect and pointed, [. . .] nostrils flaring, [. . .] lips slightly parted and pressed against white teeth" (60).   As in Kate's rituals, the female body becomes the bridge to an ecstasy and understanding that directly connects women to the divine.   In such a scheme, male religious intermediaries like Moses Barton lose their authority.

When Moses's vision of a black god and racial supremacy is challenged by one trumpeted by a nameless socialist agitator who advocates a classless, raceless, egalitarian society, Moses believes he must crucify himself to redeem Hebron and "assure its continuance" (239) as an earthly kingdom of the black Father-God's elect.   He thus attempts to use his body as that which, according to his deluded logic, will win favor in heaven for his people. Yet his Christ-like sacrifice is little more than a ruse. Under cover of conscious martyrdom, he is able to covertly commit a suicide that allows him to escape from his perceived failure as a spiritual leader. In what the agitator says, Moses senses future defeat: "The words that the man had spoken remained in (the Cockpit Center inhabitants') hearts, prepared them for the coming of others of whom he was only the forerunner; as Moses had been his" (222). For Kate and May-May, the divine has no race or class; it merely exists as part of them and of the natural world they inhabit. For Moses, however, notions of God is tied up with power and control, which themselves play out in a colonial society stratified by race, class and gender.

The one male in the New Hebron community who does eventually come to recognize the value of the feminine is Obadiah Brown, the young disciple who eventually succeeds Moses as the congregation Elder. Obadiah is as chaste as Moses is lustful. When Obadiah briefly runs away to Kingston as a young man, he is described as being afraid of the girls there and "of their hot breasts as they rubbed themselves against him, their loud laughter and their bawdy jokes" (152). Perhaps his attitude in part derives from his early life experiences with his mother May-May, who, in addition to being a Pukkumina worshipper, was also a part-time prostitute. May-May's professional activities recall Lilith's post-Adamic existence: according to Pamela Norris, Lilith took up with evil Red Sea demons and "gave birth daily to a hundred or more evil spirits." Lilith's demonic children became feared for the injuries they caused to newborns and the nocturnal emissions they caused in men.[13] However frightened Obadiah may be of females, he is also a man who has been profoundly impacted—albeit at a subconscious level—by women: specifically, by the physicality and sexuality that informs their spirituality. In one of the wood carvings he creates, he remembers his mother "as she danced at a Pukkumina meeting, her eyes wide and lost in a cold ecstasy, her breasts taut like thorns, her legs strong and powerful. . ." (149). Although he destroys that doll out of embarrassment, Obadiah, unlike any of the other New Hebronite males, also reveals a kind of unconscious admiration for the same women he fears.

Although *The Hills of Hebron* is, as critic Victor Chang has rightly claimed, a "woman's novel,"[14] the narrative itself actually centers around the awakening of a man — Obadiah Brown — to the place and importance of women in New Hebronite society. When the novel begins, Obadiah appears to be leading his congregationalists towards the same spiritual vision first set forth by Moses. Obadiah, in fact, seems to imitate Moses's act of apparent self-sacrifice by telling his congregation that for one year and one day, he will leave his wife sexually untouched to save New Hebron from further devastation, itself wrought by the hurricanes God had inflicted upon the community. Yet it is the unexpected — that is, the discovery of Rose's pregnancy — that causes Obadiah to not only face his fears regarding women and sexuality but to pay heed to the doubts he harbors about the New Hebron project: "What was this all about, Obadiah asked himself. [. . .] What were they all doing up there (in the hills above Cockpit Center), they who called themselves the New Believers. . ." (21). The public "unveiling" of Rose's swelling belly before the congregation thus heralds the start of Obadiah's personal journey towards gender enlightenment. As it does so, it also recalls the fact that New Hebron came into being because of another scandalous pregnancy: that of Rose's mother Gloria, who is raped by the white English minister of Cockpit Center, Reverend Brooke. It was this man who was able to secure for a crafty and conniving Moses the squatting rights to the land that would eventually become New Hebron.   Seen in another way, pregnant female bodies nourish both the growth of the community and its social and spiritual evolution, as exemplified in Obadiah's own transformation.

Like the mad Kate and the cursed and shunned Rose, Obadiah becomes an outsider to the community when his congregation elects Moses Barton's widow, Gatha, as the replacement Elder — at least, until her son Isaac Barton, returns from teacher training college.   He, too, experiences insanity: he becomes the "moon-struck prophet shut away from them in the troubled forests of his flesh, in a private world of jealous fantasies" (58).   The association of the moon with Obadiah's madness reinforces the idea that Obadiah himself has been "touched" by/because of a woman.   It is not until the night he nearly kills Rose in his quest to discover the man with whom she committed adultery that he realizes the magnitude of his own folly.   His revelation is accompanied by references to moonlight that transform "Hebron into a magic world" (74).   The "feminine" illumination symbolized by the moon suggests Obadiah's gender epiphany.   In such a light, he can approach what he previously did not understand — women, female sexuality — to learn from it the lessons of compassion and self-acceptance that reconcile him to Rose and allow him to plumb his own spiritual depths rather than slavishly follow the teachings of (male) religious teachers like Moses.

Through the revelation he has, Obadiah is transformed into a prophet who, unlike his namesake in the Old Testament, has a vision based not in vengeance for old wrongs, but in progress based on acceptance, connection and self-reliance.[15]   Obadiah reaches this pinnacle of wisdom when, near the end of the novel, he carves a doll for Rose's child that incarnates not only of his artistic spirit, but also the social and historical elements that made him.   In the carving, he remembers "mother" Africa, but also the folk culture of Jamaica and specifically, New Hebron.   Rather than blindly serve a white Judeo-Christian God or one refashioned with black skin by men obsessed with gaining and maintaining personal power, he recognizes that spirituality emerges from a fusion of gender, racial and cultural elements.   To be successful, it must be syncretic.   That a Jewish refugee from Germany is the one to recognize the "soul" inherent in the doll is also significant.   Not only does it suggest the coming together of communities in exodus; it suggests that survival comes about by creating links rather than divisions rooted in race, gender and/or class.

Gatha Randall, too, experiences her own kind of epiphany, which critic Janice Lee Liddell has seen as part of an heroic — or what she might term "sheroic" — journey to personal identity.[16] If as a younger woman, she was the wraith-like wife of the flamboyant Moses Barton, as a widow and Elder-elect, she has little difficulty telling the impoverished community, suffering from the effects of an extended drought, what she believes it must do to survive: buy water from Cockpit Center with money she has saved, brush the dust off their "lazy and slothful" (52) bodies and "pray for rain as you have never prayed before!" (56). But Gatha's commanding behavior comes not from any innate sense of her own qualities as a leader; rather, it emerges from her desire to secure the Eldership for her son, Isaac Barton, whom she believes will enlighten her people after himself being enlightened by education. What Gatha does not consider is the way the education — which comes from the same colonial sources as the God whom they have worshipped and colored black — has imbued her son and patriarch-in-the-making with a disgust of the peasant culture from which he has emerged. In a gesture reminiscent in its selfishness of Moses's suicide, Isaac, on holiday from school, steals money Gatha and Moses had saved for him and forces himself on Rose, vowing all the while never to return.

Wynter thereby reworks the biblical symbolism associated with Gatha's son's name. Rather than become, like the Old Testament Isaac, a father of nations who acts for the greater good of his descendants, Isaac Barton becomes a rapist who runs from responsibility in much the same way his father does. Realization of her son's nature and of the failure he represents temporarily render a dismayed Gatha silent; but once she beholds Rose's child — Gatha's grandchild — whom Kate brings to her, she comes face to face with the truth. Kate's eyes gleam "as if the wind had blown bits of the moon inside of them" (304), as if in affirmation of the feminine power Moses once tried to capture and harness for his own ends. The baby's living warmth cause "the fabric of (Gatha's) forebodings" (305) to fall away and Gatha weeps. Her tears reveal tacit acknowledgment of Isaac's crime and joy at a birth which signals the *real* new beginning for her community. By ridding herself of the delusion that Isaac is Hebron's savior, she becomes what Mary Daly might see as a patriarchal exorcist who expels the Father from her consciousness.[17] Like the rain that ends the drought at the close of the novel, Gatha's tears represent the workings of a divine order that plays itself out not just through men, but through women as well. Survival requires the participation and input of an entire society of people, not just one half who happen to be privileged by gender and/or other trait; for fleeing social and economic realities will not solve community or national problems. Hence "the paradoxical triumph of failure"[18] in this novel. For Wynter, success begins with solutions grounded in gender-inclusive material realities that in the end create an earthly domain in the here and now — rather than one in some imagined hereafter — that works for the benefit of all.

NOTES

1. See Pamela Norris, *The Story of Eve* (London: Picador, 1998) 278; see also Mary Daly, *Gyn/Ecology* (1978; Boston: Beacon Press, 1990) 86 n.

2. According to Mary Daly, what caused Lilith to leave Adam was the latter's desire that Lilith lie beneath him during sexual intercourse. She quotes from narrativized version of the Lilith/Adam story Raphael Patain presents in *The Hebrew Goddess* to highlight the struggle for equality implicit in Lilith's conflict with Adam: "'Why should I lie beneath you," she asked, "when I am your equal since both of us were created from dust?" See also Norris 278 and Theodor Reik, *The Creation of Woman* (New York: McGraw Hill Book Company, 1973) 21.

3. Critic Leota Lawrence believes that in Wynter's novel, Obadiah, unlike Moses, reacts rather than acts: he merely carries out orders and moves along pre-established paths. What Lawrence fails to observe is Obadiah's progression from reactive religious follower to active religious questioner who journeys towards a spirituality informed by his own (rather than received) experience. See "Paradigm and Paradox in *The Hills of Hebron,*" *MaComère* 1 (1998) 90.

4. Ivor Morrish, *Obeah, Christ and Rastaman: Jamaica and its Religion* (Cambridge: James Clarke, 1982) 49.

5. Daly 12-13.

6. Morrish 68-69: see also Leonard E. Barrett, *The Rastafarians* (1977; Boston: Beacon Press, 1988) 67.

7. Morrish 83.

8. Quoted in Victor Chang, "Sylvia Wynter" in *Fifty Caribbean Writers: A Bio-Bibliographical Critical Sourcebook,* edited by Daryl Cumberland Dance, (New York: Greenwood Press, 1986) 501.

9. Morrish 71.

10. Barrett 85.

11. Morrish 73-74.

12. Morrish 52.

13. Norris 330.

14. Chang 504.

15. Herbert G. May and Bruce M. Metzger note that the Old Testament prophet Obadiah's vision stems from the wrong the Edomites, descendants of Esau, did to the Israelites, descendants of Jacob when the latter were in danger. Rather than help the Israelites, the Edomites left their cousins vulnerable to the nations that plundered their wealth and brought death and destruction to the Israelites themselves. For their cowardice and cruelty, Obadiah promises bloody retribution Israelite dominion over the land of Edom. Within a Jamaican context, the Israelite/Edomite conflict translates into that of black Jamaicans against white British colonialists. See *The New Oxford Annotated Bible* (1962; New York: Oxford University Press, 1973) 1120.

16. In Liddell's view, Gatha, like the archetypal male and female heroes Joseph Campbell describes in *The Hero with a Thousand Faces,* undergoes various ordeals during what the critic sees as a journey to self-actualization. What makes her "quest" different is that she must overcome what Liddell correctly identifies as "an entrenched (black) patriarchy" (34). Hence, the heroism she displays is one that is

distinctly feminine, or, given the social and racial context, womanist. See pages 33-34 of "Voyages Beyond Lust and Lactation: The Climacteric as Seen in Novels by Sylvia Wynter, Beryl Gilroy, and Paule Marshall" in *Arms Akimbo: Africana Women in Contemporary Literature,* edited by Janice Lee Liddell and Yakini Belinda Kemp (Gainesville: University Press of Florida, 1999).
     17. Daly 3.
     18. Chang 505.

Works Cited

Austin-Broos, Diane J. *Jamaica Genesis: Religion and the Politics of Moral Orders.* Chicago: The University of Chicago, 1997.

Barrett, Leonard E. *The Rastafarians.* 1977. Boston: Beacon Press, 1988.

Chang, Victor. "Sylvia Wynter." *Fifty Caribbean Writers: A Bio-Bibliographical Critical Sourcebook.* Ed. Daryl Cumberland Dance. New York: Greenwood Press, 1986.

Daly, Mary. *Gyn/Ecology.* 1978. Boston: Beacon Press, 1990.

Lake, Obiagele. *RastafarI Women: Subordination in the Midst of Liberation Theology.* Durham, North Carolina: Carolina Academic Press, 1998.

Lawrence, Leota. "Paradigm and Paradox in *The Hills of Hebron.*" *MaComère* 1 (1998): 88-93.

Liddell, Janice Lee. "Voyages Beyond Lust and Lactation: The Climacteric as Seen in Novels by Sylvia Wynter, Beryl Gilroy, and Paule Marshall." In *Arms Akimbo: Africana Women in Contemporary Literature.* Ed. Janice Lee Liddell and Yakini Belinda Kemp. Gainesville: University Press of Florida, 1999.

May, Herbert G. and Bruce M. Metzger, eds. *The New Oxford Annotated Bible.* 1962. New York: Oxford University Press, 1973.

Morrish, Ivor. *Obeah, Christ and Rastaman: Jamaica and its Religion.* Cambridge: James Clarke, 1982.

Norris, Pamela. *The Story of Eve.* London: Picador, 1998.

Reik, Theodor. *The Creation of Woman.* New York: McGraw Hill Book Company, 1973.

Wynter, Sylvia. *The Hills of Hebron.* London: Jonathan Cape, 1962; London: Longman, 1984.

——. "One Love—Rhetoric or Reality?—Aspects of Afro-Jamaicanism." Rev. of *One Love* by Audvil King, Althea Helps, Pam Wint and Frank Hasfal. *Caribbean Studies* 12 (1972): 64-99.

23   Go Bring Down Goliath:
Biblical Reappropriation and Counter-Discourse in
Derek Walcott's
Ti-Jean and His Brothers
Jana Karika

A literature that (re)centers the perceptions of authority, culture, and morality on the wisdom of the native cultures that were marginalized during imperial rule requires the subversion of colonial assumptions imposed by the Western canon. Images of civilization, righteousness, and thus, by extension, savagery and blasphemy, were cultivated through the language and literature of the Center. By re-working the Western canon through such methods as retelling "classic" stories through an indigenous point of view or rewriting Judeo-Christian myths using native gods or rituals, postcolonial writers expose deceptive notions of universality and create an anti-colonial tool of resistance which Helen Tiffin terms "canonical counter-discourse" (97). Both the power and the vulnerability of this practice are found in the intertextuality between the literature of the oppressor and the literature of the oppressed. On one hand, by playing off of the writings of the Center, the other risks perpetuate its position on the margin. On the other hand, the hybridization inherent to postcolonial society requires that the efforts to retrieve a pre-colonial sense of dignity come together with the inescapable influences of colonization to embrace what Ashcroft, Griffiths, and Tiffin call the "cross-fertilisation between their constitutive elements" (*Reader* 184). In "Post-colonial Literatures and Counter-discourse," Tiffin articulates the potentially problematic nature of this approach: "But separate models of 'Commonwealth Literature' or 'New Writing in English' which implicitly or explicitly invoke notions of continuation of, or descent from, a 'mainstream' British literature, consciously or unconsciously re-invoke those very hegemonic assumptions against which the post-colonial text has [. . .] been directed" (96). Postcolonial readings and criticism of these counter-discursive works must recognize the genre's capacity to unmask the arrogance and usurp the authority assumed by Western thought or else they further stabilize the imperial constructs of authority which they seek to dismantle.

Because it is arguably the most influential book in colonial and postcolonial life, both for its use as a tool of oppression and for its (re)use as a resistance narrative, the Bible is a likely source for counter-discursive works. Gilbert and Tompkins say, "As a master narrative which has assisted and justified the imperial project, the Bible [. . .] necessarily figures among the chief canonical texts targeted for strategic reform" (43).

In his play *Ti-Jean and His Brothers*, Derek Walcott re-works biblical myths to create a counter-discourse which embraces hybridism while shifting the balance of power and reflecting a spirituality that is relevant and recognizable to local people. Through a series of parallels and divergences with biblical text; the tale becomes an allegory for what he calls "one race's quarrel with another's God" ("Overture" 13).

Many parallels between *Ti-Jean and His Brothers* and the Old Testament story of "David and Goliath" suggest that Walcott partially accepts the constructs of the biblical story but also reworks it to interrogate the cultural assumptions made concerning the nature of God's 'chosen' people and the role of racist, oppressive religion. Both stories are set in times of transition–"David and Goliath" during Israel's transition from being ruled by judges to being ruled by kings and *Ti-Jean and His Brothers* during the transition from colonial rule to postcolonial independence–raising questions about the extent of God's role and loyalties in matters of social transition. Both stories feature protagonists who are unlikely heroes empowered by their spirituality. In the Old Testament version, David receives God's blessing and becomes, despite his physical immaturity and lack of battle experience, the victor in a match against the war-hardened, giant Philistine, Goliath. It is a classic example of the type of story that Jews and Christians have told for centuries as evidence that the Israelites were the chosen people and that God's people can overcome any adversary. Through Ti-Jean, Walcott challenges the European assumptions about the "chosen" people by placing a native boy in the hero position against a white devil.

This displacement of the traditional biblical hero is punctuated by the similarities between Ti-Jean and David. They are both the youngest brothers in their families, and their older siblings, who don't recognize their hidden strengths, chastise them both. In the Bible, God sends Samuel to recognize and anoint the next leader of the Israelites. When Samuel looks at David's oldest brother, Eliab, he believes that Eliab will probably be the one God chooses. But God says to Samuel, "Do not consider his appearance or his height [. . .]. The Lord does not look at the things man looks at. Man looks at the outward appearance, but the Lord looks at the heart"(1 Sam 16:7). Seven brothers are rejected before Samuel finds David and anoints him as God's chosen leader for his people. David's three oldest brothers are full-time warriors for the king, but David only spends part of his time with the king and part of his time tending his father's sheep. When David shows up on the battlefield and says he will fight the Israelites' most menacing enemy, Goliath, Eliab scolds David, questioning his judgment and his intentions. Ti-Jean is also the youngest brother and seems to be the least qualified to fight his people's battle against the Devil. His oldest brother, Gros-Jean, is the strongest and boasts, "I have an arm of iron, / It have nothing, I fraid, man, beast, or beast-man" (*Ti-Jean* 106). His middle brother, Mi-Jean, is the most educated and plans to outsmart the devil. Gros-Jean and Mi-Jean both chastise Ti-Jean and accuse him of not doing his share of the work. They say, "We do all the damned work. / We do all the damned thinking. / And he sits there like a prince. / As useless as a bone" (*Ti-Jean* 92). And finally, both of these chastised younger brothers ignore the ridicule of their siblings and go into battle with a confidence that can only be attributed to inner peace and spiritual foundation. David answers Eliab's reprimand by asking, "Now what have I done? Can't I even speak?" and returns to his business (1 Sam 17:29). Ti-Jean goes into his battle telling his mother, "Yes, I small, maman, I small, / And I never learn from book, / But, like the small boy, David. / I go bring down, bring down Goliath" (*Ti-Jean* 134).

Walcott's adaptation of the protagonist of one of the better-known biblical stories reflects an influence of the Christian tradition on his writing and on postcolonial culture in general. The nature of this influence isn't one that replaces indigenous culture and tradition, but rather, one that serves to move it forward into the New World. In their description of hybridity, Ashcroft, Griffiths, and Tiffin say, "The interleaving of practices will produce new forms even as older forms continue to exist" (*Reader* 184). And Walcott himself argues that truly revolutionary writers know "that maturity is the assimilation of the features of every ancestor" ("Muse" 370). And so it is, Walcott recreates David in the form and ideology of a native boy. In a sense, *Ti-Jean* reflects Walcott's own life and mission as a postcolonial writer. The futility of the older brothers' efforts to overpower or outsmart the Devil mirrors those in postcolonial settings who seek justice without ever redefining the elements of the confrontation. The native boy, in Walcott's own image–an ordinary Caribbean boy who synthesizes his education and experience into a resistance literature that will eventually win him a Nobel Prize–redefines the notion of hero.

Walcott isn't merely incorporating the biblical tradition into his work. He is using his work to question the underlying assumptions of Western epistemology and shift the balance of power. Walcott's play diverges from the "David and Goliath" story as it recasts the players and redefines the battle to illuminate the injustices and hypocrisy of white colonial domination (an endeavor enriched by the ironic alignment of Christ with the Devil). The youngest, weakest brothers in the families are going to fight the battles of their people. They must be called the battles of their people because the significance of their prospective fights goes beyond the scope of family or personal matters. David is fighting an enemy who defies the king and, by extension, snubs his nose at the God of Israel. It is said that the king will bestow great wealth upon whoever can kill Goliath. This biblical story has traditionally been interpreted as an illustration of the inevitable victory and power of God's people over their enemies. Thus, as Walcott realigns the characters of the story so that the protagonist is a native, he shows that interpretations are subjective and can be manipulated to serve native culture as well European culture. The challenge to Ti-Jean's family is to fight the Devil himself, who wears, among others, the mask of the white Planter. A "Bolom," a spirit that is neither living nor dead, messengers the Devil's challenge. This messenger of the Devil not only introduces a native mysticism to the story, but also personifies the bitter version of the postcolonial story– the spirit that is strangled by hatred and fear and "twisted out of shape / deformed past recognition" before it can even be born (*Ti-Jean* 97). "Fulfillment, wealth, and peace" will be the reward for any brother who can make the Devil angry, but any brother who challenges him and loses will be eaten. If all three brothers die in the effort, the Bolom will be given life. Thus, Ti-Jean's struggle is that of an entire people to win on two fronts–the fight for freedom from colonial oppression and the fight to overcome the self-destructive pride and bitterness of the past.

Walcott further complicates the story by creating an adversary who is more complex than the biblical Goliath. The Devil in *Ti-Jean*, like the agents of imperial rule, dons different masks to suit his deceptive purposes at any given time in the action. At the heart of this counter-discursive work is the association Walcott makes between Christ and the Devil. There are two direct references to Christ that work to indict white Christianity and the evils committed in its name. In the first, the Devil sings, "When I was the Son of the Morning / When I was the Prince of Light [. . .] Oh, to hell with that! You lose a job, you lose a job. Yet once we were one light once up there, the old man and I, till even today some can't tell us apart" (151). This reference to Christ is a double assault on the colonizer's Christianity. First, as the Devil boasts, people cannot always tell the difference between God and the Devil. This is an attack on the hypocrisy of the religion that was forced upon the displaced Africans and Amerindians. Even as the colonizers proselytized about the heavenly reward of earthly suffering, they focused their own efforts on making money and seeking power at the expense of the indigenes. Only by questioning colonial motivations and assumptions can the postcolonial community make its own peace with God.

Second, this passage may be seen as an allusion to a fallen Christ in the world. In this case, the passage casts doubt on the Christian notion of the Savior as a living God who overcame the temptations of the Devil and was victorious over sin and death. Walcott seems to be asserting that in their zeal for power and authority, the colonizers corrupted even the holiest, most sacred of figure in their religion—in essence, they killed him. This interpretation would seem to correlate with the second reference to the "Son," when Ti-Jean's mother prays, "And if [Ti-Jean] must die, / Let him die as a man, / Even as your Own Son fought the Devil and died," and Ti-Jean says, "I'm as scared as Christ" (158). The conspicuous absence in these passages of any reference to the Christian belief of resurrection implies that Christ battled the Devil and lost on earth. The insertion of this New Testament allusion into one of the classic Old Testament testimonies of God's blessing on a "chosen" people further subverts the presuppositions of the Europeans' regard for their own chosen status and self-serving interpretations of God's will.

In addition to his alignment with the Christ figure, however, the Devil also wears various other masks to become an old man and a white planter. This dramatic device highlights not only the different faces of oppression in colonial society but also hints at an oral tradition in which one storyteller would play multiple characters. Walcott combines this element of storytelling–the Devil sometimes goes so far as to turn and speak to the audience as a narrator–with the dialogue between characters. Anne Fuchs contends that this method is especially useful in postcolonial theater to symbolize the confrontation and hybridization that surround postcolonial society. She says "the presence of two or more actors who confront each other physically is perhaps essential in a society which is one of conflict and division as opposed to the relative harmony of the tribal structures" (37).

The Devil always appears first as an old man in the woods stopping to talk to the brothers as they go off to meet the challenge. The old man speaks words of wisdom all the while hiding his cloven hoof under his skirt. In one breath, he tells Gros-Jean that "strength should have patience" and in the next he tells him, "What counts in this world is money and power" (106). The contradictions in the old man's speech are similar to the contradictions in colonial society–a society that preached about freedom through spiritual salvation for all people but profited from slavery and racially exclusionary communities. The irony is that both of the older brothers see the cloven hoof and dismiss it. The evil that stands before them is never challenged; it is accepted as an annoying anomaly of nature. Only Ti-Jean makes the connection between this old man, the voice of the deception of the past, and the Devil. In this way, the character Ti-Jean comes to symbolize the postcolonial writer who rejects the history told by the Western historians as a narrative that omits the indigenous story altogether. The postcolonial writer does not simply fill the gaps in what Walcott calls "the partial recall of the race"; he rewrites the story of past and present simultaneously, recognizing and answering the contradictions of colonial history ("Muse" 370). Helen Gilbert underscores this importance of the writer/playwright to the resistance effort by pointing out, "the essential elements which make up the theatre [. . .] suggest that drama offers significant sites from which to explore the lacunae left by imperialist representations of our past" (91).

When the brothers, one at a time, meet the Devil next, he is wearing the mask of the white Planter. The Planter is the most direct parallel with colonial rule. It is behind this mask that the Devil manipulates the brothers physically, intellectually, and emotionally. He designs arbitrary rules that serve his purposes (in this case, to make the brothers angry.) Among other things, he tasks each of the brothers with keeping track of a wandering goat and accounting for every leaf in the fields in order to give him a report at night. Gros-Jean believes he can meet the challenge with no problem because his physical strength will allow him to endure any hardship. The Old Man calls him "the spirit of war: an iron arm and a clear explanation"(108). Mi-Jean believes he will meet the challenge because he is wiser than the Devil. He plans to beat the Devil with a silent smile. He sings the "Song of Silence": "Within this book of wisdom / Hear what the wise man say: / The man who is wise is dumb/ And lives another day, / You cannot beat the system / Debate is just a hook, / Open your mouth, de bait in! / And is you they going to juck" (122). Through the strategies that these two brothers employ against the Planter, Walcott isn't merely showing the inadequacy of self-reliance (the lesson in the Bible), but also the shortcomings of the postcolonial reactions of bitterness and avoidance. Gros-Jean, "the spirit of war" and Mi-Jean, who decides it's wiser to be silent than to engage the oppressor in debate, both are eaten by the Devil.

Ti-Jean, on the contrary, beats the Devil. Like David, he seeks God's favor. But Walcott's hero does it through reverence to his ancestors and to nature—connections to indigenous spirituality—as well as through prayer. In this way, Walcott re-appropriates the themes of faith and redefinition from the David and Goliath story to create a tale that is relevant to the indigenous experience. Ti-Jean honors the faith of his mother by comforting her with the words she used to teach him as a boy, "You have taught me this strength / To do whatever we will / And love God is enough" (133). Unlike his brothers, Ti-Jean's deference toward his mother acknowledges his ancestral roots and emphasizes the wisdom of the community's elders. He asks her to pray for him, and she observes: "The first of my children / Never asked for me strength / The second of my children / Thought little of my knowledge, / The last of my sons, now, / Kneels down at my feet, / Instinct be your shield" (133). He also looks to the forest animals for education rather than cursing them and kicking them aside in the manner of his brothers. Ti-Jean's deference to the creatures of the forest shows his recognition that alone he is weak, but with the community he is empowered. By seeking the blessing and guidance of his mother and the forest animals, Ti-Jean reflects a spirituality that is congruous with pre-colonial values.

Thus empowered by his spiritual foundation, Ti-Jean meets the Devil without fear. Like David, who does not set out to fight Goliath using man's rules of engagement and carries only five stones and a slingshot into battle against the armored warrior, Goliath, Ti-Jean redefines the terms of the battle against the Planter. Rather than chase the goat around, constantly trying to re-secure the goat on his rope, Ti-Jean neuters the goat, which squelches its desire to run away. Likewise, he abstains from the frantic leaf count, and instead tells the slaves in the field to burn the entire field, thus making leaf counting unnecessary. The young boy's ability to turn the whole plantation upside down infuriates the Planter. Ti-Jean gains victory by rejecting the colonizer's rules of engagement. He steps out of the box of "accepted" behavior and embodies what Walcott calls "the second Adam, the recreation of the entire order, from religion to the simplest domestic rituals" ("Muse" 372).

The tale of *Ti-Jean and His Brothers* is an artful combination of techniques that serve to create a postcolonial work of hybridization, resistance, and cultural reflection. Derek Walcott successfully marries old culture with new and comes up with a counter-discourse that exposes the hypocrisy and injustice of colonization while celebrating the continuous redefinition of postcolonial existence.

Works Cited

Ashcroft, Bill, Gareth Griffiths, and Helen Tiffin. *The Empire Writes Back.* London: Routledge, 1989.

———. eds. *The Post-Colonial Studies Reader*. London: Routledge, 1995.

Barker, Kenneth (gen. ed.) *The NIV Bible*. Michigan: Zondervan Bible Publishers, 1985.

Fuchs, Anne. "Re-creation: One Aspect of Oral Tradition and the Theatre in South Africa." *Commonwealth: Essays and Studies* 9.2 (1987): 32-40.

Gilbert, Helen. "Historical Re-presentation: Performance and Counter-discourse in Jack Davis's Drama." *New Literatures Review* 19 (1991): 91-101.

Gilbert, Helen, and Joanne Tompkins. *Post-Colonial Drama: Theory, Practice, Politics*. London: Routledge, 1996.

Tiffin, Helen. "Post-colonial Literatures and Counter-discourse." *Kunapipi* 9.3 (1987): 17-34. Rpt. in Ashcroft, Reader 95-98.

Walcott, Derek. "What the Twilight Says: An Overture." *Dream on Monkey Mountain and Other Plays*. New York: Noonday Press, 1970. 1-40.

———. *Ti-Jean and His Brothers. Dream on Monkey Mountain and Other Plays*. New York: The Noonday Press, 1970. 81-166.

———. "The Muse of History." *Is Massa Day Dead? Black Moods in the Caribbean*. Ed. Orde Coombes. New York: Doubleday, 1974. Rpt. in Ashcroft, *Reader* 370-374.

Religion and Crypto-Jews in Mexico Through
Kathleen Achalá's *Spirits of the Ordinary***

Gay Wilentz

In an essay, "The Crypto-Jews: An Ancient Heritage Comes Alive Again," a retired school teacher who was interviewed stated that he was convinced that the family, though raised Catholic, could trace back their Sephardic Jewish ancestry: "Can you believe, 500 years and we're still looking for our identity?" As most Jews know, identifying Jewish culture solely as a religion is a limited view; however, if not a race and not merely a religion, there are familial and social traditions that connect to a matrilineal heritage for 5764 years! When the Spanish expelled the Jews during the Inquisition, many became *conversos*, who became Catholics, yet still practiced some of the family traditions in hiding; others were *anusims*, who were forced to convert but did not give up their Jewish traditional religion. So, as the opening line explores, what has happened to future generations of these crypto-Jews? And the "veil of silence" is a long history of Jewish identity and the religious practices and rituals (Metz 209).

In this chapter, I explore a recent novel by a descendent of these crypto Jews in Mexico and the way in which they continue their Jewish heritage and religion, despite the *"auto-da-fé"* coming of out the Inquisition and the executing of over 1500 Jews in the 1500-1600s. In *Spirits of the Ordinary* (1997), Kathleen Achalá examines the long history of her family's hidden Jewish traditions, practiced in secret since they were forced as *conversos*. For each generation, the children at times connect to this culture and deny it, as one son becomes an evangelical preacher in the US, yet returns to his family traditions. Achalá, who dedicates this book to her family, explores the spirituality and the hidden dysfunction of denying your identity as she unfolds the tale of generations of crypto-Jews. The question of religion and traditions once again reflects the conflicts and poignancy of this Jewish heritage. *Spirits of the Ordinary* raises the question of (re)claiming one's Jewish identity through generations and how the passing on the rituals of religion affects that 500 years of searching for the Sephardic self.

Alcalá raises the question of hiding Jewish identity and practicing religious rituals through generations and how crossing internal/external borders affects one sense of self. This work addresses a lived reality and social construct, especially complicated in terms of Latino/a Jewish identity. For the purposes of this essay, I identify Jews as a culture/ethnic group, apart from national affiliation and linked to religious beliefs as well as to a collective memory and history. According to David Theo Goldberg in *Jewish Identity*, the concept of ethnicity for Jews is a linking of *descent* (whom my ancestors are) and *assent* (what I choose to call myself), within the context of historical circumstances. For example, Goldberg lines up the concept of assent with physical attributes, familial identification, and how I am perceived by the society around me. Still, another aspect of descent/assent within Latin America and parts of the US is a concept of denial and demarcation of a hidden Judaism. In the introduction to David Gitlitz's *Secrecy and Deceit: The Religion of Crypto-Jews*, Ilan Stavans states the mysteries of identity almost from the start: "It became a kind of template among descendents of *conversos*, especially in the Southwest, northern Mexico, and Central America. To them it is a mirror that validates a suspicion" (xvii). However, what is most significant in this idea is on aspect of suspicion, which is "in the *Oxford English Dictionary* as 'a feeling or state of mind'" (Stevens xvii).

So that feeling and/or state of mind through that isolated history of crypto-Judaism is a part of this novel and a secret narrative. Recently there has been much interest in reclaiming that Jewish heritage that was lost under this veil of silence. Although many *conversos* still practiced Christian religion (usually Catholic), "it was increasingly common among later generations of crypto-Jews, whose Jewish identity was likely to be little more than a vague self-concept, a reminiscence of Jewish background, an emotional tie to 'Jewishness'" (Gitlitz 121). Even stories of Latino/as in New Mexico (as cited in my opening), who realized that their traditions (especially Friday night candles) were in fact a Jewish Sabbath, often through television like "Seinfeld" and movies about Jewish culture. Of course the situation in Latin America was very different from the US. And that history is a longer one. Many who escaped the Inquisition in Spain thought that they would be safer in the Americas; and it was true for a while until the *auto-da-fé*'s executions in Mexico and Central America. What is particularly unique now is the revitalization of this Jewish identity through an unveiling of the past. In another recent work, *Hidden Heritage: The Legacy of Crypto-Jews* (2002), Janet Liebman Jacobs tells of this reclaimed heritage while focusing on her own hidden history and gender issues. Jacobs states: "The persistence of secrecy among modern crypto-Jewish descendents illustrates the sociopsychological impact of historical oppression" (22). But there is another reality of practicing their Jewish traditions, as Jacobs notes: "As this current generation of descendants come to terms with their Jewish ancestry, it is primarily through a veil of secrecy and uncertainly that they come to understand and appreciate the extent to which danger and anxiety remain part of the legacy of crypto-Judaism" (34).

As Jacobs also notes, many of the current generation are linked through female members practicing these rituals in the family. I have also commented in my own book *Healing Narratives*, the profound significance of women's role in maintaining Jewish culture in the home. Sigmund Freud's wife Martha, when having guests on Friday night told them: "You must know that on Friday evenings good Jewish women light candles for the approach of the Sabbath. But this monster — *unmensch* — will not allow it because he says that religion is a superstition" (Gay 153). Yet, she still continue to pass on the traditions despite Freud's dysfunction with his Jewish identity.[1] Sydney Stahn Weinberg observes in *The World of Our Mothers* that the passing on of these traditions, especially the Sabbath, in this way "became a major rather than peripheral components of transmitting a sense of Jewish identification to the children" (140). The visual image of the mother lighting the Sabbath candles becomes a trope of comfort in Diasporic Jewish homes in memoirs and literature, linked to a communal sense of Jewishness. Jacobs also notes that women often passed on these hidden traditions as their role as culture bearer: "Through the performance of ritual, these women fostered a spiritual environment that has had a significant impact on the current generation of descendants who are in the process of recovering their Jewish ancestry" (66). This appears valid for many women novelists, clearly for the "current descendants"; yet, in the novel itself, the passing on of secret Judaism is more vividly centered on the men, especially the father Julio and his son Zacarias.

In *Spirits of the Ordinary*, Kathleen Alcalá examines the long history of her family's hidden Jewish traditions in their Mexican culture, practiced in secret since they were forced as *conversos* in the late 15th century. For each generation, the children at times connect to this culture and deny it, as the main protagonist Zacarias reclaims his identity and his son becomes an evangelical preacher in the US. Alcalá, who dedicates this book to her family, explores the spirituality and the dysfunction of denying your identity as she unfolds the tale of generations of crypto-Jews. Although the novel itself deals with many kinds of spirits, including those of indigenous cultures in Mexico, the focus is on the hidden legacy of the Jews that were both *conversos* and *anusim*. In addition, the Mexican Inquisition often used the term "Judaizers" for people who, like the father, Julio Caraval and the mother Mariana, clearly reflect *anusim*, as they practice their traditions The Morelos family knew that they were *Judios*, and the children blame them for putting the evil eye on their babies that die. The five boys hit Mariana with stones and call her a Christ-killer (seems as if it is being redone recently as well). She is saved by her father but after unconsciousness, she says only one word "*Angeles*" and never speaks again (81).

Alcalá may have related this fictional tale to a well-known historical family, Carvajal/Carbajal (maybe her own, but she doesn't say that). As many historians have written, these Jews were one of the most powerful families in Mexico in the 16th Century, who thought that it would be safer to leave Spain for their new country (Metz 211). In "Seal of the Mexican Inquisition," this famous family was powerful in Mexico at first, but eventually they were identified with Mexican Jewry. Other members of the family, including Mariana Carvajal was burned alive, were also executed in the auto of 1601, one of the *largest Auto-da-fé* to take place in Mexico. Also, Luis de Carvajal the younger, who was a "mystic visionary" was found guilty of Judaizing and was burned as a "unrepentant heretic" in the same auto-da-fé (Gitlitz 56). Yet with the transition of government and the auto-da-fé, the family members were executed, when they thought they were in a safe place in Mexico. Mariana Carvajal is linked to the protagonist Zacarias' mother in naming and spiritual ways. Zacarias name is Carabajal, and the mother's name is Mariana Vargas Caraval. We can see the similarities to this significant family in Mexico at the time period that the novel is placed. But the similarities go beyond the name. Mariana Carvajal actually painted the crypto-Jews that were executed, and like the younger Luis de Carvajal, she was visionary and spiritual: "In her artistic rendering, Mariana is shown at the *auto-da-fés* as she awaits strangulation, while all around her other Judaizers are already burning at the stake" (Jacobs 137). Although Mariana is burned at the auto-da-fé, Mariana, the mother in *Spirits of the Ordinary*, suffers from the anti-Semitic environment as a child. But despite this violence perpetrated on her, Mariana gains some special spiritual qualities and perceives things through the visionary angels and protects her son as he enters a world with an unclear identity and does not connect to his family or his religious practices.

Although within Jewish tradition and religion, it was often the woman who passed on the rituals in the home. But in this novel, although Mariana is a significant mother for Zacarias, it is the father Julio, who is the main person of his rituals of his culture, which fits into men's role of religion. Later, Zacarias who is lost in terms of his Jewish identity and ceremonies, becomes the most consequential person is taking the Jewish ancestry and religion to the next generation and other people like the indigenous. When Zacarias was born, he was named after the Governor Luis de Carabajal/Carvajal, who was executed in the *auto-da-fé* in 1596 (23). And perhaps this made him isolated for the positive aspects of Jewish traditions and heritage. At first, Zacarias did not connect to his Jewish background, and he married a young woman Estela, whose father let her marry him only if the children would be brought up Catholic. His father Julio is *anusim*, and what the government of Mexico called a Judaizer. But he allows his son to marry a non-Jew and then regrets it, because Zacarias is lost in every way. At first, it seems that Zacarias cannot function in any place in the world, just interested in exploring gold and wasting his wife's money. The loss of identity is not ostensibly linked to the denial of his Jewish customs and traditions, despite the fact that he remains close to his parents. Yet his parents, as well as his wife, connect his loss of home and sense of self to the loss of his Judaism. Julio is dismayed by his son's inability to connect to their Jewish heritage, and thinks that "maybe he should intervened when Zacarias wanted to marry a non-Jew. But who could tell anymore? The families, although they would not admit it, had Jewish blood" (85). But Julio goes on to talk about the community of Jews that practice Friday night Sabbath, and Julio, even with a perilous situation, keeps his religious books and practices the Cabala (Kaballah). For Julio, his commitment to his religious and cultural traditions is profound with his understanding of the Cabala. "In the afternoon, Julio tended his gardens, both actual and metaphysical, giving himself over to God's wisdom both through his creations and through the mystical teaching of the Cabala" (90). The role of Jewish mysticism has been challenged by European Jewish intellectuals,[2] but according to Gershom Scholem in *Major Trends in Jewish Mysticism*: "The development of Jewish mysticism from the time of the Spanish exodus onwards has been singularly uniform" (287). In Julio's template, what is unique is the way in which the Jewish people dealt with exile: "These new ideas combine a mystical interpretation of the fact of exile with an equally mystical theory of a path to redemption" (Scholem 287). For Julio and his wife Mariana, their Jewish traditions and mystical religion give them a path to a kind of redemption, while they are suffering from the oppression that surrounds them. But for Julio, "the landscape of Zacarias' existence troubled Julio's mind" (90). Early on, Zacarias and his father are in a conflicted situation because of the Jewish tradition and the way in which Zacarais seems lost. Their early fight is about Zacarias desire to claim gold and is not connected to his parents, his wife and his children. Julio confronts his son, as Zacarias leaves to find gold, about the gold business: "[It] is an addiction, like whisky or gambling. No one in my family has ever had an addiction before" (23). And we can see the problems with Zacarias, when he challenges his father stating that his obsession with his Torah and the Cabala is also an "addiction"; Julio ponders "this wild stranger who is his son," and returns to his studies (23). And Julio wants a scholar in his family, but Zacarias at first only cares about gold.

Although Zacarias is not very connected to his father, he is mystically connected with his mother, who cannot talk. She tries to make Julio be more sympathetic to Zacarias, and often Zacarias dreams about his mother (61), and always returns home to see Mariana. But his wife, Estela is also uncomfortable with her husband. He seems lost and is barely bonded to her and their children, since her father make sure their children would not be raised as Jews (5). Estela notes that he has always left on Christmas and Easter, while she celebrated those traditions with their children: "But Estela wondered if it wasn't his ties to his

Jewish family. Zacarias said it was not important to him, that all of that was part of a past that did not concern them, but Estela wasn't so sure" (100). And when Estela throws him out because he will not function as a husband at home and spending all of her money on his searches for gold, he enters a world that leads him back to his Jewish identity. And this is a path that is both personally healthy and seriously dangerous.

In investigating the history of crypto-Jews in Mexico, Zacarias's story is historical in terms of a connection to the indigenous people. Although there is a relationship of many indigenous groups and the Jews, because the Christians tried to end their own religions; still, in this novel, it is the Tarahumara in Northern Mexico. In realizing that he has lost his ritual and identity, Zacarias has to reconnect, so that he can heal himself and his next generation. In an Internet article called, "Where Did My People Go? Passover in Oaxaca," the essay explores about the secret history of hidden Jews but also to the relationship to the indigenous in that area: "The rest of the community remained hidden for 300 years, spreading their religion to the Indians who also had things to hide" (2). And according to a store owner who sells Menorahs and other books like the Torah translated into Spanish, he stated: "Sabbath supplies are quite popular, even among the local Indians, who practice a mutated form of Judaism" (2). But it also works in another way. As a way of hiding their tradition, the Jews use corn tortillas as their *matzas* for their Passover *Seder* (Gitlitz 57). So we see a linking of cultures and religions, as well as the fact that both groups were oppressed by the dominant society in Mexico.

While still obsessed with finding the gold, Zacarias's switchback come though his meeting with that indigenous group in Mexico, the Tarahumara, who still practice their rituals today. But an indigenous friend Matakumi tells Zacarias that he needs to go to the Casa Grande, a city of the ancients/"Las casas de los ancianos"(177), to find what he is seeking. According to David Gitlitz, one of the *conversos* would be "vacillators": "For some *conversos* the road to assimilation as Catholics was filled with switchback" (88). Zacarias thinks that what his friend is saying refers to the gold, but it is really his reclaiming of his Jewish heritage through the stories from his family and Biblical collective memory. As Zacarias decides to sleep in the ancient city, the guide says: "There are spirits here." But Zacarias is fine with that, and at dawn he begins to connect to his Jewish rituals and traditions, as his friend Matakumi had planned for him. Even though he is still obsessed with the gold, something within the city of the ancients reconnects him to his ancestry. The indigenous guide brings some children with him to see Zacarais, and since he is lonely, he tells the children about the fact that his mother, who was mute, could talk to birds. But as more children and other indigenous people come to his place, he begins to tell them about his Jewish father's relationship to the Cabala: "He told about his father writing words on a plate in an ancient, secret language [Hebrew] that would hasten the coming of the last day of the world, which would be ruled by the Messiah, the long-promised savior of his people" (178-9). Since the idea of the

Messiah coming would connect to oppressed people, the indigenous people really linked their own thoughts to Zacarias. And it is interesting that finally though his stories, he identifies with his father Julio. He begins to tell these tales to many of the Tarahumara.

Zacarias tells those who surround him about his father Julio and the Cabala as well as their hidden Jewish practices. In a very different viewpoint from Christianity, Zacarias tells of his father's comprehension of Judaism, which is one of the religions that believes in "four worlds":

> Each of these worlds emanates from God, and there is a ladder
> of ascent from the world farthest away, *asiyah*, to the closest, *atzilut*.
> We live in a world of *beriah*, ruled by the laws of the Torah of
> *beriah*. But someday, the messiah will return, and the world will be
> placed in a perfect balance, *tikkun*. On that day, everything will
> change, the divisions between all the worlds will be gone, and we
> will live in the world of *atzilut*. Then, the laws of the Torah of the
> *atzilut* will reign, because everything will be perfect. (180)

Ironically, despite the fact that Zacarias did not always accept the knowledge of his father, he learned it and passes it on to the Tarahumara. And after he spoke, an older woman, Jesusita responds: "We too, believe in four worlds" (180). As they get into more conversations, it is clear that both cultures have similarities, maybe not known earlier. Jesusita states that things are now not so bad, since "everything is changing, now that you, our vecinos, our neighbors are here. But we still have our sacred places, the caves, and the lakes where the creator spirit lives. These things, too, are secret. We must also pray in secret" (181). And as they all pass on their spiritual aspects of each other culture, Zacarais brings the Torah's version of the Old Testament that "he learned as a child from his secretive family" (181).

It is this linking together of these two cultures, with a conjoining of history and healing, that leads the government to seek out Zacarias as someone who is interfering with the "native" workers returning the mines. This horrific fiction is connected to a violent incident that actually happened in 1649, when the Jews were not only "being accused of religious heresy, also turned out to be threats to the state" (Metz 215). Of course, the irony is that Zacarias finally associates with his Jewish heritage, and like many of the Judaizers, he becomes a threat to the dominant culture linked to Christianity. And the connection with Tarahumara is also a danger to the Mexicans, who want to control then and not let them practice their own traditions. So this healing experience for both Zacarias and the Tarahumara community leads to violence and death. Although Zacarias escapes because the indigenous people tell him he has to go, since "you must live! This is our struggle" (203). Many of the Tarahumara are slaughtered, and the imagery of the blood in the river becomes a linking of the plagues done to Moses and also the flood of Noah. As the rain continues down and the flood happens, there is also the violence changing the water to red, as Zacarias looks at the murders of the indigenous people: "Below, the stream ran red not just with iron but with the blood of women, children, men, and soldiers" (206). As in the *auto-da-fés*, the violence done to Jews was also done to the indigenous people as well. But this experience led Zacarias to thank God for his savior but also feel the loss of the people he loved so much. And his transformation leads him to return home and make his youngest son a Jew. Yet, in spite of the violence, Zacarias returns home and finds his new son, whom he circumcises and calls him Noé (Noah). He sees this as his "covenant" and the promise to his father. Explaining to Estela his creation of his son as a Jew, she is furious with him. But he tells her: "It is a sign that we are apart. That we will always be faithful to Him. The way the rainbow is His sign to us that He will never again destroy the world by flood" (212). At this point Zacarias is no longer a vacillator, but now a Judaizer like his father. He has finally found himself but that is perilous as well.

At this point, the government goes after all the Jews, including his parents. Julio and Mariana. Since he keeps his books and his traditions, Julio is in very much danger as well as his wife: "Julio shivered. Ten days before he had looked in a plate made of copper only to see it turn a deep and bloody red" (215). But as Zacarias returns to his family and tell them of his experiences and his reconnection to his culture, Zacarias warns his parents: "They may bring harm upon you because of me. Because we're Jews" (217). Although Zacarias finally realizes the endowment of his Jewishness, Julio and Mariana have known that throughout their lives. Like the younger Luis de Carvajal, Julio hid his books, but they are found as Julio and Mariana escaped to Mexico City, joining friends who will protect them. But after they escape, the soldiers come in and burn down the house as well as his Hebrew books. So a part of the culture is lost, except as prayers and rituals as "passed along is the oral tradition" (Gitlitz 444). Although these rituals and prayers are often incomplete, but still they are part of that heritage to next generations.

Mariana lives, unlike the strangulation of the historical women she may be modeled after. Yet what happened is that often other Jews knew the ones who escaped, and if they were secure as hidden Jews, they protected them. According to Gitlitz, "Secret Jews, like any other clandestine group, required methods of identifying one another without disclosing their identity to the hostile larger community that engulfed them" (605). So, for Zacarias, another hidden Jewish family takes him in to save him. He realizes they are Jewish as he rides through the town and sees the house and the garden, like his father's: "[Zacarias] felt the chill wind cut through the wool of his poncho as though probing him for his identity. The sun was setting, and candles and lanterns began to appear in the cavernous windows"(233). And when he talks to them, they also identified Zacarias and invite him in to their house: "It is late, and we are about to celebrate the *Shabbos* [Sabbath]" (234).

So Zacarias is in solidarity with the other Jews, whose names are not mentioned, and he is protected from the soldiers after him. That is the last time we see Zacarias in the novel, but we recognize he has finally found a home and his identity. His wife also has to leave her town, because of the family peril, but we never find out what exactly happens to her son Noah, who was circumcised as a Jew. Yet the novel ends with an epilogue of the other son Gabriel, who is a scholar (what the father Julio wanted for Zacarias). And before the epilogue, we have a poem that begins it:

> I wait for you in the high and lonely places.
> I will peep thy secret name in my heart.
> For seventy times seventy days,
> I will sing your praises in reverence.
> My sons will praise thee, oh Lord,
> Until the hundredth generation. (236)

Alcalá does this novel as a memory of the descendents, and the poem is almost a voice of the history of the crypto-Jews. At the same time, it is also the voices of the father Julio and his son Zacarias, who finally becomes part of that Judaic tradition as Judaizers. As the crypto-Jews practice in secret for many, many generations in honor of their culture and religion. But the novel itself ends with a rather unresolved ending, which is very much part of the reality of crypto-Jews throughout the Americas. The epilogue exposes that we never learn what happens to the son Noé/Noah (despite Zacarais's attempt of making him a Jew), but the son's story of Gabriel is one that remains confused as a crypto-Jew, although his mother is not a Jewish person (maybe, always unclear)[3]. Gabriel goes to the US for school in 1877 and becomes an evangelical preacher, because of the family that boarded him. When he returns home to Mexico, his mother rejects him because he is no longer a Catholic and is evangelical. But we hear that she takes her son Noé to Mexico City, where his grandparents Julio and Mariana are, so the experience of Noé is extratextual. But as a missionary, Gabriel marries an Opate Native American Rosa Canelos, whose family was part of the Casa Grande experience with Zacarias. "Rosa's mother was present at Casa Grandes when my father was there, and seemed to trust me on that basis" (238). Therefore, we are once again revisited with Gabriel's Jewish heritage, as he reads the stories that Zacarias passed on to the Tarahumara, which the Aunt Lucy Canelos kept in a journal. She had kept the papers of Zacarias for many years, and although they were old, they w ere readable. She forced Gabriel to read the writings that were "religious in nature" (239), and he realized that the writings are part of a Jewish religion and heritage, but also a history of his own family.

As Gabriel reads the writing from his father in exile, he realizes that the writings transformed his father: "From his writing, it was clear that he had undergone a deep and profound change—a revelation if you will—that had shaken him to the very foundation of his soul and brought him back to the traditions of his family" (240). After he reads the writings of his father, he must return to Saltillo, as he prays to God (which God?) for guidance. After he visits his mother's family, he returns to the house of his grandparents, as he rides on a horse: "I knew this path by heart, the ways we remember the shape of a favorite toy or the words to a song. [. . .] I entered through a gap that had once held a curious grate and dismounted" (242). Gabriel does return to his grandfather's home (burned by the government after the violence directed at the Jews). As he sits in the garden, Gabriel's memories of his Jewish grandfather Julio mingle with him, and he has a vision that he calls a "hallucination" of all the children of his generations past. He states: "I recognize the curly black hair and the hawk noses of my family, the air of otherworldliness that marked and set us apart" (243). Although the ending is in some ways unresolved, it remains a story of the Crypto-Jews as Gabriel begins to clean up the fountain of his grandparents, while he feels their ancestral presence and their blessings. The epilogue ends with Gabriel's last statement: "The time had come to begin again" (244). And a quote from Isaiah 60: 1-3 remains after Gabriel's comment, where Isaiah tells the world that darkness will come and yet the nations will rise for our people rising.

The question of unresolved ending also reflects the whole sense of fragmented identity as many Jews are dealing with today, and especially the crypto-Jews. Jacques Lacan calls this a "fragmented body-image," an alienated self "which will mark with its rigid structure the subject's entire mental development" (4). We can see this from a cultural perspective as a fictive unified self one identifies with, but is actually something other, alien (Wilentz, "Healing the 'Sick Jewish Soul'"). At the same time, there is a complicated hidden identity, which is many ways is already alienated, since it cannot be passed it on to their community and sometimes even their family. The relationship to Jewish ancestry and traditions continues, but in some ways the hidden practices are also embedded in the future of crypto-Jews. As Socolovsky notes about another novel, *Days of Awe*, of crypto-Jews in Cuba: "We thus need to consider not only what has been left absent from dominant historical remembering, but also in what ways that absence textures the present with its ghosts and fragments" (223). Returning to the question of identity for Jewish ethnicity as set up by Goldberg and others with the concept of assent/descent, I think we can see by the writings of Alcalá that one's Jewish ancestry, heritage, and traditions is much more complicated as the crypto-Jews (re)claim a denied and loss identity, while demarcating what exactly that sense of self will mean. And as we witness with the end of the novel that maybe Gabriel will pass on the continuing traditions as he learns more about his Jewish rituals and connects to the indigenous past of the Tarahumara, since as he says, the time has begun again.

NOTES

1. What is profoundly ironic about this double bind in relation to Freud, was not only that he seems unable to identify what was going on in his own subconscious in relation to his Jewish identity, but also that he was in fact defining a discourse that would leave him and his culture group still marginalized and dis-eased. As Rothman and Isenberg point out in "Freud and Jewish Marginality," Freud saw psychoanalysis as a "universal doctrine which denies the reality of culture and of cultural differences" (47). In attempting to dislodge the foundation of prejudice by subverting the restrictive base of the dominant culture, however, Freud also reinforced the discrimination inscribed in his own discourse by denying the cultural differences that exist.

2. As Jewish people went to Europe, their aim as intellectuals were to make the relation more like Christianity rather than the Kaballah, which related more to their earlier traditions since it was not good vs. bad, but all of one's life has a mystic aspect of it.

3. As Gitlitz and the authors Alcalá and Obejas state it is hard to say who has Jewish heritage in their generations past. As the protagonist Ale/Alexandra of *Day of Awe* investigates her Jewish ancestry through her father's hidden practices in the basement, she also realizes that her mother is also a *converso*, who has given up her Jewish traditions, yet worships Santeria, a Yoruba/African religious practice in Cuba. This inquiry makes Ale more comfortable with who she is by discovering that "matrilineal stamp, I'm missing" (44).

Works Cited

Alcalá, Kathleen. *Spirits of the Ordinary*. New York: Harcourt Brace & Co, 1997.

Bloom Southwest Jewish Archives. "The Crypto-Jews: An Ancient Heritage Comes Alive Again." *Southwest Jewish History* 2.1 (Fall 1993): 1—4.

Gay, Peter. *A Godless Jew: Freud, Atheism, and Making of Psychoanalysis.* New Haven: Yale UP, 1987.

Gitlitz, David M. *Secrecy and Deceit: The Religion of Crypto-Jews.* Albuquerque: University of New Mexico Press, 2002.

Goldberg, David Theo, and Michael Krauss. Jewish Identity. Philadelphia: Temple UP, 1993.

Jacobs, Janet Liebman. *Hidden Heritage: The Legacy of the Crypto-Jews.* Berkeley, CA: University of California Press, 2002.

Lacan, Jacques. *Ecrits: A Selection.* Trans. Alan Sheridan. New York: Norton, 1977.

Metz, Allan. "'Those of the Hebrew Nation. . . .': The Sephardic Experience in Colonial Latin America." *Sephardim in the Americas: Studies in Culture and History*. Eds. Martin A. Cohen and Abraham J. Peck. Tuscaloosa: UP of Alabama, 209-33.

Obejas, Achy. *Days of Awe*. New York: Ballantine Press, 2001.

Rothman, Stanley and Phillip Isenberg. "Freud and Jewish Marginality." Encounter 43 (Dec. 1974): 46-54.

Scholem, Gershom. *Major Trends in Jewish Mysticism*. New York: Schocken Books, 1995.

Seal of the Mexican Inquisition, "A Summary of History of the Inquisition in Mexico."Hemi.nyu.edu/archives.

Socolovsky, Maya. "Deconstructing a Secret History: Trace, Translation, and Crypto-Judaism in Achy Obejas's *Days of Awe. Contemporary Literature* 44.2 (Summer 2003): 225-49.

Stavans, Ilan. "Introduction." Gitlitz xiv—xix.

Weinberg, Sydney Stahn. *The World of our Mothers: The Lives of Jewish Immigrant Women*. Chapel Hill, NC: University of North Carolina Press, 1988.

"Where Did My People Go? Passover in Oaxaca." www. Oaxacainfo.com/oaxaca/Passover. 1-3.

Wilentz, Gay. *Healing Narratives: Women Writer Curing Cultural Dis-ease*. New Brunswick: Rutgers UP, 2001.

——. "Healing the "Sick Jewish Soul': Psychoanalytic Discourse in Jo Sinclair (Ruth Seid's *Wasteland*." *literature and psychology* 47. 1-2 (2001): 68-93.

Note on the Contributors

ESTERINO ADAMI holds a PhD in English Studies and teaches English Language at the University of Turin, Italy. He has also held seminars and workshops on 'Minority Literatures', Postcolonial Literatures, and Intercultural Education. He has presented papers at national and international conferences and has also written essays and reviews, mainly on African and Indian authors. He is interested in Indian diasporic writers in Britain, the new Literatures in English, Shakespearean Drama, and Gothic Fiction.

M. M. ADJARIAN earned her degrees in Comparative Literature from the University of California, Berkeley (B.A.) and from the University of Michigan (Ph.D.). Currently, she is an Associated Researcher with the Southwest Institute for Research on Women (SIROW) at the University of Arizona, where she has also taught courses in corporeal feminist theory and in transnational gender studies for the Womens Studies Department. Her primary research interests include post-1950 Caribbean, African Diasporic and postcolonial literature: twentieth century travel writing; autobiography and feminist and postcolonial theory. She has published articles and reviews in Michigan *Feminist Studies, College Literature, Calalloo, West Virginia University Philological Papers, Palabres,* and the *African Literature Association Selected Papers.* Her book "Allegories of Desire: Body, Nation and Empire in Modern Caribbean Literature by Women" (Praeger, 2004) examines how six post-1980 Caribbean women writers critique North Atlantic imperialism through allegorical depictions of female/maternal bodies and the relationship those bodies have to cultural and discursive manifestations of colonial/patriarchal power.

TRISH CLARK teaches English at West Craven High School in Vanceboro, North Carolina. She received her MAEd in English Education, with a concentration in multicultural literature and feminist studies, in 2005 from East Carolina University. She was Craven County's 2003-2004 Teacher of the Year where she continues to teach and reside.

SEODIAL FRANK H. DEENA is Associate Professor at East Carolina University where he co-coordinates the Multicultural Literature Program and teaches multicultural, world, postcolonial, African American, and Caribbean literature, as well as the Bible as literature. He received his Ph.D. in Literature and Criticism from Indiana University of Pennsylvania and his undergraduate degree from the University of Guyana. He has published widely in professional journals such as *College Language Association Journal, UFAHAMU: Journal of the African Activist Association, Commonwealth Novel in English, Commonwealth* Review, *Indo-American Review, Afro-American Literature, The Literary GRIOT,* and *Journal of Caribbean Studies*; and has chapters in *Postcolonial Discourse* (Prestige 1996), *Literature of Nature* (Fitzroy Dearborn 1998), *Alice Walker's The Color Purple: A Reader's Companion* (Asia Book Club 2002), *Latitude 63°North* (Mid-Sweden University College 2002), and *Terranglian Territories* (Peter Lang 2000). His book, *Canonization, Colonization, Decolonization: A Comparative Study of Political and Critical Works By Minority Writers,* has been published by Peter Lang Publishing INC. in 2002. *From Around the Globe: Secular Authors and Biblical Perspectives* and *Situating Caribbean Literature and Criticism in Multicultural and Postcolonial Studies* are forthcoming in 2005. Dr. Deena has traveled to more than 50 countries, and he brings an international, intercultural, and interdisciplinary approach to his research, teaching, and service.

Dr. Deena serves as MLA Bibliographer for six postcolonial journals, and he is on the editorial boards of *Indo-American Review, The Commonwealth Review, Journal of Caribbean Studies,* and *A Turbulent Voyage.* He reads for *Journal of Commonwealth* and *Postcolonial Studies* and *Literature Interpretation Theory.*

CRYSTAL DOWNING Biography with a Ph.D. in English from the University of California, Santa Barbara. Crystal Downing has published on a wide variety of literary topics, from Shakespeare to the Brontes, and has won both national and international awards for her essays on film. Much of her recent scholarship focuses on the relationship between postmodernism and faith, an issue which informs her book "Writing Performances: The Stages of Dorothy L. Sayers" (Palgrave Macmillan 2004). Downing is Associate Professor of English and Film Studies at Messiah College in Grantham, PA, where she has been honored with the Smith Award for Excellence in Teaching.

MARIE FARR received her Ph.D. in English from the University of Washington. Dr. Farr taught at Seattle University and moved to East Carolina University in 1972, where she helped found the ECU Women's Studies Program and has, at various times, served as Acting Chair of the Department of Communication and Assistant Dean of Arts and Sciences. In 2004 Dr. Farr received the Vagina Warrior Award for her past work. She has published on such writers as Virginia Woolf, Marge Piercy, and Charlotte Perkins Gilman, and has given library talks on Randall Kenan throughout eastern North Carolina.

FRED M. FETROW is a Professor of English at the United States Naval Academy. His publications include a book on Robert Hayden (not surprisingly entitled, Robert Hayden, 1984, in the Twayne's United States Authors Series), several scholarly articles on Hayden, and diverse work on other genres and literary periods. His teaching and research interests include most notably African American literature, Shakespeare, and Eighteenth-Century British literature (he wrote his University of Nebraska 1970 Ph.D. dissertation on John Dryden's drama). He is currently working on the poetry of Michael S. Harper, correlating his relationships with Hayden and Sterling Brown with Harper's penchant for densely allusive celebratory poems on diverse African American culture heroes over the years.

LEONORE GERSTEIN earned her BA in English literature and European Philosophy at the Hebrew University in Jerusalem. She did graduate work in comparative literature, with an emphasis on French and English, at the University of Minnesota. After a twenty-year professional career in speech and language pathology (MA, Western Mcihigan University), she returned to the study of literature, earning her MA in English at Eastern Michigan University. She spent 12 formative years in Israel, hence her fluency in Hebrew and interest in modern Hebrew poetry. Her Masters thesis dealt with the reception of T. S. Eliot in Israel. She lead a seminar for retirees on American poetry in 2005 and expects to continue teaching literature and writing to non-traditional students.

YEHUDIT BEN-ZVI HELLER is a lecturer in the Jewish Studies program at Smith College as well as at the Commonwealth College at the University of Massachusetts, Amherst, where she is also a PhD candidate in Comparative Literature. Her research and teaching interests include: the poetry of Rachel Bluevstain, the Bible as literature, autobiography, Hebrew (language and Israeli poetry and literature), the female pioneer subject in American literature, and issues of exile and displacement. Yehudit Ben-Zvi Heller has published two books of poetry in Hebrew in Israel: *Kan Gam ba-Kayitz Hageshem Yored* [Here Even in the Summer it Rains] and *Ha'isha Beme-il Segol* [The Woman in the Purple Coat]. Translations of her poems have appeared in *Metamorphoses* and the *Massachusetts Review*.

JANA L. KARIKA received her M.A. in English from East Carolina University Her nine years of teaching experience includes ESL at Coastal Carolina Community College, English composition and professional writing at the U.S. Marine Corps NCO and Staff NCO Academies, and spouse's education with the Marine Corps' L.I.N.K.S. program. Her research focuses on Postcolonial Literature written in English and the relationship between Christianity and native cultures. Currently, her energy is focused on raising her two young children.

BABACAR M'BAYE received a Ph.D in American Studies at Bowling Green State University, in Bowling Green, Ohio, in 2002. He currently teaches African American Literature and African Diaspora Studies at The Evergreen State College, Olympia, Washington. His research interests include the historical and cultural connections between Africa and its Diaspora, race relations in the West, imperialism, colonialism, post-colonialism, and alternative gender constructs. His publications include: "Dualistic Imagination of Africa in the Black Atlantic Narratives of Phillis Wheatley, Olaudah Equiano, and Martin Robinson Delany" (*New England Journal of History*, 58 (3): Spring 2002. 15-32), "The Representation of Africa in Black Atlantic Studies of Race and Literature" (*Thamyris Itersecting: Place, Sex and Race*. N⁰ 11. 2003. 151-162), and "The Image of Africa in the Travel Narratives of W.E.B. Du Bois, Richard Wright, James Baldwin, and Henry Louis Gates, Jr.," (*BMa: The Sonia Sanchez Literary Review*. 9 (1): Fall 2003. 153-177).

O. QUIMBY MELTON is a *cum laude* graduate of the University of Georgia and is currently a Ph.D. candidate in the University of Nevada -- Las Vegas English Department. His dissertation is entitled "Jumping the Pond: Literary E/Immigration within Modernism's Anglo-American Exchange." His research interests include Transatlantic/Anglo-American Modernism and the intersections of the Internet and Hypertext with language and literature. A study of the Anglo-American cultural exchange in *Brave New World*, his M.A. thesis is entitled "'In That New World Which Is the Old': New World/Old World Inversion In Aldous Huxley's *Brave New World*" (UNLV 2003). As part of his Graduate Assistantship, he currently teaches classes for the UNLV Honors College and the UNLV English Department where he is also the departmental Webmaster.

DANIELLE MELVIN is a lecturer and writing consultant for the English Department at East Carolina University. Danielle received her Masters of Arts in English Literature with a concentration in Multicultural Literature from East Carolina University. Danielle's special interests include African, African American, and Latino literature. Danielle has research interest in exploring the impact of Christianity upon literatures of the world. Danielle enjoys traveling, reading, and working with children.

ALESSANDRO MONTI is Full Professor of English and Head of Department of Oriental Studies, University of Turin (Italy) and teaches Shakespearean Drama. He is the Italian translator of Raja Rao and collaborates with Indian publishers and academic institutions. He has extensively published on postcolonial literatures: among his titles, the following volumes *Durga Marga*, *The Time After Cowdust*, *Hindu Masculinities across the Ages* deal with Indian writing in English.

RANEN OMER-SHERMAN is assistant professor of English and Jewish Studies at the University of Miami. His essays on Jewish writers have appeared in journals such as *Texas Studies in Literature and Language*, *MELUS*, *College Literature*, *Journal of Modern Jewish Studies*, *Religion & Literature*, *Shofar*, and *Modernism/Modernity*. His first book, *Diaspora and Zionism in Jewish American Literature: Lazarus, Syrkin, Reznikoff, Roth* (2002) was published by UP New England. A second book, entitled *Jewish Writing and the Desert: Israel in Exile* is forthcoming this fall from the University of Illinois Press.

MELISSA MATYJASIK-PARSONS earned her MA in English from East Carolina University where she is now a lecturer. Her interests range from Medieval Literature and Religion in Literature to Science Fiction and Film Studies. She has presented essays on Angela Carter's The Bloody Chamber and Neil Gaiman's American Gods and his comic, 1602.

SHARON D. RAYNOR is currently an Assistant Professor in the Department of English and Foreign Languages at Johnson C. Smith University in Charlotte, NC. She previously taught for seven years in the English Department at East Carolina University in Greenville, NC. She completed her doctorate degree in Literature and Criticism from Indiana University of Pennsylvania in August 2003. She received both her Bachelor of Arts degree in English and her Master of Arts degree in Multicultural Literature at East Carolina University. Her doctoral dissertation is entitled, "Shattered Silence and Restored Souls: Bearing Witness and Testifying to Trauma and 'Truth' in the Narratives of Black Vietnam Veterans." From 1999-2002, she served as the Project Director for the North Carolina Humanities Council grant, "Breaking the Silence: The Unspoken Brotherhood of Vietnam Veterans" and Co-Director for the Writers Reading Series of Eastern North Carolina. She also serves as a workshop leader for the Veterans History Project sponsored by the American Folklore Society, a speaker for the North Carolina Speakers' Forum and a scholar for the "Let's Talk About It Book" Discussion Program, both sponsored by the North Carolina Humanities Council. Sharon is a member of the American Folklore Society. Her most recent publications, "The World of Female Knowing According to Georgia Douglass Johnson," appeared in College Language Association Journal (CLA) and

"Breaking the Silence: The Unspoken Brotherhood of Vietnam Veterans" appeared in NC Crossroads. Her forthcoming publications will appear in The Encyclopedia of African American Literature, The Encyclopedia of African American Folklore, and Dos Passos Review.

EDWARD J. REILLY chairs the English Department at Saint Joseph's College of Maine. His publications include *Approaches to Teaching Swift's Gulliver's Travels, The 1960s,* two books on baseball and American culture, and nine books of poetry. He currently is writing a biography of F. Scott Fitzgerald.

GAY WILENTZ is Co-Coordinator of the Multicultural Concentration and Director of Ethnic Studies at East Carolina University. She is the author of *Binding Cultures: Black Women Writers in Africa and The Diaspora* (Indiana 1992), co-editor of Africa World Press's *Emerging Perspectives on Ama Ata Aidoo* (with Ada Azodo), and book editor of Jewish immigrant writer Anzia Yezierska's 1923 novel, *Salome of the Tenements.* Her most recent work of criticism is *Healing Narratives: Women Writers Curing Cultural Dis-Ease* (Rutgers 2000). She has also published in *Literature And Medicine, College English, African American Review, Research In African Literatures,* and *MELUS,* among others. Currently, Wilentz is working on a cultural study of Black-Jewish relations in the 1920s through the friendship of Fannie Hurst and Zora Neale Hurston.

Index